Daoist Encounters with Phenomenology

ALSO AVAILABLE FROM BLOOMSBURY

Chinese and Buddhist Philosophy in Early Twentieth-Century German Thought, by Eric S. Nelson

Comparative Philosophy without Borders, edited by Arindam Chakrabarti and Ralph Weber

Confucian Ethics in Western Discourse, by Wai-ying Wong

Faith and Reason in Continental and Japanese Philosophy, by Takeshi Morisato

Imagination: Cross-Cultural Philosophical Analyses, edited by Hans-Georg Moeller and Andrew Whitehead

Daoist Encounters with Phenomenology

Thinking Interculturally about Human Existence

Edited by
David Chai

BLOOMSBURY ACADEMIC
LONDON • NEW YORK • OXFORD • NEW DELHI • SYDNEY

Bloomsbury Publishing Plc

50 Bedford Square, London, WC1B 3DP, UK

1385 Broadway, New York, NY 10018, USA

BLOOMSBURY, BLOOMSBURY ACADEMIC and the Diana logo are trademarks of Bloomsbury Publishing Plc

First published in Great Britain 2020

Cover design: Louise Dugdale

Cover image: Eric Van Horrik / EyeEm / Getty images

A catalogue record for this book is available from the British Library.

A catalog record for this book is available from the Library of Congress.

ISBN: HB: 978-1-3500-6958-9
PB: 978-1-3500-6955-8
ePDF: 978-1-3500-6954-1
eBook: 978-1-3500-6956-5

Typeset by RefineCatch Limited, Bungay, Suffolk

Printed and bound in Great Britain

To find out more about our authors and books visit www.bloomsbury.com and sign up for our newsletters.

In Memory of our Teachers

Herbert Fingarette (1921–2018)
Henry Rosemont, Jr. (1934–2017)
Vincent Shen (1949–2018)

CONTENTS

Part Three: Mature Encounters: A Forest of Ideas

Part Four: A Most Urgent Encounter: Re-Rooting Our Futural Selves

LIST OF CONTRIBUTORS

Mary I. Bockover is Professor of Philosophy at Humboldt State University, where she has taught since 1989. She created the *HSU Philosophy Forum*, a community-wide forum for discussing issues of social and moral significance, which she now cooperatively runs with the University's Associated Students organization. Professor Bockover serves on a number of ethics committees in her community. She also likes to travel, especially to China, and to the Czech Republic where she and her family spent a Fulbright year in 2004–5. Her publications are mainly in the areas of comparative philosophy, ancient Chinese philosophy, ethics, and identity theory.

David Chai is Assistant Professor of Philosophy at the Chinese University of Hong Kong. He is the author of *Zhuangzi and the Becoming of Nothingness* (2019) and *Early Zhuangzi Commentaries: On the Sounds and Meanings of the Inner Chapters* (2008), and editor of *Dao Companion to Neo-Daoism* (2020). His work has appeared in a wide variety of journals and edited anthologies. Professor Chai's research covers the fields of Chinese philosophy, metaphysics, phenomenology, hermeneutics, and comparative philosophy.

Bret W. Davis is Thomas J. Higgins, S.J. Professor of Philosophy at Loyola University Maryland. In addition to attaining a Ph.D. in philosophy from Vanderbilt University, he has spent more than a dozen years studying and teaching in Japan. He is author of *Heidegger and the Will: On the Way to Gelassenheit* (2007) and of more than sixty articles in English and Japanese on Continental, East Asian, and comparative philosophy. He is translator of Heidegger's *Country Path Conversations* (2010) and the editor or co-editor of *Japanese Philosophy in the World* (in Japanese, 2005), *Martin Heidegger: Key Concepts* (2010), *Japanese and Continental Philosophy: Conversations with the Kyoto School* (2011), *Engaging Dōgen's Zen: The Philosophy of Practice as Awakening* (2017), and *The Oxford Handbook of Japanese Philosophy* (2019).

Katrin Froese is Professor of Philosophy and Religious Studies at the University of Calgary. She is the author of *Rousseau and Nietzsche: Toward an Aesthetic Morality* (2001), *Nietzsche, Heidegger and Daoist Thought: Crossing Paths In-Between* (2006), *Ethics Unbound: Some Chinese and Western Perspectives of Morality* (2013), and *Why Can't Philosophers Laugh?* (2017).

Patricia Huntington is Professor of Philosophy and Religious Studies at Arizona State University West. Her primary areas of study include continental philosophy, phenomenology, comparative philosophy, feminist theory, and women and religion. She takes a special interest in Chan/Zen, Huayan, and Yogācāra Buddhism. She is the author of *Loneliness and Lament: A Phenomenology of Receptivity* (2009), *Ecstatic Subjects, Utopia, and Recognition: Kristeva, Heidegger, Irigaray* (1998), and co-editor with Nancy Holland of *Feminist Interpretations of Martin Heidegger* (2001).

Kwok-Ying Lau is Professor of Philosophy at the Chinese University of Hong Kong. His monograph *Phenomenology and Intercultural Understanding: Toward a New Cultural Flesh* (2016) was awarded the 2019 Edwin Ballard Prize by the Center for Advanced Research in Phenomenology, as well as the 2017 Research Excellence Award by the Faculty of Arts at the Chinese University of Hong Kong. His other monographs include *Traces of French Phenomenology: From Sartre to Derrida* (in Chinese, 2018), and *Persona: Figures of Contemporary European Philosophers, From Husserl to Lyotard* (in Chinese, forthcoming). He is co-editor with Chung-Chi Yu of *Border-Crossing: Phenomenology, Interculturality and Interdisciplinarity* (2014) and *Phenomenology and Human Experience* (2012), with Chan-Fai Cheung and Tze-Wan Kwan of *Identity and Alterity. Phenomenology and Cultural Traditions* (2010), and with John Drummond of *Husserl's Logical Investigations in the New Century: Western and Chinese Perspectives* (2007).

Sarah A. Mattice is Associate Professor in the Department of Philosophy and Religious Studies at the University of North Florida, specializing in comparative and East Asian philosophy. In addition to her book *Metaphor and Metaphilosophy: Philosophy as Combat, Play, and Aesthetic Experience* (2014), recent publications related to Daoism include: "A Metaphorical Conversation: Gadamer and Zhuangzi on Textual Unity" (2015), "The *De* of Levinas: Cultivating the Heart-Mind of Radical Passivity" co-authored with Leah Kalmanson (2015), and "Daoist Aesthetics of the Everyday and the Fantastical" in *Artistic Visions and the Promise of Beauty: Cross-Cultural Perspectives*, edited by Higgins, Maira, and Sikka (2017).

Eric S. Nelson is Professor of Humanities at the Hong Kong University of Science and Technology. He works on Chinese, German, and Jewish philosophy. He is the author of *Chinese and Buddhist Philosophy in Early Twentieth-Century German Thought* (2017) and *Levinas, Adorno, and the Ethics of the Material Other* (2020). He is editor of *Interpreting Dilthey: Critical Essays* (2019). He is co-editor with François Raffoul of the *Bloomsbury Companion to Heidegger* (2016) and *Rethinking Facticity* (2008), with John Drabinski of *Between Levinas and Heidegger* (2014), and with Antje Kapust and Kent Still of *Addressing Levinas* (2005).

Graham Parkes taught Asian and comparative philosophy at the University of Hawaii for twenty-five years, punctuated by three years as a visiting scholar and fellow at Harvard. He is now a Professorial Research Fellow at the Institute of Philosophy, University of Vienna. He has published extensively in the fields of Chinese, German, Japanese, and environmental philosophies, and has just finished a manuscript with the title *Climate Crisis and China: A Philosophical Guide to Saner Ways of Living*.

Martin Schönfeld is Professor in the Department of Philosophy and in the College of Global Sustainability at the University of South Florida. He teaches environmental ethics, comparative philosophy, and future-oriented philosophical courses related to the Anthropocene. He writes on climate change, civil evolution, and pathways of wisdom for transitioning to a stabilized Earth System. His papers have appeared in science venues such as *Earth System Dynamics*, and journals in comparative philosophy and the history of philosophy. He is the editor of *Journal of Global Ethics*.

Mario Wenning is Associate Professor at the University of Macau and Vice President of the Karl Jaspers Society of North America. His work focuses primarily on social and political philosophy as well as aesthetics from an intercultural perspective. He has published in, among others, *Comparative Philosophy*, *Journal of Chinese Philosophy*, *Philosophy East and West*, *Confluence*, and *Studies in Philosophy and Education*, and is currently completing a book manuscript on natural agency East and West. Apart from his scholarship, Professor Wenning has also translated modern German philosophers into English (including Jaspers, Tugendhat, and Sloterdijk).

Jason M. Wirth is Professor of Philosophy at Seattle University, and works and teaches in the areas of Buddhist Philosophy, Aesthetics, Continental Philosophy, Environmental Philosophy, and Africana Philosophy. His recent books include *Nietzsche and Other Buddhas* (2019), *Mountains, Rivers, and the Great Earth: Reading Gary Snyder and Dōgen in an Age of Ecological Crisis* (2017), a monograph on Milan Kundera (*Commiserating with Devastated Things*, 2015), *Schelling's Practice of the Wild* (2015), and the co-edited volume (with Bret W. Davis and Brian Schroeder) *Japanese and Continental Philosophy: Conversations with the Kyoto School* (2011). He is the associate editor and book review editor of the journal *Comparative and Continental Philosophy*.

ACKNOWLEDGMENTS

I am honored to be joined by such an illustrious group of contributors, without whom this book would not have come to fruition. To Mary, Bret, Katrin, Patricia, Kwok-Ying, Sarah, Eric, Graham, Martin, Mario, and Jason, I thank you for joining me on this journey of intercultural comparative philosophy, and for helping me amplify Daoism's edifying voice above the din of the modern world. My thanks also to Colleen Coalter and Becky Holland at Bloomsbury for their support of this project and for making its realization a smooth and enjoyable process.

Editor's Introduction

When Matteo Ricci arrived on the shores of China in 1583, he would open a new chapter in Western civilization's engagement with the East. Struck by the wisdom of Chinese thought, the Jesuits would translate the canonical works of China into Latin and these, in turn, would be rendered into other European languages. As these translations made their way through Europe, some of them found their way into the hands, or were whispered into the ears, of the greatest thinkers of the early-modern and modern periods.[1] One would think the texts of Confucianism would have garnered the greatest interest given their moral-political content but that was not the case. It was the naturalistic thought of Daoism that caught people's attention, a naturalism that is cosmological and aesthetic, spiritual and phenomenological. What is more, Daoism addresses both the sayable and unsayable, the visible and invisible, as well as the knowable and unknowable. It is, in other words, a philosophical tradition concerned with things and non-things alike and humanity's ability to comprehend this inseparable, binomial nature of reality.

When it comes to the topic of this book—phenomenology—far greater attention has been paid to its reception in Japan than China. Of the works written to date about Chinese phenomenology in English, they have either been limited in scope to Edmund Husserl,[2] or were done at a time that their findings are in need of refreshing.[3] What is more, there has not been a single book-length study in English devoted to Daoism and phenomenology.[4] The present work will not only remedy this neglect, it will argue that Daoism's inherently phenomenological nature makes it the perfect foil to question the Western tradition's self-assuredness and domination of the modern global philosophical stage.

This is not to say that the West's grip on phenomenology should be eradicated simply to make room for that of the East: quite the contrary. Phenomenology has and continues to demonstrate a willingness to adapt to the challenges put before it by thinkers and traditions within and beyond the Western realm.[5] Having said as much, it should be stated that the present work is neither an apology for, nor a history of phenomenology, but an encounter between two historically and culturally unique understandings of the phenomenological world. Thus while Daoism does not belong to the school of phenomenology per se, it touches upon issues found in the latter's philosophical system in such a way that the two traditions mutually resonate with one another. In this way, the intercultural encounter that guides this work has been designed to provoke questions about human existence in such a way that the answers arrived at will be globally relevant and not limited to either East or West. Daoism thus acts as the protagonist, poking and prodding the West to justify its reasoning and methodologies. Such being the case, the first objective of this book is to debunk the mischaracterization of Daoism as nothing more than mystical gibberish; the Daoist rendition of phenomenology is as valid as it is ancient. A second objective is to highlight how Western phenomenology, as represented by the figures included in this volume, is closer in spirit to Daoism than it is apart. The book's third and final objective is perhaps the hardest to realize in that it not only asks us to think phenomenologically, it challenges us to make Daoism part of our life praxis.

While the Western side of our discourse is flexible as concerns which figures are discussed, the Daoist side is limited to either Laozi 老子 (c. sixth century BCE) or Zhuangzi 莊子 (fourth century BCE). Laozi is associated with a text entitled *Daodejing* 道德經 (Classic of Dao and Virtue) and Zhuangzi with the *Nanhua Zhenjing* 南華真經 (True Classic of Nanhua), or simply the *Zhuangzi*.[6] Since an overview of phenomenology will make this introduction unwieldy, I shall outline the major concepts of Daoism instead.[7]

Of primary concern to Daoism is learning how to comprehend and follow Dao 道. Perhaps the most profound of Chinese concepts to explain in English, Dao literally means "path" or "road" and has the extended meaning of "Way." The Chinese character is comprised of two parts: a head (首) and a pair of feet (辶). The feet carry the head and, in so doing, create a path in the world. When one lets their feet transport their head, as opposed to using the head to determine where the feet should go, the "Way" to proceed naturally presents itself. The second meaning bestowed to Dao is that of primal creator or mother (*mu* 母). All things in the universe (i.e., the myriad or ten thousand things, *wanwu* 萬物), as well as the universe itself, arise and decline because of Dao; however, this cosmic birthing is neither a divine act nor one of predetermination. Although the lifespan of things is fated according to their form (*xing* 形), what determines whether its end is reached or cut-short prematurely is not Dao but each thing itself. Exhaustion of the body (*ti* 體 or *shen* 身) and (heart-) mind (*xin* 心), illness, natural or human inflicted calamity, there are any number of ways a thing's finitude can be concluded. For Daoism, death is inevitable and since everything in the universe must die at some point in time, there are no grounds to justify the fear humanity harbors of what is essentially a natural occurrence.

Dao makes possible the occurrence of life (*sheng* 生) and death (*si* 死), and the innumerable changes (*hua* 化 or *bian* 變) that take place in-between, but it does not manipulate or interfere with them. From this we derive the concepts of naturalism or spontaneity (*ziran* 自然), and non-interference or non-action (*wuwei* 無為). These, in turn, give rise to the notions of selflessness and forgetting (*wang* 忘). To be in harmony with Dao is hence to be in accordance with the collective natural world (i.e., Heaven and Earth, *tiandi* 天地). In order to do this, Daoism states that humans must abandon our dependency on certain models of thinking and acting whilst experiencing the world. If we are to return to things themselves, we cannot do so if we continue to view ourselves as being separate or different from the collectivity of said things. Daoism is thus a proponent of cosmic holism wherein no one thing has priority over all others.

In order to best illustrate this life praxis, Daoism offers us the model of the sage (*shengren* 聖人). The sage reveals the nature of things by allowing them to display their phenomenological uniqueness and harmony with Dao. Acting as the mirror of the world, the sage allows things to shine in the light of Dao whilst remaining dark himself, allows things to sound forth whilst remaining silent himself, and stands still so that the world may revolve around him. In this way, the sage helps preserve the root of Dao in the world by showing the latter the true extent of the former's potential. Without the sage, the "Way" of Dao will become lost to humanity and when that happens, humanity will descend into chaos and destruction.

In sum, the Daoist worldview is a phenomenological experience not predicated on a knowledge-based self; rather, Daoism seeks to liberate human knowing and thinking by discarding the subjective self, dogmatic norms, and non-inclusionary theories of reality. In this way, Daoist phenomenology contributes to the Western notion of the term by shifting the plane of truth from the human sphere to the onto-cosmological realm of Dao *qua* ultimate reality. Daoist phenomenology is thus simultaneously mundane and transcendental, this-worldly and non-worldly, appreciative of things as they naturally are while also being sensitive to what said things were and may become. It is a mode of living alongside the beings and non-beings of the world without being affected by their attributes or propensities, all the while appreciating said qualities as perfectly natural and in accordance with each thing's inborn nature.

To conclude, the chapters comprising this book can be read independent of one another and in any particular order. Although they are organized chronologically according to the lifetime of the Western figure and divided into three groups indicating the approximate development of phenomenology—in the context of this book that is—what remains consistent throughout is the edifying voice of Daoism.

Notes

1   See the following: Eric S. Nelson, *Chinese and Buddhist Philosophy in Early Twentieth-Century German Thought* (London: Bloomsbury Academic, 2017); Graham Parkes, ed., *Heidegger and Asian Thought* (Honolulu: University of

Hawaii Press, 1987); Graham Parkes, ed., *Nietzsche and Asian Thought* (Chicago: University of Chicago Press, 1991); Lin Ma, *Heidegger on East-West Dialogue: Anticipating the Event* (New York: Routledge, 2007); and Reinhard May, *Heidegger's Hidden Sources: East-Asian Influences on His Work*, trans. Graham Parkes (New York: Routledge, 1996).

2   See Kwok-Ying Lau and John Drummond, eds., *Husserl's Logical Investigations in the New Century: Western and Chinese Perspectives* (Dordrecht: Springer, 2007).

3   See Anna-Teresa Tymieniecka, ed., *Phenomenology of Life in a Dialogue Between Chinese and Occidental Philosophy* (Dordrecht: Kluwer Academic Publishers, 1984). Although the publication of this book was ground-breaking at the time for introducing to the world the field of Chinese phenomenology, only two of its twenty-five chapters dealt with Daoism. What is more, in the time that has since passed, not a single work on phenomenology has appeared in which Daoism has been given more than the briefest of analysis.

4   Even though the works of Hegel, Husserl, and Heidegger have been available in Chinese for some time, Chinese scholars have been just as derelict as their Western counterparts when it comes to direct comparisons between Daoism and phenomenology. Two notable exceptions are: Rujun Wu, *Daoist Hermeneutics and the Forceful Purity of Phenomenology* (Taibei: Taiwan Xuesheng Shuju Youxian Gongsi, 2011); and Zhenyu Zhong, *Daoist Phenomenology of Qi* (Taibei: Zhongyang Yanjiuyuan Zhongguo Wenzhe Yanjiusuo, 2016).

5   For more on phenomenology in its traditional and contemporary guises, see Dan Zahavi, ed., *The Oxford Handbook of the History of Phenomenology* (New York: Oxford University Press, 2018); Dan Zahavi, ed., *The Oxford Handbook of Contemporary Phenomenology* (Oxford: Oxford University Press, 2012); Dermot Moran and Lester Embree, eds., *Phenomenology: Critical Concepts in Philosophy* (London: Routledge, 2004); Anna-Teresa Tymieniecka, ed., *Phenomenology World-Wide: Foundations, Expanding Dynamics, Life-Engagements: A Guide for Research and Study* (Dordrecht: Kluwer Academic Publishers, 2002); Dermot Moran, *Introduction to Phenomenology* (London: Routledge, 2000); and Robert Sokolowski, *Introduction to Phenomenology* (Cambridge: Cambridge University Press, 2000).

6   We will not concern ourselves with the historical dates of Laozi or Zhuangzi, or the compilation and editing of their texts, as these are beyond the scope of this work.

7   More comprehensive introductions are available in: Hans-Georg Moeller, *Daoism Explained: From the Dream of the Butterfly to the Fishnet Allegory* (La Salle: Open Court, 2004); Eske Mollgaard, *An Introduction to Daoist Thought* (New York: Routledge, 2011); and Steve Coutinho, *An Introduction to Daoist Philosophies* (New York: Columbia University Press, 2013).

References

Coutinho, Steve. (2013), *An Introduction to Daoist Philosophies*, New York: Columbia University Press.

Lau, Kwok-Ying and John Drummond, eds. (2007), *Husserl's Logical Investigations in the New Century: Western and Chinese Perspectives*, in *Contributions to Phenomenology* (vol. 55), Dordrecht: Springer.

Ma, Lin. (2007), *Heidegger on East-West Dialogue: Anticipating the Event*. New York: Routledge.

May, Reinhard. (1996), *Heidegger's Hidden Sources: East-Asian Influences on His Work*, Graham Parkes (trans.), New York: Routledge.

Moeller, Hans-Georg. (2004), *Daoism Explained: From the Dream of the Butterfly to the Fishnet Allegory*, La Salle: Open Court.

Mollgaard, Eske. (2011), *An Introduction to Daoist Thought*, New York: Routledge.

Moran, Dermot. (2000), *Introduction to Phenomenology*, London: Routledge.

Moran, Dermot and Lester Embree, eds. (2004), *Phenomenology: Critical Concepts in Philosophy*, London: Routledge.

Nelson, Eric S. (2017), *Chinese and Buddhist Philosophy in Early Twentieth-Century German Thought*, London: Bloomsbury Academic.

Parkes, Graham, ed. (1987), *Heidegger and Asian Thought*. Honolulu: University of Hawaii Press.

Parkes, Graham, ed. (1991), *Nietzsche and Asian Thought*. Chicago: University of Chicago Press.

Sokolowski, Robert. (2000), *Introduction to Phenomenology*, Cambridge: Cambridge University Press.

Tymieniecka, Anna-Teresa, ed. (1984), *Phenomenology of Life in a Dialogue Between Chinese and Occidental Philosophy*, in *Analecta Husserliana* (vol. 17), Dordrecht: Kluwer Academic Publishers.

Tymieniecka, Anna-Teresa, ed. (2002), *Phenomenology World-Wide: Foundations, Expanding Dynamics, Life-Engagements: A Guide for Research and Study*, in *Analecta Husserliana* (vol. 80), Dordrecht: Kluwer Academic Publishers.

Wu, Rujun 吳汝鈞. (2011), *Daoist Hermeneutics and the Forceful Purity of Phenomenology* 道家詮釋學與純粹力動現象學, Taibei: Taiwan Xuesheng Shuju Youxian Gongsi.

Zahavi, Dan, ed. (2012), *The Oxford Handbook of Contemporary Phenomenology*, Oxford: Oxford University Press.

Zahavi, Dan, ed. (2018), *The Oxford Handbook of the History of Phenomenology*, New York: Oxford University Press.

Zhong, Zhenyu 鍾振宇. (2016), *Daoist Phenomenology of Qi* 道家的氣化現象學, Taibei: Zhongyang Yanjiuyuan Zhongguo Wenzhe Yanjiusuo.

PART ONE

Precursory Encounters: Unearthing Fertile Seeds

1

Daoism and Hegel on Painting the Invisible Spirit:

To Color or Not?

David Chai

1. Introduction

To look upon the world is to see an astonishing array of colors. Indeed, the colors that fall under our gaze bewitch our eyes and intoxicate our hearts and yet, if we were to sweep away said coloration, turning the world into a monochrome palette, would we still be enraptured by its bedazzling visuality? What would we make of a world lacking the emotional, psychological, and religious signification of color? Based on the bond between color and these states of human realization, we confidently ascribe each an array of identificatory markers. With this toolkit at our disposal, we take the world at large to be constructed in a similar manner, forgetting the fact that all outward manifestations of inner potential are fleeting in nature; moreover, what makes each thing a particular thing—its spirit—is colorless. The foggy translucency of spirit is not because it is impervious to color; rather, by embodying colors in their collectivity, spirit colors the world such that it transcends conventional representation. The challenge, therefore, lies in conveying spirit's resistance to literal expression.

One aspect of spirit commonly seen in the world's great works of art is freedom—not of the social, political, or religious kind, but that belonging to humanity as a whole—and nowhere is freedom felt more than in Nature. The artwork that merely imitates Nature, however, is but a decorative image insofar as it lacks spirit. Ornamental art fails to encourage its viewer to contemplate its painted scene, even though it might be pleasurable to look at, because it does not bring said viewer a sense of inner freedom. In order for art to be spiritually transformative, it needs to uplift our sense of self-awareness, in terms of not just who we are as individuals, but who we are as members of the collective being of spirit.

In discussing painting and spirit, one cannot but turn to the German philosopher Hegel. In his *Aesthetics: Lectures on Fine Art* (hereafter, *Aesthetics*), Hegel proclaims painting has united what was formerly two distinct spheres of art: that of the external environment (architecture), and that of the embodied spirit (sculpture). The color of a painting, he says, gives the spiritual inner-life its appearance by rendering the invisible visible. While this chapter is not concerned with Hegel's account of the history of art, nor with his discussion of the different styles of art or particular artists, it is interested in exploring his thesis that a painter literally colors the living sensuousness of an object. Neither drawing technique nor the clever use of light and shadow can match the effect color has on spirit. While Hegel's discourse on the role of color in painting is an admittedly minor aspect of his corpus, when compared to the writings of Alexander Baumgarten (1714–62) and Johann Gottfried Herder (1744–1803), it is just as stimulating and phenomenologically innovative.

Many centuries before Hegel, Chinese painters had come to an altogether different conclusion regarding painting and color. For them, inner-spirit was brought to life through brushwork, not color. Indeed, the influence of Daoist philosophy on Chinese painting made color antithetical to the naturalness of the depicted scene. What is of utmost importance is the spiritual resonance between the painter and her subject. Although color was used in early Chinese painting, it was done so sparingly in order to avoid masking the brushwork delimiting the figures or scenes therein. Indeed, the blank canvas was just as important to a painting as its content, so much so it became a vital component of the finished work. In this way, when early Chinese artists speak of the harmony between the white canvas and the black ink applied to its surface, they were pointing to a human–cosmic harmony reflective of the non-coloration of Nature. Daoist-inspired painting thus draws observers into the collective spirit of Dao *qua* ultimate reality by freeing them to partake in the naturalness of the painter's heart-mind. In what follows, we will compare the Hegelian and Daoist appropriation (or lack thereof) of color and how it bears upon the standing of spirit in both its human and worldly form.

2. Spirit as Art's Foundation

Amongst his writings on art, Hegel's analysis of painting in his *Aesthetics* has received an inappropriately low amount of scholarly attention.[1] Although he might not formally belong to the phenomenological tradition associated with Husserl, Hegel nevertheless speaks of the coloration of painting in a manner that can be construed as phenomenological. His approach to art is decidedly European in orientation however, and while Hegel claims "the Chinese, Indians, and Egyptians acquired fame on the score of their paintings,"[2] he undermines himself when he says "the Chinese, Indians, and Egyptians, in their artistic shapes, images of gods, and idols, never get beyond formlessness or a bad and untrue definiteness of form."[3] The reason why they were incapable of mastering true beauty, Hegel says, is because the content of their art lacks that which is absolute in itself (i.e., spirit). One must then ask, what is this true beauty Hegel speaks of? In his *Aesthetics*, he writes that painting has united the disciplines of architecture and sculpture through its use of color; to be specific, the painter colors spirit by making visible its invisible nature. This bringing to light what was formerly dark is spiritual resonance, what Hegel calls shining (*scheinen*). We will interrogate Hegel's claim that the painter colors the living sensuousness of a subject via the Daoist doctrine that color handicaps access to spirit. To support this claim, it will be argued that the non-coloration of Daoist painting allows for a deeper level of harmonization between the painter and her subject such that the latter marks the naturalness of the former's heart-mind (*xin* 心). In this way, Chinese monochrome painting transcends color thereby bringing it and those who gaze upon it to a higher realm—not the shining of spirit as Hegel would have it—but that which gives rise to spirit: Dao 道.

The ancient Chinese term for painting (*huatu* 畫圖) is used only once in the classical texts of Daoism, specifically chapter 21 of the *Zhuangzi* 莊子. Said passage reads:

> Prince Yuan of Song wanted some new paintings. A crowd of clerks gathered before him and having receiving their easels, separated into several lines. Moistening their brushes and ink-sticks, there were so many of them that half had to stand outside [the hall]. One clerk arrived late, casually entering [the hall] without the slightest concern. Upon receiving his easel, he did not join the others in line but returned to his quarters. When Prince Yuan sent someone to check on this clerk, they found him sitting on the floor, legs stretched-out before him, naked. Excellent, said the Prince, this is a real painter![4]

There is not much to be gleaned from this passage on the nature of painting, or how it manages to encapsulate the spirit of Dao. What we are able to discern is that a person who carries Dao within their heart-mind has nothing to burden them on the outside. This is why the clerk did not rush to the side of the Prince, eager to please his every wish, but orders his life in accordance with the cosmic rhythm of the world. It might also explain why he practices his craft naked! Needless to say, only when the painter is spiritually liberated does the resultant painting reflect said freedom; only when the painter's spirit wanders between the realms of Nature and the canvas does the painted scene touch the spirit of others. As we shall see, Daoist-inspired painting does not fixate on the technical particularities of perspective, light and shadow, color saturation, and so forth, but on the suggestiveness conveyed through brushwork.

In this regard, Daoism's influence on artists, poets, and philosophers of the Wei-Jin, Tang, and Song dynasties can be attributed to its emphasis on the invisible attributes of the world in that to be hidden is to be mysterious, and mystery lights the way to Dao. In other words, what is authentic (*zhen* 真) does not belong to the world of the visible, a world where suggestiveness is erased by crude pursuits of self-gain and recognition, and where the hidden is trampled on by the vanity of the known and dispersed by the false knowledge of spoken words. It is likewise absent from the line of clerks awaiting their Prince's command; rather, to be authentic entails a metaphorical stripping-off of one's clothes, and by implication the rank and honor associated with them, so as to reveal one's true self underneath. Herein lies the difference between the Daoist and Hegelian views of painting—the former sees spirit permeating the entirety of reality while the latter locates it in the carnality of human flesh.

Why does it fall to the painter, as opposed to the sculptor, to successfully capture human spirit? The following passage from Jean-Luc Marion gives us some food for thought:

> The painter grants visibility to the unseen, delivering the unseen from its anterior invisibility, its shapelessness. But why is it the painter who manages to do this—he and he alone? How does he seize the power to make the unseen appear? By what gift does one become a painter? Certainly, it is not enough to be able to see, to be on duty with a gaze, so to speak, to have an eye for the visible already available and on display every day, since in that case every non-blind person would know how to paint. If the painter rules over the access of the unseen to the visible, his gift thus has nothing to do with his vision of the visible but with his divination of the unseen. The painter, like the blind man, sees more than the visible, painting and seeing par excellence.[5]

Perhaps Hegel had something similar in mind when he noted how "art liberates the true content of phenomena from the pure appearance and deception of this bad, transitory world, and gives them a higher actuality, born of the spirit."[6] It would seem that the art of painting is indubitably tied to spirit, so let us examine in greater detail what this relationship entails.

3. The Art of Painting

Nowhere is Hegel's opinion on the art of painting more succinctly presented than the following: "The universal need for art ... [lies in] man's rational need to lift the inner and outer world into his spiritual consciousness as an object in which he recognizes again his own self."[7] We can contrast this with what the Chinese painter and art theorist Xie He 謝赫 (fl. fifth century CE) wrote:

> Spiritual nature is conveyed by instilling vitality (*qiyun shengdong* 氣韻生動); inner quality is suggested through skillful handling of the brush (*gufa yongbi* 骨法用筆); correspondence with reality is achieved through the representation of forms (*yingwu xiangxing* 應物象形); accordance to type is accomplished by application of colors (*suilei fucai* 隨類賦彩); layout and composition are determined by careful positioning and placement (*jingying weizhi* 經營位置); and similitude and accuracy are dependent upon faithful modeling and depiction (*zhuanyi moxie* 傳移摹寫).[8]

Xie He's "Six Laws" (*liu fa* 六法), like Hegel's statement quoted before them, place spirituality front and center; unlike Hegel, however, who held that painting was about giving expression to human spirit by rendering it visible through color, Xie He took brushwork to be of greatest importance. Xie He is indicative of the early Chinese attitude toward art. Though he would prove to be a highly influential figure, he was not the only one to correlate painting and spirit. Take, for example, the great Tang poet and painter Wang Wei 王維 (699–761 CE):

> Now those who speak of painting ultimately focus on nothing but appearances and positioning. Still, when the ancients made paintings, it was not in order to plan the boundaries of cities or differentiate the locale of provinces, to make mountains and plateaus or delineate watercourses. What is founded in form is fused with soul (*ling* 靈), and what activates movement is the heart-mind (*xin* 心). If the soul cannot be seen, then that wherein it lodges will not move. If eyesight is limited, then what is seen will not be complete. Thus with one reed brush I simulate the form of the Great Void (*taixu* 太虛); with differentiated shapes I paint the perceptions of the inch-wide pupils.[9]

Wang Wei lived at a time when painting had only just begun to be the domain of the literati class in China, and among said persons, ink-wash landscapes rapidly became the medium of choice. Indeed, "it was exclusively to the ink-wash that the Chinese literati assigned the play of variation between pale and dark, dry and wet, between there is and there is not, to render the evanescent character of things in the process of emergence or resorption."[10] Working with black ink did not hamper the creative rendering of painting for the early Chinese. In fact, they made up for the lack of color by devising six "colors" appropriate to their monochrome take on the world: black, white, dry, wet, thick, and thin.[11] These three pairs allowed for more subtle modes of expression to come to light: condensed, opaque, material, distilled, hazy, and lively.[12]

Zhang Yanyuan 張彥遠 (c. 815–907 CE) was another notable name in early Chinese art theory. On the issue of spirit in painting, he said: "Contemporary painters are roughly good at describing appearances, attaining formal likeness but without its spirit resonance; providing their colors but lacking in brush method. How can such be called painting?"[13] The allusion to spirit resonance and brushwork was not accidental; indeed, it indicates a pattern amongst early Chinese intellectuals and artists: naturalism is sought over and above technical realism. Zhang's quote might be sparse in detail but we can nevertheless make a comparison to Hegel's statement that: "[Painting is] . . . the formation of a picture by means of particular colors whereby the form of the object as our vision sees it is transformed from the shape of something real into a pure appearance artistically created by the spirit (of the artist)."[14] For Hegel, painting is about the discovery of human essence in that which is beautiful, a beauty inscribed and imposed upon the world through color. What is more, color lies at the heart of painting in a way that stone cannot lie at the heart of sculpture: it transforms the tangibly visible into the intangible invisibility of spirit. This spirituality, however, is not a resonating of the mysterious pulse of Nature but an embodiment of the free human soul. Zhang Yanyuan's view, that a painting lacking in spirit resonance and correct brushwork does not merit being called a painting, stands apart from what Hegel has in mind in that the brush serves as a conduit through which the painter's spirit can reverberate in their work, reducing the use of color to second-order importance.

We can add yet another observation, that despite one's technical skill in using a brush, so much so that the likeness between a scene and its portrayal is beyond reproach, this does not imply one has successfully captured its ineffable spirit. To quote Zhang once more:

One may be said to have fulfilled one's aim when the five colors are all present in the management of ink alone. If one's [heart-] mind dwells on the five colors, then the images of things will go wrong. In painting things, one should especially avoid meticulous completeness in formal appearance and coloring, and extreme carefulness and detail that display skill and finish. Therefore one should not deplore incompleteness but rather deplore completeness. Once one knows a thing's completeness, where is the need for completing it in painting? This is not incompleteness. Should one not recognize a thing's completeness, that is true incompleteness.[15]

This textual passage is inspired by none other than the *Zhuangzi*. For example, the corruption of images by way of the five colors is derived from chapter 8 which says: "One who is web-toed in eyesight will be confused by the five colors, bewitched by patterns and designs, by the brilliant blues and yellows on embroidered robes, is this not the case?"[16] On the need to preserve the incompleteness of things, this takes after the example of true forgetting seen in chapter 5 of the *Zhuangzi*: "When men do not forget what can be forgotten but forget what cannot be forgotten, this is called true forgetting."[17] Painting, therefore, is not tasked with literal reproduction, either in content or coloration, but mastering the skill of incompleteness. In other words, painting, as a creative act, can only be natural and a spiritual embodiment of its subject when the scene is left partially un-rendered. It is here, in the blankness of invisibility, where the spirit dwells for Daoism, Daoist-inspired painters, and, one might add, for Hegel who believes: "The heart of pictures is not the subjects themselves but the liveliness and soul of the subjective treatment and execution, the mind of the artist which is mirrored in his work and provides not only a mere copy of these external things but at the same time himself and his inner soul."[18] In the words of Stephen Houlgate: "Painting [for Hegel] fulfills its task as art, therefore, not when it accurately reproduces what is given in nature, but when it creates a new reality that is itself ensouled . . . rendering human character and subjectivity concretely visible."[19] The first half of Houlgate's explanation represents another commonality between the Daoist and Hegelian theory of painting, whereas the second half marks their point of departure: Hegel seeks to strengthen our self-understanding through a process of internalization, while Daoism endeavors to weaken our dependency on selfhood by conjoining the self of humanity with the collective spirit of Nature.

In the above discussion we touched upon one of the most fundamental principles of painting for the Chinese—spirit resonance (*shenyun* 神韻), the first of Xie He's six laws; however, there are two benchmarks not included in Xie's laws to which all early Chinese painters aspired: the breath of spirit (*shenqi* 神氣) and the breath of life (*shengqi* 生氣). It is interesting to note that Xie He's *shenyun* does not appear in the two principal texts of Daoism (i.e., the *Daodejing* 道德經 and *Zhuangzi*) nor does *shengqi*, while the term *shenqi* appears in only two chapters of the *Zhuangzi*: 12 and 21. Quite clearly, then, thinkers in Xie He's time were working with their own conceptual toolbox that not only emulated ideas found in the *Zhuangzi*, but developed new ones specifically suited to the art of painting. To put the terms *shenqi* and *shengqi* into context, here is how Zhang Yanyuan portrays them:

> The [brush] strokes of Gu Kaizhi 顧愷之 (345–406 CE) are strong in firmness and uninterrupted in continuity, circling back upon themselves in abrupt rushes. His tone and style are untrammeled and varied; his atmosphere and flavor sudden as lightning. His conception was formulated before his brush [was used], so that when the painting was finished the conception was present. Thus he completed the breath of spirit (*shenqi*) . . . Wu Daozi 吳道子 (680–759 CE) kept watch over his

spirit, concentrating upon his own unity. Being in harmony with the work of creation itself, [his spirit] could borrow Master Wu's brush. This is [described as] formulating the conception before the brush is used, so that when the painting is finished the conception is present . . . Now, if one makes use of marking line and ruler, the result will be dead painting. But if one guards the spirit and concentrates upon unity, there will be real painting. Is not plain plaster better than dead paintings? Yet even one stroke of a real painting will show the breath of life (*shengqi*). Now, the more one revolves thought and wields the brush while consciously thinking of oneself as painting, the less success one will have when painting. If one revolves thought and wields the brush without ideas fixed on painting, one will have success. [Painting] does not stop in the hand, nor freeze in the [heart-] mind, but becomes what it is without conscious realization.[20]

There is certainly a lot to be said about this long passage but the key idea seems to be this: over-reliance on ink masks the authentic nature (spirit) of the subject, wiping out the painter's brushwork in the process. The opposite is also true: a weak painting is one whose use of ink is too sparse and whose brushwork is too feeble. In order to avoid these extremes, spirit resonance is essential, for only concentrated spirit leads to clarity of thought, and when both of these are present, the painter will envision the painting before her brush even touches the canvas. In this way, the idea exists before the brush is grasped, and what is grasped by the heart-mind is responded to by the hand, as Zhang Yanyuan so eloquently stated.

Should we jump forward in time to the last dynastic period of China, the Qing, we find all of the above ideas echoed in Shitao's 石涛 (1642–1707) *Treatise on the Philosophy of Painting* (*hua yulu* 畫語綠). For example, in the fourth of his *Treatise*'s eighteen brief essays, Shitao famously declares that when "a painting receives its ink, ink is then received by the brush, the brush is then received by the wrist, and the wrist is received by the heart-mind."[21] In his seventh essay, Shitao says: "When brush and ink meet, this is known as indistinct intermingling. When what indistinctly intermingles is not separated, this is called undifferentiated wholeness. To penetrate such undifferentiated wholeness, what better way to do so than with the primal brushstroke?"[22] Brush and ink thus form an inseparable pair, in the same way that Yin and Yang, Heaven and Earth do; what threads them together is the spirit of Dao. The authentic painter, Shitao writes in his sixteenth essay, "perceives things beyond their physical form and when composing such forms, reveals no trace of his efforts."[23] The key is to manipulate ink and brush in such a way that they free and revitalize the spirit of the subject being painted: the spirit of Nature is hence one and the same with the spirit of all things therein.

Returning to Hegel, he says nothing about brushwork but turns his attention to the spatiality of the canvas:

[Painting allows] space to persist and extinguishes only one of the three dimensions . . . This reduction of the three dimensions to a level surface is implicit in the principle of interiorization which can be asserted, as inwardness, in space only by reason of the fact that it restricts and does not permit the subsistence of the totality of the external dimensions . . . [Painting's] content is the spiritual inner life which can come into appearance in the external only as retiring into itself out of it . . . [hence] painting has to renounce the totality of space.[24]

John Sallis offers some astute observations on the unique spatial nature of painting: "The visible forms and colors of the painting itself serve to project, beyond the painting, a visible configuration depicting things that either actually are and could actually be seen or that, even if only imaginary, are imagined as visible. In effect, painting engages three successive planes of visibility: the forms and colors on the canvas, the visible scene thereby composed and projected, and the actual or imaginary scene thereby depicted."[25] A second point Sallis makes is that "a painting can present the invisible in the very midst of the visible, that it can let something that never appears to the senses—that cannot appear as such to the senses—be presented in and through the very shining of the sensible."[26] He continues: "What comes to appear on the surface as mere shining becomes also a trace pointing back to spirit in its retreat; and, as painted, the trace is presented as a trace. Painting presents spirit not as circumscribed or imaged there on the painted surface, but only by way of the traces that from that surface point back to spirit in its retreat."[27]

The trace Sallis speaks of is also found in the Chinese tradition, such as this detailed descriptive passage by the Tang dynasty theorist Jing Hao 荊浩 (*c.* 870–930):

Spirit is obtained when your [heart-] mind moves along with the movement of the brush and does not hesitate in delineating images. Resonance is obtained when you establish forms, while hiding [obvious] traces of the brush, and perfect them by observing the proprieties and avoiding vulgarity. Thought is obtained when you grasp essential forms, eliminating unnecessary details [in your observation of nature], and let your ideas crystallize into the forms to be represented. Scene is obtained when you study the laws of nature and the different faces of time, look for the sublime and recreate it with reality. Brush is obtained when you handle the brush freely, applying all the varieties of strokes in accordance with your purpose, although you must follow certain basic rules of brushwork. Here you should regard brushwork neither as substance nor as form but rather as a movement, like flying or driving. Ink is obtained when you distinguish between higher and lower parts of objects with a gradation of ink tones and represent clearly shallowness and depth, thus making them appear natural as if they had not been done with a brush.[28]

Here, the trace is not directly bound-up in spirit but points the way to it through brushwork. A subtle yet important difference, to be sure. The thing we need to take away from Jing Hao's account is that spirit does not lie dormant within a painting, hidden amongst its colors, but flows with the movement of the painter's brush—here weak, there strong, here forcefully visible, there subtly invisible. Chapter 22 of the *Zhuangzi* can be cited as but one of many potential sources of inspiration: "The bright and shining is born from deep darkness; the ordered is born from formlessness; and pure spirit is born from Dao."[29] What is to be treasured in a painting is not the forms inscribed on the canvas but the brushwork underlying said forms. In other words, the painted forms should convey a degree of incompleteness because only then does spirit have freedom of movement as the observer's eyes traverse from one section of the canvas to another, forming a complete yet fluid image in their heart-mind. This is what Jing Hao means by resonance. We find the same rationale expressed by Su Shi 蘇軾 (1037–1101) in a colophon he wrote on a painting by Li Gonglin 李公麟 (1049–1106): "There is Dao and there is skill. If one has Dao and not skill, although things have been formed in one's heart-mind, they will not take shape through one's hands."[30]

Having spirit alone is, therefore, not enough to make someone a genuine artist, for such persons have mastered the skill of letting the hand follow the heart-mind's intuition, not using the heart-mind to control the hand. In this way, the true painter allows her spirit to flow freely between hand and heart-mind such that both come to assume the personality of the depicted subject. One becomes the mountain, the bamboo, and so forth, the result of which is a naturalism perfectly harmonious with Dao: "Let your heart-mind wander in simplicity, blend your vital breath with that which is vast, follow along with things as they are, and leave no room for personal views."[31] Such an approach to painting means Chinese artists can produce works of art that are neither technically driven nor color dependent. As for why Daoist-inspired painters abstained from color while Hegel took it to be the highest marker of the artist, this is a question we shall now try to answer.

4. Painting's Coloration and the Shining of Spirit

Due to the immense influence of Daoist philosophy on the visual arts in medieval China, the use of color in painting, particularly landscapes, was quickly abandoned. The reason for this comes from the Daoist belief that color corrupts one's vision. Textual evidence of this is found in both the *Daodejing* and *Zhuangzi*, the latter of which writes:

What can be looked at and seen are but forms and colors; what can be listened to and heard are but names and sounds. How sad, that the people of the world take form and color, name and sound, as sufficient for expressing the truth of things![32]

The truth referred to by Zhuangzi is not that of knowledge but spirit. Every encounter with an object or person produces in us an emotional response, even if it is only on a subconscious level. This emotive reaction, however, seldom forces us to ponder the unquantifiable, spiritual aspect of said encounter, and so we happily take things as they are presented at face value, ignorant of what lies within. No matter if it is color, sound, appearance, or words that beguile us, none pave the way to completeness in Dao. This is because spiritual wholeness *qua* the shining of Dao can only be reached when one subsists in the world colorlessly, silently, formlessly, and emptily. To be colorless is to openly receive color, to allow it to namelessly change of its own volition. The decision of the Chinese to paint in black ink was hence not a random act. Black was seen as the only color capable of harmoniously circumscribing the whiteness of the canvas beneath, creating the possibility for other colors to thereupon fill this newly emergent space. Said differently, the spirit of Dao does not lie with ink or canvas individually but the application of the former, which takes place in sweeping and fleeting moments of action, onto the latter, whose inherent blankness is a constant receptivity akin to the harmony between Dao and the myriad things of the world. In this way, it is the painting and not the painter that invites the viewer to imaginatively fill-in any required color. Had the painting already been replete with color, there would be nothing for the observer to meditate upon, nowhere for their spirit to wander, for the spirit of Dao does not dwell in what is full and active but the empty and placid. The whiteness of the empty canvas thus represents the dark, mysterious nature of both Dao and the spiritually enlightened painter.

Hegel, conversely, holds that "light becomes the physical principle of painting."[33] As to why this is so, he says it is because "light makes objects known in their differences of shape, [makes them] distant from one another, and it does this by irradiating them; it lightens to a greater or lesser extent their darkness and invisibility."[34] Color, for Hegel, thus becomes the true material of painting while coloring is its principle. What is more, he speaks of color as the dark whereas form, distance, expression, and other manners of visible and spiritual character, are light. Light as such remains colorless; it is the pure indeterminacy of identity with itself.[35] Adding color to a canvas is hence to bring to the foreground what was previously unseen. However, coloring is more than simply contrasting black and white, which would render a painting flat and lifeless—it is what allows a painting to shine. Shining, therefore, is not merely light but lightness darkened by color. In other words, the two-dimensional painting regains its lost third dimension, not through tricks of drawing, but the act of coloring. "It is color, coloring, which makes a painter a painter,"[36] Hegel writes, and "it is only by the use of color that painting gives to the life of the soul its really living external appearance."[37] Is this to say, then, that without color the Hegelian soul cannot be knowable to the world via painting? If the shining of spirit is the result of a painter's coloring, does this not imply that the painter, and by extension works of painting, are dependent upon and limited by color?

Hegel's understanding of light and dark, and color generally, was without doubt influenced by the work of Johann Wolfgang von Goethe (1749–1832). Indeed, in his *Philosophy of Nature*, Hegel often praises Goethe while viciously criticizing the work of Isaac Newton (1642–1727):

> We have to thank Goethe for the conception of color which conforms to the Notion. Goethe was drawn into a consideration of colors and light very early, mainly as the result of his interest in painting. The simple purity of his feeling for Nature, which is the prime faculty of the poet, was bound to resist the barbarity of reflection one encounters in Newton.[38]

As for what, precisely, Hegel found so attractive in Goethe's analysis of color, the following offers a succinct explanation:

> The main feature of Goethe's theory is that light is for itself, and that darkness is another principle, which is external to it. White is visible light, black is visible darkness, and grey is their primary and purely quantitative relationship, which is therefore either a diminution or augmentation of brightness or darkness. In the second and more determinate relationship however, in which light and dark maintain this fixed specific quality in face of each other, the deciding factor is which of the two is basic, and which constitutes the dimming medium. There is either a bright base present with a more shaded principle imposed upon it, or vice versa. It is this that gives rise to color.[39]

Goethe's account of light is relevant to our discussion in that light and dark partake in a fixed and oppositional pairing. The diminution or augmentation, as Hegel puts it, of light and dark involves one overpowering the other; color is thus squeezed-out as a by-product of this violent encounter. Bright, vibrant colors symbolize the triumphant embodiment of lightness while dark, dull colors epitomize the submission of light to darkness. Dramatic, yes, but Goethe assists our understanding of why Hegel writes what he does about coloration and shining.

It would be wrong of us to assume Hegel's discussion of light and dark was metaphysically motivated. Nevertheless, we can raise some interesting points of comparison with Daoism. For example, Daoism does not subscribe to the view that light and dark are fixed in position; rather, one is embedded in the other, creating a permanent state of transformative possibility. This idea, that white houses black and black houses white, is a nod to their cosmological model of constant change and transformation. The Daoist worldview lacks the binary perspective of either white or black but embraces the multi-perspectival fluidity of grayness. Chinese ink-wash paintings are thus a seamless blending of white, black, and gray because doing so not only portrays the interwoven spiritual harmony of the natural world, it also reinforces the idea that Dao is beyond clear-cut delimitation and conveyance. The mystery *qua* spirit of Dao is, therefore, a shining of the self-embracement of things in the world; it is none other than a mutual and simultaneous enlightening and darkening of its own authenticity that does not strive to overcome the external things it creates, but abides in nourishing its own invisible root.

Returning to Hegel, in contrast to the plastic arts or poetry, the beauty of a painting is derived exclusively from its color. What makes a painting special is the ability of color, not the forms portrayed therein, to speak to and push the viewer to reflect upon the state of her spirit. Said differently, "painting thus opens the way for us to regard what we see not just as material presence, but as the manifestation of what is immaterial and inward, as the 'shining forth' of the human spirit."[40] This is why Hegel writes that the space captured in a painting is not true, nor is it supposed to be; rather, it is merely a shining of Nature reflecting the spirit of painter and humanity alike. On this point, Chinese painters would agree; however, they would disagree with Hegel when he argues that "shape, distance, boundaries, contours, in short all the spatial relations and differences of objects appearing in space, are produced in painting only by color."[41] What is more, Hegel declares that "oil color not only permits the most delicate and soft fusion and shading of colors, with the result that the transitions are so unnoticeable that we cannot say where a color begins and ends ... [they produce] a translucency of different layers of color."[42] Owing to its translucency through layering, color is able to touch the viewer's spirit in ways poetry and architecture, for example, cannot. The reason for this, Hegel writes, is due to the unique properties of light:

> Light illumines, the day drives away darkness; as the simple blending of brightness with present darkness, this duskiness generally gives rise to grey. In coloring however these two determinations are combined in such a way, that although they are held asunder, they are to the same extent posited in unity. Although they are separate, each also shows in the other. This is a combination which has to be called an individualization; it is a relationship which resembles that considered in what is called refraction, in which one determination is active within another, and yet has a determinate being of its own.[43]

For Chinese painters inspired by Daoism, not only did they learn to work with monochromatic tones, they came to prefer them over their colored alternatives. Wang Wei is a case in point: "Among the ways of painting, monochrome is by far superior. It originates in the nature of the self-existent and perfects the efforts of the creator. Thus in the few inches of a painting, a hundred thousand miles of scenery may be drawn. East, west, south, and north seem to be before the eyes; spring, summer, autumn, and winter are produced under the brush."[44] The self-existent Wang Wei is referring to is Dao, but Dao is only evident to those whose heart-mind has been properly attuned to it. The *Zhuangzi* explains: "He who embodies Dao will have all the gentlemen of the world gather around him. As for Dao . . . one may look for it but it has no form; listen for it but it has no voice. Among those who discuss it, it is called darkly profound. Thus the Dao that is discussed is not [the authentic] Dao"[45] Since Dao is dark and unknowable, Chinese painters tried to capture its natural self-concealment via visual incompleteness. Rather than darkening what is light by applying color, Chinese artists used light to enhance the mystery of the dark. Painting in monochrome thus required deftness of the brush not found in works of color if it was to avoid appearing dead. Jing Hao elaborates:

> Painting is equivalent to measuring . . . One must not take the outward appearance and call it the inner reality. If you do not know this method [of understanding truth], you may even get lifelikeness but never achieve reality in painting . . . Lifelikeness means to achieve the form of the object but to leave out its spirit. Reality means that both spirit and substance are strong. Furthermore, if spirit is conveyed only through the outward appearance and not through the image in its totality, the image is dead.[46]

In other words, if one wishes to capture the inner-spirit of a subject or scene by portraying it in as lifelike a manner as possible, this will inevitably result in failure. How curious, then, that Hegel should also speak of the "living movement" of light, one that belies the false lifelikeness of a painting but which comes about as a result of the inner-shining of spirit:

> White is the corporeal fixation of brightness and is as yet achromatic; black is the materialization and specification of darkness; color occurs between these two extremes. It is the combination of light and darkness, and particularly the specification of this combination, which first gives rise to color. Outside this relationship both light and darkness are as nothing. Night holds all powers within it as self-dissolving ferment and deracinating strife, it is the all-embracing and absolute possibility, the chaos in which matter has no being, and whose annihilation therefore contains all things. Light is purity of form, and it is in its unity with night, which is the mother and nourisher of all, that it has its initial being. All powers stand in awe of night and shift and tremble quietly before it; the brightness of day is the self-externality of night, which has no inwardness, and which is shed and dissipated as a spiritless and powerless actuality. As has become evident however, the truth lies in the unity of both and is not the light which shines in the darkness, but that which is penetrated by darkness as by its essence, and is thereby substantiated and materialized.

It does not shine into darkness, and it neither illumines it nor is it blended by it; it is rather the inwardly disrupted Notion, which as the unity of light and darkness displays itself in the differences of its moments. This is the gay realm of colors, the living movement of which brings forth a variety of hues and constitutes, in its further development, the realized actuality of color.[47]

To paint the living sensuousness of spirit is to paint the living movement of color, to capture light's purity of essence is to penetrate and disrupt the spirit-depriving power of darkness. One cannot help but notice a religious undertone to Hegel's description, a valorization of spirit in the grandest of terms. The same is also true of Daoist-inspired painters. A case in point is when Zhang Yanyuan, whose description we read earlier, elucidates the role of light and color in portraying the ephemeral nature of Dao:

Mysteriously evolving without speech, [Dao's] work operates by itself. Grasses and trees spread forth their glory without depending upon cinnabar and azurite; clouds and snow whirl and float aloft and are white with no need for ceruse. Mountains are green without needing malachite, and the phoenix is iridescent without the aid of the five colors. For this reason, one may be said to have fulfilled one's aim when the five colors are all present in the management of ink alone. If one's heart-mind dwells on the five colors, then the images of things will go wrong. In painting things, one should especially avoid meticulous completeness in formal appearance and coloring, and extreme carefulness and detail that display skill and finish. Therefore one should not deplore incompleteness but rather deplore completeness. Once one knows a thing's completeness, where is the need for completing it? This is not incompleteness. Should one not recognize a thing's completeness, that is true incompleteness.[48]

Taking inspiration from the *Zhuangzi*,[49] Zhang reveals the importance of balancing the blank canvas with its partially painted surface, a balance that also serves as a beacon of the painter's spiritual shining. We should note that the Chinese gentry since antiquity were schooled in six traditional arts, one of which was calligraphy, and calligraphy required perfecting the choice and use of paper, brush, ink-stick, and rubbing stone, skills that would be transferred to the craft of painting. Without understanding the ratio of water to ink, or the amount of pressure to apply to one's brush, the calligrapher and painter alike will fail to capture the free-flowing spirit of Dao. Color is hence an obstacle to releasing the heart-mind of the artist in terms of what a painting can be; by holding the color spectrum to black, white, and gray, the painted subject can be left incomplete—to melt into the canvas—and such being the case, it actualizes itself with every glance thrown its way. In other words, it falls upon the observer to imaginatively recapture the spiritual shining of the painter during the act of painting, and the best way to free the observer's imagination is to commence their dream in black and white.

Hegel, on the other hand, holds the opposite is true: "The sense of color must be a property of the artist, an individual way of looking at and conceiving tones of color as they really exist; it must as well be an essential feature of reproductive imagination and invention."[50] In his discussion of color, Hegel notes three things: first, light and dark colors share a reciprocal relationship; second, harmony between colors gives us a sense of satisfaction; third, carnality represents the magic of color's pure appearance.[51] Skin-tone is the most revered color because it allows others to shine through it, undisturbed. However, carnal color succeeds best when it is lusterless as this befits the pure appearance and emanation of the soul, which is why Hegel argues it is amongst the most difficult things known to painting.[52]

The painting of flesh stands out for Hegel because it alone acts as the shining of spirit, and shining is "the middle between the immediate sensible and ideal thought."[53] What is more, the ability of color to reveal the shining of human spirit means it also determines the sensible in art, a relationship brought together by magic:

> In general, it may be said that the magic consists in so handling all the colors that what emerges is an inherently objectless play of shining, which forms the extreme hovering summit of coloring, an interpenetration of colors, a shining of reflections that shine in other shinings and become so fine, so fleeting, so soulful that they begin to pass over into the sphere of music.[54]

The sensibility of painting does not arise from the canvas surface but from color's coloring; indeed, a painting's surface "is liberated from the scaffolding of its mere materiality,"[55] thus giving way to the shining of the sensible. Based on the above passage, the shining is none other than appearing, but an appearing that points to nothing material; it is, one can say, the play of sensibility. Since art, for Hegel, "brings forth only a shadow-world of shapes, sounds and sights . . . [it] affords satisfaction to higher spiritual interests since it has the power to call forth from all the depths of consciousness an echo and a resounding in the spirit."[56] Said spiritual resounding does not commence with shining and proceed outward into the world of objects whereupon it is imprinted as an image; rather, the shining shines the image of consciousness.

We see something similar in the Chinese tradition, albeit without dependency on the mind. The *Zhuangzi* speaks of the primal shining of Dao, but unlike Hegel and his sensibility of human soul, the spirituality attained by following Dao is onto-cosmological in nature:

> All that have faces, forms, voices, colors—these are but mere things. How could one thing and another be far removed from each other? How could any thing be worth taking as a predecessor? They are forms, colors—

nothing more. But things are born from that which is formless and find their end in that which is unchanging.[57]

Hegel's argument that the goal of art is not to imitate Nature, which would preclude the shining of the sensible, mirrors the Chinese view; however, the preparation required of a painter before painting is a point of divergence. According to Hegel, the painter should "get to know and copy with precision the colors in their relation to one another, the effects of light, reflections, etc., as well as the forms and shapes of objects in their most minute nuances."[58] Given early Chinese painters did not openly embrace working with color, and so had no need to realistically mimic shadows, reflections, and the like, they could devote themselves to how best to represent the intangible spirit of Dao. Herein lies the dilemma for Hegel: if the non-reductive sensibility of painting consists of the shining of color, and said shining illuminates the inwardness of spirit as "the mirror of externality,"[59] then removing color removes any hope of what John Sallis calls "an affective disclosure of the inward spirit to itself."[60] If we truly wish to resolve this dilemma, perhaps we should admit the fact that, in the words of Jean-Luc Marion:

[Painting] breathes in the distance between the unseen and the visible before presenting a new visible (and sometimes without presenting anything), hides every object from the gaze, or better, delivers the gaze from the objective restraints of an object. The painting confronts us with a non-object, unavailable, unmanageable, unable to be (re)produced, unable to be mastered. A non-object admittedly, a counter-object and not a simple anti-object, where the successive destruction of all the dimensions of the pictorial object reinforces by right the rule of objectivity, as its horizon remains intact.[61]

5. Conclusion

Unlike the people of old, modern society takes color for granted. We color the world as we wish it to be colored and pounce on those whose vision differs from our own. Color is now so heavily symbolic and metaphorically-laden that we have forgotten its original, non-human roots. Daoism has shown us the pitfalls of color-dependency and we have seen how painters and art theorists have applied this way of viewing the world to create artworks that free one's heart-mind and spirit of bias and blindness. Whereas the Chinese subscribed to the doctrine of incompleteness in painting, Hegel argued the opposite: to paint is to color and to color is to paint the unhindered spirit. This is achieved by restoring the third dimension to painting, to enrich and enliven what would otherwise be flat and stale.

In light of the neglect given to Hegel's discourse on the coloration of painting, it is hoped the present study will inspire others to embark on analyses of their own. The Chinese, on the other hand, have written a great deal over the centuries about painting, and these works are readily available, including English translations. What is not readily available, and where this chapter makes a significant contribution, is the indebtedness of Chinese aesthetic theory to Daoism, especially when it comes to color. To this end, the goal of this chapter was not to dismiss Hegel but to use his brilliant insights on art and color as fodder for our analysis of the Chinese view. That we learned something new about Hegel as a result of this cross-cultural engagement is a gift worth treasuring all the more.

Notes

1   See the opening pages of Pippin for textual issues surrounding Hegel's *Aesthetics*.

2   G.W.F. Hegel, *Aesthetics: Lectures on Fine Art* (London: Oxford University Press, 1975), vol. 2: 799.

3   Hegel, *Aesthetics*, vol. 1: 74.

4   Qingfan Guo, ed., *Collected Explanations to the Zhuangzi* (Beijing: Zhonghua Shuju, 1997), 719. Translations of Chinese texts are my own unless stated otherwise.

5   Jean-Luc Marion, *The Crossing of the Visible* (Stanford: Stanford University Press, 2004), 26–7.

6   Hegel, *Aesthetics*, vol. 1: 9.

7   Ibid., 31.

8   Victor Mair, "Xie He's 'Six Laws' of Painting and their Indian Parallels", in *Chinese Aesthetics: The Ordering of Literature, the Arts, and the Universe in the Six Dynasties*, ed. Zongqi Cai (Honolulu: University of Hawaii Press, 2004), 94–5; Jianhua Yu, ed., *A Compilation of Texts on Chinese Art Theory* (Beijing: Renmin Meishu Chubanshe, 1986), 355.

9   Susan Bush and Xiaoyan Shi, *Early Chinese Texts on Painting* (Hong Kong: Hong Kong University Press, 2012), 38–9; Yu, *A Compilation of Texts*, 585.

10 François Jullien, *The Great Image Has No Form, or On the Nonobject through Painting* (Chicago: University of Chicago Press, 2009), 194.

11 Ibid.

12 Ibid.

13 Bush, *Early Chinese Texts*, 55; Zicheng Shen, ed., *Historical Collection of Treatises on Painting from Famous Works* (Beijing: Wenwu Chubanshe, 1982), 36.

14 Hegel, *Aesthetics*, vol. 2: 801.

15 Bush, *Early Chinese Texts*, 62–3; Shen, *Historical Collection of Treatises*, 38.

16 Guo, *Zhuangzi*, 314.

17 Ibid., 216–17.

18 Hegel, *Aesthetics*, vol. 2: 804.

19 Stephen Houlgate, "Presidential Address: Hegel and the Art of Painting," in *Hegel and Aesthetics*, ed. William Maker (Albany: State University of New York Press, 2000), 68.

20 Bush, *Early Chinese Texts*, 60–3; Shen, *Historical Collection of Treatises*, 39–40.

21 Jianhua Yu, ed., *Shitao's Treatise on the Philosophy of Painting* (Beijing: Renmin Meishu Chubanshe, 1962), 5.

22 Ibid., 7.

23 Ibid., 12.

24 Hegel, *Aesthetics*, vol. 2: 805.

25 John Sallis, *Transfigurements: On the True Sense of Art* (Chicago: University of Chicago Press, 2008), 11.

26 Ibid., 14.

27 Ibid., 91–2.

28 Bush, *Early Chinese Texts*, 170; Shen, *Historical Collection of Treatises*, 50.

29 Guo, *Zhuangzi*, 741.

30 Susan Bush, *The Chinese Literati on Painting: Su Shi to Dong Qichang* (Hong Kong: Hong Kong University Press, 2012), 37.

31 Guo, *Zhuangzi*, 294.

32 Ibid., 488–9. See also the passage from note 16.

33 Hegel, *Aesthetics*, vol. 2: 808.

34 Ibid., 809.

35 Ibid., 810.

36 Ibid., 838.

37 Ibid., 839.

38 G.W.F. Hegel, *Philosophy of Nature* (London: George Allen & Unwin, 1970), vol. 2: 148.

39 Ibid.

40 William Maker, ed., *Hegel and Aesthetics* (Albany: State University of New York Press, 2000), 64.

41 Hegel, *Aesthetics*, vol. 2: 810.

42 Ibid., 847–8.

43 Hegel, *Philosophy of Nature*, vol. 2: 138.

44 Bush, *Early Chinese Texts*, 172; Yu, *A Compilation of Texts*, 592.

45 Guo, *Zhuangzi*, 755.

46 Bush, *Early Chinese Texts*, 146; Yu, *A Compilation of Texts*, 605.

47 Hegel, *Philosophy of Nature*, vol. 2: 142.

48 Bush, *Early Chinese Texts*, 62–3; Shen, *Historical Collection of Treatises*, 38.

49 Guo, *Zhuangzi*, 216–17.

50 Hegel, *Aesthetics*, vol. 2: 849.

51 Ibid., 841–5.

52 Ibid., 847.

53 Hegel, *Aesthetics*, vol. 1: 38.

54 Hegel, *Aesthetics*, vol. 2: 848.

55 Hegel, *Aesthetics*, vol. 1: 79.

56 Ibid., 39.

57 Guo, *Zhuangzi*, 634.

58 Hegel, *Aesthetics*, vol. 1: 45.

59 Hegel, *Aesthetics*, vol. 2: 801.

60 Sallis, *Transfigurements*, 93.

61 Marion, *The Crossing*, 42.

References

Bush, Susan and Xiaoyan Shi. (2012), *Early Chinese Texts on Painting*, Hong Kong: Hong Kong University Press.

Bush, Susan. (2012), *The Chinese Literati on Painting: Su Shi to Dong Qichang*, Hong Kong: Hong Kong University Press.

Cai, Zongqi, ed. (2004), *Chinese Aesthetics: The Ordering of Literature, the Arts, and the Universe in the Six Dynasties*, Honolulu: University of Hawaii Press.

Guo, Qingfan 郭慶藩, ed. (1997), *Collected Explanations to the Zhuangzi* 莊子集釋, Beijing: Zhonghua Shuju.

Hegel, G.W.F. (1970), *Philosophy of Nature*, M.J. Petry (trans.), London: George Allen & Unwin.

Hegel, G.W.F. (1975), *Aesthetics: Lectures on Fine Art*, T.M. Knox (trans.), London: Oxford University Press.

Houlgate, Stephen. (2000), "Presidential Address: Hegel and the Art of Painting," in William Maker (ed.), *Hegel and Aesthetics*, 61–82, Albany: State University of New York Press.

Jullien, François. (2009), *The Great Image Has No Form, or On the Nonobject through Painting*, Jane Marie Todd (trans.), Chicago: University of Chicago Press.

Mair, Victor. (2004), "Xie He's 'Six Laws' of Painting and their Indian Parallels," in Cai Zongqi (ed.), *Chinese Aesthetics: The Ordering of Literature, the Arts, and the Universe in the Six Dynasties*, 81–122, Honolulu: University of Hawaii Press.

Maker, William, ed. (2000), *Hegel and Aesthetics*, Albany: State University of New York Press.

Marion, Jean-Luc. (2004), *The Crossing of the Visible*, James Smith (trans.), Stanford: Stanford University Press.

Pippin, Robert. (2014), *After the Beautiful: Hegel and the Philosophy of Pictorial Modernism*, Chicago: University of Chicago Press.

Sallis, John. (2008), *Transfigurements: On the True Sense of Art*, Chicago: University of Chicago Press.

Shen, Zicheng 沈子丞, ed. (1982), *Historical Collection of Treatises on Painting from Famous Works* 歷代論畫名著彙編, Beijing: Wenwu Chubanshe.

Yu, Jianhua 俞劍華, ed. (1962), *Shitao's Treatise on the Philosophy of Painting* 石濤畫語錄, Beijing: Renmin Meishu Chubanshe.

Yu, Jianhua 俞劍華, ed. (1986), *A Compilation of Texts on Chinese Art Theory* 中國畫論類編. Beijing: Renmin Meishu Chubanshe.

2

Two Portrayals of Death in Light of the Views of Brentano and Early Daoism

Mary I. Bockover

1. Introduction

This chapter is divided into two main parts. The first part is Western in perspective and begins by examining Brentano's thesis, which attempts to distinguish mental from physical phenomena. In sum, Brentano (1838–1917) argues that mental or "intentional" phenomena entail objects "within themselves" that are characterized by what is called "intentional inexistence," whereas physical phenomena are characterized by having extension and spatial location. After discussing this distinction in depth, I offer a clarification of Brentano's view, as well as my own account of how conscious experience forms an irreducible unity—where how one is conscious entails what one is conscious of, or about—but not the other way around. The object of each intentional event exists "within it" in this (unidirectional) sense. Insights from the discussion of Brentano's view are then applied to how death might be understood and treated in the West.

Next, I transition to the second Daoist part of this chapter by critiquing Brentano's distinction between mental and physical phenomena in a way that brings out what objectivity would mean in that context. Specifically, I argue that all phenomena are a function of our conscious experience, including physical phenomena that are experienced *as if* they have an independent existence (i.e., outside of the mind). I also show how this lays the groundwork for understanding dreams as intentional events that can serve a unique function in helping us to consider who we are within the larger context of this thing that we call "the real world." This view is then compared to the role of dreaming in the *Zhuangzi* 莊子, based on some stories found therein. We end the first part of this chapter by finding, in light of this comparison, that dreaming is a rich and engaging mental process that can inform us about our own lives and the mysterious qualities of life and death in general.

The second part of this chapter goes on to provide a Daoist understanding and treatment of death based on two great Daoist classics, the *Daodejing* 道德經 and the *Zhuangzi*. This discussion shows how an adequate understanding of the role of death in these texts first requires understanding the worldview or "metaphysical"[1] framework expressed therein; one which sees things as being essentially interconnected or as being varying aspects of the same thing, process, or way of change. A basic assumption of Daoism is that Dao 道 (the "Way" or what I call the Great Maker) "contains" and produces all things. For Daoists, Dao is the Ultimate Reality: what is ultimately real and true about existence in general, and life and death in particular.

This comparative discussion of metaphysics and phenomenology achieves a number of goals. For one, it shows how our most basic assumptions will deeply influence how we view reality, life and death. It will also show how Daoist philosophy can be sharply contrasted with the Western view that tends to focus on, and to privilege the life of the mind—conscious experience, reason, or the pervasive sense of subjectivity that distinguishes us from other people and things. Namely, we will see how the basic Western tendency to conceive of ourselves as being self-contained, independent, or as existing in isolation from other things both living and nonliving, differs from the Daoist view that sees life as a mystery and a miracle populated with living beings that are mutually connected and supporting. We will also see how these two very different worldviews can be applied to what it means to live and die well.

2. Brentano's Thesis: The Distinction between Mental and Physical Phenomena

In *Psychology from an Empirical Standpoint*, Franz Brentano (1838–1917) developed the notion of "intentionality," which was originally introduced by scholastic philosophers to refer to a concept. According to Brentano, intentionality distinguishes mental phenomena so that they are directed at objects or states of affairs that do not need to exist or be true about the physical world. The objects of mental phenomena are characterized by "inexistence," meaning that they exist "in the mind" even though they may be *of*, or *about* physical objects.[2] Brentano held that only mental phenomena are characterized by intentional inexistence and cannot be reduced to physical phenomena for this reason. This key excerpt captures Brentano's thesis on intentionality:

Every mental phenomenon is characterized by what the Scholastics of the Middle Ages called the intentional (or mental) inexistence of an object, and what we might call, though not wholly unambiguously, reference to a content, direction towards an object (which is not to be understood here as meaning a thing), or immanent objectivity. Every mental phenomenon includes something as object within itself, although they do not all do so in the same way. In presentation something is presented, in judgement something is affirmed or denied, in love loved, in hate hated, in desire desired and so on. This intentional inexistence is characteristic exclusively of mental phenomena. No physical phenomenon exhibits anything like it. We could, therefore, define mental phenomena by saying that they are those phenomena which contain an object intentionally within themselves.[3]

By contrast, Brentano claims that physical phenomena have extension and spatial location in the "real" external world. Physical phenomena are often the objects or events to which mental phenomena are directed, but not always, because one can be conscious of something that is fictitious or abstract. Stated generally, mental phenomena make up the world of conscious experience in all of its variety. The intentional objects of mental phenomena are what our experiences are of, or about—from our most basic sensations to our most complex ideas (and every kind of experience in-between).

To explain Brentano's thesis further, every mental phenomenon is an act of inner perception, even when referring to the external world. External sensory perception is the way of being conscious that allows us to experience presumably real physical phenomena; we hear a sound, smell an odor, feel hot or cold, see colors, figures, and the like. The intentional object is what we hear, smell, feel, or see; the physical phenomena would be the sound that is heard, the odor that is smelled, the hot or cold that is felt, and the color that is seen. Our sensations, like all acts of inner perception, are indubitable according to Brentano, which is to say that we can be sure that we are having a sensation, but cannot be at all sure that what we are sensing is true of the external world. Stated simply, our sensory experiences can be doubted, which is why they can be thought of as having intentional inexistence.

For this reason, Brentano, for most of his life, held in his theory of perception that external sensory perception can only yield hypotheses about the perceived de facto world, but not truth. Physical phenomena may be what such external sensory experiences presumably are of—the feeling of warmth, the smell of lavender, the sight of Mount Shasta, for example—but whether our external perceptions accurately or correctly tell us anything about the actual external world being perceived, simply cannot be conclusively established. This is shown by the fact that our perceptions of the same thing can vary dramatically; for instance, what feels warm to one person may not feel warm at all to another. In addition, we know that our senses can be notoriously deceptive and as such, that what we perceive as real may actually be just an illusion. A similar view was previously held by René Descartes (1596–1650) who also argued that the senses cannot be trusted when it comes to establishing truth.[4]

Brentano's concept of intentionality includes a huge variety of conscious experiences; indeed, every conscious act is an intentional act, and "every mental phenomenon includes something as an object within itself," which is what the experience is of, or about. We have also seen that intentional objects are centrally defined by their "inexistence," which means that they are mental or psychological objects as opposed to physical ones, even when referring to, or being directed upon physical objects. Brentano also held that all intentional acts form a unity, which is to say that all of the various modes by which one may experience a situation—such as seeing, smelling, feeling, and even thinking about it—are taken together in the conscious act to create one overall experience. For instance, I may be seeing and smelling some lavender at the fields by Mount Shasta, while at the same time feeling the texture of the plant and thinking about how nice it would be to plant some at my own home. But I do not experience these phenomena—what I see, smell, feel, and think about—as separate events. They are experienced as a unified event.

I would like to offer another way to think about the unity of intentional phenomena, which is this: mental events entail their objects but not the other way around.[5] That is, this entailment is unidirectional; the mental event entails the object it is directed upon, but the intentional object does not entail that a particular *kind* of experience is had in virtue of its content alone. One can believe something, can fear the same thing, can hate or love it, desire it, speculate about it, dream about it, and so on. The intentional object—what the experience is of, or about—does not tell us about the kind of mental state it is an object of. Quite clearly, mental events may also give rise to radically different, even incommensurable experiences while being directed at the same object. For instance, it would be difficult for one to be happy and sad about the exact same thing at the same time, although one may be happy about certain aspects of that thing and sad about others. One's feelings about that thing may also change with the passage of time and the accumulation of new experiences.

I think Brentano's view of intentionality can be further clarified by looking more closely at the relation between mental events and their objects. For while Brentano used "intentional object" and "content" interchangeably, I suggest that this must be stipulated since there is a sense in which the content of experience might be thought to include *what kind of experience it is or the more specific way something is experienced*, which the object alone typically leaves out. For example, consider this intentional object, "that his friends will make good parents," and notice that he may speculate about this without necessarily believing that they will. He may also be happy that his friends will make good parents, which does entail that he believes it will be the case. He may also believe that they will make good parents but need not be happy about it, for he may be envious of what he perceives to be their potential to be better parents than he is. This example shows the following about intentional events: stipulating that their "contents" and "objects" can be used interchangeably, both only refer to *what the experience is of, or about,* and not the way it is being experienced. Stated another way, they form a unity that is *unidirectional*: each event must entail an intentional object, but these objects do not in themselves account for the more specific kind of experience being had. Quite often the object does not reveal anything more than what the experience is directed upon.

This is also the case for sensory experiences, once we accept Brentano's distinction between mental and physical phenomena. Recall that in Brentano's view, physical phenomena would include warmth and cold. Warmth and cold are physical phenomena that exist in the external world; for example, the ice was cold (i.e., freezing) until it was warmed up enough to become liquid. Warmth and cold are located in the ice and then the water that the ice becomes after being warmed up. Given Brentano's theory of perception, however, the warmth and cold are physical phenomena that we cannot know anything about based on *feeling* them because external sense perception is so unreliable. If we want to get an objectively clearer idea about how cold the ice is, or how warm the water is, we could use a reliable thermometer to take their temperature. In this way, we gain evidence about how warm or cold the object really is.

Physical pain is interestingly different than warmth and cold insofar as it is an essentially *embodied* experience. Pain is located in the bodies of sentient beings, all of which have extension and spatial location (this includes the sense organs). But pain is also the way we describe what we feel—in this case, it is an intentional sensory experience *of* certain bodily events. We also use "warm" and "cold" in the same way: to refer to our experience of a physical event. The difference, then, is that with *physical* pain, the object— the pain—is in our living conscious bodies.

3. The Phenomenological Paradox and Ambiguity of Death

Brentano's view suggests that the world becomes a world for us only through our experience of it: through sense perception as well as all of the other modes on intentionality that make up the psychological content of the mind. For this reason, I think of him as the father of phenomenology, although it was his student Edmund Husserl (1859–1939) who has been largely credited with this role. We must be clear that Brentano's view is not strictly subjectivist, however, because we live in a world of physical phenomena that we can more or less access through our experience of it. This de facto world contains physical objects that become intentional *for us* through our distinctively human experience of them. This does not reduce the actual object to our experience of it however. As discussed earlier, our experience is largely *of*, or *about* the objective physical world. For instance, we judge that things are true about the physical world with more or less accuracy (i.e., with more or less evidence).

In effect, Brentano's view does not deny that there is an independent, objective world of physical phenomena; on the contrary, his distinction between mental and physical phenomena depends on it. He would, however, have us see that we cannot know anything conclusively about that world. We can form hypotheses about it, share our experience of it, and construct evidence about it, but we will never know it with the veracity of intentional inner perception. When having an experience, we cannot doubt that the experience is ours; that it is one's "self" having the experience (as it is a function of one's own consciousness). Absolute truth is experienced *only* in this "mental" or psychological domain of intentionality or inner perception, while the objective physical world—although encountered and even shared—will essentially remain a mystery.

What does this have to do with the phenomenology of death? More specifically, how can Brentano's view be applied to our encounter with death? A fact about our nature as self-aware beings is that we develop a sense of mortality. We can ask questions about our own mortality, about our own death. Most of the time we ask such questions without having a clear idea of what we mean by "death." This should come as no surprise, since we have no clear idea of what "life" is either. Ironically, life—the thing that animates our bodies—can be just as mysterious as death. And like life, death can be an object for various modes of conscious experience; we can fear death, ponder death, and perhaps even sense death (etc.). Death as a physiological phenomenon has been an object of scientific research as well. But even when death is "observed" and rigorously studied in this way, exactly what is being observed and studied in many ways remains an enigma. Brentano's view is consistent with this idea. When it comes to what we think about death, various kinds of hypotheses may be offered, with some being more or less empirically supported, but like our encounter with life, the real "truth" of the matter will remain inescapably speculative.[6]

A distinct problem of giving a phenomenological account of death should be apparent from the start. I call it the phenomenological paradox of death: from the point of view of living persons, we are not able to say what death is because we have not directly experienced it for ourselves. More precisely, most of us have not experienced *our own death* and lived to tell about it.

Our experience does tell (most of) us that we are embodied living conscious beings. So how might we come to understand our own death? We might think—or rather, speculate—that death brings a complete and final end to our conscious experience.[7] But again, it depends upon what is meant by "death." Consider that within the last half-century there have been cases where "people" have physically undergone "higher brain death" and have been given life support that only serves a "maintenance function," or that keeps other bodily functions active or alive but offers no reasonable hope of returning them to sentient life. In the West, and based on such cases, the biomedical definition of death itself changed along with the criteria used to measure it. Previously death had largely been viewed as a bodily *event* based on the presence or absence of cardiovascular activity, making death more easily conceived as different in kind from life. One is alive at one moment and dead the next—when their heart stops beating or they take their last breath. But because death came to be defined and measured by brain activity, it became easier to think of it as a *process*—where one is more or less dead by being more or less brain dead. In addition to this, even with a healthy body and brain, death is a vital part of maintaining our health and well-being; for example, cells must die for new ones to be generated. As such, death can be conceived as being *essential* to life instead of as being its opposite, or instead of being conceived as an event that annihilates life altogether.

To continue, and in light of recent brain death cases, the question about what makes us *persons* is raised again. We do not have to conclusively know what the connection is between mind and body, or more specifically between consciousness and brain activity, to reasonably suppose that brain damage goes hand-in-hand with diminished cognitive functions.[8] Higher brain death seems to go hand-in-hand with the cessation of consciousness, which for Homo sapiens includes self-awareness and a whole host of intentional experiences, such as the sensory experiences of pleasure and pain. We may still be thought of as living human beings even after undergoing higher brain death, but if our identity as persons depends on having higher brain functions, when these are irreversibly lost then the once living person can be thought of as having already died (even though in some sense the body may still be alive).

In short, having a living human body may not be enough to make us persons, or may not be enough to invest our lives with the kind of quality and dignity vital to living a full human life. For that, self-awareness may be required: the ability to see ourselves as the subject of our own experience. Put another way, a certain type of consciousness is required, which gives us the ability to experience ourselves as standing in relation to others—to other people, life forms, and a whole host of other objects and events. This reflective awareness is also essential to our being able to ask questions about the meaning of death and life. Regardless of our questions though, it seems fair to say that how we come to *value* life and death will intimately be bound up with our subjective experience. And at least in the West, what makes us fear death so often is that it may completely and irreversibly take that subjective experience away.

4. Transition from a Western to a Daoist Phenomenology of Death

We can now understand how Brentano's view that inner perception is the only kind that yields absolute truth, is indebted to Descartes's idea that the only thing one can know with complete veracity is that one exists as a thinking—(self) conscious—being. We become indubitably aware that we are conscious beings through the very act of being conscious, even though we cannot be sure about the truth of the content of our experiences, since the senses can deceive and conceptual "truths" may also be misguided. The truth of our own subjectivity cannot be doubted. Even in the act of doubting, that we are having an experience is indubitable.

My complaint against Brentano is that he equivocates what in truth is the mind-dependent domain of physical phenomena with an (allegedly) real or de facto external world that our mental phenomena are typically of, or about. Just for example, is the figure, or sound, or heat *really* in the external world? I tend to agree with Immanuel Kant (1724–1804), who distinguishes between *noumena* and *phenomena*, or between reality as it exists "in itself" or independent of our experience of it, and reality as it is formed in virtue of our experience, respectively.[9] Kant argues that anything we can know comes to light for us only in virtue of the specific intuitions and categories we have for understanding the nature of things. This *understanding* resides "in the mind" as *phenomena*, not in the independent and "ultimately real" world of *noumena*.

Brentano could fairly respond to this complaint simply by saying that he is much more an empiricist than Kant—that there *is* an actual, physical world that can be more than taken for granted, since we can experience it, and even consistently measure it, with more or less accuracy. He might say that I might not like his use of terminology—namely, his use of "physical phenomena"—but that his overall view is still preferable to one that takes reality to be a function of how we are conscious of it. But Kant did not hold that we construct reality (for there is *noumena*); we construct our understanding of reality, which is all that we can know of it. Thus any notion of there being an actual external physical world will boil down to an article of faith—a presumption of what is real only. In any case, which side of this debate you come down on will depend on what you think ultimately has reality in its own right.

Brentano also held that both physical and mental phenomena were suitable for scientific investigation. In fact, he advocated for a rigorous empirical or objective approach to studying psychological subject matter. Brentano offered the following distinction as a way of understanding how this can happen. *Genetic psychology* is the study of psychological phenomena from a third-person point of view that laid the groundwork for fields such as empirical psychology and cognitive science today. *Descriptive psychology* is the study of psychological phenomena from a first-person point of view—through the systematic observation of the contents of one's own mind—using a method called "introspection."[10] Brentano's notion of descriptive psychology would significantly influence the development of phenomenology.

So, unlike how subjective events are commonly viewed today, Brentano held that mental events—comprised of the contents of one's own mind or experience—were amenable to objective, scientific study. They were empirical phenomena insofar as they could be observed, although from a first-person point of view. By contrast, what it now means for something to be empirical no longer just refers to what can be observed. To constitute reliable evidence, data has to be repeatedly observed and replicated with increasingly rigorous standards. Results came to be thought of as needing to stand on their own and not be driven by the subjects performing the tests; in effect, the more persons who perform a test and get like results, the better. In this way, the modern notion of "empirical" became conceptually more restrictive. All of this went hand-in-hand with radical developments and refinements in the scientific method, which now requires a multipronged system of third-person verification to objectively test its subject matter. In this way, subjective first-person "data" has even come to be conceived by many as inherently biased and counter to the aims of objectivity. In effect, and even by definition for the "hard" sciences, the subjective contents of our own minds are no longer considered to be appropriate subject matter for scientific investigation (for materialist reductionists, physical phenomena are thought to be the only "real" phenomena). In general, this is how the philosophical discipline of phenomenology came into prominence—so human experience could continue to be rationally and objectively examined from a first-person point of view.

Regardless of what we can *know* though, we experience life as if there is a real world outside of ourselves. This experience seems different from the mental world we experience within. And even though we cannot absolutely determine anything about the external world (and both Brentano and Kant would agree here), except that under sound circumstances we have an inescapable sense that it exists, that does not necessarily reduce it to, or elevate it from being mere illusion.

Even more, it may not be unreasonable to believe in "things" that cannot be perceived, at least not directly through the senses. There may also be other ways of objectively perceiving that do not take standard physical phenomena (especially according to today's standards) to be their only possible objects. In any case, and whatever its nature may be, we have a *strong sense* that there is a life and world beyond ourselves that has its own reality. But if we cannot ultimately know about that reality, our judgments *about* it may be as illusory as our perceptions *of* it.

In the second part of this chapter, we will see that Daoism seems more optimistic about our ability to experience Ultimate Reality, even if we cannot know it as an empirical object. However, while we may have the capacity to experience Dao, on some (e.g., spiritual) level, this is spoken of as being extremely rare for those of us in the land of the living. We find this in the *Zhuangzi*:

> Lady Li was the daughter of the border guard of Ai. When she was first taken captive and brought to the state of Jin, she wept until her tears drenched the collar of her robe. But later, when she went to live in the palace of the ruler, shared his couch with him, and ate the delicious meats of his table, she wondered why she had ever wept. How do I know that the dead do not wonder why they ever longed for life?
>
> He who dreams of drinking wine may weep when morning comes; he who dreams of weeping in the morning may go off to hunt. While he is dreaming, he does not know it is a dream, and in his dream, he may even try to interpret his dream. Only after he wakes does he know it was a dream. And someday there will be a great awakening when we know this is all a great dream.[11]

We will see why this is the case in what follows in the second part of this chapter, but let me suggest now that death may bring the great awakening Zhuangzi refers to in this excerpt. From the point of view of the living, death looks like something to weep over, as Lady Li did when she had her life as a border guard's daughter stolen from her. But if death allows us to return to Dao, then the transformation from life to death may be a tremendous benefit. This is supported later in the *Zhuangzi* with the following story:[12]

> When Zhuangzi went to Chu, he saw an old skull, all dry and parched. He poked it with his carriage whip and then asked, "Sir, were you greedy for life and forgetful of the reason, and so came to this? Was your state overthrown and did you bow beneath the axe, and so came to this? Did you do some evil deed and were you ashamed to bring disgrace upon your parents and family, and so came to this? Was it through the pangs of cold and hunger that you came to this? Or did the springs and autumns pile up until they brought you to this?" When he had finished speaking, he dragged the skull over and, using it for a pillow, lay down to sleep. In the middle of the night, the skull came to him in a dream and said, "You chatter like a rhetorician and all your words betray the entanglements of a living man. The dead know nothing of these! Would you like to hear a lecture on the dead?" "Indeed" said Zhuangzi. The skull replied, "Among the dead there are no rulers above, and no subjects below, and no chores of the four seasons. With nothing to do, our springs and autumns are as endless as Heaven and Earth. A king facing south on his throne could have no more happiness than this!" Zhuangzi could not believe this and said, "If I got the Arbiter of Fate to give you a body again, make you some bones and flesh, return you to your parents and family and your old home and friends, you would want that, would you not?" The skull

frowned severely, wrinkling up its brow. "Why would I throw away more happiness than that of a king on a throne and take on the troubles of a human being again?" it said.

Let me point out, in light of the previous excerpt, that Zhuangzi's dream could include an interpretation within it, but in the dream, he does not experience this; the message comes from the skull and is something that Zhuangzi "could not believe." One question this story raises is: Where do we draw the line between what is "real" and what is "illusory"? First, dreams—with their transformative power to move us and inform us—are a type of mental phenomenon. Moreover, the intentional content of dreams only differs in degree from that of waking experience. Like Brentano, Zhuangzi takes waking reality as it is ordinarily experienced to not be ultimately (or absolutely) real at all, and he refers to people who believe that it is as "stupid,"[13] because they do not understand that compared to Dao, to Ultimate Reality, this life—regardless of whether we are dreaming or awake—is just a "great dream" or illusion.

Both the *Daodejing* and *Zhuangzi* describe a certain kind of subjective experience—of Dao—as taking one beyond the illusory character of life as it is ordinarily experienced. This will also be discussed in our examination of these two classical Daoist texts. First though, I want to share a couple of thoughts by comparing how the role of dreaming can be understood from a Western subject-oriented view, with the Daoist Dao-oriented view that will be discussed in more depth in the second part of this chapter.

As we can see in light of the material from the *Zhuangzi* above, Zhuangzi did not take one's dream life to be irredeemably illusory; on the contrary, dreaming is potentially a source of great insight. Many are familiar with the butterfly dream in which Zhuangzi cannot tell if "he was Zhuang Zhou who had dreamt he was a butterfly, or a butterfly dreaming he was Zhuang Zhou."[14] This is to say, in light of his subjective experience he cannot tell the difference, although he goes on to say, "between Zhuang Zhou and a butterfly there must be *some* distinction! This is called the Transformation of Things."[15] The significance of this passage is not clear, but it may suggest that as far as awareness or consciousness itself is concerned, we are essentially the same despite our differences; we are conscious beings united in that fact. But who is the subject here? Is it Zhuang Zhou, who upon waking experienced himself as solidly and unmistakably Zhuang Zhou? Or is it the butterfly "flitting and fluttering around, happy with himself and doing as he pleased"?[16] Whoever was having the experience seemed to be the same in either case, or the question could not have been raised, even in the context of a dream, for it is the subject of the dream who is asking the question. This is not to radically distinguish between embodied consciousness and the bodies it imbues with the capacity for subjective experience. One cannot be a subject of experience without being uniquely and existentially situated in a world filled with all kinds of objects (whatever "world" is supposed to mean here!). Rather, and as the passage suggests, I think it is meant to draw our attention to Dao and its mysterious transformative powers. Namely, regardless of the particular lives at hand or the bodies that they animate, they are all the same in being united in Dao. Despite their differences, they all have the power to change of their own accord in virtue of being alive.

I believe that the phenomenon of dreaming is extremely important, and often because of what it doesn't answer or resolve. I think dreaming acts as a gateway to deeper mysteries, as Zhuangzi's dream about the roadside skull was for him. Dreams allow us to confront a part of ourselves that is a mystery to us and that informs us that we are part of something larger—something beyond the self that is also a part of the self, as Dao is in each of us but is also (eternally) beyond any one of us.[17] If we are lucky, our reflections may bring insight to our waking lives, but the deeper insight is that our lives, our experience, our very selves are a part of this great mystery that Daoists simply refer to as Dao.

Why should we automatically privilege our waking life over our dream life when it comes to forming a relationship with Ultimate Reality, which goes beyond them both? Of course, this is completely anecdotal, but numerous reports from near death experiences refer to a tunnel being traversed in a dreamlike state, and of experiences happening during that state that had bearing on one's current life—even regarding things of which one was previously unaware. In that state, something also happened that brought that person back to the land of the living. Who knows what we will experience (if anything) as we pass into death from life; as we will see shortly, Daoism views life and death as mysteries that can be deeply, even spiritually, appreciated so long as we open ourselves up to them. Both the *Zhuangzi* and *Daodejing* tell us that in order to do this, we must start from a place of not knowing—to be open to possibilities never before experienced—and that preconceived notions will only keep us from taking them in. Shall we welcome the mysteries even when death comes our way?

5. Towards an Understanding of Death in the *Daodejing*: First, the "Metaphysic" or View of "Reality" Expressed Therein

In this second part of this chapter I am ultimately interested in the view of death expressed in the *Daodejing*, sometimes translated *The Way and its Power*, and the *Zhuangzi*. Understanding death in these texts first requires understanding their "metaphysic" or view of reality though, or more specifically, gaining insight into the significance of death from these Daoist perspectives requires knowing how it fits into their larger worldviews.

Chapter 1 of the *Daodejing* contains a very brief account of how the "universe" came to be—that is, the philosophical universe or Ultimate Reality, which goes far beyond the physical universe. I realize that I am using Western language here when referring to Dao as Ultimate Reality, for Chinese metaphysics generally portrays reality in terms of generative processes or "ways of change"—in terms of relations and patterns of change—whereas in the West it is generally understood in terms of static essences or separate substances. Despite this cultural difference, Dao is the source and sustainer of *everything*, which paradoxically is typically cast as "what is not"—as what cannot be seen, heard, or known, at least not in the sense that we may come to know physical objects and events. More importantly, while Dao is repeatedly referred to as "something" that cannot be fathomed or measured, it is also referred to as that which creates all things and sets the course for how they change as long as they exist. In other words, the Dao is the creative "principle"[18] of the universe itself. Here is what chapter 1 says about Dao:

> The Dao that can be spoken of is not the constant Dao; the Dao that can be named is not the constant name. The nameless was the beginning of Heaven and Earth; the named was the mother of the myriad creatures. Hence always rid yourself of desires in order to observe its secrets; but always allow yourself to have desires in order to observe its manifestations. These two are the same but diverge in name as they issue forth. Being the same they are called mysteries, mystery upon mystery—the gateway of the manifold secrets.[19]

The nameless Dao was the beginning of Heaven and Earth, the images of the first two hexagrams of the *Yijing* 易經 (*Book of Changes*), which are Creativity and Receptivity respectively.[20] Dao birthed them as a mother gives birth to her progeny. Dao is the *mother* of the *myriad creatures*—all that was, is, and will be. These are the "manifestations" that we can observe, if we desire to do so. But Dao includes more than what is made manifest and can be named, for Dao includes "what is not" and "what will not be," since all non-things could also have existence if only Dao would make it so. In other words, everything is possible for Dao, even if all things are not made actual (or manifest); Dao has the *de* 德 or *power* to do anything, and through Dao all things are done, even though not all things are done. These "things" (or non-things) may have no observable existence, but they are real and "exist" as possibilities, as the *potential* Dao has to bring things into existence *or not*.

We also read in chapter 42 of the *Daodejing*:

> Dao begets one, one begets two, two begets three, and three begets the myriad creatures. The myriad creatures carry on their backs the Yin and embrace in their arms the Yang, and are the blending of the generative forces of the two.[21]

Dao is often translated as "one" (often capitalized to show its significance), but in this excerpt is said to beget one, which I take to mean that the idea of there being one already implies that there is something else, such as two, or three, or 10,000 things (here, called the myriad creatures). In other words, the "one" is what we call Dao once we give it a name, but if we hold to "its" being nameless, it admits of *no distinction whatsoever*. This is one way of thinking about Dao. Dao in this sense is called "one" to name the nameless way of change, also characterized as "changeless" because there is truly nothing from which it can be distinguished. What we observe is not *change itself*, but the effect that change has had on things. These two aspects of reality—the *changeless change* that can only be observed in virtue of the effect it has on what Dao has created, and the things that are observed *as changing* because Dao has made it so—are in practice inescapably interdependent. There is no change unless there is something to be changed. Or, the changeless (way or *dao*) of change is activated only once it has something to act upon. The changeless way of change still exists and is real even before there is anything to be changed though. This is the ultimate power of Dao: to create something out of nothing. Would this be out of nothing in an absolute sense? No: it is Dao's power to create and make things manifest in the world.

Now, referring back to chapter 1 of the *Daodejing*, as soon as we speak about Dao—as soon as we give the nameless a name—we distinguish it as "something," which mistakenly makes the infinite source and sustainer of reality appear to be a definite object to be experienced as other manifest objects of experience are. So, as soon as we start to talk about Dao, we misrepresent the very "thing" we are trying to fathom. Consider this excerpt from chapter 25 of the text:

> There is a thing confusedly formed, born before Heaven and Earth. Silent and void it stands alone and does not change, goes round and does not weary. It is capable of being the mother of the world. I know not its name so I style it "the Way."[22]

The "thing" that "stands alone and does not change" is the changeless change just explained, that was "born before Heaven and Earth" or before anything was actually created. In fact, to say it was born may be off, since Dao is consistently referred to as eternal or "always so." What is this "way" more specifically though? We go back to chapter 42 and see: from Dao came something in contrast to it, which then became further differentiated into two primal forces (Yin and Yang) that interact ("the three" that "goes round and does not weary") to produce everything else. In short, this is the way the world changes. This is the way things move from the "silent and void" or *not being* of Dao into *being* or observable reality. Ultimately though, the primal forces of "what is not" and "what is" are absolutely interrelated, as we will soon see in more depth. For now, we can see why the primal force of

Yin that powers all change is likened more to the silent emptiness of the Primal Mother than to the ostensible and observable changes we can see and name (Yang). Still, Yin and Yang are always interdependent, as these basic metaphysical "ingredients" for change must *interact* for anything to change at all.

To explain the view of reality found in the *Daodejing* in more depth, Yin originally referred to "darkness" in contrast to the "lightness" of Yang, but now the Yin–Yang relation applies to any pair of related "opposites" that are in reality mutually implying complements. In fact, they are just different aspects of the same "thing," or more accurately, the same way of change. For example, creativity (the image is Heaven) and receptivity (the image is Earth) are simply different aspects of the same "creative" process. We focus on *what is created* because we can see, hear, or experience it in a more tangible way. But the *Daodejing* makes it clear that *inactivity* (*wuwei* 無爲) is a necessary aspect of any activity (activity and inactivity are also mutually entailing); nothing could be created without it possessing an element of receptivity within itself. Something comes into being out of something it was not, and the "place" into which it moves as an existing thing has to be receptive to its being (there). For example, it is not possible to have a creative thought without first being open to the possibilities of things not yet thought. The mind has to be "silent and void" in order for something new and different to enter. Similarly, it is the empty space between the notes that makes manifest the sound. Here's an excerpt from *Daodejing* chapter 2:

> Thus Something and Nothing produce each other; the difficult and easy complement each other; the long and the short offset each other; the high and the low incline toward each other; note and sound harmonize with each other; before and after follow each other.[23]

My claim is that these complements do not just produce, offset, incline toward, or harmonize with each other. These "opposites" refer to the same "thing," or more precisely, they are varying aspects of the same creative process or way of change. For example, Nothing is *not* logically inconsistent with Something; it is a vital aspect of what anything is, including what it can do. Think again about the generative power of Dao. Everything that exists first had the potential to exist, and was at some point brought into existence from *what it was not*. Moreover, things and processes can be distinguished from others only by virtue of what they are not, making each thing definite (one is not two, two is not three, etc.). Therefore, Nothing is *not* Nothing in an absolute sense. Nothing is not the negation of Something, rather, it is *essential* to what makes it what it is, including the way it can change. The same holds true for any mutually entailing pairs of "opposites." Consider that dark is just *less* light. Place one instance of "less light" beside another that is even less light, then the first instance becomes "dark" by comparison. These qualities refer to the same thing that we call lightness or darkness depending on our focus and how we desire to make use of them, but they are different only in degree, existing on a continuum and manifesting as definite qualities because of what they are not (and by contrast). Mainly, each thing or quality has a "way" that is useful only in virtue of Nothing. Chapter 11 of the *Daodejing* makes clear this point:

> Thirty spokes share a hub. Adapt the nothing therein to the purpose at hand, and you will have the use of the cart. Knead clay in order to make a vessel. Adapt the nothing therein to the purpose at hand, and you will have the use of the vessel. Cut out doors and windows in order to make a room. Adapt the nothing therein to the purpose at hand, and you will have the use of the room. Thus what we gain is Something, yet it is by virtue of Nothing that this can be put to use.[24]

To conclude, the Dao cannot be fathomed in any ordinary way, for the very reason that it is not an object of ordinary experience. However, if we expand our focus beyond the specific purpose or desired end we may have in mind, we can experience the mysteries of Dao on what could be called a spiritual level.[25] Experience on this level allows us to observe more than how things and processes manifest in the world; it also allows us to *feel our connection* with the magnificence of creation itself. The *Daodejing* does not just critique our myopic human view of things; we can experience the unity of things and how they have their source in Dao, if, like Dao, we make our minds "silent and void." Then our minds may be pervaded with a profound appreciation for the mysteries of Ultimate Reality. In this way, we have phenomenological access to the Mother of Creation that produces all things and brings them to completion, not in knowing the details of the process but in having *our very being moved* by being part of creation itself. This may be the strongest sense of connection one can feel—that "one" is not really one at all but a vital aspect of "something" that goes far beyond the "self."

Because of this, I think the central aim of the *Daodejing* is to evoke in us a deep appreciation for what it is to be alive. We do not live our lives as much as life is living us. From this perspective, we are not so much subjects of consciousness as we are subjects of life, a life that is *given* to us, and it is a false sense of agency and overabundance of desire that make us think that we are the ultimate source of our own vitality. We live for as long as Dao carries us, and then we return to that great source. This realization should dramatically impact how we experience and value life: as for our own existence, there was an almost infinitely greater chance of our *not being*, but here we are. Life is truly a miracle, a dimly visible reality from which we move, and breathe, and have our being. Life may be the most profound mystery of all. Of it, how can we not stand in awe?

6. The Phenomenology of Death in the *Daodejing*

As light and dark are mutually implying complements, so too are life and death. They are just different aspects of the same "thing," process or event, or way of change. Death is just "less life" as life is just "less death." They exist as aspects of something we call "life" because we, as living, conscious beings are drawn to what makes more sense to us—to what we perceive, think about, and name. Here is another key point in the *Daodejing*: what we perceive and name shapes the world *as we experience it*. This is the "human way" (*rendao* 人道) that constructs a uniquely human reality built of ideas, conventions, and artifacts that can give us an overrated sense of our own importance as living members of this world. Our power to create a human world can never match the power of Dao though, which has ultimate power over our lives and the lives of all beings, although it need not make a show of it. Dao and its power are beyond our control, no matter how much we would like to think otherwise. Dao produces all things, including our natural capacity to live as we uniquely do as human beings. We can create only because Dao has created us to do so.

Our nature is to create, which rests on our innate capacity to distinguish things. We name them based on our unique way of experiencing them as separate and distinct. Then we construct new things by putting the parts together in new and different ways. Dao has given us this human way, but it has become unbalanced and unhealthy. This is one of the most important points that the *Daodejing* makes: we are consumed by desire to construct more and to have more, and as a result we are losing our connection with each other as well as with Dao, the Great Maker who has given us our very lives. The Yin–Yang relation has become unbalanced in us, and too much Yang energy is making us sick. This is why the *Daodejing* reminds us to embrace the Yin—to welcome the dark, to return to our roots, to live simply and be receptive to the source and sustainer of life itself.

In a way, the emptiness, stillness, and silence of Dao is more like death than life. Paradoxically, this "dimly visible"[26] aspect of life is life in its fullness in a key respect. Dao's infinite power to create rests upon *what is not*—what does not exist and is brought into being; the inactivity needed for activity to rest, be restored, and to achieve its very best; the Nothing that is the vital part of Something that makes it *what it is*; the "death" that changes something into something else so it can go from one "state of being" to another—that is to say, so it can live. Without such transformation, nothing could live or exist in the first place. Based on this, I think of death as being the "secret essence" of life. Here is an important analogy that I will now explain: death is the essence of life as Dao is the essence of All Things.

Dao is the essence of all things; it is Ultimate Reality even though we may not be able to experience it like the things it brings into being. I have said that life is perhaps the most miraculous of all created things, which is why it is of such central importance in the *Daodejing*. But death is the process whereby living things return to Dao. This is why both Dao and death are almost always referred to with Yin language and imagery; they seem changeless, empty, and darker than any mystery. Most critically, death is not the absolute negation of life. As Dao is the essence of being, death is the essence of life in being its source (we come into being from not being), its sustainer (change requires the death of what came before), and its ultimate secret. And this is nothing short of ironic.

The *Daodejing* is infused with paradoxes or apparent contradictions designed to bring out the truly ironic quality of life. We have already seen this in relation to Yin–Yang, inaction and action, nothing and something, empty and full, etc. It is the *inaction* in action that activates change and allows it to produce maximum results. Without death life would not be as full, and this is nothing short of ironic, for death gives our lives value and meaning exactly because we do not know just what it is or what it has in store for us. "Death" is a word that refers to a change so mysterious that it leaves us with no words, and no way to conclusively account for it. This is profoundly ironic because if we think death is a mystery, what on earth do we think life is!

7. Towards an Understanding of Death in the *Zhuangzi*: First, a Comparative Account of *Zhuangzi's* "Metaphysic" or View of "Reality"

As we have already seen in the *Daodejing* and will see in the *Zhuangzi*, if one stands in awe of being alive, and of the extraordinary depths this experience can offer, then one has realized—phenomenologically—the beauty of being alive, regardless of what life has in store. I think this is one key truth that the *Daodejing* and *Zhuangzi* were trying to convey, not as a conceptual or epistemic truth, but as an experiential realization.

In any case, the traditional metaphysic of ancient China schematized Dao as being tripartite: a Dao of Heaven (*tian* 天), Humanity (*ren* 人), and Earth (*di* 地). This traditional account saw humanity as bridging the gap between Heaven and Earth, in a sense as ministering for Dao so that prosperity, civility, and peace could be achieved. Human power was taken to be an extension of the power of Dao. The problem was that the humans in power seriously abused this natural gift and virtue, and the result was profound self-centeredness and social disorder.[27]

I think this is why the *Daodejing* radically and explicitly revised how we understand Dao to consist of the unspeakable Dao, Heaven, and Earth. That is, as a metaphysical category, humanity was removed and presumably relegated to the realm of Earth and the myriad creatures that Dao has populated on it. We have seen this from the beginning of the text, wherein the constant Dao birthed its primal progeny of Heaven and Earth—with no mention of humanity; no metaphysical elevation of humanity above the other myriad creatures.

Indeed, the *Daodejing* generally critiques the human way as having lost its way by creating imbalance and disorder instead of harmoniously blending with others in the human community and the rest of the world. We humans were demoted in not living up to the calling, in not being true to the mandate of Heaven. The *Zhuangzi* maintained the traditional language of the Dao—of Heaven, Humanity, and Earth—but still offered a clearly Daoist solution for restoring the good life: we must return to Heaven's (or Nature's) Way, to harmoniously blend with the rest of life.

Why must we turn our attention to Heaven? So that we can gain power over others? No, and this is precisely why we fail to hear the Dao. If our lives are aligned with Dao, then we will be able to live a good life *by cultivating a general state of well-being* on a personal, social, and spiritual level. Zhuangzi characterizes this way of being as one of ease and true contentment that comes from being lost in the Dao. In order to do this, however, one must lose oneself. From chapter 2 of the *Zhuangzi* we see this exchange between Ziqi and Ziyou:

> Ziqi of Nanguo sat leaning on a low table. Looking up to Heaven, he sighed and seemed to be at a loss as if his spirit had left him. Yan Cheng Ziyou [his pupil], who was standing in attendance in front of him, said, "What is the matter? The body may be allowed to be like dry wood but should the mind be allowed to be like dead ashes? Surely the man leaning on the table now is not the same man leaning on the table before." "Aren't you asking a good question!" Ziqi replied. "Do you know that I have just lost myself? You have heard the music of man but not the music of Earth. You may have heard the music of the Earth but not the music of Heaven." . . . Ziyou said, "Since the music of Earth consists of sounds produced in the various hollows, and the music of man consists of sounds produced in a series of flutes, what is the music of Heaven?" "The wind blows in a thousand different ways," replied Ziqi, "but the sounds are all produced in their own way. They do so by themselves. Who is there to rouse them to action?"[28]

Both the *Daodejing* and *Zhuangzi* acknowledge that we are created by Dao to create artifacts and conventions for interacting in a human context. But we have forgotten that we are *subjects* of Dao and its power, subjects of life, and this should be humbling as well as uplifting. We should be humbled by the realization that we are not as great as we may think regardless of the power and status that the human world may give us. We are like all other living things in coming from Dao, returning to Dao, and in being subjected to its power at all times. At the same time, we should be uplifted by the realization that we can rest in that which gives us our life, what gives us our very being and efficacy. We have been given this gift, and life will live itself as sound produces itself. What rouses them all to action? Dao is truly the Great Maker who will provide for us if only we let go of ourselves and turn our attention to Heaven. This is key to cultivating a good life: to not let an inflated sense of self-worth get in the way.

According to Zhuangzi, there is an unmediated spiritual knowledge that the "perfect person" (i.e., the sage) experiences, that allows one to fully appreciate the boundless unity and perfection of Dao that is foundational to living a good life, and that naturally leads one to *live a life of ease and contentment*. "Knowing" Dao so intimately is highly paradoxical though. It does not entail knowing Dao in the sense that we gain immediate and total access to all of the details of objective reality (that is, all that Dao creates). I think the spiritual—or mystical—sense of "knowing" refers to an experience for which an awareness of self does not get in the way of experiencing a close and vital connection with Ultimate Reality. Such a spiritual experience of Dao is "pure"—a kind of "unknowing" where the mind is filled up, but not with ordinary objects, mental or physical. Instead, one becomes aware of Dao's miraculous creative potential, so that what is "dimly visible" or not fathomed at all by most of us becomes illuminated. This experience is of the infinite Way of change itself, which is beyond all (relative) perceptions and distinctions. As the traditional account of the tripartite Dao suggests, we humans are a vital part of creation and have a special role to play in it; to fully appreciate our connection with the source and sustainer of reality and to be naturally guided by it. Knowing "this" puts us at ease in feeling Dao's power to carry and support us where our own limited self-will cannot. In this way, one can abide by the power to act not out of self-will but as a vehicle for Dao and the harmonious blending and ease of action it makes possible. Is this easy? . . . When it comes to our own dying? I think not, for all we have to do is be at ease with losing our very "selves"!

8. A Comparative Account of the Phenomenology of Death in the *Zhuangzi*

According to Chinese philosophy in general, knowledge does not just make certain kinds of experience possible; it is directly connected with living a good life and acting in a particular kind of way. A main theme in both the *Daodejing* and the *Zhuangzi* concerns what I will call excellence in action— "actionless action" (*wuwei*) in the *Daodejing* and "natural" or "spontaneous" (*ziran* 自然) action in the *Zhuangzi*. In both texts, this action is executed with such refined skill that it looks easy. One may even refer to such action as "perfected" in using just the right amount of effort to achieve the best possible results (or at least what appear to be). The *Zhuangzi* makes clear that one has to have a "knack" for acquiring such skill; conversely, that for some, no matter how much effort and practice they put into it, they may not be able to acquire a particular skill, not to mention reach the perfected ability possessed by true savants. Both texts discuss how extraordinary skill can be applied to specific areas of action as well as to living life more generally. As far as specific talents are concerned, actions become "second nature" since we are creatures of artifact—we do not just act directly according to what nature has given us. For us, life embodies this paradox: nature gives us the ability to create of our own doing.[29] We "by nature" create realities, both material and conceptual. We construct our world, our cultures, our roles, and our "selves." We construct ideas and meanings. And by nature, we try to grasp the meaning of life and death.

Excellence in action is not just a capacity in either text, however. In the *Zhuangzi*, the knack for developing a skill is perfected by one's being a committed participant in the activity. It is a living embodiment of skill always borne out in action, so consistently that persons possessing such skill are often identified in virtue of it. This is the human way: we are creatures of artifact who do not just directly respond to the promptings of nature; rather, we take what nature provides and then imaginatively create something out of it that fulfills some desired purpose.[30] Some examples from the *Zhuangzi* include fishermen, potters, cooks, woodworkers, and the like. Here is what Cook Ding has to say about his skill in chapter 3:

> What I care about is Dao, which goes beyond skill. When I first began cutting up oxen, all I could see was the ox itself. After three years I no longer saw the whole ox. And now—now I go at it by spirit and don't look with my eyes. Perception and understanding have come to a stop and spirit moves where it wants. I go along with the natural makeup, strike the big hollows, guide the knife through the big openings, and follow things as they are. So I never touch the smallest ligament or tendon, much less a main joint. A good cook changes his knife once a year because he cuts. A mediocre cook changes his knife once a month because he hacks. I've had this knife of mine for nineteen years and I've cut up thousands of oxen with it, and yet the blade is as good as though it had just come from the grindstone.[31]

Cook Ding describes how he has applied Dao to develop his special talent. His knack is brought to life in an extraordinary way, not because *he* is so great, but because his "perception and understanding have come to a stop" for him, so the spirit or power of Dao itself can guide his action. His action becomes an extension of Dao because his "self" does not interfere with what he is doing and its aim. This truth can be generalized (more or less) to any excellence in action. Dao can best act through us because the focus is on the object and how to achieve it and not on how *we* are making it happen.[32] Consult your own experience. When you act in a way that today might be referred to as "being in the zone," when you "just do it" with ease and skill but without thinking, notice that your perception of "you doing the thing" has vanished. Your focus is "actionlessly" and spontaneously on the action and its aim, in a way that does not involve an explicit awareness of what *you* are doing or what *you* are aiming for. Truly, it is as if the "you" does not figure into the experience at all. Your living conscious body—not your "self"—becomes a conduit of Dao's power to create, to produce, and to achieve excellent results. This is how to live well, applied to specific skills or talents. It also applies to the art of living and dying.

For contemporary purposes, I think the sage is a person who has come to master life. To say that the sage has a "mastery" in the art of living may not be using a very Daoist word, but the point is still made: the sage is a spiritual being who is "pure" in focus, despite the challenges life might offer up; "perfected" in the ability to be connected to, and to derive (even extraordinary) strength from Dao. But like so many themes, "strength" here is to be understood in its paradoxical fullness. In both texts, Daoist strength may appear by conventional standards to be weak. In the *Zhuangzi*, the sagely ability to "let go" of the self in order to take sustenance from Dao is a prime example. The sage experiences Dao and its power directly—and is humbled by experiencing the true nature of things, that inseparably creates great ease and contentment with any change that Dao may bring their way. But feeling at ease in the face of death? How can this be easy? Feeling at ease with this change we call death can occur when one realizes that Dao or the great Way of change is ultimately good. That truth is anticipated in the following excerpt from chapter 6 of the *Zhuangzi*:

> Life and death are fated—constant as the succession of dark and dawn, a matter of Heaven. There are some things which man can do nothing about—all are a matter of the nature of creatures. If man is willing to regard Heaven as a father and to love it, then how much more should he be willing to do for that which is even greater! If he is willing to regard the ruler as superior to himself and to die for him, then how much more should he be willing to do for the Truth![33]

What is "that which is even greater" than Heaven or Nature? It is the power that Dao gave Heaven to have things act and change according to their nature. What power did Dao imbue in matter in order for it to *live*? It is the power to change of its own accord (and according to its own specific *li* or principle): the power of self-transformation. Life and death, draped in conventionally ritualized dressing, are only the veneer of the miraculous and mysterious power of creation itself. Knowing this truth—embodying this truth as a lived reality—allows one to be content with what even by conventional standards would be the saddest of circumstances. To state this central truth found in the *Zhuangzi* in more detail: experiencing Dao and its

miraculous power generates a deep and abiding faith in its workings—
namely, a faith that Dao is good in a way that human conventions cannot
touch. This profound faith and the comfort it entails is expressed in an
excerpt concerning Master Lai, who is gravely ill, and Master Li who has
come to visit.

> Soon afterward Zilai fell ill, was grasping for breath and was about to
> die. His wife and children surrounded him and wept. Zili went to see him.
> "Go away," he said. "Don't disturb the transformation that is about to
> take place." Then, leaning against the door, he continued, "Great is the
> Creator! What will he make of you now? Where will he take you? Will he
> make you into a rat's liver? Will he make you into an insect's leg?" Zilai
> said, "Wherever a parent tells a son to go, whether east, west, south, or
> north, he has to obey. The Yin and Yang are like man's parents. If they
> pressed me to die and I disobeyed, I would be obstinate. What fault is
> theirs? For the universe gave me this body so I may be carried, my life so
> I may toil, my old age so I may repose, and my death so I may rest.
> Therefore to regard life as good is the way to regard death as good."[34]

Feeling at ease in the face of death is one thing. But it is not disconnected
from what many if not most of us get practice in during our lives—how to
manage and even feel comfort in times of what by conventional standards
would be considered misfortune. Consider Cripple Shu who had his "chin
stuck down in his navel, shoulders above his head, pigtail pointing to the
sky, his five organs on the top . . ." Even crippled as he was, he went on to
"finish out the years that Heaven gave him" with "crippled virtue," which I
take to be the skill of living one's life as best one can despite such limitations.[35]
Then there is Shentu Jia without a foot, Mr. Lame-Hunchback-No-Lips, Mr.
Pitcher-Sized-Wen, and many others who populate the *Zhuangzi* and who
are True Persons or persons of virtue despite their abnormalities. We also
meet Master Yu who fell ill and was amazed when the Creator made him
"all crookedy." He did not resent it at all, but instead was "calm at heart and
unconcerned."[36] He responded in awe, imaging all of the wonderful things
that he could do with whatever the Creator might make of him—such as
transforming his left arm into a rooster, or his right arm into a crossbow
pellet, or his buttocks into cartwheels. These seem like absurd possibilities,
but I think the point is this: life is unpredictable and can do anything. The
question is, what will we make of it? Will we live virtuously or the best we
can despite what life might throw at us?

These cases also communicate a crucial message: there is something
inherently good about life, come what may. Despite its spectacular variety
and unpredictability, life is still a gift—a miracle and mystery that gives us
the chance to act, change, and grow into something new and different. This
transformation can be extraordinary. Recall that the *Zhuangzi* begins with
a story of the Kun fish who transforms into the Peng bird—a radical

transformation that may be just as radical as the transformation of life to death. In a sense the Kun fish dies when the Peng bird emerges. We have analogously radical transformations when we look at natural evolution over time. If space and time are relative, lodged in a perspective that is species-specific and specific to any given life, then all these distinctions become somewhat blurred in the grand scheme of things. That too may be the case with the relation between what we call life and death. But one thing seems clear: that life entails death, or what we "know" of what we call "life" involves a process or event that we call "death," that seems to be quite unlike it. Since living entails dying, living well entails dying well, which the *Zhuangzi* tells us involves a mindset of contentment and ease; a willingness to freely go with the change regardless of what it may bring.

9. Conclusion

A question that may arise from the examples and stories in the *Daodejing* and *Zhuangzi* is what the relation is between the self—our awareness of our existence as living things—and the material form that our lives animate. In the first part of this chapter, I critiqued Brentano's thesis that mental and physical events are different in kind; where mental events are thought to exist in the mind only, while physical objects (such as our bodies) exist in the external physical world. My point was that "physical phenomena" have to be experienced by subjects in order for them to exist for us at all (they are phenomena), and to that extent they are "mental" objects too, even though they are experienced as if they have an independent existence. In addition, the mental phenomenon of dreaming shows how even more varied and ambiguous conscious experience can be—because until we wake up, dreams can seem as real as any waking experience, while waking life can sometimes feel like a dream. In any case, for humans, we are not only conscious of, or about things; we can see ourselves as figuring into the content of our own experience. This is where the sense of "I" comes from that Zhuangzi refers to in various places.[37] The *Zhuangzi* does not discuss the question of what the relation is between our "selves" and our bodies in any depth however. I think this is because our consciousness, mind, or experience, is never conceived in isolation from our bodies, that are existentially necessarily for us to have a place in the world and that are constantly changing. Nor are we conceived as metaphysically separate from the other "external" people, places, things, and events that make up our ever-changing world.

To explain further, my focusing on, and defining the "self" as a self-aware subject of experience displays a cultural bias. We have seen that the *Zhuangzi* refers to actual embodied characters no matter how extreme or absurd— who in each case cannot be understood in absence of their story or situation. I think if we could ask Zhuangzi, he might reply that ideas such as mind or self are just abstractions, and perhaps misleading ones when considering what is real. Exactly what does it mean to have a mind or self? Of course, we are able to be aware and to act according to the limitations of our nature, which for humans mean we can reflect on our experience and actions, as well as our role in bringing them about or changing them in the future. But do these concepts merely refer to certain species-specific capacities? Then where is the real person in this, when what is most essential to our having a particular life is abstracted away? Life is to be lived and not just postulated. I think Zhuangzi might say that such abstractions, especially when taken to be independent realities, fail to do justice to our experience as living human beings. We are not minds with selves; and even if we posit that we have these, they will not define what makes us who we most essentially are; they will not capture what makes existence unique for each and every one of us.

To continue, I think Zhuangzi might say that the subject–object distinction as Brentano saw it, or as I have redefined it, does more than fail to do justice to our experience. While we might agree that experience has to be of, or about something, there is no good reason to privilege the experience of *our own minds* or conscious activities over the things that make up our world— the one we live and die in. I see the overall matter this way: Western metaphysics or accounts of reality tend to be biased or lodged in a "mentalistic" and hence "individualistic" worldview. So, we become preoccupied with what might happen to our individual (self) consciousness when we die. By contrast, Daoist worldviews tend to be biased in favor of the concept of Dao or framed in a perspective that sees this Ultimate Reality that produces and sustains all things as needing no explanation. Dao and its power to create is ultimately what is real. Moreover, if we consult our experience, we can clearly observe that nothing real exists alone or in isolation, which would include our so-called minds or selves.[38] Dao or the unfathomable way of change is ultimately real, so all other questions, such as ones about the self are of secondary or no real importance. To state the matter simply: for Daoists we are subjects of life, not subjects of objects.

We do know that both the *Daodejing* and the *Zhuangzi* see life as a miracle and mystery that cannot be fathomed. We can appreciate it fully and be at ease with its changes, but we cannot know the infinite Dao as we might "know" definite things. As the *Daodejing* says in its opening chapter, we can "observe" Dao's secrets, which I take to mean that we can "see" and be awed by them, but we cannot know them. We can only know that they are good in coming from Dao. In effect, we can have *faith* in Dao and its power to change us into whatever it will. Dao is the way of change, including the change of life into death. So there is nothing to fear; nothing ultimately to be sad about.

Zhuangzi's wife died. When Huizi went to convey his condolences, he found Zhuangzi sitting with his legs sprawled out, pounding on a tub and singing. "You lived with her, she brought up your children and grew old," said Huizi. "It should be enough simply not to weep at her death. But pounding on a tub and singing—this is going too far, isn't it?" Zhuangzi said, "You're wrong. When she first died, do you think I did not grieve like anyone else? But I looked back to her beginning and the time before she was born. Not only the time before she was born, but the time before she had a body. Not only the time before she had a body, but the time before she had a spirit. In the midst of the jumble of wonder and mystery a change took place and she had a spirit. Another change and she had a body. Another change and she was born. Now there's been another change and she's dead. It's just like the progression of the four seasons, spring, summer, fall, winter. Now she's going to lie down peacefully in a vast room. If I were to follow after her bawling and sobbing, it would show that I don't understand anything about fate. So I stopped."[39]

Zhuangzi's wife dies, then she "lies asleep in the great house (the universe)."[40] This passage expresses Zhuangzi's faith in the workings of Dao, in Heaven or Nature, and in our destiny within that larger context—of human life and the death it necessarily entails. So, what can we say about death according to the *Zhuangzi*? We are told that death is peaceful, restful, and perhaps the greatest transformation in the process or way of change that living things undergo. Dao or the Great Maker made life, and human life evolved from that, which now includes each one of us as well as those we care about. We also are told that the Great Maker is Good, and that anything it does is all right, even though it may not seem that way from a human perspective. Zhuangzi wept for his wife, and presumably we will weep for those we love if their time comes to pass into the Great Unknown before us.

The Great Maker also made us so that we might try to know ourselves—to plumb the depths of our being even if we come up with just a deeper mystery. Now imagine this as a kind of thought experiment. Imagine that your time to die has come and the door to the vast room, the great house, opens in front of you. If you could, if it was within your power to do so, would "you" willingly pass through that door with eyes wide open and ears attuned? Would you choose to go and see?

Notes

1   I put the word "metaphysics" in quotes since the worldview in ancient China did not see the distinction between the physical and so-called metaphysical world as being one of kind.

2   Mental objects need not be real or physically exist either; for example, we can be conscious of fictitious or abstract ideas, images, and objects too.

3   Franz Brentano, *Psychology from an Empirical Standpoint* (London: Routledge, 1995), 88–9.

4   See Descartes's "First Meditation" wherein he uses his Dream Hypothesis to consider that everything his senses tell him is true about reality may actually be false or just a dream. This hypothesis is used to show that since the senses can deceive, they cannot be trusted to get at what is true beyond a doubt.

5   I discussed this in depth in my Ph.D. dissertation called *Emotionally Relevant Feelings*. Among other things, I show how there is an intentional sense of feeling that is not to be understood as either a (bodily) sensation, or as a judgment, or as a combination of the two. These "emotionally relevant feelings" constitute a distinct type of intentional event in their own right.

6   "Truth" here would mean beliefs that we have about death that we have shared empirical evidence for believing.

7   See Epicurus' argument concerning death that basically concludes that death cannot harm us since, in order to be harmed, we must be able to have experiences, which death prevents.

8   Ample evidence supports this, but there are also accounts suggesting that one may be conscious of a lot more than has been assumed. For instance, see recent testimony by Eben Alexander (1953–present), e.g., *Proof of Heaven*.

9   Immanuel Kant, *Critique of Pure Reason* (Cambridge: Cambridge University Press, 1998), chapter 3.

10   Some other introspectionist philosophers were William James (1842–1910) and Wilhelm Wundt (1832–1920).

11   Zhuangzi, *Zhuangzi: Basic Writings* (New York: Columbia University Press, 2003), 42–3.

12   See Chai 2016 for a deeper appreciation of the significance of this story.

13   Zhuangzi, *Basic Writings*, 43.

14   Ibid., 44.

15   Ibid.

16   Ibid.

17   I think dreaming is akin to meditating and praying, as a tool for increasing awareness, agency, and peace of mind in a world not defined by materialist reductionist values.

18   I put "principle" in quotes because it is a Western way of referring to something that according to Chinese metaphysics is ultimately and completely real. Indeed, even using the term "metaphysics" as it is often distinguished from "physics" may suggest a distinction of kind where a general Chinese worldview would see such a difference more in terms of degree.

19   Laozi, *Daodejing* (London: Penguin Books, 1963), chapter 1.

20   *Yijing* is often translated "The Way of Changes," but A.C. Graham, a noted scholar of Chinese philosophy, translated the "Yi" in the title as "Divination Made Easy."

21   Laozi, *Daodejing*, chapter 42.

22   Ibid., chapter 25.

23 Ibid., chapter 2.

24 Ibid., chapter 11.

25 This "spiritual" level may actually be most basic and primal—while human objectification may disconnect or alienate us from each other and the world we live and die in.

26 Laozi, *Daodejing*, chapter 6.

27 This is very much the case around the Warring States Period (475–221 BCE).

28 Wing-Tsit Chan (trans.), "The Mystical Way of Chuang Tzu," in *A Source Book in Chinese Philosophy* (Princeton: Princeton University Press, 1963), 179–80.

29 One could point out that non-humans also creatively respond to the callings of nature, such as female Grizzlies who will "act against their nature" in order to protect their young [see the video, Bear 71]. But humans take this to a different level, and both the *Daodejing* and *Zhuangzi* cite this as being potentially very problematic. I think both texts indicate that the problem lies in the fact that nature has given us a sense of "self" that we then misconceive as deserving far too much power. That is, the problem lies in our seeing our elevated metaphysical status as being a product of our own efforts instead of as being a gift from Dao. We have transformed this gift into an Achilles' heel that will lead to our downfall as a result—precisely because we abuse instead of nurture our lives and our special connection to Dao.

30 Recall chapter 1 of the *Daodejing*, "always rid yourself of desires in order to observe its [Dao's] secrets; but always allow yourself to have desires in order to observe its manifestations"; that is, so we can make use of them to accomplish some imagined purpose.

31 Zhuangzi, *Basic Writings*, 46.

32 Self-consciousness may actually interfere with our ability to "just do" the action with excellent results.

33 Zhuangzi, *Basic Writings*, 76.

34 Chan, "The Mystical Way of Chuang Tzu," 197–8.

35 Zhuangzi, *Basic Writings*, 61–2.

36 Ibid., 80.

37 Ibid., 32–3.

38 This culturally biased assumption has many moral and political implications. In the West, conceiving of oneself as independent and autonomous has unpleasant results despite the positive ones.

39 Zhuangzi, *Basic Writings*, 115.

40 Chan, "The Mystical Way of Chuang Tzu," 209.

References

Alexander, Eben. (2012), *Proof of Heaven: A Neurosurgeon's Journey into the Afterlife*, New York: Simon & Schuster Inc.

Bockover, Mary. (1991), *Emotionally Relevant Feelings*, Ph.D. dissertation, University of California at Santa Barbara.

Brentano, Franz. (1995), *Psychology from an Empirical Standpoint*, Linda McAlister (trans.), London: Routledge.

Chai, David. (2016), "On Pillowing One's Skull: Zhuangzi and Heidegger on Death," *Frontiers of Philosophy in China*, 11.3: 483–500.

Chan, Wing-Tsit, trans. (1963), "The Mystical Way of Chuang Tzu," in *A Source Book in Chinese Philosophy*, Princeton: Princeton University Press.

Descartes, René. (1960), *Meditations on First Philosophy*, Laurence Lafleur (trans.), Indianapolis and New York: The Bobbs-Merrill Company, Inc.

Graham, A.C. (1989), *Disputers of the Tao: Philosophical Argument in Ancient China*, La Salle: Open Court.

Kant, Immanuel. (1998), *Critique of Pure Reason*, Paul Guyer and Allen Wood (trans.), Cambridge: Cambridge University Press.

Laozi. (1963), *Daodejing*, D.C. Lau (trans.), London: Penguin Books.

Yijing. (1950), Richard Wilhelm and Cary Baynes (trans.), Princeton: Princeton University Press.

Zhuangzi. (2003), *Zhuangzi: Basic Writings*, Burton Watson (trans.), New York: Columbia University Press.

3

In the Light of Heaven before Sunrise:

Zhuangzi and Nietzsche on Transperspectival Experience

Graham Parkes

The world is overfull of beautiful things, but nevertheless poor, very poor, in beautiful moments and unveilings of these things.
NIETZSCHE[1]

Zhuangzi *and* Nietzsche. The names have similar cadences and rhyme on the last syllable.[2] But what is the point of the *and*? In a context like this, it sounds like a compare-and-contrast exercise. But again—so what? Well, with Nietzsche and Zhuangzi the consonances are remarkable, between what they say *and* how they say it. These have been remarked on before, in the first comparison (as far as I know) of these two thinkers' ideas: an article called "The Wandering Dance: *Zhuangzi* and *Zarathustra*," published in *Philosophy East & West* in 1983. But before considering this essay, whose point is "to enhance our understanding of both philosophies," let's first ask the question, which the essay fails to ask, whether Nietzsche was familiar with Zhuangzi's ideas. Then, after comparing Zhuangzi's and Nietzsche's views on what's going on at the deepest philosophical level, we'll inquire into how a comparison might highlight aspects of their thought that have generally gone unnoticed—especially on the question of whether and how perspectives beyond the human might be attainable. Finally, I'll point to a correspondence between the physical practices underlying their philosophical ideas.

The occasional comments Nietzsche makes about China suggest that he didn't know much more about Chinese culture than one would expect from a well-educated German of his time. He mentions Chinese philosophers only twice, both times at the end of his career. In a letter to a good friend he wonders whether The *Laws of Manu*, an ancient Hindu text that he has just read with enthusiasm, might have influenced "Confucius und Laotse [Laozi]"—unlikely, since scholars now date the text to not much earlier than the second century BCE, a few centuries *after* the golden age of classical Chinese philosophy. And in a discussion of Christ the Redeemer in *The Antichristian*, he claims that the allusive language of the Holy Bible corresponds to the language of the Sankhya School of philosophy in India and Laozi in China.[3]

This claim suggests that the basis for the mentions of Laozi may have been the German translation of the text by Victor von Strauss, published in 1870. Strauss compares the "saying" connotation of the Chinese term *dao* 道 with the Biblical "In the beginning was the Word"; and although he leaves the term untranslated, he writes in his Preface that the only being to whom you could ascribe everything that Laozi ascribes to *dao* is: "God, and only God!" According to Strauss, Laozi was possessed of "a surprisingly grand and profound awareness of God, a sublime and very definite concept of God that is consistently congruent with the revealed concept of God." This wholesale projection of Christian ideas onto the ancient Chinese text results in misleading mistranslations that give the text a religious and moralistic flavor that's quite foreign to the original. This would surely have discouraged Nietzsche from taking the book, if he read it, as serious philosophy.[4]

1. The Wandering Dance

"The Wandering Dance" begins by acknowledging "the disparate historical circumstances" of the *Zhuangzi* 莊子 and *Zarathustra*, and then draws numerous parallels—between the literary styles, dramatic episodes, conversations and dialogues, irony, humor, parody, and above all their imagery. The significance of these parallels (which the essay doesn't mention) is that Zhuangzi and Nietzsche are thinkers who highlight the limitations of language with respect to a world of radical becoming, and employ language in new and poetic ways to help transform our experience.

In both cases it's *images* rather than concepts that articulate the thought, with images of natural phenomena predominating—sky, earth, fire, water, plants, animals, moon, sun, and stars. The imagery reflects a common antipathy to anthropocentrism: both authors believe that we become fully human (or "Overhuman" in Nietzsche's case) by getting over the ludicrous prejudice that we are the center of the universe.

On an abstract plane, the anti-anthropocentrism is connected with their perspectivisms, which are remarkably similar and raise the question of how to go beyond human perspectives—or whether that's even possible. They are both thinkers of flux and transformation, philosophers of becoming rather than Being. And on the question of what, ultimately, is going on, they offer comparable suggestions. "The Wandering Dance" deals with this question, claiming early on that "Nietzsche's later understanding of will to power as an interpretive energy inherent in all things comes close to the panpsychism that informs the *Zhuangzi*."[5]

This is the basic philosophical question: when the *Zhuangzi* says "Just open yourself to the one energy that is the world," and Nietzsche says "This world is the will to power—and nothing besides! And you yourselves are also this will to power—and nothing besides!" are they saying more or less the same thing?[6]

"The Wandering Dance" is surely heading in the right direction, but the formulations are sometimes imprecise. Rather than "an interpretive energy inherent in all things" the energy *is* all things: that's what they are. And "panpsychism" isn't quite the right term for Zhuangzi's view that everything is *qi* 氣 energy. The Daoists' "one energy that is the world" isn't just a matter of "life energy," since *qi* exceeds the animate and animal realms to become rivers and rocks—what we regard as "inanimate" matter—as well.[7] The closest equivalent to *qi* in Western philosophy before Nietzsche is probably the notion of *aer* proposed by Anaximines, but "panaerism" doesn't sound quite right for the idea of the world as a field of energies. "Panenergism" perhaps?

The wandering dancer develops the idea further: "Just as for Nietzsche every being manifests will to power—primarily through interpreting and construing the world in terms of values—so, too, for Zhuangzi every being has its own perspective, determined by the conditions particular to it."[8] Better to say that every being *is* will to power, because "manifests" suggests that they could be separate from it. Otherwise this is fine, though the author doesn't provide much textual justification for the claim that Nietzsche understands will to power as "interpreting" and "interpretive energy." There is only—but significantly—a citation of the first mention of will to power in *Thus Spoke Zarathustra*, in "On the Thousand Goals and One." Zarathustra speaks thus:

> A tablet of things held to be good hangs over every people. Behold, it is the tablet of its overcomings; behold, it is the voice of its will to power.[9]

The values that inform our world, the points on which a people overcomes itself, are collective interpretations, different in different cultures, of what is good, or praiseworthy, holy, or evil.

But this only gives us "will to power as interpretation" in the human realm, which needs to be extended to the non-human as well—and that's where "The Wandering Dance" takes us.

Just as for Nietzsche everything in existence is a manifestation of the will to power, so in the *Zhuangzi* there is a correspondence between the universal *dao* and the idea of *de* 德, or power, which is the manifestation of the *dao* in particular existents.[10]

If we drop the "manifestations" again, and "the universal" before *dao*, we'll be on track: *dao* refers to the whole process, together with the way, or patterning, of its unfolding—and so not to something that could exist independently of its manifestations. We could say, then, that corresponding to *dao* as total patterning of particular *des* would be the world as will to power as a field for particular things as configurations of will to power.

2. The Field of *Dao-De*

A colleague of the wandering dancer at the University of Hawaii, Roger Ames, developed this theme in an essay from 1991 with the title "Nietzsche's 'Will to Power' and Chinese 'Virtuality' (*De*): A Comparative Study." For the thinkers behind the classical Daoist texts, according to Ames, "Existence is a ceaseless and continuous process or field of change (*dao*) made determinate in the interdependent particulars (*de*) that constitute it." And for each of these particulars, "the range of its particularity is variable, contingent upon the way in which it is *interpreted* both by itself and by other environing particulars." This means that *de* is continuous with *dao*: "a variable field or focus of potency in the process of existence. As viewed from the perspective of any particular, this dynamic process *in toto* is called *dao*, but when discussed as individuated existents, these particulars are *de*."[11] These fine formulations, which remain central to Ames's reading of Daoism, open up a helpful way of understanding the philosophy of *qi* as the field of *dao* and *de*.

Turning to Nietzsche, Ames suggests that "perhaps the most felicitous way of describing the 'part–whole' relationship in will to power is to invoke the language of 'field and focus' we used for describing *dao-de*." Most felicitous indeed. Insofar as Nietzsche understood existence "as a force-field: dynamic quanta of interconnected relationships" (Ames again), the particulars as *de* would be configurations of will to power such as rocks, trees, animals, human beings and so forth. Whereas the essay focuses on these particulars as *de*, it's just as significant that the whole field of *dao* would be equivalent to "the world as will to power" for Nietzsche.[12] For example, one of our wisest Nietzsche scholars, in discussing Nietzsche's rejection of materialistic atomism in favor of a view of "the world as will to power," supposes that "it can be shown with some probability that to be is to be energy in an always shifting energy field."[13]

What is more, in a passage that Ames doesn't cite, Nietzsche entertains a view of existence as "interpretation" similar to what Ames ascribes to the Daoists (any particular is "interpreted both by itself and by other environing particulars"). In an aphorism in *The Joyous Science* titled "Our New 'Infinite,'" Nietzsche asks "whether all existence isn't essentially interpreting existence." If we open ourselves up to perspectives beyond the human, he writes, we find that "the world has become 'infinite' for us again, insofar as we cannot reject the possibility that it contains infinite interpretations."[14] Since this means not only multiple interpretations from each human being, but also from all other beings, we're in a world that's a lot more like Zhuangzi's than Ames appears to acknowledge.

Ames goes on to invoke the stark contrast in tone and language between the Daoists and Nietzsche: with the former we have a sense of mutuality, coherence, coordination, harmony, integration; and from Nietzsche's side we get overcoming, mastery, contest, conquest, domination. Yes, this contrast is valid to some extent—and derives from the differing contexts. The Daoists (Laozi especially) advocate, in view of the horrors of the Warring States period (475–221 BCE), maintaining a low profile and withdrawing rather than confronting or contending; while Nietzsche, faced with two millennia of Platonism and Christianity, engages the war of ideas in a more aggressive mode.

Ames cites the infamous characterization of "life as will to power" from *Beyond Good and Evil*: "Life itself is *essentially* appropriation, injury, overpowering what is alien and weaker, suppression, hardness, imposition of one's own forms, incorporation and at least, at its mildest, exploitation."[15] Critics of Nietzsche who cite this statement as evidence of the man's moral turpitude miss the point by taking it as prescriptive rather than descriptive. And on this point, I have to part company with my friend Roger Ames. Yes, Nietzsche characterizes life as appropriation, injury, and so forth, but this doesn't mean that he's *advocating* a human life—especially a philosophical one—dedicated to murdering, raping, and pillaging. The question is this: given that life is essentially appropriation—how, as human beings, do we deal with that? How are we to live *our* lives?

Ames concludes his essay with what he sees as the main contrast between the Nietzschean and Daoist ideals:

> The attitude of the Nietzschean *Übermensch* who engages his world by asserting his will to power against both his environments and himself might be regarded by the person of virtuality as one who squanders his considerable energies by failing to respect the complementarity and synchronicity of things.[16]

In the philosophical "compare-and-contrast" exercise, the more interesting is often the "contrast" phase—but in this case it's coming too soon: the parallels extend further. The comparative approach prompts us to look for correspondences that may not immediately be apparent: domination in Daoism, for example, and harmonious integration in Nietzsche. Leaving the former topic aside for now, let's see whether we might find in Nietzsche a Daoist sense for "the complementarity and synchronicity of things"—not only in his texts but also in (what we know of) his experience as a plausible basis for the ideas found in his works.

A reason to suppose that there is such a sense there comes from a well-known note from 1885 that prefigures Nietzsche's paramount presentation of the teaching of will to power in *Beyond Good and Evil* 36. "This world," he writes, is

> an ocean of energies . . . flowing out from the simplest forms into the most manifold, from the stillest, most rigid, and coldest into the most incandescent, wildest, and most self-contradictory, and then again returning home from abundance to the simple, from the play of contradictions to the pleasure of harmony.[17]

3. A Net of Light

When Nietzsche discovered the Upper Engadine (in the south east of Switzerland) in 1879, "at the end of [his] thirty-fifth year," he felt himself "surrounded by death"—his father had died at 35 of a brain tumor, and Nietzsche's susceptibility to migraines made him think that he might suffer a similar fate. But at the same time, he felt himself profoundly *related* to the landscape: "The nature here," he wrote, "is related to my own." This resonates not only with the Daoists' ideal of a natural spontaneity in the human being which is attuned to the powers of Heaven and Earth, but also with the Stoics' project of living "according to our human nature as well as the nature of the universe." Marcus Aurelius liked to remind himself that "our own natures are parts of the nature of the whole," and so the task is to integrate them harmoniously.[18]

Nietzsche likes to remind those who are proud of the human spirit that their pride rests on the mere prejudice of human superiority to all other beings. For most of human history, he remarks, spirit (*Geist*) pervaded the human and natural realms equally. "There was thus no shame attached to being descended from animals or trees . . . and one saw spirit as that which connected us to the natural world rather than what separated us from it." Such a view is still possible in the modern age, as long as we're open to the idea, and experience, of what Nietzsche calls "Nature as *Doppelgänger*": the idea that "in many a part of nature we discover ourselves again, with enjoyable horror." And in the part called the Engadine, he is fortunate to be able to say: "This part of nature is intimate and familiar to me, related by blood, and even more."[19]

We're not going to get that sense of intimacy and quality of experience as long as we remain in what Nietzsche regards as the natural attitude—in which we simplify and thereby falsify our experience in order to get by, getting from the natural world what we need, and taking care of human business. We need to shift out of our "life" perspective to a "death" view of the world: uncouple for a while the drive for self-preservation so that we can just look, or contemplate, without wanting or aiming at anything. In an aphorism of *The Wanderer and His Shadow* that was composed amidst the magnificent landscape of the Engadine, Nietzsche writes of himself in the third person, graced by a vision of the great god Pan asleep "At Midday":

> Upon a meadow hidden among the woods he sees the great God Pan asleep; all the things of nature have fallen asleep with him, an expression of eternity on their faces—so it seems to him. He wants nothing, he frets about nothing, his heart stands still, only his eyes are alive—it is a death with open eyes. Now the man sees much that he has never seen before, and for as far as he can see everything is spun into a net of light, and as it were buried in it.[20]

The world as a net of light, *ein Lichtnetz*: things of nature buried in the light, the Earth illumined, everything dissolved into a network of interactions—a field of *dao* and *de*.

Letting the heart stand still and not wanting anything is a way of getting beyond the all-too-human perspective: "To think oneself away out of humanity, to unlearn desires of all kinds: and to employ the entire abundance of one's powers in *looking*."[21] The Daoists engage in a corresponding practice, which Zhuangzi calls "fasting the heart"—a matter of emptying the mind of what we humans bring to our engagement with the world in the way of prejudices and preconceptions, inclinations and aversions, all of which get in the way of our experiencing what is actually going on. Talking of hearing rather than seeing (which Nietzsche as an "ear" rather than an "eye" person would appreciate), Zhuangzi recommends (through the person of "Confucius") "coming to hear with the vital energy [*qi*] rather than the heart" because "the heart is halted at whatever verifies its preconceptions." This fasting of the heart bypasses human prejudices and lets one experience through the openness of *qi* "the presence of beings."[22]

Returning to Nietzsche, another world of light, "pure and crisp," shines forth in another passage that evokes the mountain landscapes of the Engadine, *Et in Arcadia ego*: "Even here, I [death] am." The ground is "bright with flowers and grasses" yet also shadowed by death, as in the painting by Poussin that Nietzsche alludes to. He describes a scene of beauty that "made one shudder and mutely worship the moment of its revelation," a "pure, crisp world of light, in which there was no longing, expecting, or looking forward and back."[23] Another "enjoyable horror," a shudder in the face of light—reminiscent of the shuddering and divine delight that Lucretius experienced on understanding Epicurus' vision of natural activity going on throughout the void.[24]

But how is it that the everyday world seems so much more substantial than light most of the time, so full of things, some of which can get in the way? It's a matter of where our attention is: on figures (things we have to cope with to survive) or ground (the background contexts). The *Zhuangzi*'s take on this is succinctly summed up by Brook Ziporyn in the Introduction to his translation, and in distinctly phenomenological terms:

> Our attention is directed away from the foreground purposes of human activity and toward the background, that is, what normally escapes our purpose-driven awareness. This move reorients our focus toward the spontaneous and purposeless processes in nature and man that undergird and produce things, begin things, end things, compose the stuff of things, and guide things along their courses by not deliberately guiding them at all.[25]

It's a matter of broadening our perspectives, expanding the "natural light" (*lumen naturale*) of human understanding to become co-extensive with what Zhuangzi calls the "broad light of Heaven."[26] Viewing things in this light lets us see them impartially, since the light of Heaven is above all indifferent to what it illuminates. But how would such a broadening of perspective work in Nietzsche's case?

4. Driving Reality

A year after writing of his experience of the "net of light" Nietzsche remarks that we tend to get caught in a very different net, imprisoned by the restricted range of our sense-apparatus, its location in a particular place, and the projections of our minds.

> The habits of our senses have woven us into the lies and deceptions of sense-perception . . . from which there is no escaping, no hidden bypaths into the *actual* world! We are in our own nets, we spiders, and whatever we may catch in it, we cannot catch anything that does not allow itself to be caught in *our* own net.[27]

As spiders we spin webs of concepts from our own mental substance and project them into the world—also images, schemata, narratives, categories, persons—where they support the fleeting stuff of our lives and lend it some kind of structure, providing some measure of regularity on which we can depend.

In a context where preconceptions prevent us from being flexible in the perspectives we entertain, and in the uses for things that we envision, Zhuangzi describes this situation as "a lot of tangled weeds clogging up the mind." He uses similar terms to characterize the obscuring effects of notions of right and wrong, and ingrained Confucian virtues such as humaneness and responsibility—effects that Nietzsche would also regard as restrictive. In one of the *Zhuangzi*'s Outer chapters there's the question: "What is the use of throwing humaneness and responsibility into the midst of the Course [*dao*] and its virtuosity [*de*], trying to fasten everything together as if with glue and knotted cords? All it does is cast the world into confusion."[28] Projections of moral values and attempts to fix things into some kind of conceptual framework are fruitless exercises—because as Nietzsche as well as Zhuangzi will say: they are already fastened together. We would see this if we opened up and paid closer attention.

On another level of description Nietzsche highlights the crucial role of the drives (*Triebe*) in constituting our experience—for example, the drives for distinction, understanding, predominance, security, play, peace and quiet, justice, truth, and so forth.[29] On the basis of the play of nervous stimulation on the system, the drives interpret nerve-impulses by imagining their causes—and they do this as much, and more freely, when we are asleep and dreaming as when we're awake.[30] In contrast to the spider's web of dry concepts, the play of drives produces *images*, and is described in terms of images—especially of vegetation. The activity of the drives introduces a strong dose of poetic or imaginative *invention* into our experience.

In one of his more incisive provocations, Nietzsche invokes the power of past experience as he ridicules the realists' naïve belief in their ability to be totally objective:

> That mountain there! That cloud there! What is "real" about those? Try taking away the phantasm and the entire human *contribution*, you sober ones! Yes, if only you could do *that*! If you could forget your heritage, your past, your training—your entire humanity and animality! For us there is no "reality"—nor for you either, you sober ones.[31]

In other words, it is impossible to extract from our current awareness the sedimentations, accumulated over millennia, of previous animal as well as cultural experience, impossible to escape the ways in which "some phantasy, some prejudice, some unreason, some ignorance, some fear and who knows what else" have woven their way into our "every feeling and sense-impression."

Zhuangzi would agree, but he doesn't emphasize the archaic or historic dimension to this contribution, in part because the weight of tradition appears to lie less heavily on his shoulders. Yes, he was aware of the power of tradition invoked by the Confucian thinkers who came before him, but Nietzsche is confronted by over two millennia more of cultural development.

On the one hand Nietzsche appears to have lost touch with the net of light and resigned himself to being caught, if not in a spider's web of concepts, then at least in the inventive play of interpreting drives. But on the other, while he was composing this passage about the inevitable contribution from our archaic heritage, he was also thinking of ways to subvert it. We find a number of passages in his writings suggesting that it may be possible after all to check that ancient positing, perhaps through some kind of phenomenological *epoché*, and let natural phenomena like mountains and

clouds simply show themselves, from themselves—and perhaps even as they
are in themselves?

5. Opening up the Angle

Nietzsche elaborates the idea of knowing things as they are in themselves,
rather than as human awareness construes them, in a remarkable series of
notebook entries from 1881. "The task: to see things as they are! The means:
to be able to see with a hundred eyes, from many persons!" We can adopt a
multiplicity of perspectives because we consist in a multiplicity of drives,
which often manifest themselves as inner persons. But in order to "think
oneself away out of humanity" it's necessary to acknowledge as well the vast
inscape of the human soul, which consists in land and sea, rocks and waves,
wind and stars.[32]

After praising "wanting to know things as they are [as] the only *good*
inclination," Nietzsche writes: "What is needed is *practice* in seeing with
other eyes: practice in seeing apart from human relations, and thus seeing
factually [*sachlich*]! To cure human beings of their delusions of grandeur!"[33]
If we are to "know things as they are" we have to get out of the anthropocentric
mode of approach and regard things from the perspective of the thing
itself—*die Sache selbst*. To see *sachlich* is to see from the viewpoint of
the thing in the sense of "the matter," the affair, the concern, the whole
situation.

Zhuangzi appreciates not only the benefits of seeing with other eyes but
also of fluttering with other wings, swimming with other fins, and waving
one's boughs in the winds. Stories of talking animals, insects, and even trees
abound in the *Zhuangzi*, and invite us to entertain the perspectives of other
inhabitants of the world. The "free and easy wandering" of the opening
chapter involves a play of transformations and a dance through diverse
perspectives. We tend to get stuck in the human perspective because the
heart "is halted at whatever verifies its preconceptions."[34]

Nietzsche suggests in a similar vein that "we only see what we're *familiar*
with," and that the greater part of what we see "is not a sense-impression
but a *product of fantasy*." This highlights the unnoticed role of the imagining
drives in the play of the world that is our experience: they make much of it
up as we go along. Practice in seeing with other eyes weakens the sense of
the ego, unsettling the faith that it's I who own the show or me who runs it.
If we can free the I from what Nietzsche calls the self-deception of possession,
we can come to "recognize the affinities and antagonisms among things,
multiplicities therefore and their laws."[35] *That* would really be something to
recognize, those four items. And affinities and antagonisms among the
myriad things are exactly what the ancient Chinese thinkers were concerned
to understand, articulating such patterns in images of Yin and Yang, as
exemplified especially in the *Yijing* 易經, or *Book of Changes*.

Nietzsche apparently stayed with the idea of "seeing with other eyes" through to his later work, as exemplified by the often-cited sentence from *On the Genealogy of Morality*:

> There is only a perspectival seeing, only a perspectival "knowing"; the *more* affects we are able to put into words about a thing, the *more* eyes, various eyes we are able to use for the same thing, the more complete will be our "concept" of the thing, our "objectivity."

That makes sense. But if we forget about concepts and the intellect that employs them, can't we attain a *complete* experience of things as they are? A reason to suppose that we can is Zarathustra's saying, at "Midday," that "The world is complete."[36] So how does it get that way?

To be a good "student of nature," Nietzsche writes in *The Joyous Science*, one needs to "get out of one's human corner" and go beyond the "one-sided" view that sees life as "a struggle for existence," in order to appreciate the overflowing abundance of the natural world as "will to power."[37] To get out of one's *Winkel* is to open up the human *angle* on things to 360 degrees, as it were, while somehow shifting the center so that the perspective is no longer anthropocentric. And this is a point at which a comparison with Zhuangzi raises a further question: yes, multiplying perspectives all around is enlightening—but can't we thereby go further to some kind of perspectiveless experience?

6. The Light of Heaven

Here's a related question, which arises from an examination of the "Equalizing Assessments of Things" (*qiwulun* 齊物論) chapter of the *Zhuangzi* along with the "Before the Sunrise" and "At Noon" chapters of *Zarathustra*: How does the Daoist sage's "letting all things bask in the broad daylight of Heaven" compare with Zarathustra's blessing, "to stand over each and every thing as its own Heaven" and his experience of the world's becoming "complete—round and ripe"? Complete: *vollkommen*, or "perfect."

In the *Zhuangzi*'s second chapter the sage is said to begin from accepting his perspective as "this," and then to proceed to entertain so many "that" perspectives in relation to his own that he begins to see through the relativity and interdependence of all "thises" and "thats." In the end "he doesn't proceed from any one of them alone but instead lets them all bask in the broad daylight of Heaven."[38] (The Chinese term for "Heaven" [*tian* 天] is often used as shorthand for "Heaven and Earth," which means the natural world. Like Zarathustra's *Himmel* it has no transcendent or otherworldly connotations.)

Zhuangzi then adds the retroflective comment: "And that too is only a case of going by the rightness of the present *this*"—emphasizing that these pronouncements about thises and thats are also made from a particular perspective. It's worth noting that Nietzsche makes a similar rhetorical move when he accuses the physicists of his day of misunderstanding the natural world through their anthropomorphic perspective: they only see nature as "lawful" because they project "the democratic instincts of the modern soul" onto the object of their study. "Everywhere equality before the law!" From his beyond-anthropocentric perspective Nietzsche understands the natural world as "will to power," as having a "necessary" and "predictable" course [*Verlauf*], *not* because laws reign in it but because laws are absolutely *absent*, and every power draws its ultimate consequence in every moment.

Every particular thing or process, as a configuration of interpreting will to power, is at every moment construing all other things and is the product of their manifold interactions. The Daoist sage would understand this talk of the course of nature as both "necessary" (which is "freedom itself," Zarathustra says, "blissfully playing with the thorn of freedom") and "predictable" (intuitively, once you understand the rhythms and cadences).[39]

But having dismissed the physicists' "naïvely humanitarian" interpretation of nature and proposed his own view of the world as will to power instead, Nietzsche then adds this final twist: "Given that this is also only an interpretation—and you will be eager enough to raise this objection?—well, all the better.—"[40] The last dash is there to give us time to reflect on what he's doing here.

Both Zhuangzi and Nietzsche say the world unfolds in an array of diverse perspectives and interactions—*and* acknowledge their claims as perspectival, though proffering not just any perspective but one that affirms the plurality of perspectives and the possibility of entertaining that plurality. In both cases: yes, another interpretation—but in each case so powerful as to be not just *any* other interpretation. Their interpretations make good sense of what's going on—but on the understanding that it's in the nature of interpretations to be superseded. After all, the secret of life as will to power, which the figure of Life herself intimates to Zarathustra, is this: that she is *"that which must always overcome itself."*[41]

Returning to "the broad daylight of Heaven": the Daoist sage goes along with the play of perspectives it reveals, "using various rights and wrongs to harmonize with others and yet remaining at rest in the center of the Potter's Wheel of Heaven." Zhuangzi explains what's going on here by elaborating the image:

> When "this" and "that"—right and wrong—are no longer coupled as opposites—that is called the Course as Axis, the axis of all courses. When this axis finds its place in the center of the ring, it responds to all the endless things it confronts, thwarted by none.[42]

The "Course" is Brook Ziporyn's translation of *dao*, or "Way," and so it's a matter of finding the axis of the Way things are unfolding, some kind of still center in the cyclical patterning of events and processes.

The same point can be made with reference to the other great classic of philosophical Daoism—the *Daodejing*—which uses the image of a cartwheel: "Thirty spokes are united in one hub. It is in its emptiness that the usefulness of the cart resides."[43] Just as a wheel can only rotate if its center is empty (otherwise you'd only have a disc or a potter's wheel), so the world can go round, and things come and go in cyclical fashion, only thanks to emptiness within it. We generally experience through perspectives on the rim of the wheel, as it were, and often fail to appreciate that with a turn of the world—in a day, or a year, or a sequence of years in a lifetime—we can find ourselves on the opposite side, where "there" has become "here," and "that" has become "this." Most experience affords this opportunity, and with practice we realize there's a point in the middle from where we can appreciate both. If it's a circle cycling, the calmest place is the center—as long as you rotate on your axis.

After extension and expansion to the peripheries, this withdrawal to the center, the axis of the Course, the still point of the turning world (where the dance takes place), allows us to go beyond our customary, restricted, all-too-human perspectives, and get a sense of the whole. Not a transcendence to a God's-eye view, nor a view from everywhere or nowhere, this drive to the heart of things, or withdrawal to the center, may let us see "the world from the inside," as Nietzsche puts it when he writes of "the world as will to power—and nothing besides."

The Daoist sage is wise thanks in part to his virtuosity in changing perspectives. In one of his last works, Nietzsche congratulates *himself* on a corresponding ability, acquired through long practice, to "*switch perspectives.*"[44] And just as the sage can let all those perspectives bask in that way because he has made himself "one with Heaven," so Zarathustra "Before the Sunrise" is on the deck of a ship out on the open sea, where the horizon affords the greatest expanse of sky—so vast as to be absorbing. By casting himself up into the light-abyss of the sky he is able to merge with his "friend," with which he has so many things "in common." Here and in "At Midday" depth and height "are no longer coupled as opposites" but come together in a *coincidentia oppositorum*.

7. Before the Sunrise

Zarathustra rises before dawn to speak to the sky all around him, addressing it as a familiar: "O Heaven above me, so pure! so deep! You abyss of light! Beholding you I shudder with godlike desires."[45] His own depth, he tells Heaven, comes from casting himself *up* into the height of the sky. Opposites can now come together, in part because no Heavenly bodies are visible: no sky Gods—nor even one God—no providential forces loom behind or beyond.

"You do not speak," Zarathustra remarks: this is how Heaven reveals its "wisdom." Openness and reticence are likewise a central characteristic of Heaven in the Chinese philosophical tradition. Early on, when a student of Confucius asked him why he wished he didn't have to speak, the Master replied: "Does Heaven ever speak? And yet the four seasons turn and the myriad creatures are born and grow within it. Does Heaven ever speak?"[46]

The reticence of the Chinese Heaven comes from its impartiality: it casts its light, not to mention rain, evenly on all things. A remarkable feature of the pre-dawn sky (also true of post-sunset dusk) is the quality of light in the absence of direct sun: more so than on an overcast day, things appear to shine with their own light. When they are illuminated by the sun (symbol of the Idea of the Good) the light always comes from a particular direction, making one side of things bright and leaving the other in shadow. This would correspond in the *Zhuangzi* to perspectives that afford us a "this" and a "that." By contrast the illumination of the pre-dawn sky is uniform and without directionality: no bias, no light casting dark shadow, and instead of exclusive opposites a smooth continuum.

Rising into the light-abyss of Heaven, Zarathustra reaches the ranks of those who "bless":

> And this is my blessing: to stand over each and every thing as its own Heaven, as its round roof, its azure bell and eternal security: and blessed is he who blesses thus!
>   For all things are baptized at the fount of eternity and beyond good and evil.

With respect to each particular thing that he encounters, Zarathustra stands as impartially and non-judgmentally as Heaven stands to him when he is open to it. When we deal with things from the perspective of utility, we confine them and restrict their possibilities. But Zarathustra's new stance lets things be what they are, insofar as he frees and "redeems them from their bondage under Purpose."

> Verily, a blessing it is and no blasphemy when I teach: "Over all things stands the Heaven Accident, the Heaven Innocence, the Heaven Contingency, the Heaven Exuberance."

Zarathustra is able to stand as Heaven over things together with these four other liberating Heavens because he is one with them: Heavens are like horizons in being non-obstructive.

Zarathustra calls Heaven "a dance-floor for Divine accidents," showing his stance to be dynamic rather than static: he realizes that things chafe under the yoke of determination by something other than themselves and want instead "to *dance* on the feet of chance." The Daoist thinkers call this freedom from necessity *ziran* 自然, "so of themselves," spontaneous, or—

because it's a dynamic condition—"self-so-ing." It's significant that in modern Chinese (and Japanese) this is the term chosen to translate the English word "nature."[47]

There's a story in the *Zhuangzi* that anticipates Zarathustra's point in almost a mirror-image. It's a retelling of the ancient tale of how one day, when ten suns rose in the sky at once and threatened to scorch the Earth, the mythical sage-ruler Yao saved the world by having nine of them shot down by the legendary archer Yi. Since the sun is sometimes said to "govern" humans, the idea is that ten rulers are too many and one is best. But Zhuangzi turns it around: "Once upon a time, ten suns rose in the sky at once, and the ten thousand things were all simultaneously illuminated. And how much better are many virtuosities than many suns?" Multiple *de*'s means many perspectives, as well as sages who entertain them.

The Confucian philosopher Wang Fuzhi 王夫之 (1619–92) commented: "When the ten suns shone, there was no this and that, no large and small, no right and wrong." And Ziporyn could almost be referring to Nietzsche when he notes:

> Yao thinks ten different standards of "rightness" will lead to chaos—there must be a single unified truth, a single ruler. Zhuangzi here allows all things their own rightness—and thereby there will be all the more illumination, with each thing its own sun.

A few episodes later in the *Zhuangzi*, there is this description of the sage:

> He is there taking part in the diversity of ten thousand harvests, but in each he tastes one and the same purity of fully formed maturation. For to him each thing is just so, each thing is right, and so he enfolds them all within himself by affirming the rightness of each.[48]

—Again turning out to be just like Zarathustra, who realized early on there was no point in wasting his time with followers: "Companions the creator seeks, and fellow harvesters: for all that is with him stands ripe for the harvest. But the hundred sickles are lacking."[49] And Zarathustra later affirms the rightness of all things on the grounds of their being "beyond good and evil."

"Before the Sunrise" ends with Heaven's blushing and Zarathustra's realizing that the pre-dawn sky is about to disappear, to give way to day and its light. It's then that he says: "The world is deep—and deeper than ever the day has thought."[50] The day and life perspectives reveal things we need to know to get through, to make it; while the night and death perspectives—deeper because they reveal the underworld we inhabit nightly in our dreams and dreamless sleep—complement and complete our experience. They round it out. Just as in the *Zhuangzi*, where life and death are often said to belong together, and waking life and dream are interchangeable.[51]

Images of roundness, ripeness, and stillness abound in a chapter of *Zarathustra* "At Midday," which is a reprise of the themes in the earlier "At Midday" and invokes the God Dionysus as well as Pan. Speaking hypnagogically to his own soul, Zarathustra says:

> Do not sing! Still! The world is complete . . . a moment's glance [*Augen-Blick*]—a *little* makes for the *best* happiness. What? Did the world not just become complete? Round and ripe? Oh the golden round hoop—whither does it fly? . . . Still! Did the world not just become complete? Oh the golden round ball![52]

The golden round hoop is a larger version of the ring of eternal recurrence, which is generated by those moments when life assumes such fullness that one can want it to come around again, and innumerable times again. If you can get into the gateway of the moment the right way—behind which "all things have happened, and been done, and passed by already"—you realize that "all things are fastened together so tightly that this moment draws after it *all* things that are to come."[53] And so by affirming this moment, you are in a position to affirm all things.

There's a passage in the *Zhuangzi* that resonates with the Potter's Wheel of Heaven image discussed earlier, and seems strangely to anticipate Nietzsche's thought of eternal recurrence. In the course of a description of the sage, who "gets through to the intertwining of things, so that everything forms a single body around him," the text invokes the intense joy of contemplating "the old homeland, the old neighborhood." (Perhaps also a matter of realizing one's original nature.) And how much greater the joy "if you could still see what you had once seen and hear what you had once heard there"—which could happen if those moments came around again, if they recurred. How this might happen is suggested by a reversion to the sage who "found the center of the ring":

> He brought himself to completion by following along with things, staying right there with them no matter how they ended or began, no matter what their impulse or season. It is the one who constantly changes together with all things who is always one and unchanging—when has he ever had to abandon them for even a moment?[54]

When the center of the ring was found back in the second chapter of the *Zhuangzi*, the Axis of the Way was able "to respond to all the endless things it confronts, thwarted by none."

The center of the ring can accommodate the axis and its endless turning because it's empty, and we can find a place there only if *we* are empty of tangled weeds and conceptual clutter. The *Zhuangzi* suggests that you know you've fasted the heart well enough if what moves you to activity is not your self, but the forces of Heaven and Earth moving through the body unimpeded.

Here are the final pieces of advice concerning the practice of dealing with things—and people—after emptying the mind:

> Concentrate on the hollows of what is before you, and the empty chamber within you will generate its own brightness. Good fortune comes to roost in stillness. To lack this stillness is called scurrying around even when sitting down ... This is the transformation of all things, the hinge on which [the sage-emperors of old] used to move.

As one of the Outer chapters advises: "Let your body be moved only by the totality of things."[55] Paying attention to the openness that's before us is a matter of realizing that things are empty of essences, that they are what they are only in relation to others and thanks to "the affinities and antagonisms" among them. Just as one can scurry around even when sitting down, one can also, with practice, stay still while moving about. The benefits of finding still points are praised in the *Daodejing* as well as the *Zhuangzi*. And to get in touch with our inner stillness, it helps to sit still for a while every now and then. A few words, then, on practice, before we conclude.

8. Methods and Practices

As is usual for East-Asian philosophies, the ideas in the *Zhuangzi* are rooted in certain kinds of physical or somatic practice.[56] There are allusions in the text to breathing techniques, but the main task is "fasting of the heart" (*xinzhai* 心齋), emptying it and keeping it empty of all the mental and emotional furniture that obstructs the flow of experience. The practitioner also learns, whether through meditation or the consummate practice of crafts, to experience not through the senses and the heart-mind but rather through *qi* energies.[57] The practices thus range along a spectrum from "passive" (as in sitting still) to active (as in carving awesomely beautiful bell-stands).

Nietzsche engaged in corresponding practices at either end of this spectrum: vigorous and prolonged hiking in the open air on the one hand, and what he calls "incubation" on the other. Incubation was the practice, in the cult of the divine healer Asclepius, of sleeping in sacred places in order to receive a dream, the interpretation of which would cure one's ills. In Nietzsche's case his migraine headaches would put him indoors and flat out on his back, often for three days at a stretch. "The poor guy," people often say, but here's what he himself had to say about this affliction.

> Illness *gradually liberated me, cleaning me out* ... Illness likewise gave me the right to a complete change in my habits ... it bestowed on me the *needfulness* to lie still, to be idle, to wait and be patient ... But that's what is called thinking![58]

There's a good deal of lying still in the Nietzschean philosophical corpus, especially in *Thus Spoke Zarathustra*, where the protagonist is laid out flat before each intimation of the thought of eternal recurrence. Yes, Nietzsche thought best, perhaps, with the body in vigorous motion, but also when immobile and supine.

At the active end of the spectrum was Nietzsche's hiking—or *marching*, he often called it—"six to eight hours" in the open air, a meditative exercise that emptied and opened out the mind and smoothed the body into energetic flow. He reports that his greatest creativity came when the muscles were working at their most supple pitch, such that the body is experienced not as recalcitrant matter but as a dynamic configuration of energies.[59]

The point of the preceding exercise has not been to deny the harder or harsher aspects of Nietzsche's thought, but rather to show how the comparison with Zhuangzi highlights complementary aspects of "harmony" and "interconnection" in Nietzsche's thought that are often overlooked. Restrictions of space and time permit no more than a brief look at how the comparison can reveal, conversely, the "creative" aspect to Zhuangzi's philosophy, which is often regarded as calmly reflective and quietistic.

9. Creative Experience

When we ask what kinds of experience are the basis of an interpretation of the world as will to power or a field of *dao* and *de*, there comes a point where the views of Nietzsche and the Daoists appear to diverge. The Daoist sage practices fasting the heart and emptying the mind so that he can reflect the actual ongoing situation without distortion. And for Nietzsche, "seeing apart from human relations" and from a "death" perspective can lead to "knowing things as they are." But then what are we to make of Nietzsche's occasional praise of creative experience and repudiation of "mirror"-like perception?

In a chapter of *Zarathustra* titled "On Immaculate Perception" (or "Understanding"), the protagonist appears in a rather un-Daoist light when he ridicules those philosophers who aspire to "the immaculate perception of all things." Their ultimate aspiration, he says, is

> to look upon life without desire and not like a dog with its tongue hanging out . . . To love the Earth as the moon loves her, and to touch her beauty with the eye alone . . . [and to be able to say] "I want nothing from things, except that I may lie there before them like a mirror with a hundred eyes."

Such knowers Zarathustra brands unproductive because they have lost touch with "the unexhausted procreative life-will" that is will to power, and are thus incapable of loving the Earth "as creators, procreators, or enjoyers of becoming."[60] As a conduit for the procreative life-will that is will to power, as a conductor of the drives that play through the human body, the Nietzschean creator contributes to the play of life through understanding and acting.

But if, by contrast, the Daoist sage's mind is to reflect the actual situation without distortion, wouldn't this prevent him from being a creator and an enjoyer of becoming? After all, at the end of the Inner Chapters there is this injunction:

> Fully realize whatever is received from Heaven, and never have personal gain in sight. It is just being empty, nothing more. The utmost man uses his mind like a mirror, rejecting nothing, welcoming nothing: responding but not storing. Thus he can handle all things without harm.[61]

Without harm to him or to them. As long as the mirror reflects the broad daylight of Heaven, it impartially lets the things it reflects show themselves as they are, rather than as the partial mind would have them be—insofar as the partial mind rejects bad stuff and welcomes good things, and stores by holding on.

A lot depends of course on where the utmost man situates his mirror-mind. Think of the creativity of the great photographer, who gets the camera in the right place at the right time, and pointing in the right direction, before clicking the shutter. This is the registration moment of experience, but there is also the activation moment, which makes for creativity. The "Fathoming Life" chapter says that, if one is able to "let go of the world" and not hold on,

> you are reborn along with each presence that confronts you ... When the body is intact and the seminal quintessence of vitality restored, you are one with Heaven ... Making the quintessence of vitality still more concentrated and quintessential, you return to the source, thereby *assisting in the operations of Heaven.*[62]

In this way, the good Daoist can expand her awareness throughout the whole field, and through "sympathetic resonance" (*ganying* 感應) get the hang of what's really going on.

This passage is followed by accounts of the awe-inspiring virtuosities of a cicada catcher, a ferryman, a maker of bell-stands, a charioteer, and an artisan. At the conclusion of these stories, a Master says of the conduct of the Consummate Person (or Daoist sage): "This is called taking action but not relying on it for any credit, helping things grow but not controlling them."[63] There are of course passages in the *Zhuangzi* that can be cited in favor of a more quietist reading, where the sage is detached from the human realm. But the comparison with Nietzsche reveals a more engaged aspect of the philosophy, where the sage practices non-attachment rather than detachment. I find this aspect more appealing, and more relevant, because the way things are going these days, they need all the help we can give them.

The last sentence of Parkes (1983) trusts that "at least a few steps have been made along the way of the wandering dance." The Dionysian move out of oneself, and into other persons and things of nature, requires a "lightness of foot" that's attuned to the music of the world. As Zarathustra says, "the dancer has his ear—deep down in his toes!"[64] Zhuangzi, wandering freely among diverse perspectives, is foremost among those few well-attuned thinkers who were able to go beyond talking the talk, and even walking the walk, to *dancing the dance*—in the light of the Heavens above and around.

Notes

1   Friedrich Nietzsche, *The Joyous Science*, 339 (*KSA*, 3: 569). Translations of Nietzsche's texts are my own, for the sake of preserving the imagery. References to the published works are by section number, so that the passages can be found in any edition, followed by the volume and page number of the *Kritische Studienausgabe* (*KSA*) of the collected works. References to the unpublished notes are in the *KSA*, by volume and page number, and to the letters in the *Kritische Studienausgabe* of the *Briefe* (*KSB*).

2   The last syllables of both names rhyme with the last syllable of "feature" without the "r" sound, rather than with "(kim)chee." In citations I have changed Wade-Giles romanization to Pinyin for the sake of consistency.

3   Nietzsche, letter to Heinrich Köselitz, May 31, 1888 (*KSB*, 8: 325); *The Antichristian*, 32.

4   Laozi, *Lao-Tse's Tao Te King* (Leipzig: Fleischer Verlag, 1870), xxxii–xxxvii; see also the commentary to the first chapter on page 3.

5   Graham Parkes, "The Wandering Dance: Zhuangzi and Zarathustra," *Philosophy East and West*, 33.3 (1983): 237.

6   Zhuangzi, *Zhuangzi: The Essential Writings with Selections from Traditional Commentaries* Brook Ziporyn (trans.) (Indianapolis: Hackett Publishing, 2009), 22 (86); Nietzsche, *KSA*, 11.610 = *Will to Power*, 1067 (1885). References to the *Zhuangzi* are to the chapter, followed by the page in Brook Ziporyn's translation in parentheses.

7   Zhuangzi, *Essential Writings*, 22 (86).

8   Parkes, "The Wandering Dance," 240.

9   Nietzsche, *Zarathustra*, 1:15, "On the Thousand Goals and One." For more on will to power as interpretation, see xxi–xxii.

10 Parkes, "The Wandering Dance," 246–7.

11 Roger Ames, "Nietzsche's 'Will to Power' and Chinese 'Virtuality' (*De*): A Comparative Study," in *Nietzsche and Asian Thought*, ed. Graham Parkes (Chicago: University of Chicago Press, 1991), 133, 134 (emphasis added), 136.

12 Ibid., 143–4.

13 Laurence Lampert, *Nietzsche's Task: An Interpretation of Beyond Good and Evil* (New Haven: Yale University Press, 2001), 41.

14 Nietzsche, *The Joyous Science*, 374. In German he asks "ob nicht alles Dasein essentiell ein auslegendes Dasein ist."

15 Ames, "Nietzsche's 'Will to Power'," 147, citing *Beyond Good and Evil*, 259.

16 Ibid., 146–8.

17 Nietzsche, *KSA*, 11.610 = *Will to Power*, 1067, 1885. (I'm admittedly enhancing the resonances with Daoism by rendering the word *Kraft* as "energy" rather than "force.")

18 Nietzsche, *Letters*, B4: 441, 430. Marcus Aurelius, *Meditations*, C.R. Haines (trans.), (Cambridge: Harvard University Press, 1916), 12.26.

19 Nietzsche, *Dawn of Morning*, 31; *The Wanderer and His Shadow*, 338. Nietzsche also writes of how closely *related* he feels to the landscape in several of the letters he sent to family and friends during his first stay in the Engadine (June–September 1879). See also *WHS* 14, 17, 51, 57, 115, 138, 176, 205, 295, 308, and 332.

20 Nietzsche, *The Wanderer and His Shadow*, 308.

21 Nietzsche, *KSA*, 9: 454.

22 *Zhuangzi*, 4 (26–7).

23 Nietzsche, *The Wanderer and His Shadow*, 295. The aphorism's title comes from a painting by Poussin, *Les bergers d'Arcadie*, showing a group of Arcadian shepherds examining the inscription *Et in Arcadia ego* on a sarcophagus. An earlier version has a skull on top of the sarcophagus, but here a shepherd points instead to the shadow of his companion's head. Available online at: https://en.wikipedia.org/wiki/Et_in_Arcadia_ego

24 Lucretius, *De Rerum Natura*, 3.15–30; translation in Pierre Hadot, *Philosophy as a Way of Life* (Cambridge: Blackwell, 1995), 88.

25 *Zhuangzi*, "Translator's Introduction," xv.

26 *Zhuangzi*, 2 (12).

27 Nietzsche, *Dawn of Morning*, 117. He first uses the spider's web image in connection with Parmenides in his long essay on the Presocratic thinkers (*KSA*, 1: 844), and in "On Truth and Lie in the Extramoral Sense" (*KSA*, 1: 882, 885).

28 *Zhuangzi*, 1 (8), 2 (18).

29 Some drives Nietzsche mentions in works from the so-called middle period: the drive to contradict; drive for justice, drive for truth, curiosity, fear of boredom, resentment, vanity, the drive to play (the *Untimely Meditation* on History, section 6); drive for security (*The Wanderer and His Shadow*, 16); drive for preponderance (*Übergewicht*) (31); drive to be sociable (70); the same drive: cowardice/humility (*Dawn of Morning*, 38); the drive to understand (45); the drive for calm, fear of shame, love (109); the drive for distinction (113).

30 Nietzsche, *Dawn of Morning*, 117. For a detailed discussion of the nature and function of the drives, see chapter 8 of Graham Parkes, *Composing the Soul: Reaches of Nietzsche's Psychology* (Chicago: University of Chicago Press, 1994).

31 Nietzsche, *The Joyous Science*, 57.

32 Nietzsche, *KSA*, 9: 466, 9: 454. For a description of Nietzsche's inscapes, see Parkes, *Composing the Soul*, chapter 4.

33 Nietzsche, *KSA*, 9: 443–4.

34 *Zhuangzi*, 4 (26). We hear, for example, a talking cicada and turtle-dove in chapter 1 (4), and a talking tree in chapter 4 (30).

35 Nietzsche, *KSA*, 9: 445–6, 9: 450–1.

36 Nietzsche, *On the Genealogy of Morality*, 3.12; *Zarathustra*, 4.10, "At Midday."

37 Nietzsche, *The Joyous Science*, 349.

38 Nietzsche, *Ecce Homo*, "Why I am so Wise," 1. *Zhuangzi*, 2 (12). For "one with Heaven" see *Zhuangzi*, 19 (77), "Fathoming Life."

39 Nietzsche, *Zarathustra*, 3.12, "On Old and New Tablets," 2.

40 Nietzsche, *Beyond Good and Evil*, 36.22.

41 Nietzsche, *Zarathustra*, 3.12, "On Self-Overcoming."

42 *Zhuangzi*, 2 (12), 19 (77).

43 Laozi, *Daodejing*, 11. Hans-Georg Moeller has elucidated the significance of the cartwheel image in Hans-Georg Moeller, *Daoism Explained: From the Dream of the Butterfly to the Fishnet Allegory* (La Salle: Open Court, 2004), 27–35.

44 Nietzsche, *On the Genealogy of Morality*, 3.12; *Ecce Homo*, "Why I am So Wise," 1. The German for switching perspectives is *Perspektiven umstellen*, to turn them round or reverse them.

45 Nietzsche, *Zarathustra*, 3.4, "Before the Sunrise."

46 Confucius, *Analects*, 17.19.

47 I discuss this topic in Graham Parkes, "Zhuangzi and Nietzsche on the Human in Nature," *Environmental Philosophy*, 10.1 (2013): 1–24.

48 *Zhuangzi*, 2 (17); Ziporyn, 17n24; *Zhuangzi*, 2 (19).

49 Nietzsche, *Zarathustra*, Prologue, section 9.

50 "The world is deep" prefigures *Zarathustra*, 3.15, "The Other Dance-Song" (section 3).

51 Life and death: *Zhuangzi* chapters 1, 5, 6, 22, 23, and 25; dream and waking: 2 (numerous discussions) and 6.

52 Nietzsche, *Zarathustra,* 4.10, "At Midday."

53 Nietzsche, *The Joyous Science*, 341; *Zarathustra*, 3.2, "On the Vision and the Riddle."

54 *Zhuangzi*, 25 (108).

55 Ibid., 4 (27), 23 (99).

56 See Graham Parkes, "Awe and Humility in the Face of Things: Somatic Practice in East-Asian Philosophies," *European Journal for Philosophy of Religion*, 4.3 (2012): 69–88.

57 *Zhuangzi*, 4 (26).

58 Nietzsche, *Ecce Homo*, "Why I write such good books," "Human, All-Too-Human," 4.

59 Nietzsche, *Ecce Homo*, "Why I Write such Good Books," "Thus Spoke Zarathustra," 4.

60 Nietzsche, *Zarathustra*, 2.12, "On Self-Overcoming"; 2.15, "On Immaculate Perception."

61 *Zhuangzi*, 7 (54).

62 Ibid., 19 (77) (emphasis added).

63 Ibid., 19 (83).

64 Nietzsche, *Zarathustra*, 3.15, "The Other Dance-Song."

References

Ames, Roger. (1991), "Nietzsche's 'Will to Power' and Chinese 'Virtuality' (*De*): A Comparative Study," in *Nietzsche and Asian Thought*, Graham Parkes (ed.), 130–50, Chicago: University of Chicago Press.

Hadot, Pierre. (1995), *Philosophy as a Way of Life*, Michael Chase (trans.), Cambridge: Blackwell.

Lampert, Laurence. (2001), *Nietzsche's Task: An Interpretation of Beyond Good and Evil*, New Haven: Yale University Press.

Laozi. (1870), *Lao-Tse's Tao Te King*. Victor von Strauss (trans.), Leipzig: Fleischer Verlag.

Laozi. (2007), *Daodejing*. Hans-Georg Moeller (trans.), La Salle: Open Court Publishing.

Moeller, Hans-Georg. (2004), *Daoism Explained: From the Dream of the Butterfly to the Fishnet Allegory*, La Salle: Open Court Publishing.

Nietzsche, Friedrich. (1980), *Sämtliche Werke: Kritische Studienausgabe*, München: de Gruyter.

Nietzsche, Friedrich. (1986), *Sämtliche Briefe: Kritische Studienausgabe*, München: de Gruyter.

Nietzsche, Friedrich. (2005), *Thus Spoke Zarathustra: A Book for Everyone and Nobody*. Graham Parkes (trans.), Oxford: Oxford University Press.

Parkes, Graham. (1983), "The Wandering Dance: Zhuangzi and Zarathustra," *Philosophy East and West*, 33.3: 235–50.

Parkes, Graham, ed. (1991), *Nietzsche and Asian Thought*, Chicago: University of Chicago Press.

Parkes, Graham. (1994), *Composing the Soul: Reaches of Nietzsche's Psychology*, Chicago: University of Chicago Press.

Parkes, Graham. (2012), "Awe and Humility in the Face of Things: Somatic Practice in East-Asian Philosophies," *European Journal for Philosophy of Religion*, 4.3: 69–88.

Parkes, Graham. (2013), "Zhuangzi and Nietzsche on the Human in Nature," *Environmental Philosophy*, 10.1: 1–24.

Zhuangzi. (2009), *Zhuangzi: The Essential Writings with Selections from Traditional Commentaries*, Brook Ziporyn (trans.), Indianapolis: Hackett Publishing.

PART TWO

Early Encounters: Nourishing the Sprouts of Possibility

4

The Pre-objective and the Primordial:

Elements of a Phenomenological Reading of Zhuangzi

Kwok-Ying Lau

1. Anti-Rationalist, Skeptic, or Mystic: Is Zhuangzi Unintelligible?

The eminent Western scholar of Chinese Philosophy A.C. Graham presents Zhuangzi as an "anti-rationalist," albeit a "great" one.[1] To Graham, Zhuangzi's entire intellectual effort consists in nothing other than conducting an "assault on reason" and "dismiss[ing] reason for the immediate experience of an undifferentiated world, transforming 'all are one' from a moral to a mystical affirmation."[2] One of the arguments Graham puts forward to substantiate his diagnosis of Zhuangzi as an anti-rationalist is that this pre-Qin Daoist philosopher always refuses to practice rational thought by means of analytic thinking. As Graham sees it, one of Zhuangzi's persistent thoughts is that "in accepting what fits in with one's ideas as 'this' and rejecting what does not, analytic thinking lights up only a lesser whole around the thinker and casts the rest into darkness."[3] Graham explains further his rather pejorative diagnosis of Zhuangzi in the following terms: that this pre-Qin Daoist philosopher

> shares that common and elusive feeling that the whole is more than the sum of its parts, that analysis always leaves something out, that neither side of the dichotomy is wholly true.[4]

Thus he sums up Zhuangzi's whole doctrine as skepticism.[5] This diagnosis of Zhuangzi has received a large following among scholars who plunge into the difficult text known as the *Zhuangzi* 莊子.[6]

For me, to label Zhuangzi as an anti-rationalist, skeptic, and even a mystic, is nothing surprisingly new. The *Zhuangzi* has always been presented in such a manner by its Western readership.[7] To defend rational thinking is the vocation of a philosopher; however, is Graham's understanding of rational thinking as a somewhat narrowly defined form of analytic thinking not too exclusive? When he criticizes Zhuangzi of holding the view that "the whole is more than the sum of its parts," is he aware of the fact that Gestalt theories since the first decades of the twentieth century have shown precisely the truthfulness of what he thinks as absurdity? Taking into account the basic structural components of elementary perception, namely the differential relation between the figure and the ground of a perceptual object, the whole is precisely greater than the summation of its parts. And the acknowledgment of this kind of perceptual truth gives rise to the acknowledgment that the logic of perception as a logic of perceptual meaning is irreducible to the logic of physical properties as a logic of mathematical summation.

The most well-known illustrative examples of Gestalt psychology (i.e., lines of Müller-Lyer; figures of multistability) reveal the following stunning truth: that one identical geometric figure can give rise to two entirely different perceptual objects with two different perceptual meanings. This discovery of Gestalt theories leads to the discovery of the pre-objective order of things, an order which goes beyond, or more precisely beneath the order of empirical visible objects: the perceptual field is not formed by the simple addition or juxtaposition of physical elements. It is rather structured by the two heterogeneous elements of the figure and the ground. It is only upon this phenomenal field, which is itself not of the order of the visible object, that any empirical object can come to appearance and be visible to the naked eye. The pre-objective order is an order of things which organizes itself into meaningful appearances prior to the active intervention or interpretation of the reflective perceiving subject. Thus this is an order of things incomprehensible to objective thought, the mode of thinking prevalent in modern scientific and positivistic thought, which relies on formal logical deduction and judgment of the reflective knowing subject on empirical visible objects. The truth of Gestalt theories has been acknowledged by Edmund Husserl, the father of modern phenomenology, in his *Logical Investigations* of 1900–1[8] and by Maurice Merleau-Ponty in his *Phenomenology of Perception* of 1945.[9] In his magnum opus, Merleau-Ponty seeks to go deeper than the level of objective thought in order to understand in its fuller extent the operation of rational thinking and, at the same time, the works of great thinkers such as those of Husserl. While some commentators have seriously criticized Husserl, Merleau-Ponty defended him against those who applied a so-called objective critique of Husserl's doctrine by subjecting it "to analytic observation or out-of-context thinking."[10] This latter attitude is positivistic in nature, an attitude which "requires the meaning of [a man's] work to be wholly positive and by rights susceptible to an inventory which sets forth what is and is not in those works."[11] To Merleau-Ponty, by adopting a purely positivistic and analytic attitude one will end up destroying the heritage of Husserl the thinker. On the example of Merleau-Ponty with regard to the works of Husserl, we would like to adopt a similar attitude toward the works of Zhuangzi in order to understand them philosophically. In the rest of this chapter we will attempt a phenomenological approach to the reading of the *Zhuangzi* text in order to go into the pre-objective order of things to which we think that this text conveys us. By proposing such a reading, we hope to render *Zhuangzi* more comprehensible to a contemporary reader.

2. Epoché: From Getting Rid of Prejudice to "Fasting of the Mind" and "Sit and Forget"

What does it mean by adopting a phenomenological approach with regard to a famous classical text such as the *Zhuangzi*? It means first of all that we are guided by the motto "going back to the things themselves" and follow strictly the principle of description prior to interpretation.[12] In concrete terms we carry out the epoché, i.e., suspension of judgment with regard to any prejudice and any unexamined thesis about these texts, be they a result of traditional or modern authoritative exegetes, prior to our own examination.[13] We let the texts speak for themselves and describe what they reveal to us in a language as close and faithful as possible to the state of affairs thus revealed.[14] In this regard, we find that the opening paragraph of chapter 2 (*qiwulun* 齊物論) of the *Zhuangzi* shows precisely that the author of this text advocates a critical attitude with regard to those who pronounce their opinions on cognitive and moral issues in an irresponsible manner. To Zhuangzi it is simply impossible to attain truth for all those who profess a cognitive judgment (affirmative or negative about a state of affairs) or a moral judgment (that an action is just or unjust) if they remain in the pre-reflective mundane attitude of everyday life. Zhuangzi guards us against the attitude of upholding unexamined prejudices which is prevalent in our pre-reflective everyday life. Let us listen to Zhuangzi:

> If we follow our prejudices and take them as our guide [or teacher], who will not have his own guide [or teacher]? Why should only those who are intelligent enough to know the laws of change by heart maintain their own guiding principle? The foolish do the same thing. If one makes an affirmation or a negation prior to the judgment by the cognitive mind, it

is just as [absurd as] saying that one sets out for the Southern lands today but arrived there yesterday. To do so is to make something out of nothing. Making something out of nothing is a state of affairs that even the sage Yu is unable to understand. How could I alone make sense of it?[15]

At the outset of considering whether ordinary opinions can attain truth, Zhuangzi makes a preliminary distinction between two kinds of attitude held respectively by the foolish and the wise man. The wise man possesses knowledge of the laws of change by heart whereas the foolish does not. While the wise man lets himself be guided by the reflective judgment conducted by the exercise of his faculty of cognition in accordance with the laws of change, i.e., the laws of nature, the foolish lets himself be guided by prejudices. The attitude of the wise man is reflective, while that of the foolish is unreflective which leads to absurdities. Here Zhuangzi announces a first principle for true cognition: do not let yourself be guided by prejudices otherwise you will result in absurdities which even the sage cannot resolve. This vigilant attitude is comparable, and arguably equivalent to, the practice of epoché, the basic phenomenological attitude advocated by Husserl and his phenomenological followers. With the practice of epoché there is not only the theoretical distinction between the non-reflective attitude of natural life and the reflective attitude as methodological guidance to true knowledge, there is also the call for transformation of the unreflective attitude into the reflective attitude. This self-transformation of the subject is the fruit of the spiritual exercise of self-examination of the wise man. Wisdom or intelligence is thus not generated nor demonstrated through a kind of formal logical deduction, but by the practice of spiritual exercise of the subject on herself who engages herself in critical reflections. But the term "reflection" here has a connotation which is not merely theoretical, but also practical and moral. In the Chinese language, theoretical reflection is *fansi* 反思, whereas reflection in the practical and ethical sense of the term is *fanxing* 反省. The reflections brought about and highlighted by Zhuangzi are not of the purely theoretical order, but belong to the practical and ethical order too.

But how can we guard against our prejudices as we are always preoccupied by all kinds of mundane practical interests in our everyday existence? The first step is to abstain from pursuing activities motivated by mundane life interests. Below is what Zhuangzi reports from someone who claims to have learned the Dao (*wendao* 聞道) in chapter 6 (*dazongshi* 大宗師):

In any event, it should have been easy to teach the Dao of a sage to someone with the ability of a sage. Still, I had to instruct him and watch over his practice. After three days, he could get rid of all mundane preoccupations. Once he was able to get rid of mundane preoccupations, I continued to watch over his practice. After seven days, he was able to remain unaffected by the concern of external things. Once he was able to remain unaffected by the concern of external things, I continued to watch over his practice. After nine days, he was able to abstain from any concern about life [and death]. Once he was able to abstain from any concern about life [and death], he was able to achieve enlightenment comparable to the clarity of the morning. Achieving enlightenment comparable to the clarity of the morning, he could then envision the Unique. Envisioning the Unique, he could transcend [the historical time of] past and present. Transcending [the historical time of] past and present, he could gain access to the state of [spiritual] immortality.[16]

In this step-by-step progressive process of spiritual exercise in seven stages which leads to the learned acquisition of Dao, all begins by abstaining from the preoccupation of mundane interest. This first step leads to the giving-up of concern over external things and hence to the liberation from reification of the mind. Once the mind is liberated from the effect of reification by external things, it passes onto the stage of abstention from concern about mundane life and death which is the precondition for enlightenment of the mind and the vision of the Unique, another name for the Dao. The attitude of abstention from all sorts of mundane interests, material concerns as well as concerns of the mundane life span is the attitude of epoché with regard to all mundane life interests. It is the gateway to enlightenment and the visioning of the Dao. The talk about "fasting of the mind" (xinzhai 心齋) in chapter 4 (renjianshi 人間世)[17] and "sit and forget" (zuowang 坐忘) in chapter 6[18] should both be understood along this line: they are practices of spiritual asceticism which, beginning by the epoché of all mundane life interests, bring about self-transformation of the subject and lead in turn to enlightenment and ultimately to experience of partaking of the vision of the Dao.

"Fasting of the mind" and "sitting and forgetting" are two modes of spiritual exercise or self-cultivation that manifest a quasi-religious attitude of asceticism. But if these celebrated practices are quasi-religious in nature, one may raise the following query: how can they be assimilated to the phenomenological epoché of Husserl who has invented this methodological device with the explicit epistemological purpose of acquisition of knowledge with scientific rigor? In other words, how can the epoché which, in its original form, was epistemologically oriented, be extended to a usage which is practically and quasi-religiously oriented?

While it is true that Husserl had at the beginning understood the epoché purely from the epistemological standpoint, his invention of this method was first inspired by the aesthetic attitude as one that abstains from any practical and pragmatic interest with respect to the object of aesthetic contemplation.[19] In the early 1920s, Husserl began to see that the epoché is at the basis of the religious attitude of Buddhism, which is a quasi-transcendental attitude. In fact, it is through the practice of prayers and meditations that a Buddhist practitioner strives to overcome all mundane life interests.[20] Toward the end of his life, notably in the unfinished but important work *The Crisis of European Sciences and Transcendental Phenomenology*, Husserl explicitly recognizes the convergence between the phenomenological epoché and religious conversion by stating that "the total phenomenological attitude and the epoché belonging to it are destined in essence to effect, at first, a complete personal transformation, comparable in the beginning to a religious conversion."[21] So there is a profound proximity between the usage of epoché in the epistemological domain, the aesthetic domain, as well as the religious domain in terms of their common attitude in relation to mundane life interests: abstention or indifference. If we take into account the fact that this attitude is also at the basis of the ascetic attitude of Stoicism as a philosophic school prevalent in Western antiquity, we can see that the attitude underlying the epoché is both a cross-cultural phenomenon (as shown in Chinese pre-Qin Daoism, Indian Buddhism, Greek-Roman Stoicism, and contemporary European phenomenology) and a multi-domain technique of the self (*technique de soi*), to use the terminology of Foucault, observable in philosophical reflection, aesthetic contemplation, and religious practice, because all these activities necessitate a pre-requisite process of self-transformation experienced through and through by the subject of philosophical meditation, aesthetic appreciation and religious *askesis*.

Our analyses of the *Zhuangzi* passages above show that the practice of the epoché through spiritual exercise is not only a guiding principle for the formation of true and sound cognitive judgments, it is also the condition *sine qua non* for achieving enlightenment of the mind as a pre-requisite for envisioning the Dao and gaining access to the state of spiritual immortality. In this regard, Zhuangzi shows a great sense of rigor in terms of methodological considerations with respect to ascertaining sound and true cognitive judgments, as well as securing systematic execution of progressive practical steps which lead to spiritual self-transformation as the precondition to the learned acquisition of the Dao.[22]

3. Description: Return to the Pre-Objective and the Primordial Order of Things

Though Zhuangzi is good at argumentation, as seen from his celebrated debates with his friend Hui Shi, and subtle analysis, he always proceeds by way of description. In the following, I will take three well-known passages from the *Zhuangzi* as examples to show what is meant by the pre-objective and the primordial order of things. They are taken respectively from the passages about the Cook Ding in chapter 3 (*yangshengzhu* 養生主), about the Wheelwright Pian in chapter 13 (*tiandao* 天道), and about the swimmer in chapter 19 (*dasheng* 達生).

3.1. Cook Ding's Technique of the Self-Cultivation Toward Perfection

Cook Ding's technique of self-cultivation is a body-schema *qua* knowledge of the pre-objective order, coincidence of the capacity to know, and the capacity to act, integration of theory and practice:

Cook Ding was cutting up an ox for Lord Wenhui. Wherever his hand touched, his shoulder leaned, his foot stepped, his knee nudged, the flesh would fall away with a swishing sound. Each slice of the cleaver was right in tune, zip zap! He danced in rhythm to the Mulberry Grove; moved in concert with the strains of the Managing Chief. Ah, wonderful! said Lord Wenhui, that skill can attain such heights! The cook put down his cleaver and responded, what your servant loves is Dao, which goes beyond mere skill. When I first began to cut oxen, what I saw was nothing but whole oxen. After three years, I no longer saw whole oxen. Today, I meet the ox with my spirit rather than looking at it with my eyes. My sense organs stop functioning and my spirit moves as it pleases. In accord with the natural grain, I slice at the great crevices, lead the blade through the great cavities. Following its inherent structure, I never encounter the slightest obstacle even where the veins and arteries come together or where the ligaments and tendons join, much less from obvious big bones. A good cook changes his cleaver once a year because he chops. An ordinary cook changes his cleaver once a month because he hacks. Now I have been using my cleaver for nineteen years and have cut up thousands of oxen with it, but the blade is still as fresh as though it had just come from the grindstone. Between the joints there are spaces, but the edge of the blade has no thickness. Since I am inserting something without any thickness into an empty space, there will certainly be lots of room for the blade to play around in. That is why the blade is still as fresh as though it had just come from the grindstone. Nonetheless, whenever I come to a complicated spot and see that it will be difficult to handle, I cautiously restrain myself, focus my vision, and slow my motion. With an imperceptible movement of the cleaver, plop! and the flesh is already separated, like a clump of earth collapsing to the ground. I stand there holding the cleaver in my hand, look all around me with complacent satisfaction, then I wipe off the cleaver and store it away. Wonderful! said Lord Wenhui. From hearing the words of the cook, I have learned how to nourish life.[23]

In this celebrated passage, there is a widely shared understanding that it shows Zhuangzi's indifference and even negative attitude toward both cognitive and moral activities, for what is essential for Zhuangzi is nurturing life, which is a kind of practical activity in which neither the cognitive interest nor the moral concern comes to the fore. In this regard, cognitive and moral activities are both harmful to achieving the ultimate end of nurturing life. Thus it is often understood that Zhuangzi's whole orientation is to repress both the cognitive and the moral dimension of human activity. Yet if we return to this famous tale in the *Zhuangzi*, we find that it contains meticulous descriptions about the Dao and the progressive steps leading to the technique of self-cultivation in the profession of a cook who is in fact a butcher. These descriptions contain rich elements of an ethic of self-cultivation in terms of the perfect coordination of the body and the mind in view of attaining a maximum degree of self-mastery in the exercise of the art of dissection of an ox. Ethic is the term employed to capture the relation of the moral subject to herself. Thus if one can say that Zhuangzi is an a-moralist in the sense that he does not care about conventional moral norms, it is difficult to maintain that Zhuangzi has no ethical concern. On the contrary, we can even say that Zhuangzi's ultimate concern is an ethic of self-cultivation.

However, this very expression "ethic of self-cultivation in Zhuangzi" needs clarification, as there will be questions about the sense of self in the *Zhuangzi*. Is there a unitary sense of self as identity in this Daoist philosopher who always emphasizes the change and transformation (*hua* 化) of things? By emphasizing change and transformation, is Zhuangzi not rather a thinker of non-identity? And if Zhuangzi is a thinker of non-identity, how can we talk about the self in the sense of a form of identity of the subject in the *Zhuangzi*? All of these are not easy questions to answer. Their complete clarification needs another work which we cannot undertake here. But we can at least address this issue in a preliminary way by borrowing the distinction between two forms of identity proposed by the eminent French phenomenological philosopher Paul Ricoeur: identity as *idem* and identity as *ipse*. *Idem*-identity is identity understood along the lines of sameness by reference to externally identifiable properties or characters. This is identity understood from the point of view of whatness, proper for a thing or the static character trait of a person. When the physical properties of a certain thing change, it will probably be changed into another thing. *Ipse*-identity is identity of an individual (or even a group) from the perspective of "who." It refers to the identical pole of an acting subject immersed in a plurality of actions that manifests a selfhood despite the fact that her external and physical features undergo constant changes. As a living being, a human person is an individual who undergoes constant changes but who still keeps a sense of identity as a self. More importantly, a human subject is also a being of possibility and desire: she tries to be someone she is not yet. That means a human being is also a being of promise: she promises to the others but first of all to herself to be the one she projects to be. The realization of promise must be enacted through time. Understood in this sense, the selfhood of a person is not established outside of time but within time. Thus identity of a person, or simply personal identity, is *ipse*-identity on the basis of *idem*-identity. In this way, for a human being who expresses her identity as a self, there is no contradiction between her sense of selfhood and the changes—

physical, physiological, and psychological—she constantly experiences.[24] According to Ricoeur, personal identity cannot be attained by external description in the manner of description of a physical object; rather, it can only be done so by construction of the permanence of the selfhood in time through narratives. Thus personal identity is a kind of narrative identity.[25] Ricoeur's distinction between *idem*-identity and *ipse*-identity, as well as his introduction of the notion of narrative identity, contribute considerably to the clarification of the puzzle around personal identity since Hume.[26]

With Ricoeur's concept of narrative identity in mind, the fact that although Zhuangzi emphasizes change and transformation, there is still room to speak of the self, and thus of practices of self-transformation which are an integral part of his ethic of self-cultivation. In light of this, let us return to the technique of self-cultivation which attains a degree of perfection as professed by Cook Ding. Cook Ding's action of dissecting the ox is not guided by a degree of perception perceptible by the naked eye, but by some sort of vision of the whole body of the ox animated by the spirit. When his vision is guided by the spirit in coordination with the vision of the whole body of the ox, what is in front of him is no more an ordinary empirical object, but the texture and inner structure of this object. His action is thus no more exercised at the surface of the empirical object but goes deep-down into its inner space. Thus Cook Ding is able to act, or more precisely to articulate his various gestures within this inner space. This is no more an action guided by some sort of representational thinking, i.e., a mode of thinking characterized by the attentive fixation of the eyes on the object seen or that of the mind on the object of thought through some sort of idea or image. Cook Ding's dissection of the ox can be better understood by the Merleau-Pontian term of "body-schema" (schéma corporelle) put forward in his master work *Phenomenology of Perception* (we will return to this again a bit later).

Zhuangzi's description of the inner space of the object as the deep-structure of the thing in terms of void and fissure reminds us of the term "écart" employed by Merleau-Ponty in his description of the flesh (*la chair*).[27] This is a term which is used to describe the ontological character of a level of being which is pre-objective. A thing is not only a compact composition of positivities and fullness; it consists also of void and fissure. In other words, in a thing there is a certain form of absence which is yet not a pure absence. This is part and parcel of the texture and inner structure of a thing. Yet this level of being is no more that of an object understood in the sense of empirical sciences, but at a level which is underneath it while also supporting it. The term pre-objective serves to describe this state of affairs. Only in this way can we understand the world as a world structured by texture and depth, and not merely as one composed of flat beings. It is tempting to use the Merleau-Pontian term "flesh" to describe the flesh of the ox revealed under the spiritual vision of Cook Ding. In any case, the concept of "matter" employed by the positive sciences is unable to do justice to the state of affairs revealed in the description of the pre-objective order of things of the world. Merleau-Ponty calls being at this pre-objective level "brute being," that is, being not yet domesticated by objective thinking. The latter is a mode of thinking shared by objective sciences and intellectualist philosophy; it is a mode of thinking from a bird's-eye perspective which is a massive view on the things of the world. This latter being consists merely of objects of a pure spectacle laid out before our naked eyes, however, this mode of being is ignorant of the depth of things and the depth of the world. It is also incapable of understanding void and fissures as negative elements constitutive of the structure of the things and of the world of the pre-objective order. To Merleau-Ponty this level of pre-objective brute being does not belong to materiality, but to sensibility: "the sensible (*le sensible*) is the universal form of brute being."[28]

It is manifest that the representational mode of thinking at the basis of the operation of objective thought in the Merleau-Pontian sense, which remains an act of attentive fixation on the empirical object, is far from being able to understand the spiritual vision demonstrated by Cook Ding when his technique of ox-dissection attains perfection. We think that Merleau-Ponty's concept of body-schema better captures this kind of technique as shown by Cook Ding, which is a perfect coordination between the mind and the different senses of the body guided by a certain non-representational spiritual vision. Let us first look at the way Merleau-Ponty explains the term body-schema:

> If the need was felt to introduce this new word [body-schema], it was in order to express that the spatial and temporal unity, the inter-sensorial unity, or the sensorimotor unity of the body is, so to speak, an in principle unity, to express that this unity is not limited to contents actually and fortuitously associated in the course of our experience, that it somehow precedes them and in fact makes their association possible ... the body schema will no longer be the mere result of association established in the course of experience, but rather the global awareness of my posture in the inter-sensory world, a "form" in Gestalt psychology's sense of the word.[29]

There is a global form which gives unity to the different senses distributed over the body-subject, such that these different bodily senses can coordinate with one another to achieve the execution of an action. But how is this global form generated? The body-subject is a subject-in-the-world who is polarized by her tasks to be accomplished through her non-representational body movement. "Psychologists often say that the body schema is *dynamic*. Reduced to a precise sense, this term means that my body appears to me as a posture toward a certain task, actual or possible."[30]

With the concept of body-schema, not only can we understand the possibility of basic bodily gestures, which the practical necessity of daily life requires us to accomplish at the pre-reflective level, we can also better understand the execution of complicated and sophisticated bodily techniques which are not in a state of absence of knowledge, but knowledge integrated with bodily skills and gestures, such as that of martial arts, dance, gymnastics, playing musical instruments, calligraphy, painting, and so forth. The execution of bodily gestures required by these kinds of arts is motivated by the purpose of accomplishing tasks, notably artistic tasks. They are either below or above the level of objective thought. They have to mobilize the body-schema as knowledge of the pre-objective order, which is a certain form of articulation between the capacity to know and the capacity to act, as well as integration of theory and practice. The technique of ox-dissection at the level of perfection demonstrated by Cook Ding is an eminent example of the realization of perfect integration of the knowing and acting capacities of the body with the mind through the body-schema.

3.2. Further Illustration via the Story of Wheelwright Pian

> Duke Huan was reading in the upper part of his hall and Wheelwright Pian was hewing a wheel in the lower part. Setting aside his hammer and chisel, the wheelwright went to the upper part of the hall and inquired of Duke Huan, saying, I venture to ask what words Your Highness is reading? The words of the sages, said the Duke. Are the sages still alive? They are already dead said the duke. Then what my Lord is reading are merely the dregs of the ancients. How can you, a wheelwright, comment upon what I am reading? asked Duke Huan. If you can explain yourself, all right. If you cannot explain yourself, you shall die. I look at it from my own occupation, said Wheelwright Pian. If the spokes are loose, they will fit sweet as a whistle but the wheel is not solid. If they are too tight, you will not be able to insert them no matter how hard you try. To make them neither too loose nor too tight is something you sense in your hand and feel in your heart. There is a knack to it that cannot be put into words. I have not been able to teach it to my son, and my son has not been able to learn it from me. That is why I'm still hewing wheels after seventy years. When they died, the ancients took with them what they could not transmit. So what you are reading are the dregs of the ancients![31]

In this passage, what Wheelwright Pian faces is also the pre-objective order of things which is beyond verbal expression in the sense that it cannot be entirely objectified by linguistic means. That is why this art cannot be transmitted in the mode of objective knowledge because the technique of hewing wheels is on this side of objective representation. Wheelwright Pian tries to explain to Duke Huan that the art of hewing wheels is incomprehensible from the cognitivist or intellectualist mode of thinking. To solve his problems, Wheelwright Pian has to mobilize a certain kind of technical knowledge which is best understood as arising out of his body-schema, and not from a cognitivist or intellectualist mode of thinking, the only mode of thinking that Duke Huan has in mind. Thus both the examples of Cook Ding and Wheelwright Pian show the anti-cognitivist or anti-intellectualist approach of Zhuangzi.

4. Back to Primordial Nature: Critique of Over-Civilization, Praise for Wild Being and Savage Spirit

Let us begin with the example of the surprising observation of Confucius on the wild swimmer in chapter 19 (*dasheng* 達生):

> Confucius was observing the cataract at Spinebridge where the water fell from a height of thirty fathoms and the mist swirled for forty tricents. No tortoise, crocodile, fish, or turtle could swim there. Spotting an older man swimming in the water, Confucius thought that he must have suffered some misfortune and wished to die. So he had his disciples line up along the current to rescue the man. But after the man had gone several hundred yards, he came out by himself. With disheveled hair, he was walking along singing and enjoying himself beneath the embankment. Confucius followed after the man and inquired of him, saying: I thought you were a ghost but when I looked more closely, I saw that you are a man. May I ask if you have a special way for treading the water? No, I have no special way. I began with what was innate, grew up with my nature, and completed my destiny. I enter the very center of the whirlpools and emerge as a companion of the torrent. I follow along with the way of the water and do not impose myself on it. That is how I do my treading. What do you mean by began with what was innate, grew up with your nature, and completed your destiny? asked Confucius. I was born among these hills and feel secure among them—that is what is innate. I grew up in the water and feel secure in it— that is my nature. I do not know why I am like this, yet that is how I am—that is my destiny.[32]

This passage describes in stunning language a mode of being and a state of mind exemplified by the wild swimmer. He is entirely at ease with the wild Nature in which he has lived since birth. I would borrow the terms of "wild being" and "savage spirit" from Merleau-Ponty to describe them in order that they can be more intelligible than the term "spontaneity" used by A.C. Graham and others. This is a mode of being and a state of mind which remains in close contact with primordial Nature, i.e., the nature which is not yet domesticated by civilization. The wild swimmer is unable to explain in a civilized language, the language of Confucius, how he acquired this capacity, and accomplished actions and techniques unimaginable for a civilized man. The only thing he can do is to demonstrate it in accordance with the capacity he acquired by his close contact with primordial Nature since his birth. Confucius is the representative of civilization at its maturity, following in each life-situation the rituals and social norms prevalent under the reign of Zhou. In doing so, he has lost any contact with primordial Nature. His potentiality of being is thus immensely limited according to Zhuangzi. Here Zhuangzi makes an implicit critique of over-civilization, a term I borrow from the Czech phenomenologist Jan Patočka.[33] There is an explicit critique of over-civilization in the famous parable of the Emperor Hundun 渾沌 in chapter 7 (*yingdiwang* 應帝王) of the *Zhuangzi*.[34] The Emperor Hundun is killed by the goodwill of other self-esteemed civilized emperors. This is because the other civilized emperors think that the face of the Emperor Hundun lacks the seven orifices which are characteristics of the face of a civilized being, and only a civilized being is dignified enough to be an emperor. To qualify Zhuangzi's position as critique of over-civilization means that he is not against any form of civilization. The examples of Cook Ding and Wheelwright Pian show that to Zhuangzi, the techniques of self-cultivation are essential for leading a good life. Thus the affirmation and highlighting of some form of civilization is still important for Zhuangzi.

We are even tempted to say that if Zhuangzi can be understood as some kind of social reformer, the social reforms he would propose necessitate a certain form of cultural renewal. This form of cultural renewal is not the further development of the very anthropocentric conception and practices of human civilization, but regaining inspiration from primordial Nature, from the "wild being" and the "savage spirit" embedded within it. In this regard we can also find some resonances from Merleau-Ponty when he expresses his praise of Husserl with reference to the latter's contribution to cultural renewal: "Willy-nilly, against his plans and according to his essential audacity, Husserl awakens a wild world and a savage mind."[35] This wild world and this savage mind are not yet domesticated by the classical rationalism of objective thinking. I think the greatness of Zhuangzi is to have revealed this wild world and savage spirit in his own way more than two thousand years ago through stories and parables in a non-intellectualist way, without relying on conceptual analysis as seen in Husserl, Merleau-Ponty, and others.

6. Conclusion

In the reading and analysis exposed above, we have shown that certain passages of the *Zhuangzi* text demonstrate a meticulous sense of method. Zhuangzi emphasizes the necessary change of attitude, namely the getting rid of prejudices and pre-reflective mundane opinions and interests in order to ascertain the formation of sound and true cognitive judgments. Zhuangzi also advocates systematic execution of methodological procedures in a step-by-step manner as a way to lead to spiritual self-transformation which is the precondition for the learned acquisition of the Dao. These methodological procedures begin by abstaining from any concern about mundane life interests. The change of attitude leading to the doing away with prejudices and abstaining from mundane life interests is Zhuangzi's version of the phenomenological epoché.

The *Zhuangzi* text also shows a great sense of faithful description of the state of affairs belonging to the pre-objective order and the order of primordial Nature. It is an order of things inaccessible to the intellectualist mode of thinking of the objective positive sciences. Resuming contact with primordial Nature will enable us to rediscover the "wild being" and the savage spirit embedded in our originary mode of being not yet tamed by over-civilization. Against all kinds of social conventions and institutions as a result of over-civilization, Zhuangzi proposes the re-actualization of the potentialities of a "wild being" and a savage mind which are the sources of cultural renewal. Understood in this manner, the *Zhuangzi* is neither anti-rationalist nor skeptic nor mysterious, but highly intelligible.

Notes

1   A.C. Graham, *Disputers of the Tao: Philosophical Argument in Ancient China* (La Salle: Open Court, 1989), 176.

2   Ibid.

3   Ibid., 178.

4   Ibid., 180.

5   Ibid., 186.

6   See, for example, Paul Kjellberg and P.J. Ivanhoe, eds., *Essays on Skepticism, Relativism, and Ethics in the Zhuangzi* (Albany: State University of New York Press, 1996).

7   One of the first full English translations of the *Zhuangzi* was published by Herbert Giles under the title: *Chuang Tzu, Mystic, Moralist, and Social Reformer* (Shanghai: Kelly and Walsh, 1889). James Legge (Oxford: Oxford University Press, 1891), the other early English translator of the *Zhuangzi*, uses the generic title of "The Sacred Books of China" before the specific title of "The Texts of Daoism" in his translation of the *Daodejing* and the *Zhuangzi*. Legge thus presented these works as belonging to religion, comparable to works of Christianity. Martin Buber was among the few Western thinkers in the early twentieth century to have presented Zhuangzi as a philosopher in his own right. This is expressed in the "Afterword" to his 1910 German translation (Leipzig: Insel-Verlag, 1910) of the *Zhuangzi* (*Reden und Gleichnisse des Tschuang-tse*): "Zhuangzi may perhaps be compared to the entirety of Greek philosophy, which completed that which he only adumbrated—the Greek

philosophy which expanded the teachings from the sphere of the real life to the sphere of the explanation of the world, of the knowable, and of the ideological construct, and thereby indeed created something very individual and very powerful of its own." Buber, 103. For an in-depth discussion of Buber's relation to Zhuangzi, see Jonathan Herman, *I and Tao: Martin Buber's Encounter with Chuang Tzu* (Albany: State University of New York Press, 1996).

8   Edmund Husserl, *Logische Untersuchungen,* III. "Zur Lehre von den Ganzen und Teilen," II/1 (Tübingen: Max Niemeyer Verlag, 1901), 225–93. For the English translation, see Edmund Husserl, *Logical Investigations*, J.N. Findlay (trans.), vol. 2, Investigation III, "On the Theory of Wholes and Parts" (London: Routledge, 1970), 435–89.

9   Maurice Merleau-Ponty, *Phénoménologie de la Perception* (Paris: Gallimard, 1945), 12. For the English translation, see Maurice Merleau-Ponty, *Phenomenology of Perception*, Donald Landes (trans.), (London: Routledge, 2012), 6.

10   Maurice Merleau-Ponty, *Signes* (Paris: Gallimard, 1960), 202. For the English translation, see Maurice Merleau-Ponty, *Signs*, Richard McCleary (trans.), (Evanston: Northwestern University Press, 1964), 160 (translation modified).

11   Ibid.

12   Husserl himself has explained this motto in different places. In the *Logical Investigations*, he writes: "Meanings inspired only by remote, confused, inauthentic intuitions—if by any intuitions at all—are not enough: we must go back to the 'things themselves.'" Husserl, *Logical Investigations*, vol. 2, 252; German original: "Bedeutungen, die nur von entfernten, verschwommenen, uneigentlichen Anschauungen—wenn überhaupt von irgendwelchen—belebt sind, können uns nicht genug tun. Wir wollen auf die 'Sachen selbst' zurückgehen." Husserl, *Logische Untersuchungen*, Bd. II.1, 6. In *Ideas Pertaining to a Pure Phenomenology and Phenomenological Philosophy, First Book* (The Hague: M. Nijhoff, 1982), Husserl says: "But to judge rationally or scientifically about things signifies to conform to the things themselves or to go from words and opinions back to the things themselves, to consult them in their self-givenness and to set aside all prejudices alien to them." Husserl, *Ideas*, 35; German original: "Vernünftig oder wissenschaftlich über Sachen urteilen, das heißt aber, sich nach den *Sachen selbst* richten, bzw. von den Reden und Meinungen auf die Sachen selbst zurückgehen, sie in ihrer Selbstgegebenheit befragen und alle sachfremden Vorurteile beiseitetun." See Edmund Husserl, *Ideen zu einer reinen Phänomenologie und Phänomenologischen Philosophie, Erstes Buch, Allgemeine Einführung in die reine Phänomenologie* (Tübingen: Max Niemeyer Verlag, 1913), 35. See Martin Heidegger, *Sein und Zeit* (Tübingen: Max Niemeyer Verlag, 1927), 27. For the English translation, see Martin Heidegger, *Being and Time*, John Macquarrie and Edward Robinson (trans.), (New York: SCM Press, 1962), 50. See also Merleau-Ponty, *Phénoménologie de la Perception*, iii / *Phenomenology of Perception*, 8.

13   Husserl, *Ideen I*, 56–7 / *Ideas I*, 60–1.

14   Ibid., 139–41 / Ibid., 167–70.

15   For the Chinese, see Guying Chen, ed., *Modern Commentary and Annotations to the Zhuangzi* (Hong Kong: Zhonghua Shuju, 1997), 49. Although the

translations in this chapter are my own, I have benefitted from those by Victor Mair, A.C. Graham, Burton Watson, and Brook Ziporyn.

16 For the Chinese, see Chen, *Zhuangzi*, 184.

17 Ibid., 117.

18 Ibid., 205.

19 See Kwok-Ying Lau and Thomas Nenon, eds., "Aesthetic Attitude and Phenomenological Attitude: From Zhu Guangqian to Husserl," in *Logos and Aisthesis: Phenomenology and the Arts* (Cham: Springer, 2020).

20 See Kwok-Ying Lau, *Phenomenology and Intercultural Understanding: Toward a New Cultural Flesh* (Dordrecht: Springer, 2016), 56–9.

21 Edmund Husserl, *Die Krisis der Europäischen Wissenschaften und die Transzendentale Phänomenologie* (The Hague: M. Nijhoff, 1954), 140. For the English translation, see Edmund Husserl, *The Crisis of European Sciences and Transcendental Phenomenology*, David Carr (ed.) (Evanston: Northwestern University Press, 1970), 137.

22 The step-by-step sense of progression of the technique of self-cultivation leading to enlightenment by the Dao is also shown in the following descriptive passage in chapter 6 (*dazongshi* 大宗師): "Wherever did you learn all this? asked Sir Sunflower of Southunc. I learned it from the son of Assistant Ink. Assistant Ink's son learned it from the grandson of Ready Reciter. Ready Reciter's grandson learned it from Bright Vision. Bright Vision learned it from Agreeable Apprehension. Agreeable Apprehension learned it from Ascetic Service. Ascetic Service learned it from Sighing Chanter. Sighing Chanter learned it from Murky Mediation. Murky Meditation learned it from Contemplating the Unique. Contemplating the Unique learned it from Commencing Doubt." For the Chinese, see Chen, 184. This step-by-step process of progression can be retrieved in the following order: from writing or script (*fu mo* 副墨) back to reading aloud (*ge song* 洛誦), then back to understanding (*zhan ming* 瞻明), then back to apprehension by the mind (*nie xu* 聶許), then back to ascetic practice (*xu yi* 需役), then back to chanting admiration before the universe (*yu ou* 於謳), then back to meditation (*xuan ming* 玄冥), then back to contemplation of Unique (*can liao* 參寥), then back to the commencing doubt (*yi shi* 疑始). It is interesting to note that the term "the commencing doubt" reminds us of the *thaumazein*, i.e., wonder and puzzlement as the origin of the philosophical attitude in Plato and Aristotle.

23 For the Chinese text, see Chen, 95–6.

24 Paul Ricoeur, *Soi-Même comme un Autre* (Paris: Seuil, 1990), 137–66.

25 Ibid., 167–98.

26 For a concise presentation and critical evaluation of Ricoeur's contribution to the issue of personal identity, see Philippe Cabestan, "Qui suis-je? Identité-ipse, identité-idem et identité narrative," *Le Philosophoire*, 1 (2015): 151–60.

27 Merleau-Ponty, *Signes*, 217 / *Signs*, 172.

28 Ibid.

29 Merleau-Ponty, *Phénoménologie de la Perception*, 115–16 / *Phenomenology of Perception*, 102.

30 Ibid.

31 For the Chinese text, see Chen, 357–8.

32 For the Chinese text, see Chen, 486–7.

33 See Jan Patočka, "La Surcivilization et son Conflit," in *Liberté et Sacrifice: Ecrits Politiques* (Grenoble: Jérôme Millon, 1990), 99–177.

34 Chen, 228.

35 Merleau-Ponty, *Signes*, 228 / *Signs*, 180.

References

Buber, Martin. (1991), *Chinese Tales, Zhuangzi: Sayings and Parables and Chinese Ghost and Love Stories*, Alex Page (trans.), London: Humanities Press International.

Cabestan, Philippe. (2015), "Qui suis-je? Identité-*ipse*, identité-*idem* et identité narrative," *Le Philosophoire*, 1: 151–60.

Chen, Guying, ed. (1997), *Modern Commentary and Annotations to the Zhuangzi* 莊子今注今譯, Hong Kong: Zhonghua Shuju.

Graham, A.C. (1989), *Disputers of the Tao: Philosophical Argument in Ancient China*, La Salle: Open Court.

Heidegger, Martin. (1927), *Sein und Zeit*, Tübingen: Max Niemeyer Verlag.

Heidegger, Martin. (1962), *Being and Time*, John Macquarrie and Edward Robinson (trans.), New York: SCM Press.

Herman, Jonathan. (1996), *I and Tao: Martin Buber's Encounter with Chuang Tzu*, Albany: State University of New York Press.

Husserl, Edmund. (1901), *Logische Untersuchungen*, III. "Zur Lehre von den Ganzen und Teilen," II/1, Tübingen: Max Niemeyer Verlag.

Husserl, Edmund. (1913), *Ideen zu einer reinen Phänomenologie und Phänomenologischen Philosophie, Erstes Buch, Allgemeine Einführung in die reine Phänomenologie*, Tübingen: Max Niemeyer Verlag.

Husserl, Edmund. (1954), *Die Krisis der Europäischen Wissenschaften und die Transzendentale Phänomenologie*, W. Biemel (ed.), The Hague: M. Nijhoff.

Husserl, Edmund. (1970), *The Crisis of European Sciences and Transcendental Phenomenology*, David Carr (ed.), Evanston: Northwestern University Press.

Husserl, Edmund. (1970), *Logical Investigations*, vol. 2, Investigation III, "On the Theory of Wholes and Parts," J.N. Findlay (trans.), London: Routledge & Kegan Paul.

Husserl, Edmund. (1982), *Ideas Pertaining to a Pure Phenomenology and Phenomenological Philosophy, First Book, General Introduction to Pure Phenomenology*, F. Kersten (trans.), The Hague: M. Nijhoff.

Kjellberg, Paul and P.J. Ivanhoe, eds. (1996), *Essays on Skepticism, Relativism, and Ethics in the Zhuangzi*, Albany: State University of New York Press.

Lau, Kwok-Ying. (2016), *Phenomenology and Intercultural Understanding: Toward a New Cultural Flesh*, in *Contributions to Phenomenology* (vol. 87), Dordrecht: Springer.

Lau, Kwok-Ying and Thomas Nenon, eds. (2020), "Aesthetic Attitude and Phenomenological Attitude: From Zhu Guangqian to Husserl," in *Logos and Aisthesis: Phenomenology and the Arts*, Cham: Springer.

Merleau-Ponty, Maurice. (1945), *Phénoménologie de la Perception*, Paris: Gallimard.

Merleau-Ponty, Maurice. (1960), *Signes*, Paris: Gallimard.

Merleau-Ponty, Maurice. (1964), *Signs*, Richard McCleary (trans.), Evanston: Northwestern University Press.

Merleau-Ponty, Maurice. (2012), *Phenomenology of Perception*, Donald Landes (trans.), London: Routledge.

Patočka, Jan. (1990), "La Surcivilization et son Conflit," in *Liberté et Sacrifice: Ecrits Politiques*, Erika Abrams (trans.), Grenoble: Jérôme Millon.

Ricoeur, Paul. (1990), *Soi-même comme un Autre*, Paris: Seuil.

5

Martin Buber's Phenomenological Interpretation of Laozi's *Daodejing*

Eric S. Nelson

1. Introduction: Buber's Daoism

Martin Buber's engagement with Chinese philosophy, religion, and culture is a significant example of intercultural encounter and dialogical exchange in early twentieth-century philosophy.[1] His early interpretations and selected translations of the *Zhuangzi* 莊子 and the literary work *Strange Stories from a Chinese Studio* (*Liaozhai Zhiyi* 聊齋誌異) of Pu Songling 蒲松齡 (1640–1715), were informed by his own philosophical, cultural-political, and religious context and concerns.[2] His approach to Chinese thought is structured by questions of mystical and dialogical experience, natural spontaneity and technological mechanization, and the this-worldly corporeal spirituality disclosed in Hasidic and Daoist sources. His intercultural engagements in turn informed the development of his own dialogical philosophical project, as Buber himself recognized and as is evident from the Daoist traces visible in his classic work *I and Thou* (*Ich und Du*, first published in German in 1923).[3]

Buber is primarily remembered as a thinker of Jewish religious experience, an advocate of ethical personalism, and a philosopher of dialogical communication. Additionally, furthermore, Buber practiced a preliminary form of intercultural philosophizing, did not limit the sense and range of the ethical to human persons, and interpreted communication through a phenomenology of interpersonal and embodied encounter, engagement, and conversation.

First, in contrast to his friend and collaborator Franz Rosenzweig, as well as later thinkers such as Emmanuel Levinas, Buber did not explicitly reject

(Rosenzweig) or casually dismiss (Levinas) Asian and other so-called "non-Western" discourses.[4] He engaged from his early to late works with mythic, religious, poetic, and philosophical sources and what they taught and transmitted (their teaching, *Lehre*) through image, word, and concept.[5] Buber's vision of "Daoism" is as a "teaching of the way" that is taught through a full range of communicative media.[6]

Second, Buber's "ethical personalism" does not rely on or entail a limited concept of the person that only includes other humans. His experiential and dialogical models, developed in part in relation to the *Daodejing* 道德經 attributed to Laozi 老子 and the *Zhuangzi*, encompass the "myriad things" (*wanwu* 萬物): stones, trees, animals, other humans, and spiritual realities.[7] Buber's expansive model of the "thing" and the possibility of ethically encountering it diverge from other accounts of "ethical personalism." Buber's relational approach to the thing and the other are linked with his assessment of these two early pre-Qin Daoist sources.[8]

Third, Buber conceives of dialogue as corporal, experiential, and personal. It occurs through (insofar as they can be distinguished) interpersonal and "interthingly" encounters, engagements, and exchanges. This phenomenological and to an extent semi-Daoist description and interpretation of communicative events continues to be a radical alternative to the abstract formalistic paradigms that dominate the philosophy of language and communication. Buber is not a practitioner of phenomenology understood as following the phenomenological school and methods inaugurated by Edmund Husserl. He does, nonetheless, practice phenomenology in the sense of describing and interpreting what is revealed in and what exceeds experience. These descriptions draw on his own personal experience, self-reflection, and a variety of global philosophical and non-philosophical sources and discourses. Of these, the *Daodejing* and the *Zhuangzi* play a noteworthy role, particularly in the 1910s and 1920s.[9]

2. The *Daodejing* as Natural Philosophy, Cosmology, and Ontology

Buber's initial systematic interpretation of Daoism is articulated in his 1909 essay "The Teaching of the *Dao*" ("Die Lehre vom Tao") that became part of his afterword to his 1910 edition of the *Zhuangzi*.[10] In this early account, the *Daodejing* is portrayed as the more embryonic beginning of the teaching of the Way, and the *Zhuangzi* as its communicative culmination.[11] Laozi is taken here to be a more primitive and less perfect teacher of the Way, because the *Daodejing* lacks the fuller use of language and the communicative fulfillment of the Way that Buber attributed to the *Zhuangzi*. However, in discussions in 1924 ("Besprechungen mit Martin Buber über Lao-tse's

Tao-te-king") and 1928 ("China und Wir"), his translation of selected political passages into Hebrew in 1942 ("Lao Tzu al hashilton" [Laozi on Governing]), and references in later works, it is the *Daodejing* that occupies Buber's attention.[12]

Buber offered a seminar devoted to the *Daodejing* to a private group in Ascona in southern Switzerland from August 10 to 31, 1924. The transcripts for this seminar were published in 2013 in volume 2.3, *Schriften zur Chinesischen Philosophie und Literatur*, of the new on-going edition of Buber's collected works.[13] The archivally accessible yet previously unpublished 1924 manuscript has received considerably less attention than his other writings concerning Chinese philosophy and literature. It unfolds striking threads for elucidating Buber's interests in Daoism and phenomenological interpretation of the *Daodejing* that he based on Victor von Strauss's 1870 translation and commentary and, rarely in this text, Richard Wilhelm's 1921 edition.[14]

Buber commenced his philosophically oriented commentary on this Chinese classic with an introduction that considers two reoccurring themes: (1) the Chinese conception of heart (*xin* 心) identified as the feeling of taste and sensuous contact with the external world that is both directional and relational, in contrast to the Western notion of interiority; and (2) Laozi as a thinker of return.[15]

This introduction indicates that the *Daodejing* is not a form of mysticism in at least two senses: it does not maintain a radical submersion into interiority and subjectivity, the depths and dark night of the soul, or an otherworldly mysticism directed into a transcendent super-sensuous realm. Instead, the *Daodejing* teaches the relational interconnection of heart and world. Accordingly, in commenting on the first chapter of the *Daodejing* that Strauss entitled the realization or fulfillment of the *dao* ("Verwirklichung des Tao") and Wilhelm the embodiment of sense ("Verkörperung des Sinns"), Buber defined the Chinese word *dao* 道 as path (*Bahn*) and way (*Weg*) and as change/exchange (*Weschsel*) and change/transformation (*Wandel*).[16]

Already in his reading of the first chapter, Buber traces three dimensions of Laozi's way: (1) It is a natural philosophy of the regularity of nature, the movement of the stars, the change of seasons, the growth of plants, and rhythmic return; (2) It is a cosmology of the structuring whole of circles within circles, cycles within cycles, that is a chaos of transformations and an interconnected structured cosmic order; and (3) It is an ontological teaching distinguishing (a) the *dao* that can be spoken, the *dao*'s finitization as pathway and manifestation as transformation (cosmology), and (b) the unsayable and limitless *dao* that exceeds it.[17]

It is at this point in his commentary that Buber enters into a reflection on naming and encountering that reflects a significant *topos* in his own path of thinking.

3. Naming, Encountering, and the Thing

A standard theory of language construes names as arbitrarily designated conventional terms that are reified when taken to indicate the actual essences of things. This account is often applied to early Daoist texts in contemporary philosophy, and Daoist words are classified as conventions and its philosophy of language as nominalist. Buber, in this commentary and in *I and Thou*, contests this abstract epistemological and impersonal model of language with the counter-argument that such conventional names are not genuine names. There is a distinction in the *Daodejing* between inconstant conventional names, associated with fluctuating finite paths, and so-called "eternal" or "constant" names (*changming* 常名) mentioned in chapter 1 of the text.

Buber sketched an intriguing phenomenological interpretation of Laozi's "constant name." Eternal names are those that are "not constructed but discovered" in encounter (*Begegnung*) and in "the reality of the relation."[18] The mutuality of "the thing and the I" is necessary for this relation in which the name operates as the being-between (*dazwischen*) *this* specific being and myself. This sense of "self" is what Buber described in *I and Thou* as the relational participating self. Things search for words through us as participatory intermediaries. The movement from things to names requires their being encountered by me from and in themselves. There is accordingly, Buber notes, an "interiority of the name that arises from things themselves."[19]

Buber offers a phenomenological description of the encounter with the tree, an illustrative example that is also deployed in *I and Thou*.[20] In the latter classic text from 1923, he distinguishes perceiving and representing the tree as an object, as an "it," from encountering the tree as a relational other, as a "thou." "Relation is reciprocity" ("Beziehung ist Gegenseitigkeit") with respect to the encountered tree, and consequently other "non-human" beings. In the *Daodejing* commentary from 1924, he recognized how the tree, insofar as it is encountered as *this* being, is not subsumed under a conceptual category or regarded through a nominal conventional name. On the contrary, the tree is encountered as "*this* tree" and "something for itself" "insofar as it is something for me."[21]

The description of the I–thou relation between human and thing in *I and Thou* corresponds in word and tone with his portrayal of the thing, encompassing both animate and inanimate beings, in the *Zhuangzi* in 1910 and the *Daodejing* in 1924. Relation signifies an ethical relation and naming is an ethical response to the thing's own path and way of being itself (that is, its self-so-ness or *ziran* 自然).

To draw a preliminary conclusion at this moment, one that will receive further contextualization in what follows, Buber's "interpersonal ethics" draws in part on his analysis of the relationality of and responsiveness toward things, does not exclude the "interthingly" and non-human from the ethical encounter and interbodily relationship, a problem that places into question the appropriateness of other overly anthropocentric varieties of "personalist ethics" that neglect the non-human in the ethical encounter.[22]

4. Broken Words and Namelessness

Buber has been criticized by Levinas, who endeavored to distance his own project emphasizing asymmetrical responsibility from Buber's ostensible idea of "symmetrical reciprocity," for inadequately attending to the alterity, asymmetries, and distances between self and Other in the I–thou relationship.[23] However, this critique is off the mark to the extent that Buber appears deeply concerned with the singularity of the thing and the other in the encounter, the asymmetries between the myriad things (including the non-human) rather than only the human other, and indeed the non-encounters and distances between I and thou, and between name and named. These dimensions of Buber's thought are apparent in *I and Thou* and in this introduction to the *Daodejing*.

Continuing to comment on the initial verse of the *Daodejing*, Buber draws on Western religious thought, such as the notion of divine glory and human distance from it, in introducing questions of the name's distance from what it would name. His clarification of the mutuality of name and thing in the *Daodejing* is accordingly reoriented with a reflection on human inadequacy in each encounter with the thing and the brokenness intrinsic to names and words. Buber specifies the limitations of naming and language that transpire even in the modality of the encounter: "our names do not deliver the consummate essence" of the thing and, restating the opening lines of chapter 1 of the *Daodejing*, "the name that can be named is the broken name."[24]

Buber noted how: "Every image contains an element of brokenness."[25] But not only the image is broken: broken words and mutilated bodies, such as the disfigured bodies of the *Zhuangzi*, reappear in Buber's discussions of Jewish and Chinese sources, and Buber compares Judaism to a body disfigured by its wandering from the Orient to the Occident and persecution in his 1915 essay "The Spirit of the Orient and Judaism."[26]

Buber's deployment of the language of fragmentation, brokenness, and human alienation from naturalness is not the conclusion of his analysis, as it is linked—as it is in the *Zhuangzi*—with transformation. Human brokenness is a point of transition and allows a pivot from the cosmological world of names and things to what Buber designates the ontological: "the name is a step toward the consummate name, the many a hint of the one, and the broken an indication of the unbroken."[27]

Line four of chapter 1 of the *Daodejing* discloses that this transition is interconnected with the questions of the status and appropriate role of the human. Buber differentiated three fundamental themes of the *Daodejing* from which all the others are constructed.[28] These three spheres exhibit a process of alienation from and return to nature and the nature of things: (1) The law (*das Gesetz*), the *dao* of heaven that consists of things happening from themselves; (2) The human (*der Mensch*), as estranged from nature; and (3) The kingdom (*Reich*), as the construction or formation (*aufbauen*) of a realm in which natural order is recreated,[29] or—as he clarified later—a community.[30] The third sphere is the sphere of the good (*das Gute*) to which we will turn in the next section. In the daily renewal of creation,[31] humans emerge, as evident in his other writings on Zhuangzi and Judaism, as ethical beings who are co-creators of creation through formative participation in it.[32]

The formative recovery of the natural in the third sphere is associated with the ontological truth of the nameless. Victor von Strauss translated the third line of chapter 1 of the *Daodejing*, "無名天地之始；有名萬物之母," as "Das namenlose ist des Himmels und der Erde Urgrund, Das Namen-Habende ist aller Wesen Mutter." Buber focused in his remarks on this originary ground (*Urgrund*): the consummate, the one, and the unbroken intimate the nameless originary ground that is the mother of all things through the emergence of names—identifying rather than distinguishing the nameless (*wuming* 無名) and name-having or forming (*youming* 有名).

The nameless exceeds all designations, thingliness, and serial causality, including being posited as a beginning or first cause. Buber did not explicitly mention the Chinese character *shi* 始 that is often translated as beginning or origin. Following Strauss's translation, *shi* 始 is interpreted as not signifying a causal or ontic beginning or origin in any sense. Antedating Martin Heidegger's phenomenological elucidation of "ground," Buber explicates the originless "originary ground" as a necessarily non-causal ontological truth through which name and thing, language and world, become possible.[33] In the *Daodejing*, this ground appears as an abyssal lack of ground (*Abgrund*), a swirling groundless depth ("schwingende, grundlose Tiefe"), as indicated by the key Daoist image of water.[34]

Even though Buber's depiction primarily relies on Strauss's rendition of the *Daodejing*, he did not exclusively rely on it. For instance, in his portrayal of line four of the first chapter of the *Daodejing*, he rejected Strauss's translation of *xuan* 玄 as "deep," noting that it means "dark" (*dunkel*) and secret or mystery (*Geheimnis*).[35] Wilhelm, for example, speaks of *Geheimnis* and wonder in his rendition of this chapter. The German word *Geheimnis* used to translate *xuan* means secret as well as mystery. This deeper secret within the secret, the depth deeper than depth, Buber noted, is the genuine gateway (*Pforte*). The threshold or the portal is a pivot and point of transition. The *Daodejing*'s "return" (*Rückkehr*) is not as a recovery of a primitive past or repetition of a previous state, but—as will be addressed further below—the turning around (*Umkehr*) of transition and transformation.[36]

5. The Law, the Human, and the Kingdom

Buber presented the *Daodejing* in his 1924 lectures as a teaching of the law, humanity, and the kingdom that he defined as community (*Gemeinschaft*).

First, the sphere of the law, as mentioned previously, is the immanent self-regulating self-occurring of things. The thing is transformed into a mere object of desire and use when they are broken from the encounter and taken out of the fullness of their relational context.[37]

Second, the human sphere has distanced itself from the life of things. It has alienated itself from the law (the cosmological functioning of the *dao*) through non-genuine life, which includes morals, rituals, political regulations, and other fixations. This *Daodejing* repeatedly problematizes ordinary Confucian virtues and the conventional morality of good and evil: the posited good is complicit with the evil that is necessarily co-posited along with it, the relative good is interdependent with the bad, and the stated propositional and moralistic good cannot adequately grasp the *dao*'s originary richness and fullness.[38]

Buber did not conclude that this problematization of morality entails amorality, immorality, or attitudes of ethical indifference, skepticism, and nihilism. Such interpretations of Daoism, which have become prevalent in contemporary Western philosophical approaches, are opposed to Chinese commentarial transmissions as well as Buber's assessment that the Daoism of the *Daodejing* and the *Zhuangzi* is a radical teaching of the good. The fullness of the *dao* is not opposed to the good; it is originary goodness itself—linked with images of the mother and the feminine—in contrast to non-genuine, broken, and partial ways of enacting it associated with the partiality of the masculine.[39]

What about the third sphere? Buber designated it the kingdom, realm, or empire (*Reich*), evoking Jewish and Abrahamic conceptions of the "kingdom of God" (Hebrew: *malchut* תוכלמ). In his 1928 essay "China and Us," Buber contends in the face of the increasing destructiveness of modern technological civilization and its self-assertive will to power that Western humanity needs to relearn in its own terms and situation the Daoist teaching of "non-action." In this 1924 context, Buber elucidates how one cannot do the good but how the good transpires through "doing-non-doing" (*tun nicht tun, weiwuwei* 爲無爲). The holy or sagely person, through whom the good is enacted and the third sphere of the kingdom fulfilled, neither imposes nor withdraws, and is neither active nor passive in relation to the world. Rather, the sage is spontaneous and responsive, responding in being called (*angerufen*).[40]

In this discussion, in addition to the 1928 essay, Daoism appears to offer a unique and significant philosophical and religious response to the problematic of modernity and the human condition. Hence, first, whereas Buber portrays the Buddhist ideal as one of self-redemption, the Daoist ideal is one of world-redemption through the happening of the *dao*, of the good, which is neither in nor reducible to time and history.[41] Daoism does not demand the denial and the de-individuation of the self (*Entselbstung*); it points toward the constitutive relationality and sociality of the individual and the individual's fulfillment (*Vollendung*) in the *dao*.[42]

6. The Anarchy of the Good and the Fulfillment of the Kingdom

Buber construed the Daoist good as fundamentally ethical and social; it is equally both interthingly and interpersonal, as no absolute distinction can be drawn between things, organisms, and persons.[43] The good is fulfilled in the kingdom, interpreted as a free relational community. Moreover, the Daoist good becomes messianic (that is, it concerns the genuine king to come) and prophetic (that is, it concerns the earthly fulfillment of the good) in this elucidation. These are "weak," intercultural and secularized (as primarily ethical), delineations of the messianic and prophetic moments: (1) The messianic is glimpsed in the figure of the sage-king (*shengren* 聖人) who lets the self-generating self-relating community become itself through *weiwuwei*; and (2) The prophetic is apprehended in the originary ethics of the enactment and practice of the good.

The *Daodejing*'s message is neither mystical nor monistic absorption into the totality of the one.[44] It does not offer a phenomenology of experience, consciousness, or Dasein, but suggests a different phenomenological strategy of tracing encounters within relational reality. Buber's reconstruction of Daoism resonates with his own ethical and this-worldly interpretation of Judaism, in particular in its Hassidic forms that share a more intimate affinity with Daoism in Buber's early works. Buber's Hasidic Judaism and Daoism enact the divine in everyday communicative and corporeal life. Second, however, crucial differences remain: Buber states that Daoism teaches through nature itself, through encountering immanent reality, what Judaism and early Christianity attempt to teach through ethical prescriptions.[45]

Daoism (or at least its pre-Qin variety) is neither primitive nor pagan, according to Buber's response to these monotheistic criticisms in his correspondence with Rosenzweig.[46] Buber, as an intercultural theopolitical philosopher, can recognize it as a teaching of fulfilled life, evoking the Jewish conception of a restored world (Hebrew: *tikkun olam* עולם תיקון) that encompasses both the natural and the human.[47]

Buber's *Daodejing* is a teaching of the good as messianic or prophetic anarchism.[48] The social fulfillment of the good, the teaching of the kingdom is in a non-doing and letting in which the ruler lets the people come to themselves and to life.[49] The non-coercive sage-king is a messianic figure in embodying the authority of a teacher and an exemplary model, as well as the "lonely one" called to responsiveness and responsibility to and for others.[50]

The distinction between authority and freedom governs Buber's juxtaposition of Confucius and Laozi in his depictions of the two in 1924,[51] 1928, and in 1951. Buber's Confucius teaches human politics consisting of intentional, calculative, judgmental, and moralistic ritual and justice based on distinction (rank) and distance. In contrast to Confucius, who appears limited in Buber's Daoist-oriented perspective, Laozi communicates the originary ethics of the good: the radical intentionless spontaneity of proximity and love.[52] This assessment is reconfirmed in his 1951 essay "Society and the State." Buber continued to distinguish between Confucian authoritarian and statist rule by elites and the self-generating self-organization of the people in love and proximity.[53] Buber's Daoism is communitarian and anarchistic.

While Confucius is an educator through externally imposed prescriptive laws and life-rules, in which the dead dominate the living, Laozi is a teacher of the internally motivated, self-generating, and living incalculable good. This good and its community do not occur through my own action, deliberation, and judgment. The partial and non-relational masculine human self damages and destroys itself and others through self-assertion.[54] Absorbed in itself and its own anxieties, calculations, and concerns, the self of the second sphere (humanity) is estranged from the law and the kingdom. It is in this context that the estranged self should become again like the newborn child through non-intentional non-coerced non-doing. The good occurs through the freedom of naturally and relationally being what one is in doing-non-doing understood as non-assertion, non-imposition, and non-striving.[55]

The *Daodejing* appears to intimate a utopian ideal of an ethical community motivated by love and oriented toward the self-generating good instead of the self-assertive willfulness and external regulations that lead to estrangement and destruction.[56] However, this is not an empty speculation for "beautiful souls" for Buber.[57] In his discussion of *Daodejing* chapter 20, Laozi emerges as a prophetic witness speaking from out of the truth of the *dao* in the abandonment, brokenness, and suffering of the human sphere.[58] Daoism, as a consequence of this prophetic witnessing, has a social-critical dimension to it in relation to the suffering and injustices of the present.[59]

7. Origin, Movement, and Fulfillment

The fulfillment of the *dao* transpires immanently in the midst of earthly human life through the transition from human partialness, lack, and deficiency to balancing in the grace and other-power of the *dao*.[60] The *dao*'s grace (*Gnade*) and nourishing power is taken to be "religious" in the sense of its being independent of individual willing and willfulness.[61] The *dao* that nurtures and nourishes all things (sphere one) also heals (sphere three). Playing on the etymological kinship between the German words *heil* (healing) and *heilig* (holy), Buber identified the "holy" with that which heals the wound, and with a restorative becoming whole in the face of brokenness.[62]

This "turning" is a process of transformation: in the movement through negativity and opposition, there is no "return" to or pure reproduction of the condition of the spontaneous automatic law that is enacted in things. Buber maintained that the law's fulfillment occurs in the genuine love and responsiveness of the living communicative kingdom.[63] Buber's *dao* proceeds from the law to love via the moment of human brokenness. The *dao* is an anarchistic originary ethics of the good in and for itself.[64]

What is the logic of the *dao*'s motility? Laozi's Daoism does not promote a return as a reduction to the primitive in Buber's account. The *Daodejing*'s language of return is a discourse of transitions and transformations that does not abandon humanity in the movement toward fulfillment in the *dao* nor multiplicity in the return to the one.[65] Given this attention to transitions and transformation, and resting in mobility, the *Daodejing* offers models of dynamic relational wholes instead of a monistic static unitary oneness.

How then should the notion of "return" be interpreted? *Fan* 反 (return, reversal) only appears four times in the standard version of the *Daodejing* (chapters 25, 40, 65, and 78). Due to its being identified with the movement of the *dao* itself in chapter 40 (反者道之動；弱者道之用), it serves as a central concept in interpreting the *Daodejing*'s logic or dialectic. As noted previously, in Buber's exposition return (*Rückkehr*) signifies turning. It is misinterpreted when taken as a mere arrival back at a prior or previous point in a series; it is a point of transition, a turning around (*Umkehr*) as culmination.[66]

Thus to briefly introduce the examples of the newborn and the seed considered in Buber's commentary: (1) The *Daodejing*'s images of the flexibility, spontaneity, and vitality of the newborn baby do not entail a return to that initial state; and (2) Nor is it a return to the state of being a seed in the origin. Comparing it to the primordial light (*Urlicht*) described in the *Talmud*, "return" is a resting in the origin and the movement of the whole relational nexus of things.[67] "Return" is for that reason not a reduction to an embryonic or primeval original condition. The movement of the *dao* through reversals and returns is the formation by humans (sphere two) of a fulfilled life in the good (sphere three) that is no longer merely law (sphere one).

8. Conclusion: Intercultural Philosophy and the Phenomenology of the Encounter

It is noteworthy that Buber adopted this notion of return in his intercultural assessment of the significance of Daoism. This interpretation of turning in the *Daodejing* is employed as a model for how the West can encounter and learn from the teaching of the *dao*.[68] As in his other works examining early pre-Qin Daoism, Buber repeatedly—in 1909, 1924, and 1928—connects the Daoism of Laozi and Zhuangzi to the dilemmas of modern technological civilization, contending that the teaching of the way addresses the contemporary European precisely in this sense of "turning around" rather than demanding a return to a supposedly more primitive and primordial way of living.[69]

Further, as Buber noted in reflecting on chapter 29 of the *Daodejing*, this "turning around" toward the thing and the other is a practical question. The possibility of genuine community is not only confronted with individual self-absorption and estranged separation. Buber presciently noted that it is all the more needful given the willfulness and sickness of peoples in nationalism and racism.[70]

Can classical Chinese philosophies such as Confucianism and Daoism resolve the destructiveness of the modern West, as experienced by Buber in the crisis-ridden Weimar Republic? Buber explicitly began "China and Us" with the argument that they cannot.[71] Nevertheless, he added, Daoist *wuwei* is the teaching that Western modernity, in its willfulness and will to dominate persons and things, lacks and is in need of learning in its own sense and context in dialogue with this Chinese discourse.[72] To this extent, intercultural dialogue is a moment in this "turning around," revealing previously unrecognized paths. This is not a return, in the narrow sense of the concept, as the path is to be encountered and enacted anew.

In addition to intercultural communication and philosophizing, a turn to a phenomenology of the encounter and the communicative relational event is required. Buber described in his 1924 discussion, explored in this chapter, how the *Daodejing* provides a model of the encounter. This poses us with a significant question in Buber's analysis: how can we encounter what the *Daodejing* is modeling? Buber concluded his 1928 essay with the demand to encounter for ourselves the reality exhibited in the *Daodejing* and that is indicated by expressions such as "non-doing."[73] What is called for to "turn around" is the encounter with things and persons themselves, and therefore a philosophy that is a phenomenology of the encounter itself. Buber's classic work *I and Thou* is such a phenomenology of the encounter in which self and other are recognized as fundamentally relational realities.

In conclusion, Buber's interpretations of the *Daodejing* (examined in this chapter) as well as the *Zhuangzi* (which was not discussed here) remain an evocative historical example of intercultural hermeneutics. His readers can trace how Buber honed his own unique philosophical project in intercultural dialogue with Daoist and a diverse variety of philosophical and religious discourses. His art of philosophy, as an interculturally informed phenomenology of the encounter and the communicative event, can itself be interpreted as an exemplary model to be enacted and transformed anew.

Notes

1   As I demonstrated in my book: Eric S. Nelson, *Chinese and Buddhist Philosophy in Early Twentieth-Century German Thought* (London: Bloomsbury Academic, 2017).

2   Originally published as: Martin Buber, *Reden und Gleichnisse des Tschuang-Tse* (Leipzig: Insel, 1910); and Martin Buber, *Chinesische Geister- und Liebesgeschichten* (Frankfurt: Rütten und Loening, 1911).

3   See Martin Buber, *Werke I: Schriften zur Philosophie* (Kösel: Lambert Schneider, 1962), 8. There are a number of works exploring Buber's engagement with Daoism and Chinese thought: Irene Eber, "Martin Buber and Taoism," *Monumenta Serica*, 42.1 (1994): 445–64; Maurice Friedman, "Martin Buber and Asia," *Philosophy East and West*, 26.4 (1976): 411–26; Jonathan Herman, *I and Tao: Martin Buber's Encounter with Chuang Tzu* (Albany: State University of New York Press, 1996); and, in this volume, Jason Wirth, "Martin Buber's Dao." On the fascination with China among Central European Jewish intellectuals, see Shuangzhi Li, "'Wenn ich ein Chinese wäre': The Austrian-Jewish Imagination of China around 1900 revisited," *Austrian Studies*, 24 (2016): 94–108.

4   See Israel Aharon Ben-Yosef, "Confucianism and Taoism in *The Star of Redemption*," *Journal for the Study of Religion*, 1.2 (1988): 25–36; Nelson, *Chinese and Buddhist Philosophy*, 213–15.

5   Nelson, *Chinese and Buddhist Philosophy*, 115.

6   Although Buber did not accept the artificial and ahistorical division between a "philosophical" and "religious" Daoism, he does distinguish "early" and "late" Daoist texts. His few remarks on later Daoist sources such as the *Book of Purity and Rest* (*Qingjing Jing* 清靜經) indicate that he considered them limited and narrower in their understanding of the Way and language. See Martin Buber, *Schriften zur Chinesischen Philosophie und Literatur*, ed. Irene Eber (Gütersloh: Gütersloher Verlagshaus, 2013), 117.

7   Note that I examine these issues in the early Daoist context further, and contest the dichotomy of humanism and anti-humanism, in: Eric S. Nelson, "Questioning Dao: Skepticism, Mysticism, and Ethics in the *Zhuangzi*," *International Journal of the Asian Philosophical Association*, 1 (2008): 5–19; Eric S. Nelson, "The Human and the Inhuman: Ethics and Religion in the *Zhuangzi*," *Journal of Chinese Philosophy*, 41.S1 (2014): 723–39.

8   On early Daoist notions of the thing, see the helpful analyses of David Chai, "Meontological Generativity: A Daoist Reading of the Thing," *Philosophy East and West*, 64.2 (2014): 303–18; Sai-Hang Kwok, "Zhuangzi's Philosophy of Thing," *Asian Philosophy*, 26.4 (2016): 294–310.

9   Nelson, *Chinese and Buddhist Philosophy*, 109–29.

10   See Irene Eber's introduction in Buber, *Schriften zur Chinesischen Philosophie*, 23.

11   Compare Jeffrey S. Librett, "Neo-Romantic Modernism and Daoism: Martin Buber on the 'Teaching' as Fulfilment," in *China in the German Enlightenment*, eds. Bettina Brandt and Daniel Purdy (Toronto: University of Toronto Press, 2016), 181–98.

12 "Besprechungen mit Martin Buber über Lao Tse's *Tao-te-king*" (hereafter, BMB) and "China und Wir" (hereafter, CW) are published in Buber, *Schriften zur Chinesischen Philosophie*; Martin Buber, "Lao Tzu al hashilton," *Hapo'el Hatsa'ir*, 35 (1942), 6–8.

13 Buber, *Schriften zur Chinesischen Philosophie*.

14 Victor von Strauss, *Lao Tse's Tao Te King* (Leipzig: Verlag von Friedrich Fleischer, 1870); Richard Wilhelm, *Tao Te King: Das Buch des Alten vom Sinn und Leben.* (Jena: E. Diederichs, 1921).

15 Buber, "BMB" in *Schriften zur Chinesischen Philosophie*, 227.

16 Ibid.

17 Ibid., 228.

18 Ibid.

19 Ibid.

20 Martin Buber, *Ich und Du* (Stuttgart: Reclam, 2002), 7–8.

21 Buber, "BMB" in *Schriften zur Chinesischen Philosophie*, 228.

22 On the concept of ethical personalism, see Cheikh M. Gueye, *Ethical Personalism* (Berlin: De Gruyter, 2011); for a more extensive interpretation of the interpersonal ethics and the inhuman in Levinas, see part one of Eric S. Nelson, *Levinas, Adorno, and the Ethics of the Material Other* (Albany: State University of New York Press, 2020).

23 For Levinas's critical assessment of Buber, see the first three chapters of Emmanuel Levinas, *Outside the Subject*, trans. Michael B. Smith (Stanford: Stanford University Press, 1994). On Levinas's conception of asymmetry and alterity, see Nelson, *Levinas, Adorno, and the Ethics of the Material Other*.

24 Buber, "BMB" in *Schriften zur Chinesischen Philosophie*, 229.

25 Ibid., 273.

26 "Der Geist des Orients und das Judentum" has been republished in volume 2.1 of the *Werkausgabe*: Martin Buber. *Mythos und Mystik: Frühe Religionswissenschaftliche Schriften*, ed. David Groiser. Gütersloh: Gütersloher Verlagshaus, 2013, 187–203. See my discussion of the broken body in Buber and Zhuangzi in Nelson, *Chinese and Buddhist Philosophy*, 127.

27 Buber, "BMB" in *Schriften zur Chinesischen Philosophie*, 229.

28 Ibid., 230.

29 Ibid., 229–30.

30 Ibid., 259–61.

31 Ibid., 247.

32 On co-creation and nourishing life in Buber's interpretation of Daoism and Judaism, see Nelson, *Chinese and Buddhist Philosophy*, 115–17.

33 Buber, "BMB" in *Schriften zur Chinesischen Philosophie*, 229.

34 Ibid., 232, 256.

35 Ibid., 229.

36 Ibid., 263.

37 Ibid., 232.

38 Ibid., 230, 270.

39 Ibid., 230, 234.

40 Ibid., 230.

41 Ibid., 231.

42 Ibid., 235.

43 Ibid., 243–4.

44 Ibid., 234.

45 Ibid., 231, 235.

46 Martin Buber, *The Letters of Martin Buber: A Life of Dialogue* (Syracuse: Syracuse University Press, 1996), 275.

47 On Buber's "theopolitics" or "political theology," see Samuel H. Brody, *Martin Buber's Theopolitics* (Bloomington: Indiana University Press, 2018).

48 Buber, "BMB" in *Schriften zur Chinesischen Philosophie*, 255.

49 Ibid., 231.

50 Ibid., 254–5, 266.

51 Ibid., 255.

52 Ibid., 251.

53 Martin Buber, *Pointing the Way: Collected Essays*, ed. and trans. Maurice S. Friedman (New York: Harper and Row, 1957), 163. See also Nelson, *Chinese and Buddhist Philosophy*, 36.

54 Buber, "BMB" in *Schriften zur Chinesischen Philosophie*, 235, 238.

55 Ibid., 238.

56 Ibid., 242.

57 Ibid., 250.

58 Ibid., 242–3.

59 On Daoism and social critique, see Mario Wenning, "Daoism as Critical Theory," *Comparative Philosophy*, 2 (2011): 50–71.

60 Buber, "BMB" in *Schriften zur Chinesischen Philosophie*, 247, 250.

61 Ibid., 250.

62 Ibid., 257.

63 Ibid., 247–8.

64 Ibid., 250–1.

65 Ibid., 240.

66 Ibid., 263.

67 Ibid., 240–1.

68 Ibid., 263.

69 See chapter four of Nelson, *Chinese and Buddhist Philosophy*, for an account of the thematic of Daoism and technology in Buber and Heidegger.

70 Buber, "BMB" in *Schriften zur Chinesischen Philosophie*, 261.

71 Buber, "CW" in Ibid., 285–6.

72 Ibid., 288.

73 Ibid.

References

Ben-Yosef, Israel Aharon. (1988), "Confucianism and Taoism in *The Star of Redemption*," *Journal for the Study of Religion*, 1.2: 25–36.

Brody, Samuel H. (2018), *Martin Buber's Theopolitics*, Bloomington: Indiana University Press, 2018.

Buber, Martin. (1910), *Reden und Gleichnisse des Tschuang-Tse*, Leipzig: Insel.

Buber, Martin. (1911), *Chinesische Geister und Liebesgeschichten*, Frankfurt: Rütten und Loening.

Buber, Martin. (1942), "Lao Tzu al hashilton," *Hapo'el Hatsa'ir*, 35: 6–8.

Buber, Martin. (1957), *Pointing the Way: Collected Essays*, Maurice S. Friedman (ed. and trans.), New York: Harper and Row.

Buber, Martin. (1962), *Werke I: Schriften zur Philosophie*, Kösel: Lambert Schneider.

Buber, Martin. (1996), *The Letters of Martin Buber: A Life of Dialogue*, Syracuse: Syracuse University Press.

Buber, Martin. (2002), *Ich und Du*, Stuttgart: Reclam.

Buber, Martin. (2013), *Mythos und Mystik: Frühe Religionswissenschaftliche Schriften*, David Groiser (ed.), Gütersloh: Gütersloher Verlagshaus.

Buber, Martin. (2013), *Schriften zur Chinesischen Philosophie und Literatur*, Irene Eber (ed.), Gütersloh: Gütersloher Verlagshaus.

Chai, David. (2014), "Meontological Generativity: A Daoist Reading of the Thing," *Philosophy East and West*, 64.2: 303–18.

Eber, Irene. (1994), "Martin Buber and Taoism," *Monumenta Serica*, 42.1: 445–64.

Friedman, Maurice. (1976), "Martin Buber and Asia," *Philosophy East and West*, 26.4: 411–26.

Gueye, Cheikh M. (2011), *Ethical Personalism*, Berlin: De Gruyter.

Herman, Jonathan. (1996), *I and Tao: Martin Buber's Encounter with Chuang Tzu*, Albany: State University of New York Press.

Kwok, Sai-Hang. (2016), "Zhuangzi's Philosophy of Thing," *Asian Philosophy*, 26.4: 294–310.

Levinas, Emmanuel. (1994), *Outside the Subject*, Michael B. Smith (trans.), Stanford: Stanford University Press.

Li, Shuangzhi. (2016), "'Wenn ich ein Chinese wäre': The Austrian-Jewish Imagination of China around 1900 revisited," *Austrian Studies*, 24: 94–108.

Librett, Jeffrey S. (2016), "Neo-Romantic Modernism and Daoism: Martin Buber on the 'Teaching' as Fulfilment," in Bettina Brandt and Daniel Purdy (eds.), *China in the German Enlightenment*, 181–97. Toronto: University of Toronto Press.

Nelson, Eric S. (2008), "Questioning Dao: Skepticism, Mysticism, and Ethics in the *Zhuangzi*," *International Journal of the Asian Philosophical Association*, 1: 5–19.

Nelson, Eric S. (2014), "The Human and the Inhuman: Ethics and Religion in the *Zhuangzi*," *Journal of Chinese Philosophy*, 41.S1: 723–39.

Nelson, Eric S. (2017), *Chinese and Buddhist Philosophy in Early Twentieth-Century German Thought*, London: Bloomsbury Academic.

Nelson, Eric S. (2020), *Levinas, Adorno, and the Ethics of the Material Other*, Albany: State University of New York Press.

von Strauss, Victor. (1870), *Lao Tse's Tao Te King*, Leipzig: Verlag von Friedrich Fleischer.

Wenning, Mario. (2011), "Daoism as Critical Theory," *Comparative Philosophy*, 2: 50–71.

Wilhelm, Richard. (1921), *Tao te King: Das Buch des Alten vom Sinn und Leben*, Jena: E. Diederichs.

6

Martin Buber's Dao

Jason M. Wirth

1. Introduction

What are we to make of Martin Buber's (1878–1965) occasional but enduring, although somewhat apprehensive, relationship to the Daoist teaching of Laozi 老子 and Zhuangzi 莊子? The grounds for answering such a question demand that we first articulate the grounds upon which we would evaluate any of his claims.

The difficulty of doing so is unavoidable with Buber's seminal work, *Ich und Du* (1923). Are its claims true to lived experience? This approach would relegate the issue at the heart of the book to the confines of the I–It attitude in which an inquiring subject evaluates the veracity of a given object. "The world as experience belongs to the grounding word [*Grundwort*] I-It."[1] Does one then seek recourse to some privileged mystical access? This would ignore the work's trenchant critique of mystical absorption and its sublation (in the sense of Hegel's *Aufhebung*) of the I–You relationship. Moreover, nothing is gained by replacing the experiences that govern the I–It relationship with a special class of "mysterious" experiences. "O furtiveness without mystery [*Heimlichkeit ohne Geheimnis*], o amassment of information! It, it, it!"[2] Does one then have to assume some sort of fidelity to a particular religion in order to render Buber's approach credible, even intelligible? Buber counters that he is speaking of a reality that no religion owns, including Judaism. Even language itself is fraught with obstacles. "Pathetic are those who leave the grounding word unspoken, but miserable are those who instead of that address these ideas with a concept or a catchphrase as if that were their name."[3] One rather can only *utter the grounding word*—I and You—"with the whole of being [*mit dem ganzen Wesen*]."[4]

It is not that I experience something in particular or that I endeavor to transcend the particularities of experience by making an effort with the fullness of my own being. Rather, the fullness of my being stands in relationship to the bi-fold fullness of being itself. One neither sinks into this fullness nor absorbs it. Out of the abstract petrification of the subject–object relation emerges the intimacy of non-dual unity—not oneness, but a bi-fold unity that, as such, is always two without resolution into a higher unity. Although this opposition cannot be reconciled, it is not because its poles are discrete, self-standing, and separable. They are themselves by virtue of each other. Buber's great work hints at and speaks from this all-encompassing non-duality, that is always two, but also not just two, but somehow one, in an effort to awaken the reader to its *living* reality and to the reality of its *life*.

My emphasis on a language of non-duality also intentionally evokes major strands of Asian thought, most of which too often languish in disciplines like religious studies or area studies and still struggle in many circles to establish that they matter *as* philosophy. Buber's own thought exemplifies this challenge to philosophy in three ways: (1) It does not originate in discursivity, personal experience, or the intellectual assent that comes with religious belief; (2) As such, it is steeped in non-dual approaches, ancient and contemporary; and (3) Standing in relationship to these traditions, Buber's "philosophy" challenges us to reconsider both the ground upon which we engage non-dual traditions philosophically and what it means to evaluate them. In what follows, I will engage this problem via a case study: Martin Buber's formative and lifelong relationship to the Daoism of Laozi and Zhuangzi.

2. Approaching Buber's Dao

Given his voluminous writings, Buber wrote relatively little about Asian thought of any kind. His most sustained study of Daoist teaching was the 1910 essay, "Die Lehre vom Tao,"[5] written in the early and still developing stages of his thought to accompany his translation of selections from the *Zhuangzi*. It appears shortly after his translations of Hassidic mystical tales and parables, *Tales of Rabbi Nahman* (1906), and *The Legend of Baal Shem* (1907), and belongs to what he later characterized as his "mystical" period.

Buber, like Thomas Merton after him (who also produced an edition of the *Zhuangzi*[6]), was not a Sinologist and, admittedly, his work on the *Zhuangzi* is not admissible in this respect. His *Reden und Gleichnisse des Tschuang-tse* (Leipzig: Insel Verlag, 1910) was largely translated from the English of James Legge and Herbert Allen Giles, not from the Chinese original, although he reported in the improved 1951 edition that he had "the help of Chinese colleagues."[7] The translation itself is tendentious and conspicuously selective and in no way serves to produce a German version of the *Zhuangzi*. Granted the legitimacy of these concerns, they do not amount to grounds for dismissing the text. We should also remember that Buber was a great writer, as evidenced by the fact that he was nominated for the Nobel Prize in Literature ten times and won the Goethe Prize in 1951.

This is not to imply, however, that his engagement with the *Zhuangzi* is a kind of Chinese mirror in which he gazes upon his own thinking or unduly appropriates Chinese thought for his own purposes. As Jonathan Herman argues, "his linguistic and historical limitations do not prevent him from evincing a tremendous sensitivity to the subtleties of Chinese thought."[8]

How then do we characterize the manner of this confrontation when it is neither an early exercise in Sinology nor an assimilation of the *Zhuangzi* into Buber's early Hassidic ontology?

3. Dao as Teaching

In the 1915 lecture-essay, "The Spirit of the Orient and Judaism," Buber argued that Judaism was closer to Asian traditions than to more conventionally recognizable European ones, especially in its overcoming of the "diremption [*Entzweiung*]" of self and world.[9] Indeed, according to Irene Eber, Buber "may have been first among Jewish philosophers who appropriated ideas from Daoism and integrated these into a specifically Jewish philosophical discourse."[10] In so doing, Buber assiduously avoids the stereotype that Jewish religiosity is otherworldly and obsessed with transcendence while Asian thought is saturated in immanence. As Eric Nelson argues in his important new book on the reception of Chinese thought in early twentieth-century German language philosophy, Buber brings forth an "Hasidic Zhuangzi," which "perceives in both Hasidic Judaism and Lao-Zhuang Daoism tendencies toward the humanistic actualization of the transcendent in the immanent, of the sacred in the mundane, in everyday life through exemplary figures and genuine teachers teaching the needful and the authentic life."[11]

At the heart of Buber's "Die Lehre vom Tao" is a reflection on *die Lehre*, or teaching, itself. The latter is not a proposal concerning what is (as in a science) nor is it a series of arguments about what we ought to do (as in ethics). *It is not about anything other than itself.* It "proclaims what it is: Unity as necessity."[12] This is not a metaphysical position or a philosophical claim or any kind of "content." It was not a position that "Jesus or Buddha or Laozi" wanted to "express." It is rather "*der Sinn und der Grund*," the sense and the ground, of these men.[13] Their respective teachings were not about the meaning or the content of the words they expressed, but rather "this word's life and this word itself in its unity."[14] Daoist proclamations are not therefore metaphysical speculations or claims about the world and the nature of its things. When the *zhenren* 真人, a compound that appears nineteen times in the *Zhuangzi* to name the consummate, true, and real person,[15] speaks, she is not making a philosophical claim or otherwise producing a philosophical argument. Were the *zhenren* somehow to speak directly, she could only communicate to other *zhenren*. The *zhenren* consequently does not explain how to become a *zhenren*, but rather speaks of and from Dao in such a way so as to awaken interlocutors and readers to their own unrealized *zhenren*. The *zhenren*, so to speak, can only speak *zhenren* to *zhenren*.

Furthermore, in itself, "naked unity is mute."[16] To utter it is contradictory, an impossible mute speaking. The word has to somehow express itself in the world without sacrificing its unity, and, in so doing, awaken the one who receives the teaching not to its content, but to its unity. For Buber, the *zhenren* therefore speaks in parables, that is, *die Einstellung*, the mental or spiritual attitude or frame of mind or quality of consciousness, of "the absolute in the world of things."[17] This is an ongoing process rather than something that can be established once and for all—*die Lehre beginnt ewig von neuem*, the teaching eternally begins anew.[18]

The parable expresses the duality of eternity expressing itself as *new life*. The word enters the realm of things by speaking of and with things, and hence the unified word is also multiplicity, that is, the things and persons of which it speaks and the manners in which they are distinguished and conveyed in language. This is the inherent paradox of the parable: one as many and many as one; silence as words and words that speak to a silence beyond all words. The silence that is spoken in the parable (as well as in the later Zen *kōan*) is a silence from a paradoxical time of absolute silence, *in der Stunde der Stille* [an eternal silence that can only be thought in time, we here note]. This is the time before the day—presumably here evoking Genesis and the "time" before the "days" of creation—"*wo noch kein Du ist als das Ich*," where the I does not yet have a You or where the only You is the I. There is only solitary discourse in the darkness from and toward the abyss.[19] To speak this at all is to speak as parable (or in Laozi's unitary utterances that lift one out of a lopsided identification with the worldly). At the heart of the parable—and here we already sense *Ich und Du* on the horizon—is not the solitary I but rather I and others, I and creation, the abyss and the days of coming into being. The unity can only be spoken in a two-fold manner. The word of the parable holds together night and day, the hour of stillness and lived time, I and You. Still, one can detect that in these early formulations an "I" that is not yet fully also "You." This I that is everything but nothing in particular will also be an increasing source of trouble for Buber as he increasingly realizes the ineluctable primacy of the two-fold I and You. There *is* no pure I save for its relationship to the beings of the world. The I can only *be* as You.

The *zhenren* does not bring anything new to teaching, but fulfills it. This means that she raises it from the unrecognized to the recognized, from the conditional to the unconditional. The *zhenren* "lives [*erlebt*] and experiences [*erfährt*] Dao directly";[20] in the *zhenren*, "the unknowable and the unified human life, the first and the last, come into contact."[21] There is no knowledge *of* unity, as if unity were something to know, but rather the reverse: "unity is knowledge [*Erkenntnis*]" and, as such, *Erkenntnis* is not knowing (*Wissen*) but rather being (*Sein*).[22] Language is inadequate; all concepts fall short; all values lack certainty, even though each person tends to falsely assume the universality of their own language and considers their own concepts and values to be *the* concepts and *the* values. The *zhenren* does not look at the ten thousand things as various things, but rather regards them from the unity of *Erkenntnis*, from the non-discriminating lens of the *Dao-Lehre* or Dao-teaching. It elevates each thing that it "contemplates [*betrachtet*] out of its appearance [*Erscheinung*] and into being [*Sein*]."[23]

Such contemplation is an all-embracing love and affirmation, above and beyond all contradictions and oppositions. Beyond the partiality and deontological obedience of justice and ethical commands, the *zhenren*'s "love" spontaneously, effortlessly, and inclusively affirms the whole of being out of its own shared unity. It is "entirely free and unrestricted" and knows "no choice," and, as such, is *unbedingt*.[24] The complex deployment of the latter term merits brief embellishment. One detects three interlocking threads in Buber's use of this standard term from German Idealism: (1) in the conventional sense, we can say this is *unconditional* love," ἀγάπη, love that loves without restriction; (2) it does so because it is *unconditioned*, that is, absolute, love; it is not love that emerges from human motives or from conditional appearances; it loves the conditioned from an unconditioned perspective; in a different idiom, we could say that it loves the world the way God loves the world; and (3) it is literally a love that has not been turned into a thing (*Ding*) and, as such, it incipiently anticipates *Ich und Du* where love absolutely loves all beings (*Wesen*) intimately and relationally, that is, not as things and not in an I–It relationship. Love is not a motivated activity, but rather the *wuwei* 無爲 of unity where all beings (*Wesen*) are affirmed intimately and spontaneously both in their unknowable depths and in their dynamically evolving manifestations. Love absolutely and without action affirms the *ten thousand*—all *Wesen*—as expressions of Dao.

4. Dao as Relation

Although Buber in *Ich und Du* will distinguish (mystical) love as "identification" from love as "relation,"[25] that is, the "responsibility of an I for a You,"[26] he continues to distinguish love from a feeling or an experience (experience remains in the realm of the I–It). It is rather *ein welthaftes Wirken*, acting within the confines of the world to open it up to the I–You. It cannot be blind for that would mean that "it does not see a *whole* being [*Wesen*]."[27] Only hatred can be blind because only hatred is selective, demanding not the whole, but the parts that it loves and the parts that it rejects. As Herman argues, rightly in my view, although *Ich und Du* represents a maturation and refinement of Buber's earlier so-called "mystical" perspective, it nonetheless remains intimately intertwined with the early *Dao-Lehre*:[28] "Buber argues that Dao is a singular and ineffable cosmic principle that is accessible in the form of an obliterating oneness that nevertheless provides an ontological basis for the transformation of things, which is an ongoing process of renewal and recreation, an ongoing repetition of successive cosmogonic moments."[29]

Nonetheless, Buber articulated some serious reservations about his "mystical" embrace of Dao. Almost four decades later in a 1957 Foreword to *Pointing the Way*, a collection of essays assembled by Maurice Friedman, Buber argued that the *zhenren*

> loses the sure knowledge of the *principium individuationis*, and understands this precious experience of his unity as the experience of *the* unity. When this man returns into life in the world and with the world, he is naturally inclined from then on to regard everyday life as an obscuring of the true life . . . he constantly flees from it into an experience of the unity . . . he thereby turns away from . . . the existence into which he has been set, through conception and birth, for life and death in this unique personal form . . . in the "lower" periods he regards everything as a preparation for the "higher." But in these "higher hours" he no longer knows anything over against him: the great dialogue between I and Thou is silent; nothing else exists than his self, which he experiences as *the* self.[30]

Buber nonetheless regarded this essay as important enough to include it in the English collection of essays, as well as the earlier German collection, *Hinweise: Gesammelte Essays*, the 1953 collection from which *Pointing the Way* is drawn. It is also included in the 1951 reissue of the translation. Friedman includes the essay with other early essays in the same chronological order that they appeared in *Hinweise*, but drops the 1913 essay on the Finnish mythic founding epic, the *Kalevala*, and then dubs the subsection of essays, "Towards Authentic Existence." Buber called this necessary "stage I had to pass through," the "mystical" in the sense of a "belief in the unification of the self with the all-self, attainable by humans in levels or intervals of their earthly life."[31] And if one holds Buber to the letter of his word, he is not associating this characterization of a necessary but not sufficient mystical stage with either the *Laozi* or *Zhuangzi* per se, but with the 1910 *Dao-Lehre* essay. This particular reading of the *Zhuangzi*, as well as the principle of selection that governed which "sayings and parables" he "translated," is what is simultaneously indispensable yet immature. Indispensable and immature with regard to what? Buber's own thinking, of course. One could and should not hold Buber responsible for not thinking what he freely confesses he was unable to think at the time.

It is also critical to insist that Buber is not criticizing the *Dao-Lehre* from the outside, opposing it with a superior position. He is thinking within a living unity, exploring and clarifying and rethinking the relations between its elements. One could even say that he is thinking in and between the Dao and the ten thousand, that is, refining not only their non-duality, but also the manner of their unified *duality*. He does this in at least two critical ways: a criticism of mystical immersion and an ontological engagement with the problem of good and evil.

5. Beyond Mystical Immersion

Given the tenor of his 1957 self-criticism of his "mystical" reading of the *Dao-Lehre*, namely, that the *zhenren* regards "everyday life as an obscuring of the true life" and therefore "constantly flees from it into an experience of the unity," we can see that this is precisely Buber's critique of "mystical immersion" in the third part of *Ich und Du*. Here Buber warns against obscuring the I–You relationship in the "religious act" of *Versenkung*, which he clarifies as *die Einwandlung in das Selbst*.[32] *Versenkung* is to sink down into something, like a ship going down at sea. More metaphorically, it is to get lost in an activity, as when one is immersed in a film or a book or even driving. One is no longer aware of oneself: there is only the activity. *Versenkung* might describe Buber's implicit understanding of Cook Ding from chapter 3 of the *Zhuangzi*, and his versatility with the cleaver—there is no Cook Ding, just the unobstructed activity of cleaving. One also speaks of a contemplative, prayerful, or mystical *Versenkung*. Ecstatic prayer or Buddhist *samādhi* would be examples.

Einwandlung is archaic: to transform or change or even transubstantiate. It is here the transubstantiation of the two-fold, of I and You, into the single self before creation, into the 1910 *Dao-Lehre*'s time "*wo noch kein Du ist als das Ich*," where the I does not yet have a You. Buber distinguished the two ways in which this *Versenkung* can come about: either the opposition between I and You is dialectically sublated (in the Hegelian sense of *Aufhebung*) into the You or into the I. Either the I disappears altogether—some kind of mystical ecstasy where there is no me, just the pure, originary You—or one ascends to the One Great Self beyond all beings like *Atman* rising to *Brahman*—I am now the unity. "Both maintain a beyond of the I and You ... Both sublate [*aufhebt*] the relationship. The first does so dynamically, so to speak, through the becoming swallowed up of the I by the You so that there is no longer even a You, but rather that which alone has being [*das Alleinseiende*]. The other does so statically, so to speak, as the I dissolves into the Self of the knowing, which alone has being [*das Alleinseiende Erkennen*]."[33] This is not unity but rather "annihilation [*Vernichtung*]."[34] Buber's Buddha, whom he calls the "consummate"[35] one, recalling his characterization of the *zhenren* in 1910, wants to resolve *duḥkha* by dissolving into the Great Self. Hence in its "innermost," it tends toward the sublation of the You, indeed the sublation of the very ability to say "You" (*Dusagenkönnen*).[36] *Samādhi* sinks out of the two-fold into the pure I.

In the I–It relationship, I am separated from the world and regard it objectively, as mere things. I am my own thing, an *Eigenwesen*, and, as such, opposed to all other things. In *Versenkung*, however, the chrysalis of the I–It relationship does not let the butterfly of the I–You relationship emerge, but rather misses the mark and mystifies our relationship with the intimacy of the world. Losing one's self in the One (the pure "You" or the pure "I") is to lose one's own actuality. To lose the world in the One is to sacrifice its actuality. "Let us love the actual in all its dread, which does not want to be sublated. Let us just dare to embrace it with the arms of our spirit: and our hands will meet the hands that maintain it."[37]

Buber's criticism of the dangers of *Versenkung* is powerful and salutary, although it is less clear that his alignment of the Buddha, the *zhenren*, and Atman-Brahman with the sublation of the I into "the Self of the Knowing, which alone has being" is fair to these traditions. It is certainly fair to his reading of these traditions and, as such, the confrontation with *Versenkung* is critical to the evolution of Buber's own discourse on unity. We might here recall the famous *tat tvam asi*, you are that, from the *Chandogya Upanishad*, which Buber cites as an example of the You being sublated by the Great Unitary Self. Certainly, there is a tendency, even within Hindu spirituality, to confuse Atman-Brahman with the dissolution of all beings into the Great Self. Yet much of the tradition also runs counter to this. Śaṅkara dismissed bliss as an addiction and lived happily and compassionately in the world. The *Ox Herding* pictures in Chinese Chan Buddhism do not conclude with the overcoming of the bull and the self, but with the return to the market to "teach the withered trees to bloom." The consummate activity of Cook Ding in the *Zhuangzi* is not at all immersed in the Dao, but more intimately present to the versatile *way* of things now and here. The *zhenren* detaches from a world that is already being kept at a distance through abstraction, the over-determination of conceptualization, and a parochial sense of values, in order to reaffirm it in its immediacy, intimacy, and dynamism. Nāgārjuna—perhaps the greatest of all Buddhist philosophers— claimed in his masterpiece, the *Mūlamadhyamakakārikā*,[38] that the view, *prapañca* (hypostatization or reification), of emptiness turns that which is designed to rid one of all *prapañca* into the worst *prapañca* of all: "those for whom emptiness is a *prapañca* have been called incurable."[39] Those who hypostasize the Buddha, he later argues, are "deceived" and "fail to see the Tathāgata."[40] One jumps out of the pot and into the fire when one hypostasizes emptiness and loses the intimate dependent co-origination of all beings. "Emptiness misunderstood destroys the slow-witted, like a serpent wrongly held or a spell wrongly executed."[41] The great Japanese Rinzai reformer Hakuin warned Zen practitioners against a Zen malady that he called emptiness sickness (Jp. *kūbyō*), an attachment to *śūnyatā* or emptiness at the cost of the lived world. In a sense, this is all just to say that Buber belonged to these "teachings" at their depths more intimately than he realized.

6. Dao of Good and Evil

Tellingly, although Buber banished this early essay on Daoism to the threshold of his mature position, he did not consequently abandon his interest in Daoist thought. In his 1928 address to the China Institute in Frankfurt-am-Main, "China and Us," he respectfully distances himself from the Confucian heritage as, for better or worse, unlikely to make inroads into European culture, but he turns decisively to Daoist thought as being able to transmit something "in a living manner," namely, its teaching of *wuwei*. Unlike the Chinese sages who learned it through a transformative and positive experience, however, Europe would learn it first through the failure of its own culture. "We have begun to doubt the significance of historical success, i.e., the validity of the man who sets an end for himself, carries this end into effect, accumulates the necessary means of power and succeeds with these means of power: the typical modern Western man."[42] The ravages of Western self-assertion—slavery, the genocide of indigenous peoples and cultures, colonialism and imperialism, white male supremacy, two world wars, technological voracity and its logical conclusion, the impending ecological ruin of life as we know it—bears witness to Buber's prescience. Although he wrote these words before the Shoah, the fate of his people in the following two decades adds further poignancy to this prescience.

As this culture, built on the relentless logic of the I–It relationship, a relationship where every being, human or otherwise, is an "it" and, as such, at the disposal of the I, threatens to collapse, then the contemporary West can receive the transformative and living Daoist heritage. This is "the teaching that genuine effecting is not interfering, not giving vent to power, but remaining within one's self. This is the powerful existence that does not yield historical success, i.e., the success that can be exploited and registered in this hour, but only yields that effecting that at first appears insignificant, indeed invisible, yet endures across generations and there at times becomes perceptible in another form."[43] Alas, the collapse still has not happened and the world order continues to congratulate itself, despite the unfathomable wreckage of modern history and increasingly dire warnings about a global ecological catastrophe as the culmination of Western ideology. The West— perhaps we should now say the global world—will not first receive ancient Daoist wisdom as a confirmation of its own wisdom, but rather as the exposure of its folly. The West has tasted the Dao "in the bitterest manner; indeed, in a downright foolish manner."[44]

A year after the decisive appearance in 1923 of his mature masterpiece, *Ich und Du*, Buber lectured on Laozi's *Daodejing* in Ascona, Switzerland. From the unpublished manuscript of these discussions, we see plenty of evidence of Buber's horror at the New World Order. For example, in Soviet Russia, "a person is ... not seen in his relationship to others, or the life of the community, but as a cog in a vast, brutal, and senseless machine."[45] In 1942, as the Second World War raged and genocide loomed, Buber translated into Hebrew chapters 17, 29, 30, 31, 57, 58, 66, and 67 of the *Daodejing*, chapters that eschew the use of violence in governance.[46]

From this we can already detect Buber's second refinement, namely, his efforts to suggest what he called in 1952 "the foundation of an ontological ethics."[47] Robert Allinson argues that Buber's Hasidic perspective that "one should right wrongs" points to "what is lacking in all Daoist ones: One must include the other in the unity, then one has a good influence on him."[48] Just as love cannot be blind, only hate can, and just as the I–You relationship cannot be partial, only the I–It one can, the good is born of a recuperation of the unity of I–You. Buber did not regard anything as intrinsically evil, nor is ethics a simpleminded dedication to doing good things and avoiding evil things. "Evil is lack of direction,"[49] born of the abundance of human contingency and possibility. Good is the directionality of actions. From the Daoist perspective, one could say that it is to love the ten thousand things just as they are and, as such, to take responsibility for them, even to enter, as the mature Buber does, into dialogue with both them and Dao itself. From the Buddhist perspective it is suchness, things just as they are, and hence a calling to embrace and illuminate them as such. From the Hindu perspective, every Atman expresses Brahman and hence is precious and worthy of cherishment and care.

7. Conclusion

The directionless plight of Adam and Eve in the Garden, of the little minded ones before the *zhenren*, or the somnolence of the Buddhist marketplace, is however not yet radical evil. This happens when flowing water freezes and we take ownership of ourselves and lock the world into the I–It in order to put it at our disposal. The unitary spiritual ethicality of Daoism, of Heraclitus, of Advaita Vedanta, of Buddha Dharma, yields not only to the directionless confusion of the marketplace, but more deeply to the radical evil of sophistry. Soon, humans, as Protagoras infamously held, are the measure of all things, and Thrasymachus's world where might makes right begins to hold sway.[50] This is the great lie at the heart of radical evil: to knowingly and willingly bear false witness to being. As we teeter on the verge of ecological collapse, what better description of the prevailing global order than Buber's reflections on Psalm 12:[51] "they spin a way of thinking for them which they themselves do not follow . . . Liars as it were manufacture a special heart, an apparatus which functions with the greatest appearance of naturalness, from which lies well up to the 'smooth lips' like spontaneous utterances of experience and insight . . . Their tongues maintain them in their superiority."[52]

In response to our irresponsibility to each other and the Earth itself, Buber hints at the *wuwei* at the heart not only of his exploration of what is living in Daoist teaching, but in world philosophy itself.

Notes

1   In general, I have relied on existing translations, although sometimes I slightly emend them. Buber's language is quite singular and poetic and nowhere is this more prevalent than in *Ich und Du*. It is easy to lose the force of his singular locutions and so for this work I have relied on my own translations, and have used the original edition: Martin Buber, *Ich und Du* (Leipzig: Insel Verlag, 1923), 12.

2   Buber, *Ich und Du*, 12.

3   Ibid., 21.

4   Ibid., 9.

5   Martin Buber, "Die Lehre vom Tao," *Hinweise: Gesammelte Essays* (Zürich: Manesse Verlag, 1953), 44–83. There are at least three versions of this essay in English translation: Jonathan Herman's *I and Tao: Martin Buber's Encounter with Chuang Tzu*; Maurice Friedman's 1957 edition of *Pointing the Way: Collected Essays*, drawn from the 1953 collection, *Hinweise: Gesammelte Essays*; and the version found in Martin Buber, *Chinese Tales, Zhuangzi: Sayings and Parables and Chinese Ghost and Love Stories*, trans. Alex Page (New Jersey and London: Humanities Press International, 1991). I cite the Page translation, often with emendations and alterations, followed by the German citation.

6   Thomas Merton, *The Way of Zhuangzi* (New York: New Directions, 1965). Merton called his own efforts "free interpretive readings." See Merton, 9.

7   Buber, *Chinese Tales*, 3.

8   Jonathan R. Herman, *I and Tao: Martin Buber's Encounter with Chuang Tzu* (Albany: State University of New York Press, 1996), 127–8.

9   Irene Eber, "Martin Buber and Taoism," *Monumenta Serica*, 42 (1994): 454.

10   Ibid., 464.

11   Eric S. Nelson, *Chinese and Buddhist Philosophy in Early Twentieth-Century German Thought* (London: Bloomsbury, 2017), 117.

12   Buber, *Chinese Tales*, 86; Buber, "Die Lehre vom Tao," 52

13   Ibid.; Ibid.

14   Ibid.; Ibid., 53.

15   Laozi tends to speak of the *shengren* 聖人 or sage. Zhuangzi's *zhenren* was also later used to translate *arhat*, a Buddhist awakened person. I think it imprudent to suggest a great gap between *shengren* and *zhenren* and to hold the former as somehow more grounded.

16   Buber, *Chinese Tales*, 84; Buber, "Die Lehre vom Tao," 50; also, Buber, *Chinese Tales*, 89; Buber, "Die Lehre vom Tao," 57

17   Ibid., 84; Ibid., 49.

18   Ibid., 85; Ibid., 51.

19   See Buber, *Chinese Tales*, 89; Buber, "Die Lehre vom Tao," 57. I here differ from the Page translation, which elides the presence of an utterly solitary I (before its division into I and You) before the days of creation.

20 Ibid., 95; Ibid., 68.

21 Ibid., 97; Ibid., 71–2.

22 Ibid., 98; Ibid., 74.

23 Ibid., 99; Ibid., 75.

24 Ibid., 100; Ibid., 78.

25 As Phil Huston characterizes this moment in Buber's thinking: "This knowledge embraces all things in its being, that is, in its love . . . There is no distinction here between one person and another; there is no relation." Phil Huston, *Martin Buber's Journey to Presence* (New York: Fordham University Press, 2007), 87.

26 Buber, *Ich und Du*, 22.

27 Ibid., 23.

28 "It is, however, my contention that the fundamental ingredients of the I-Thou relation—the primacy of the existential sphere, the integrity of particular entities necessarily bound through interaction and relation, and the potential presence of the absolute within each coming together—are in fact already present within Buber's encounter with Chuang Tzu, although they have admittedly not yet coalesced or found articulate expression." Herman, *I and Tao*, 163. Herman finds the seeds of the I–You relationship already at play in the *zhenren*. "It should be noted that it is never anything less than a *oneness* that is maintained in such a state of relation; it is clearly appropriate to characterize this as a 'proto-dialogical unity', where the voice of relation is in dialectical tension with the voice of monism." Ibid., 162.

29 Herman, *I and Tao*, 154.

30 Martin Buber, *Pointing the Way: Collected Essays*, ed. and trans. Maurice S. Friedman (New York: Harper and Row, 1957), ix–x.

31 Ibid., ix.

32 Buber, *Ich und Du*, 98.

33 Ibid., 99.

34 Ibid., 104.

35 Ibid., 105.

36 Ibid., 108.

37 Ibid., 110.

38 Nāgārjuna's *Middle Way* (*Mūlamadhyamakakārikā*), ed. and trans. Mark Siderits and Shōryū Katsura (Boston: Wisdom Publications, 2013).

39 Ibid., 145.

40 Ibid., 250.

41 Ibid., 274.

42 Buber, *Pointing the Way*, 124.

43 Ibid., 125.

44 Ibid. Eric Nelson rightly notes that Buber's embrace of *wuwei* anticipates Heidegger's turn to *Gelassenheit* in the age of technology, a term that

Heidegger repurposes from Meister Eckhart, one of Buber's earliest passions. See Nelson, 123–8.

45 Eber, "Martin Buber and Taoism," 462.

46 Ibid., 462–3. See, also, Martin Buber, "Lao Tzu al hashilton," *Hapo'el Hatsa'ir*, 35 (1942): 6–8.

47 Martin Buber, *Good and Evil* (New York: Charles Scribner's Sons, 1953), foreword.

48 Robert Allinson, "Zhuangzi and Buber in Dialogue: A Lesson in Practicing Integrative Philosophy," *Dao: A Journal of Comparative Philosophy*, 15.4 (2016): 558.

49 Buber, *Good and Evil*, 130.

50 See Martin Buber, "Religion and Ethics," trans. Eugene Kamenka and Maurice S. Friedman, *Eclipse of God: Studies in the Relation Between Religion and Philosophy* (New York: Harper, 1952), 101.

51 Especially salient is the first half of Psalm 12: Help, Lord, for no one is faithful anymore; those who are loyal have vanished from the human race. Everyone lies to their neighbor; they flatter with their lips but harbor deception in their hearts. May the Lord silence all flattering lips and every boastful tongue—those who say, "By our tongues we will prevail; our own lips will defend us—who is lord over us?"

52 Buber, *Good and Evil*, 10.

References

Allinson, Robert. (2016), "Zhuangzi and Buber in Dialogue: A Lesson in Practicing Integrative Philosophy," *Dao: A Journal of Comparative Philosophy*, 15.4: 547–62.

Buber, Martin. (1923), *Ich und Du*, Leipzig: Insel Verlag.

Buber, Martin. (1942), "Lao Tzu al hashilton," *Hapo'el Hatsa'ir*, 35: 6–8.

Buber, Martin. (1952), "Religion and Ethics," in Eugene Kamenka and Maurice S. Friedman (trans.), *Eclipse of God: Studies in the Relation Between Religion and Philosophy*, 83–99, New York: Harper.

Buber, Martin. (1953), "Die Lehre vom Tao," *Hinweise: Gesammelte Essays*, 44–83, Zürich: Manesse Verlag.

Buber, Martin. (1953), *Good and Evil*, New York: Charles Scribner's Sons.

Buber, Martin. (1957), *Pointing the Way: Collected Essays*, Maurice S. Friedman (ed. and trans.), New York: Harper and Row.

Buber, Martin. (1991), *Chinese Tales, Zhuangzi: Sayings and Parables and Chinese Ghost and Love Stories*, Alex Page (trans.), London: Humanities Press International.

Eber, Irene. (1994), "Martin Buber and Taoism," *Monumenta Serica*, 42: 445–64.

Herman, Jonathan. (1996), *I and Tao: Martin Buber's Encounter with Chuang Tzu*, Albany: State University of New York Press.

Huston, Phil. (2007), *Martin Buber's Journey to Presence*, New York: Fordham University Press.

Merton, Thomas. (1965), *The Way of Zhuangzi*, New York: New Directions.

Nāgārjuna. (2013), *The Middle Way (Mūlamadhyamakakārikā)*, Mark Siderits and Shōryū Katsura (ed. and trans.), Boston: Wisdom Publications.

Nelson, Eric S. (2017), *Chinese and Buddhist Philosophy in Early Twentieth-Century German Thought*, London: Bloomsbury Academic.

7

The Dao of Existence:

Jaspers and Laozi

Mario Wenning

Karl Jaspers's in-depth engagement with non-European traditions has had surprisingly little impact. While there have been a number of studies focusing on Heidegger's hidden Asian sources, Jaspers's extensive, nuanced and open dialogue with the East remains largely unexplored.[1] This oversight is surprising, given Jaspers's radical curiosity and cosmopolitan vision. An exception among twentieth-century philosophers, Jaspers almost single-handedly expanded the scope of what was considered worthy of serious philosophical reflection by systematically turning to and engaging with East Asian thinkers, traditions, and philosophical concerns. The omission of Jaspers in most recent discussions about East–West philosophical encounters reflects a more general trend to underestimate Jaspers's contributions to engaging in intercultural philosophy from an existential-phenomenological perspective. If at all, Jaspers is mostly remembered for his political engagement in postwar Germany while his metaphysical conception of human existence seems outdated in the context of current post-metaphysical trends.[2] He has been largely forgotten among major twentieth-century thinkers associated with what he called at times philosophy of existence and reason and later characterized as cosmopolitan, global-, geo- or world-philosophy (*Weltphilosophie*).

Jaspers adopts the phenomenological pursuit of the things themselves.[3] However, the method of bracketing the world as part of an eidetic reduction proposed by Husserl, as well as the existential analytic developed by Heidegger, defies the inherently world-oriented and dialogical ethos of engaging in cosmopolitan philosophy. The theoretical reflection on eidetic essences precluded the fact that humans are primarily historically situated beings who exist in a shared world that is increasingly shaped by multiple philosophical and religious traditions, which are in need of being included in a global conversation.

In the context of the present volume's focus on a productive encounter between Daoism and phenomenology, Jaspers deserves a central position. His well-informed, systematic and original engagement opens up a radically new perspective that serves as a productive intervention in the philosophical dialogue between East and West. In what follows, this chapter will: (1) recall the motivations and outlines of the project of a world-philosophy; (2) show how, at its core, the axial age hypothesis of a shared origin overcomes the distinctive philosophical traditions East and West; (3) illustrate in what way Daoism is an axial age tradition by drawing on Jaspers's interpretation of Daoist mysticism in *Psychologie der Weltanschauungen*; (4) focus on Jaspers's discussion of the personality of Laozi as a "metaphysician who thinks from the origin" in *Die großen Philosophen* as a test case for the axial age hypothesis; (5) conclude by anticipating potential objections to the project of world-philosophy thus conceived.

1. Jaspers on the Way to World-Philosophy

Jaspers saw his unfinished attempt to integrate different philosophical traditions into a new systematic framework that he called "*Weltphilosophie*," world-philosophy, as his lasting achievement.[4] The importance Jaspers attributed to the attempt to dig up and reconstruct non-European philosophical origins of philosophy is documented in the concluding sentence of his auto-obituary: "he [Jaspers] wished to participate in the task of the times, i.e., to find the way from the end of European philosophy to a world-philosophy [*Weltphilosophie*] to come." In analogy to Goethe's concept of world literature, world-philosophy is committed to a cosmopolitan spirit that transcends particular cultural boundaries.[5] The term "*Weltphilosophie*" appears for the first time in an unpublished lecture Jaspers gave on Nietzsche in 1916. World-philosophy is distinguished from the philosophy of humans (*Menschenphilosophie*). While the latter is focused on human concerns, world-philosophy arises from a perspective on the world that transcends particular human perspectives. "*Weltphilosophie*" appears again in a radio lecture presented in 1951. Giving an account of his "way to philosophy," Jaspers states:

> We would like to participate in the transition to a new, still unknown, quickly advancing world—as individual birds in the mass of those who fly to a new age, peeking, searching. We are on the way from the glowing sunset of European philosophy through the twilight of our time to the glowing sunrise of world-philosophy.[6]

Hegel had infamously identified the progressive movement of spirit in analogy to the sun's movement from East to West. The coming of age story of how reason moves from its infant stage in China and India (where one is free) through its adolescence in Greece and Rome (where some are free) to its culmination in modern Europe (where all are free) was outdated. Similarly, the view that philosophy, symbolized for Hegel by the owl of Minerva, appears after history has come to an end was unsatisfactory. Jaspers radically revises and transforms this imagery. History has not been finished and freedom has not been realized. The philosophical as well as political task consists in overcoming the narrow focus of the European tradition if philosophy is to live up to its global vocation. At a time when it was not yet common to criticize the exclusive focus on Western philosophy at the expense of other traditions, Jaspers turned to the East in a gesture that both recovers history's diverse origins and points to the possibility of a global conversation in preparation of a future world-philosophy. World-philosophy combines a revised conception of nonlinear and nonteleological universal history with a radically cosmopolitan ethos.

The self-attributed significance of the turn to the East has been expressed in Jaspers's letters. The intensive engagement with the Chinese tradition dates back to 1937. Jaspers writes to Heinrich Zimmer, an Indologist who had introduced Jaspers to Asian sources, that "the singular nobility of Chinese Daoism" was of particular interest to him. This nobility, he continues, represents a "nobility of the soul." Jaspers acknowledged in Chinese philosophy more generally, and in Daoism in particular, an alternative to the "mad eccentricity of those wild metaphysicians" in India and to the "barbarian insensitivity of the aristocracy against pain" in Japan.[7] In 1940 Karl Jaspers writes to the classicist Erich Frank, "There is much—very much—that we need to understand in India and China. My respect for what has been thought there grows continuously. The question remains what we have abandoned in the Occident in order to make possible our grand and horrible history and what it is that could have, contrary to our situation, freely unfolded there, in the East."[8] While Jaspers's colleague Frank had escaped Nazi Germany by emigrating to the United States, Jaspers reluctantly stayed in Heidelberg and lived through a period of academic hibernation. During his internal exile, he was banned from teaching and publishing. While being prohibited from participating in public academic life, Jaspers was forced to enter an increasingly solitary period. While his home country grew increasingly foreign and hostile, he developed a "strong need for the infinitely distant, whose roots are yet familiar to us."[9] In China, Jaspers discovered "a reflection on the human condition in general" which became "almost a second home."[10] Rather than giving up philosophical work during times of political totalitarianism, he expanded his reflective grasp beyond an exclusive focus on a Europe which increasingly resembled a philosophically narrow and politically imploding cave.

Jaspers was not only deeply interested in reaching beyond Europe in a mode of Oriental admiration for the exotic other as generations of German thinkers had been in a romantic idealization of the East.[11] His interest in the traditions of China and India was one of authentic philosophical respect. He elaborated a mode of communication that anticipated a phenomenology and hermeneutics of the culturally other who makes a claim on oneself.[12] The underlying motivation for turning to the East was the attempt to unearth non-European traditions that were both significantly alien from those traditions shaping European intellectual history while pointing to common human possibilities. Under the impression of political authoritarianism and two world wars, Jaspers turned to East Asia, not to flee Europe, but to engage in a conversation that promised to overcome Western forms of nationalism in favor of a cosmopolitan spirit that would advance the task of fostering a global conversation. It was during his turn to the East that Jaspers also developed the framework for a philosophy of limitless communication in a series of lecture courses on logic, published in his magnum opus *Von der Wahrheit* (1947). The achievement of communication depends on a "loving struggle" that seeks commonality without ignoring real differences. Truth is not the property of individual convictions or standpoints, but is a relational value, which only emerges in open-ended communication that does not shy away from expressing disagreements. The engagement with Asian and especially Chinese traditions, which extends the logic of communication to the level of cultures, is enriching for the project of putting Europe into perspective since, Jaspers contends, certain dimensions of human existence could develop in Asia while they have not done so in societies influenced by Occidental rationality. Jaspers's engagement with the East is primarily existential rather than historical although it has been developed in terms of a reflection on global history. He traces the cultural origins that are the preconditions and enduring reference points in relation to which human beings can orient themselves in a common world and exercise their freedom. This focus on the communication of free individuals between and across cultural boundaries breaks with a scientific and value-free philological approach to foreign texts that has guided traditional conceptions of hermeneutics. Rather than aiming to understand a text's meaning or author's original intention, existential hermeneutics of the (culturally) other focuses on the horizon in which human beings can be free in an increasingly intercultural world by unearthing the cultural reservoirs that have given shape to the infinite potentials of human existence. For Jaspers, this horizon was constituted in terms of the assumption of a common ground that needed to be uncovered and thereby regained in a cosmopolitan philosophy of history. Such a cosmopolitan framework would break with the Eurocentric assumption of necessary historical progression that had guided Hegelian and Marxist conceptions of historical progression.

2. The Retrospective Construction of the Axial Age

The central concept of Jaspers's world-philosophy is that of the axial or pivotal age (*Achsenzeit*).[13] The self-set task triggering Jaspers's radical turn to the East consisted in responding to the political and cultural crisis of Europe. In contrast to Husserl or Heidegger, who posited that philosophy started exclusively in ancient Greece and who suggested that a rethinking would have to return to this origin, Jaspers emphasizes the existence of multiple parallel and yet independent philosophical beginnings in China, Europe, and India. A cognitive breakthrough (*Durchbruch*) occurred in the period of 800–200 BCE in these three cultural centers and is expressed in the lives and teachings of the sages, the paradigmatic founding figures of the traditions that continue to shape our conceptions of what it means to conduct one's life as a human being. For Jaspers, the roughly simultaneous lives of Buddha, Confucius, Laozi, Zoroaster, and Socrates constitutes a mystery (*Geheimnis*). The axial age theorem is not a historical truth claim, but a normative approach to reconstructing history from the perspective of the present. One ought to acknowledge and reveal the independent co-emergence of the above three cultural centers as a mystery rather than try to reduce it to a number of historical and sociological conditions such as the emergence of city states, favorable climatic conditions, or advances in agriculture and knowledge. The latter conditions might be able to explain how the breakthrough was possible, but not why it happened and why the sages lived and thought in a parallel manner about the vexing questions concerning human existence.

In spite of its phenomenological repercussions, it is not precise enough to characterize Jaspers's discovery of the axial age traditions with a broadening of horizons or a history of distinctive origins of cultures. The philosophical project of identifying and reconstructing the diverse philosophical foundations is more fittingly captured by the metaphor of philosophical construction work. Jaspers set out to uncover a foundation that was both deep and wide for the purpose of constructing an enduring world-philosophical edifice that would be supported by a number of distinctive cultural columns. As a philosophical archeologist, architect, and engineer, he not only dug vertically to temporarily distant sources, but also horizontally—or laterally—to culturally remote regions. Digging to the origins of the European tradition was thus complemented with the recovery of other origins, which had developed in an independent and yet parallel manner. These axial origins had to be connected with a diversity of subterranean tunnels, and entry and exit points, in such a way that human beings could inhabit and move between them freely. Revealing the mysteriously parallel cultural origins of the philosophical tradition meant transcending the narrow nationalisms that led to the negative climax of an imploding Occidental history. The philosophical motivation was thus no longer to get to the things themselves, as the rallying cry of the phenomenological movement had proclaimed, but to transcend one's cultural origin and reach out to the culturally diverse origins of those universal "things" which, for Jaspers, pointed to global potentials of human existence.

While Husserl and Heidegger responded to the crisis of the European sciences by turning to the origin of Western metaphysics, Jaspers's pursuit is more radical and self-critical.[14] He digs to the roots of the reflection on the human condition in the three cultural realms of China, India, and the Mediterranean, to broaden the scope of human possibilities and transcend cultural provincialism. However, it would be a mistake to reduce Jaspers's reach beyond the traditional focus on Europe to be limited to the specific war and postwar disillusionment in Europe. Unearthing European as well as non-European origins presents nothing short of a methodological revolution or paradigm shift. From the perspective of comparative philosophizing, Jaspers's approach offers important insights for an intercultural philosophy that is historically informed and normatively sound. The starting point for this quest was not primarily archeological curiosity or the sense of Oriental exoticism that has often guided the turn to Asia for European philosophers. The systematic study of the traditions of Asia—especially Buddhism, Confucianism, and Daoism—was guided by a genuine philosophical interest with a double purpose.

First, this interest was aimed at discovering a new perspective on the limits of Europe. In many respects, Jaspers was a precursor to the ongoing process of provincializing the narrow set of categories and experiences that have influenced the development of Europe and contributed to its arrogance. As Aleida Assmann has argued, "the axial age has the same meaning for the history of mankind as the 'limit situation' has for an individual's life span."[15] A focus on non-European cultural origins allows one to first become aware of the constitutive limits and thereby the very meaning of one's particular historical conditions. Decentering European philosophy from its alleged singular beginnings in Greek antiquity and its pretension to absoluteness allows the exposure of the claim to singularity of Occidental rationality as an unwarranted imposition. Jaspers was convinced that this cosmopolitan project would lead to a better understanding of Europe and pave the way for a peaceful and liberal world order, a project that is timely at a historical moment where countries and cultural spheres are claiming their distinctive moral identities against such cosmopolitan approaches. Tracing the methodological origin and impact of the axial age theorem to his conception of limit situations, Aleida Assmann also exposes the limits of Jaspers's project. In particular, Jaspers singles out only three cultural centers and ignores other potential candidates (Egypt, Mesoamerican cultures, etc.). He also adopts certain Hegelian assumptions in considering the axial breakthrough as a progress over pre-axial cultures. Moreover, according to Jaspers's historico-existential ontology, Assmann diagnoses, "the cultural human has to be stripped of his traditions and conventions before he can appear as an existential human being." She continues to contend that "(t)he concept of 'existence' aims at this human core, which needs to be stripped off completely by radically extinguishing all protective constructs and fictions."[16] While Assmann's interpretation reveals blind spots in Jaspers's universal history, there is no doubt that, for Jaspers, transcending one's cultural axis does not preclude belonging to a distinctive cultural context. While Asia, as we have mentioned above, became for Jaspers "almost a second home (*Heimat*)," he emphasizes in the lecture on "The European Spirit" presented in 1946 that, in spite of the "indispensable" task of a dialogue with the "spiritual worlds of China and India," "each return from dealing with Asian works to the Bible and to our classical texts brings us the feeling of homeliness (*des Heimatlichen*)," which he equates with the "freedom of spirit."[17] There are natural limits to distancing oneself from one's cultural background. Jaspers anticipates François Jullien's argument that it is by way of a detour through a foreign culture that one gains access to one's own culture.[18] If it is not to lead to a trans-historical form of relativism, such a detour by way of self-distancing within world-philosophy is only possible to a degree and proceeds from a distinctive time and place. Cosmopolitan philosophizing always begins from culturally marked starting points. The task is to make these conditions as explicit as possible.

In addition to making explicit one's cultural commitment to one's "home" culture in light of its relationship to other cultures, reaching beyond Europe represented, secondly, the attempt to develop a broader system of references with multiple rather than one source of philosophy. Positively stated, the conception of the axial age opened up the possibility of a humanity that, while rooted in distinctive origins, became aware of what is shared and distantly familiar in this diversity. Jaspers's concern for Asia was not limited to a focus on the key thinkers and their philosophical teachings. He turned to Asian cultures as holistic phenomena that included philosophy, literature, and the arts. The program of an archeological excavation is constructive in that it aims at connecting the diverse origins that captured the spirit of a culture to thereby expose the unity of humanity in the diversity of its manifestations.[19] Jaspers conceives of this common origin as a ground sustaining the possibility of human existence:

> If the sense of security of the in-itself connected philosophy from Parmenides to Hegel has been lost, it is still only possible to do philosophy from the one deep ground of being human, from which this thinking emerged in some sense from the passed millennia in the occident. To become aware of this ground in a different manner, we are also directed to India and China, i.e., the two other original ways of philosophical thinking.[20]

Jaspers's search was a quest for a common ground that enabled communication across different cultural traditions, however elusive the search for such a ground has become after the end of classical metaphysics. He continues in a prophetic tone of voice:

> Instead of sliding into nothingness when millennia decay, we want to sense an unshakable bottom. We want to capture historically as one that which opens the possibility as a single unitary phenomenon so that our descendants will ground the substance in a deeper way than has ever been achieved. The alternative "nothing or everything" stands as a spiritual question concerning the destiny of being human in front of our age.[21]

The project of both recovering and constructing the groundwork for a future world-philosophy was never concluded; from its inception, it was conceived of as an infinite task that remained a guiding project for modernity. The Egyptologist and thinker of cultural memory, Jan Assmann, fittingly interprets the conception of the axial age as a "founding myth of modernity."[22] The assumption of a polygenetic cultural revolution was initially discovered by the founder of Persian Studies, Abraham Anquetil-Duperron, in 1771 and further developed fifty years later by the first sinologist at the Collège de France, Jean-Pierre Abel Rémusat, who emphasized the rational dimension of Daoism and points to parallels between Laozi, Plato, and Pythagoras (1823). The axial age hypothesis was only systematically developed by Jaspers in *The Origin and Goal of History*, originally published in 1949. For Jaspers the normative (rather than historico-descriptive) implications of the axial age hypothesis are most essential. Assmann summarizes the project as follows: "Jaspers' axial humanity is a retrospective construction whose legitimation rests exclusively on the self-conception of the epoch reflecting backwards, the epoch which perceives in the axial age its true past, its true classical age in the sense of a normative past, which is to provide a present with values, norms and orientation."[23] After being ignored for twenty years, the heuristic device of the axial age has been the focus of debate in a variety of disciplines including sociology, religious studies, history, and cultural studies since the mid-1970s without truly entering discussions in philosophy. In contrast to Assmann's approach, which is informed by cultural studies, it is essential to highlight the philosophical background that Jaspers, drawing on both Kant and Weber, perceived in the both mysterious and apparent co-evolution of cultures postulated in the axial age hypothesis. This philosophical dimension consists in postulating a breakthrough to universal human potentials.[24] By extension, in contrast to the adaptation of the axial age hypothesis in an attempt to diagnose the existence of "multiple modernities,"[25] for Jaspers, the goal was to discover (or construct) unity in the midst of diversity. The cognitive breakthrough achieved by axial age traditions consists in a combination of a variety of universal developments such as: (1) an emergence of self-awareness of individual human beings, including an awareness of one's own limits; (2) a reflection on one's agency together with the emergence of historical consciousness; (3) the coexistence of different schools of philosophy and modes of living; (4) a capacity for critique; and (5) the emergence of speculative metaphysics aiming at the ultimate ground and totality of reality.[26] While scholars have primarily focused on Confucianism as an example of an axial age ethical tradition in classical China,[27] Daoism also presents an intriguing test case: the Daoist sage depicted in Laozi's *Daodejing* 道德經 is highly individuated; Laozi is aware of the limits of language, communication, and human agency, and praises non-action (*wuwei* 無為) as a form of agency; Daoism conceives of historical civilization in critical terms as having fallen away from (and as being in need of return to) Dao 道. Yet, Daoism is also highly critical of (Confucian) conceptions of cultivation; and Daoism develops a complex metaphysics. Let us now trace Jaspers's interpretation of Laozi by turning to his early depiction of Laozi as a solitary mystic during the axial age with normative implications for the present.

3. Laozi's Solitary Mysticism

While Jaspers integrated Indian and Chinese thinkers in his seminar on the history of philosophy in the 1920s, and studied them systematically starting in 1937, the beginnings of his engagement with the East date back to his first philosophical publication, which is also the first formulation of a philosophy of existence. In *Psychologie der Weltanschauungen* (*Psychology of Worldviews*), Jaspers discusses Daoism as a form of mysticism. In a typology of different modes of existence or ways of conducting one's life (*Lebensführung*) in light of the limit situations (*Grenzsituationen*) characteristic of human existence (suffering, sin, fate, struggle, etc.), Jaspers contrasts "the way of mysticism" and "the way as idea." He cites a lengthy passage from chapter 20 of the *Daodejing* to demonstrate the experience that an individual undergoes when facing masses of people who have lost the way or "the root of the absolute." Here is the passage in question, rendered into German by Richard Wilhelm:

Was aber alle verehren, das darf man nicht ungestraft beiseitesetzen. O Einöde, habe ich noch nicht deine Mitte erreicht? Die Menschen der Menge sind strahlend wie bei der Feier großer Feste, Wie wenn man im Frühling auf die Türme steigt: Ich allein bin unschlüssig, noch ohne Zeichen für mein Handeln. Wie ein Kindlein, das noch nicht lachen kann! Ein müder Wanderer, der keine Heimat hat! Die Menschen der Menge leben alle im Überfluß: Ich allein bin wie verlassen! Wahrlich, ich habe das Herz eines Toren! Chaos, ach Chaos! Die Menschen der Welt sind hell, so hell: Ich allein bin wie trübe! Die Menschen der Welt sind so wißbegierig: Ich allein bin traurig, so traurig! Unruhig, ach, als das Meer! Umhergetrieben, ach, als einer der nirgends weilt! Die Menschen der

Menge haben alle etwas zu tun: Ich allein bin müßig, wie ein Taugenichts! Ich allein bin anders als die Menschen: Denn ich halte wert die spendende Mutter.[28]

We can translate it as follows:

That which everyone praises one may not set aside without punishment. O solitude, have I not reached your center yet? Men of the crowd are radiant as if celebrating a great festival, as if climbing the towers in the spring: I alone am undecided, yet without a sign for my action. As if being a child, which is not yet capable of laughing! A weary wanderer without a home! Men of the crowd all live in abundance: I alone am as if deserted! Truly, I have the heart of a fool! Chaos, oh chaos! Men of the world are bright, so bright: I alone am as if obscure! Men of the world are so thirsty for knowledge: I alone am sad, so sad! Anxious, oh, as the ocean. Drifting around like someone who never rests. Men of the crowd always have something to do: I alone am idle like a good-for-nothing. I alone am different from men: because I hold dear the nourishing mother.

It is easy to see why this passage appeals to Jaspers. In a mode of existential solitude, Laozi expresses a sense of alienation from others. The passage combines existential solitude and unrest, which Jaspers perceives—and condemns—as a common existential mode during the axial age, as well as in modern mass society.[29] The "weary wanderer without a home" is taken in by the existential sadness over the separation from the crowd or, in modern terms, mass anonymity and isolation. In Wilhelm's translation, Laozi articulates a sense of profound existential melancholy. He sees his solitude as a legitimate punishment for not respecting the kind of valorization of distinctions that everyone appreciates and which create social cohesion. But the passage does not stop here. The self-proclaimed foolish solitaire underscores his individual uniqueness when compared to the indiscriminate masses who are imagined to be free from such feelings because they seem to pursue their lives cheerfully and at ease. Laozi engages in radical self-doubt. And yet, in a dialectical twist, the passage culminates by expressing a sense of superiority of the singular person (i.e., the sage) with regard to the masses. In his solitude, the lonely author feels as if belonging to, using Jaspers's Weberian terminology, an aristocracy of the spirit. While being detached from others, he is connected to the cosmic Dao. The mystic feels superior to the leveling morality of ordinary discriminations since he alone acknowledges the "nourishing mother" (i.e., Dao).

In Jaspers's existential rendering, this Daoist passage paradigmatically reveals the attitude of a mystic. Daoist mysticism, understood as a way of conducting one's life, is presented here in terms of the estrangement felt with regard to the community and the psychic mechanisms such self-ascribed solitude and madness give rise to. The solitary individual, Jaspers's existential-psychological interpretation contends, has not reached the wholeness of human existence. He is at once part of those masses by acknowledging that one should value what and how they value; and yet, he also has a sense of being in some sense superior to their world and modes of valorization. His profound melancholy surpasses their superficial joys. The mystic claims to be the only one who is authentically in touch with the Dao, the nourishing mother. His self-ascribed madness works like a protective shell, a cocoon that, for Jaspers, ultimately threatens to undermine a capacity for communication and taking on responsibility within the world and human society.

The mystic is trying to reach beyond communication. It is only in communication though that human beings have the capacity of taking on responsibility for their actions in a shared world in which truth and meaning only emerge within communication. In a letter to Heidegger, Jaspers mentions Laozi as an example of someone who is confronted with existential solitude. In contrast to the previous critique of irresponsible and inconsistent experience of mystic solitude in *Psychology of Worldviews*, Daoist solitude is now interpreted as standing "outside of the alternative of communication–noncommunication."[30] The Dao is not unnamable as if it would stand completely outside of the realm of meaningful communication. Rather, it transcends the division of what can and cannot be named from within communication. Turning to the Dao can foster communication, a form of transcending communication that does not take what can be said—or what cannot be said—to be fully determined or determinable: "I agree with you that the authentic (*das Eigentliche*) and essential is always 'beyond' communication and non-communication, subject and object, thinking and Being, etc.—and in that all of our thinking becomes groundless and diffuse if it loses this relation." Communication relates to the inexpressible ground and becomes meaningful precisely if it abandons the Scylla of silence and the Charybdis of the illusion of being able to fixate meaning by way of language once and for all. Humans are bound by experiencing the world according to subject–object distinctions. For this reason, Jaspers rejects Heidegger's poetic evocation of silence: "We can only speak—and communicate—within these opposites, within the appearances of what is finite."[31] For Jaspers, the philosopher of communication, it is essential that, in spite of all obstacles, we must speak and cannot, as responsible human beings, escape and hide in a mode of appealing to poetic silence or revelatory experiences of a mystic union with the divine (or Dao) beyond communication.

Jaspers emphasizes the ambivalence of mystical modes of solitary existence. An essential reason for this ambivalence arises from the valorization of passivity and non-action that is expressed in chapter 29 of the *Daodejing*. Non-action consists in a mode of conducting one's life in such a way that one not artificially privilege either the subjective or the objective dimension of an action. Experience and action depend on an absolute, which can never be identified or grasped as an object, including by way of linguistic denotation, since it is both prior and beyond the subject–object distinction. This absolute is, Jaspers claims in a rather indiscriminate manner echoing Richard Wilhelm, referred to as God or Dao. It cannot be fabricated or even evoked or followed at will. The mystic cultivates non-action in order to break the spell of willful action. For Jaspers, this emphasis on non-action and passivity is problematic when it is being absolutized and is being transformed into a method. Adopting passivity as a method leads to an irresponsible combination of escapism and quietism that is expressed in the mystic's conscious or unconscious, taking leave from logic, and revealed in his insincere attitude toward existential dissonance and self-contradictions:

> If the mystic ... becomes untrue to himself, if he becomes inconsistent, this just shows that God's ways are new ones. The world, understood as something that needs to be considered, that matters, does no longer exist for him. It may perish, whatever could happen or rather God's will shall be realized. The mystic does not contribute anything because he does not intervene. He thereby essentially believes to perform the greatest effects, even if he withdraws into himself. His authentic life is outside of the world and manifests itself in states of prayer to the point of ecstasies.[32]

This failure of the mystic to remain consistent and his connected incapacity to commit to following through with concrete tasks and paths of action in the world that is reduced to a blind process of transformation or a product of divine will finds expression in paradoxical and indirect images. Mystical teachings are formulated negatively in order to transcend finite forms of reasoning and acting.

The mystical attitude or "the way of mysticism," thus conceived, is a universal human possibility. Mysticism is not unique to Asia, but can be discovered in structurally analogous forms in different cultural and historical contexts. Jaspers discusses Daoism as a paradigmatic illustration of this mystical attitude in that the Daoist rejects the distinction between subjectivity and objectivity and embraces non-action. For Jaspers, the Daoist mystic is engaged in an "irrational way of conducting his life"[33] in that he takes leave from the life of the masses while at the same time experiencing melancholy due to his isolation. He thus both considers himself to be independent of the masses and suffering from not being part of the community. Jaspers thus sees the mystic in an existential tension that cannot be easily resolved. The mystic does not reach the level of mature selfhood and relegates responsibility to a divine dimension that is beyond his reach and possible control.[34] At the same time, Jaspers refers to "the idea of a true and fulfilled mysticism"[35] which emphasizes a spiritual dimension as well as freedom. In the last instance, though, all mystics, for Jaspers, share a formal deficiency:

> That they do not invoke reasons, principles, and tasks and that, therefore, no discussion is possible with them ... Rather they invoke a real

community with God as well as God's will, which reveals itself to them in an incomprehensible way ... The mystic does not develop, he suspends development in favor of timelessness.[36]

In this early work, Jaspers already emphasizes the normative ambivalence and logical inconsistency of the axial age tradition of Daoism. Mysticism is being introduced as a polar opposite of the (equally problematic) ideal-driven attempt to realize one's plans in the world. It embraces passivity at the price of succumbing to an irresponsible and irrational submission to a higher will or a subjection to a fateful process. In spite of his critique, Jaspers's own philosophical path reveals a proximity to mysticism that attempts to rescue its insights into existential solitude and the limits of communication and action without ignoring its constitutive blind spots. In spite of this critique, one can perceive a "mystical tendency" in Jaspers's thought.[37] His critique of mysticism is a redemptive critique. The mystic's tendency to flee the world of communication is ideally abandoned in favor of a rational, communicative, this-worldly, and yet mystical insight into the limits and potentials of human existence.

In Jaspers's early engagement with Laozi, we already see that he does not subscribe to a simplistic view of juxtaposing Orient and Occident and refrains from interpreting Asia as the wholly or radical other. Jaspers concedes that the difference between Europe and Asia is an "original polarity,"[38] which is, however, not to be transformed into a metaphysical principle. For Jaspers, this polarity is a "profound, historical mystery,"[39] which is reflected in the historical dynamics between the Greeks and Persians, the division of the Roman Empire into an Eastern and Western part, the Occident and Islam, etc. The reflection about the polarity of Europe and Asia has entered into the historical development of each of these poles. Rather than situating Daoism as an incommensurable form of mysticism, Jaspers interprets different modes or types of mysticism to be present in different cultural settings. What different forms of mysticism have in common is the emphasis on the limits of communication as well as the valorization of non-action. The originality of Jaspers's approach consists in seeing these similarities without thereby leveling difference.

Daoist motifs are also present in Jaspers's magnum opus *Von der Wahrheit* (Of Truth). What Jaspers conceives of as *"Das Umgreifende"* (the encompassing) has unmistakable similarities to the Dao. Like the Dao, the encompassing cannot be identified or captured in isolation. It transcends concrete phenomena yet permeates them. It includes all of reality and is manifest in each part, which it also transcends. It can be known and spoken about only indirectly with different provisional names (in addition to "Dao" Jaspers mentions "Pneuma").

Jaspers refers to the study of the encompassing as "periechontology" to distinguish it from traditional metaphysics and ontology, which could not perceive of the open-ended and dynamic relations of what is. In a section titled "The Consciousness of Being in Nonaction," willing is presented as inherently paradoxical: "I cannot will what I authentically (*eigentlich*) will. The ground of my will lies in the depth of that which is neither willing nor unwilling, in that which is hit upon always only indirectly in willing. If I will it directly, I disable it."[40] Analogously, true action is only possible when it is being performed indirectly by not focusing on intended outcomes. What non-action enables, in contrast, is "responsible self-transformation, opening up in inward action and self-realization."[41] The mode in which the encompassing is being experienced is a form of being receptive and trusting for what has been and is being presented as a gift. The richness of words taken from foreign languages is that they go beyond mere signs referring to a specific object or denoting a determinate meaning. Foreign words evoke an atmosphere or a mood (*Stimmung*) that opens up a kind of transcendence for a mysterious, enigmatic truth dimension: "Words always retain a residue, which is the true enigma. Their sound is not indifferent, and yet they are not sufficiently characterized in terms of their sound nor through the associations they evoke. Words from the most distant languages communicate a mood (like tabu, totem, mana, Dao, wuwei, atman)."[42]

4. Laozi as a "Metaphysician Who Thinks from the Origin"

Jaspers's most extensive engagement is developed in the discussion of Laozi at the end of *Die großen Philosophen* (1957). The entry to world-philosophy, for Jaspers, consists in the study of its most significant exemplars. In the architecture of *Die großen Philosophen*, Laozi is grouped together with Anaximander, Heraclitus, Parmenides, Plotinus, Anselm, Spinoza, and Nagarjuna. Because their thinking aims at what is perennial and thus beyond all history, Jaspers diagnoses a cross-cultural affinity (*Verwandtschaft*) among them. For Jaspers, the entry into world-philosophy through the personal dimension of these sages is important because it is their personality which draws people into the philosophical orbit they open up. Moreover, Jaspers was convinced that it is more likely to imagine a communication between these sages rather than a conversation about the dogmatic legacies that later schools of thought have developed.[43] Jaspers's interpretation of Laozi is interspersed with original quotations and interpretation that closely follows the commentary and translation of Victor von Strauss who introduced the axial age theorem to German academic circles.[44] Jaspers focuses on the metaphysics, cosmogony, ethos, as well as the politics of Laozi, but also emphasizes that this academic mode of differentiated discussion is rooted in a categorization that is somewhat foreign to the holistic spirit of Daoist thinking and the underlying metaphysics of oneness. Jaspers identifies Dao explicitly with the encompassing.[45] Those metaphysicians who are capable of thinking from the origin "enable an encounter with the ground of being. It secures the foundational knowledge, which is capable of carrying the human being who thinks in such a way every day."[46] Laozi is a "metaphysician who thinks from the origin" while the Dao is the origin that cannot be grasped by linguistic or sensuous means, and yet is present in each phenomenon and can appear in each individual existence whenever non-intentionality (*Absichtslosigkeit*) is being achieved.

While Laozi is not considered one of the paradigmatic humans (*massgebende Menschen*)—Jesus, Socrates, Confucius, Buddha—he does have a prominent role on the stage of world-philosophy. Jaspers focuses on the "life and work" of Laozi to thereby highlight existential features of his personality. Well aware of the controversies concerning the authorship of the Daoist classic, for Jaspers there is no doubt that the *Daodejing* has been created by a real human being, "a personality of the highest rank,"[47] and that this historical personality belonged to the tradition of great philosophers. It is precisely the mystery surrounding the legendary author that adds to the emphasis on the ultimately mysterious occurrence of the axial age. Laozi combines a proto-existentialist tone of voice with a metaphysical worldview into a form of proto-existential metaphysics.

Laozi first enters the stage of great philosophers as the critic and interlocutor of Confucius. Jaspers sees philosophical debate as crucial and interprets the relationship between Confucius and Laozi in analogy to the— for the development of European philosophy at least—critical encounter between Plato and the Sophists. Laozi objects to the focus of Confucius on the idealization of the past, book learning, and on ethical principles at the expense of the naturalness of following the Dao. Arguably the most original aspect of Jaspers's interpretation of the "legendary conversations"[48] between Confucius and the older and critical Laozi is that Jaspers does not treat these two positions, Confucianism and Daoism, as irreconcilable opposites as they are frequently presented by their respective followers, but as being engaged in what Jaspers, in a different context, refers to as a "loving strife."[49] The polemical and partisan reception of these two thinkers clouds their true dialogical relationship. The emphasis on the origins, and the original thinkers in particular, is a critique against any form of ideological or dogmatic belonging to schools of thought, any "isms." Confucius prior to Confucianism, and Laozi prior to Daoism, were in many respects two remarkable thinkers engaged in a conversation that revealed each other's respective blind spots. While Confucian teaching is presented as a moralistic fixation of virtues and prohibitions by Laozi, Confucius reveals the impossibility of following nature at the expense of engaging with the world of political responsibility, as proclaimed by Laozi. In spite of the appearance of an irreconcilable opposition, Confucius and Laozi resemble each other in a number of respects. Confucius, like Laozi, espouses forms of non-action and has an "inclination for world flight;"[50] Laozi, like Confucius, also offers advice to rulers.

The image of an irreconcilable struggle between opposing schools of thought was, according to Jaspers, only established after their death and characterizes the transformation of the original ideas of these personalities into dogmatic teachings. Their human traits get lost when they are being transfigured into quasi-divine founding figures of increasingly one-sided philosophical schools. The partisan confrontations between Confucianism and Daoism is at odds with the dialogical strife and the philosophical polarity of Confucius and Laozi. They signal the two poles that express possibilities of human existence. A key aspect of axial civilizations is that they provide multiple visions of the good life without leading to the partisanship and ideological confrontation that is historically, for Jaspers, closely bound to the division of orthodox and heterodox discourses. In China this ossification of discourses happened after the Warring States period (475–221 BCE) and accompanied the formation of imperial China. The instrumentalization of Laozi's teaching, for Jaspers, started when the first emperor, Qin Shi Huang, adopted not only Legalist, but also Daoist forms of subjugation, and used those for the suppression of Confucian influence. This instrumentalization of philosophy by political elites was later reversed by the adoption of Confucianism as the orthodox imperial ideology. As Jaspers emphasizes in the second volume of his *Philosophie*, which is dedicated to an elucidation or illumination of existence (*Existenzerhellung*), the philosophical focus on great personalities is intended to replace the category of political empires with that of an empire of spirits (*Geisterreich*) in which great personalities are engaged in unbounded or unlimited communication (*uneingeschränkte Kommunikation*).[51]

Jaspers is highly critical of what he interprets as a subsequent decay in the reception of these personalities. The followers of Confucius became self-interested bureaucrats while the Daoists escaped from the world of political responsibility, engaged in alchemy, and pursued magical practices. As Jörn Kroll has recently shown, Jaspers has been surprisingly one-sided in his dismissal of Laozi's most famous successor, Zhuangzi 莊子, who is characterized as a witty poet rather than a serious philosopher. "Laozi's atmosphere," Jaspers writes, "is peaceful while that of Zhuangzi is polemical, full of arrogance and mocking contempt."[52] Zhuangzi's ironic prose is edifying in Jaspers's judgment, but misses the profound suffering and the metaphysical depth of Laozi. Zhuangzi's ironic, arrogant, and superficial stories can therefore not be considered an authoritative interpretation of Laozi, the metaphysician who thinks from the origin.

For Jaspers, the followers of both Confucius and Laozi betrayed the dialogical ethos and transformed great but ordinary human beings into deities. The insight into their complementarity and inner relation has thus been lost: "Laozi and Confucius are polar opposites, but such, which belong together and necessitate each other."[53] Jaspers does emphasize that, in spite of the misleading legacy of these great humans, it remains a constant possibility to live up to the human potentials they have opened up. The possibility of preserving what binds Laozi and Confucius together survives even after their followers have at times transformed their teaching beyond recognition into a polemical battle. These polar opposites have not been integrated into a systematic philosophy, but: "The unity of both has been repeated in China by great personalities, not through a philosophy, which systematically encompassed both, but in the Chinese wisdom of a life, which illuminates itself through thinking."[54] In spite of his overall constructive reconstruction of the "great philosopher" Laozi, Jaspers sees the limit of Laozi (and "Chinese spirit" more generally) in the absence of certain "intermediary stages" (*Zwischenstufen*) to the transcendence toward Dao or the encompassing. These stages include a sense of justified ethical indignation, an understanding of tragedy and sin, as well as the "cypher of a demanding and angry, a striving God who wants strife."[55]

5. Conclusion

By way of conclusion and outlook, let me anticipate likely objections to Jaspers's engagement with Laozi as it has been laid out in this chapter. It could be argued that Jaspers's view of the limits of Laozi indirectly exposes the limits of Jaspers's own philosophical faith in the possibility of world-philosophy. In their greatness—as well as in their ultimate failure—these human sages appear as distant yardsticks of a mysterious past, which is presented by Jaspers as an eternal present and future. The axial age is thereby situated beyond time and space. Equally detached from concrete historical conditions and from the effective history the received texts have given rise to, these paradigmatic sages are also infinitely distant from the contemporary reader who, Jaspers suggests, is nevertheless to consider them as contemporary interlocutors. Indeed, Jaspers's evocation of a communication in an empire of solitary spirits can be perceived as an ahistorical and transcultural form of philosophical elitism. The gates to the empire of spirits threaten to remain closed for ordinary men and women who can, at best, peek through them and admire these geniuses from afar and in awe.

One may also object that Jaspers is indebted to some of the Eurocentric assumptions his cosmopolitan project intends to overcome, or at least put into perspective. Not only does he apply Judeo-Christian, ancient Greek, and existentialist categories in his evaluation of classical Chinese texts and authors; the philosophical approach developed in *The Origin and Goal of History* is hardly imaginable outside of an eschatological view of a history with a clear beginning and end that is foreign to classical China. Moreover, sinologists are likely to contend, Jaspers's idealization of the historical personality of Laozi and the emphasis on the legendary account of his conversation with Confucius separates the imagined authors writing in their name from actual historical fact, and ignores a complex textual corpus and the receptive history it has given rise to.

In spite of these legitimate concerns, Jaspers's turn to the East, especially his "loving struggle" with Confucius and Laozi, presents an original, systematic, and visionary attempt to prepare for a philosophical conversation at eye level, a conversation that is relevant for the future. Such a conversation is addressed at the imagined global community of possible human existence. As Jaspers remarks in a letter to Arendt, his perhaps foolish aim is to "rescue him (Confucius) not only from the banal presentations he has suffered even at the hands of sinologists but also because I found him so fruitful for us."[56]

Notes

1   While it is frequently mentioned that Heidegger attempted to translate the *Daodejing* 道德經 with the Chinese student Paul Shih-Yi Hsiao (Xiao Shiyi 蕭 師毅), he eventually dismissed this plan due to what he considered to be an unbridgeable linguistic gap. Heidegger rejected the transformative potential of a philosophical turn to and engagement with the East in an interview with *Der Spiegel* in 1966: "Only in the same place where the modern technical world took its origin can we also prepare a conversion (*Umkehr*) of it. In other words, this cannot happen by taking over Zen-Buddhism or other Eastern experiences of the word." See Martin Heidegger, "'Only a God Can Save Us': The Spiegel Interview (1966)," in *Heidegger: The Man and the Thinker*, ed. Thomas Sheehan (New Brunswick: Transaction Publishers, 2010), 62. In contrast, Jaspers emphasizes in a letter to Heidegger that he (Jaspers) considers the opening up to the East essential in spite of barriers to "knowing very well that I cannot truly (*eigentlich*) penetrate, but am inspired in a mysterious way from there." See Martin Heidegger and Karl Jaspers, *Briefwechsel 1920-1963* (Frankfurt: Klostermann, 1990), 178. On Heidegger's relationship to Asian philosophy in general and Daoism in particular, see: Graham Parkes, ed., *Heidegger and Asian Thought* (Honolulu: University of Hawaii Press, 1987); Reinhard May, *Heidegger's Hidden Sources: East-Asian Influences on His Work*, trans. Graham Parkes (London: Routledge, 1996); Guenter Wohlfahrt, "Heidegger and Laozi: *Wu* (Nothing): On chapter 11 of the *Daodejing*," *Journal of Chinese Philosophy*, 30.1 (2003): 39–59; Lin Ma, *Heidegger on East-West Dialogue: Anticipating the Event* (New York: Routledge, 2007); Bret W. Davis, "Heidegger and Asian Philosophy," in *The Bloomsbury Companion to Heidegger*, eds. François Raffoul and Eric S. Nelson (New York: Bloomsbury Academic, 2013), 459–71; David Chai, "Nothingness and the Clearing: Heidegger, Daoism and the Quest for Primal Clarity," *The Review of Metaphysics*, 67.3 (2014): 583–601; and Mario Wenning, "Heidegger and Zhuangzi on the Nonhuman: Towards a Transcultural Critique of (Post) Humanism," in *Rethinking the Non-Human*, eds. Chloë Taylor and Neil Dalal (New York: Routledge, 2014), 93–111. Noteworthy exceptions to the general omission of Jaspers's engagement with Daoism include Young-Do Chung, "Karl Jaspers und Laotse: Parallelen zwischen den Begriffen Transzendenz und Tao," *Jahrbuch der Österreichischen Karl-Jaspers-Gesellschaft*, 11 (1998): 28–43; Jean-Claude Gens, "Jaspers' Begegnung mit und sein Verhältnis zu China," in

Cross-Cultural Conflicts and Communication: Rethinking Jaspers' Philosophy Today, ed. Andreas Cesana (Würzburg: Königshausen and Neumann, 2016), 161–71; and Jörn Kroll, "Open Sky, Open Society: Zhuangzi and Jaspers on Understanding and Communicating without Closure," *Existenz* (forthcoming).

2   If mentioned, Jaspers tends to be treated as a marginal figure in twentieth-century existentialism. This was not always the case. During the 1960s, Jaspers was the most widely read philosopher in Germany—exceeding Heidegger and Adorno. He contributed and often initiated public debates concerning pressing issues including the question of German guilt, the atomic bomb, reunification and the rebuilding of the University system (see Thomas Meyer, "Mit leichter Hand," *Zeit*, available online). This political engagement might have contributed to Jaspers's image of being a popular writer and public intellectual rather than an original philosopher. For an attempt to recover Jaspers as a philosopher, see Chris Thornhill, *Karl Jaspers: Politics and Metaphysics* (New York: Routledge, 2002).

3   Karl Jaspers. *Rechenschaft und Ausblick: Reden und Aufsätze* (Munich: Piper, 1951), 327–8.

4   See Hans Saner, "Jaspers' Idee einer kommenden Weltphilosophie," in *Karl Jaspers Today. Philosophy at the Threshold of the Future*, eds. Leonard Ehrlich and Richard Wisser (Lanham: University Press of America, 1988), 75–92; Genoveva Teoharova, *Karl Jaspers' Philosophie auf dem Weg zur Weltphilosophie* (Würzburg: Königshausen & Neumann, 2005).

5   The term "*Weltphilosophie*" also resonates with Kant's distinction of a world philosophy and a school philosophy. While the term of world philosophy is never defined clearly, Jaspers considered it to be the necessary groundwork for a historically-informed and future-directed vocation to be continued by others.

6   Jaspers, *Rechenschaft und Ausblick*, 331.

7   Karl Jaspers and Heinrich Zimmer, "Briefe 1929–1939," *Jahrbuch der Österreichischen Karl-Jaspers-Gesellschaft*, 6 (1993): 24–5. Jaspers was particularly fond of Asian art, especially painting. He traces the transformation of Chinese aesthetic and philosophical motifs in different Asian contexts. When Arendt presented Jaspers with the "awfully heavy" book on Chinese painting for his birthday, Jaspers expressed his gratitude and his admiration for the "philosophical thinking of the painters." He maintains that the Chinese, "philosophizing within artistic creation and the attentive reflection on this philosophy," (see letters 204 and 205 in Jaspers, "Briefe," 245–9) finds a parallel in the occident only in Leonardo Da Vinci. He considered Da Vinci to be the philosopher among painters. See Karl Jaspers, "Lionardo als Philosoph," in *Philosophie und Welt: Reden und Aufsätze* (Munich: Piper, 1963), 211–72. Chinese philosophy, and Daoism in particular, was perfected in later Japanese painting, especially inkbrush landscape painting.

8   Karl Jaspers, Dominic Kaegi, and Reiner Wiehl, eds., *Korrespondenzen*, (Göttingen: Wallstein, 2016), 294.

9   Jaspers in a letter to his sister; see Gens, Jean-Claude., "Jaspers' Begegnung mit und sein Verhältnis zu China," in Andreas Cesana (ed.), *Cross-Cultural Conflicts and Communication: Rethinking Jaspers' Philosophy Today*, 161–71 (Würzburg: Königshausen and Neumann, 2016), 162.

10 As stated in a letter Jaspers wrote to Hannah Arendt on January 8th, 1947. See Hannah Arendt and Karl Jaspers, *Briefwechsel: 1926–1969* (Munich: Piper, 2001), 108.

11 For a nuanced reconstruction of the reception of Chinese philosophy in early twentieth-century Germany, see Eric S. Nelson, *Chinese and Buddhist Philosophy in Early Twentieth-Century German Thought* (London: Bloomsbury Academic, 2017). For the specific transformation of Daoist motifs in Western philosophy see J.J. Clarke, *The Dao of the West: Western Transformations of Daoist Thought* (London: Routledge, 2000).

12 See Emmanuel Levinas, *Le temps et l'autre* (Montepellier: Fata Morgana, 1979); Theo Sundermeier, *Den Fremden verstehen: Eine praktische Hermeneutik* (Göttingen: Vandenhoeck, 1996); and Bernhard Waldenfels, *Grundmotive einer Phänomenologie des Fremden* (Frankfurt: Suhrkamp, 2016).

13 Hannah Arendt calls the axial age "the great historical discovery" and the "foundation" of Jaspers's philosophy of history. See Hannah Arendt, "Laudatio auf Karl Jaspers," in *Menschen in finsteren Zeiten*, ed. Ursula Ludz (Munich: Piper, 2002), 109. For an overview of research perspectives invoking the axial age, see Hans Joas, *Was ist die Achsenzeit? Eine Wissenschaftliche Debatte als Diskurs über Transzendenz* (Basel: Schwabe, 2014); Johann Arnason, S.N. Eisenstadt, and Björn Wittrock, eds., *Axial Civilizations and World History* (Leiden: Brill, 2005); Robert Bellah and Hans Joas, eds., *The Axial Age and its Consequences* (Cambridge, MA: Harvard University Press, 2012); Mario Wenning, "Vom Ursprung und Ziel der Zweiten Achsenzeit", *Jahrbuch der Österreichischen Jaspers Gesellschaft*, 30 (2017): 111–29; and Jan Assmann, *Achsenzeit: Eine Archäologie der Moderne* (Munich: Beck, 2018).

14 On Husserl's and Heidegger's eurocentrism, see Nelson, *Chinese and Buddhist Philosophy*, chapters 5 and 6.

15 Aleida Assmann, "Einheit und Vielfalt in der Geschichte: Jaspers' Begriff der Achsenzeit neu betrachtet," in *Kulturen der Achsenzeit*, ed. S.N. Eisenstadt (Frankfurt: Suhrkamp), vol. 2: 334.

16 Ibid., 337.

17 Jaspers, *Rechenschaft und Ausblick*, 237–8.

18 See François Jullien, *Detour and Access: Strategies of Meaning in China and Greece* (New York: Zone Books, 2004).

19 This is a slight variation of Jürgen Habermas's (1988) description of Jaspers's project as a search for "the unity of reason within the diversity of its voices."

20 Jaspers, *Rechenschaft und Ausblick*, 340.

21 Ibid.

22 Assmann, *Achsenzeit*, 165.

23 Ibid., 281.

24 One attempt to build on Jaspers's conception of the axial age is that of Jürgen Habermas's recent work in which he, drawing on Jaspers, reconstructs the normative preconditions for a post-secular world society. See Jürgen Habermas, *Nachmetaphysisches Denken II: Aufsätze und Repliken* (Berlin: Suhrkamp, 2012).

25 See Shmuel Noah Eisenstadt, "Multiple Modernities," *Daedalus*, 129.1 (2000): 1–29.

26 The axial age hypothesis has been characterized as a breakthrough to transcendence by, among others, the sinologist Benjamin Schwartz (1975). For Jaspers, the above-mentioned five criteria were the most essential and he does not explicitly mention the role of transcendence in his discussion of the moral and cognitive breakthrough during the axial age. Arguably, the emphasis on universality and critique includes a notion of context-transcendence though, and transcendence is a major concern in Jaspers's other work.

27 See Heiner Roetz, *Die chinesische Ethik der Achsenzeit: Eine Rekonstruktion unter dem Aspekt des Durchbruchs zum postkonventionellen Denken* (Frankfurt: Suhrkamp, 1992).

28 Karl Jaspers, *Psychologie der Weltanschauungen* (Berlin: Springer, 1919), 455–6.

29 Jaspers interprets the "domination by the crowd" (*Herrschaft der Masse*) as one of the main obstacles to individual human freedom in his *Die geistige Situation der Zeit*, (Berlin: de Gruyter, 1999), 34–7.

30 Martin Heidegger and Karl Jaspers, *Briefwechsel 1920–1963* (Frankfurt: Klostermann, 1990), 183.

31 Ibid., 184.

32 Jaspers, *Psychologie der Weltanschauungen*, 454.

33 Ibid., 456.

34 Young-Do Chung proposes to conceive of Dao in analogy to Jaspers's understanding of a fugitive philosophical God who remains obscure and is distinct from the God of revelation. See Young-Do Chung, "Karl Jaspers und Laotse: Parallelen zwischen den Begriffen Transzendenz und Tao," *Jahrbuch der Österreichischen Karl-Jaspers-Gesellschaft*, 11 (1998): 42. One reason why this proposal is problematic is that, in contrast to Jaspers, the early Daoists were not aware of revealed religion and thus saw no need to distinguish themselves from it.

35 Jaspers, *Psychologie der Weltanschauungen*, 458.

36 Ibid., 459.

37 Nakayama, drawing on Hajime Tanabe, identifies a "mystical tendency" in Jaspers's thought. See Tsuyoshi Nakayama, "Jaspers und die Mystik," in *Karl Jaspers's Philosophy: Rooted in the Present, Paradigm for the Future*, eds. Richard Wisser and Leonard Ehrlich (Würzburg: Könighausen and Neumann, 1998), 179–84.

38 Karl Jaspers, *Von der Wahrheit* (Munich: Piper, 1947), 94.

39 Ibid.

40 Ibid., 180.

41 Ibid.

42 Ibid., 403.

43 See Mario Wenning, "Jaspers on Exemplary Individuals," in *Studi Jaspersiani: Rivista Annuale della Società Italiana Karl Jaspers*, 6 (2018), 151–67.

44 While he initially used Wilhelm's translations of the Chinese classics, Jaspers grew increasingly fond of Viktor von Strauß and Torney's commentary on and translation of the *Daodejing*. Von Strauß was also one of the precursors of the Axial Age theorem. See Assmann, *Achsenzeit*, chapter 6.

45 Karl Jaspers, *Die großen Philosophen* (Munich: Piper, 1957), 520.

46 Ibid., 621.

47 Ibid., 904.

48 Ibid., 181.

49 Karl Jaspers, *Philosophie*, vol. 2 (Berlin: Springer, 1956), 65–6.

50 Jaspers, *Die großen Philosophen*, 180.

51 Jaspers, *Philosophie*, vol. 2, 395.

52 Jaspers, *Die großen Philosophen*, 935.

53 Ibid., 181.

54 Ibid., 180.

55 Ibid., 937.

56 Hannah Arendt and Karl Jaspers, *Correspondence 1926–1969* (San Diego: Harvest, 1993), 324.

References

Arendt, Hannah. (2002), "Laudatio auf Karl Jaspers," in Ursula Ludz (ed.), *Menschen in finsteren Zeiten*, 101–16, Munich: Piper.

Arendt, Hannah and Karl Jaspers. (1993), *Correspondence 1926–1969*, San Diego: Harvest.

Arendt, Hannah and Karl Jaspers. (2001), *Briefwechsel: 1926–1969*, Munich: Piper.

Arnason, Johann, S.N. Eisenstadt, and Björn Wittrock, eds. (2005), *Axial Civilizations and World History*, Leiden: Brill.

Assmann, Aleida. (1992), "Einheit und Vielfalt in der Geschichte: Jaspers' Begriff der Achsenzeit neu betrachtet," in S.N. Eisenstadt (ed.), *Kulturen der Achsenzeit*, vol. 2, 330–40, Frankfurt: Suhrkamp.

Assmann, Jan. (2018), *Achsenzeit: Eine Archäologie der Moderne*, Munich: Beck.

Bellah, Robert and Hans Joas, eds. (2012), *The Axial Age and its Consequences*, Cambridge, MA: Harvard University Press.

Cesana, Andreas, ed. (2016), *Cross-Cultural Conflicts and Communication: Rethinking Jaspers' Philosophy Today*, Würzburg: Königshausen and Neumann.

Chai, David. (2014), "Nothingness and the Clearing: Heidegger, Daoism and the Quest for Primal Clarity," *The Review of Metaphysics*, 67.3: 583–601.

Chung, Young-Do. (1998), "Karl Jaspers und Laotse: Parallelen zwischen den Begriffen Transzendenz und Tao," *Jahrbuch der Österreichischen Karl-Jaspers-Gesellschaft*, 11: 28–43.

Clarke, J.J. (2000), *The Dao of the West: Western Transformations of Daoist Thought*, London: Routledge.

Davis, Bret W. (2013), "Heidegger and Asian Philosophy," in François Raffoul and Eric S. Nelson (eds.), *The Bloomsbury Companion to Heidegger*, 459–71, New York: Bloomsbury Academic.

Eisenstadt, Shmuel Noah. (2000), "Multiple Modernities," *Daedalus*, 129.1: 1–29.

Gens, Jean-Claude. (2016), "Jaspers' Begegnung mit und sein Verhältnis zu China," in Andreas Cesana (ed.), *Cross-Cultural Conflicts and Communication: Rethinking Jaspers' Philosophy Today*, 161–71, Würzburg: Königshausen and Neumann.

Habermas, Jürgen. (1988), "Die Einheit der Vernunft in der Vielheit ihrer Stimmen," *Merkur*, 467: 1–14.

Habermas, Jürgen. (2012), *Nachmetaphysisches Denken II: Aufsätze und Repliken*, Berlin: Suhrkamp.

Heidegger, Martin. (2010), "'Only a God Can Save Us': The Spiegel Interview (1966)," in Thomas Sheehan (ed.), *Heidegger: The Man and the Thinker*, 45–68, New Brunswick: Transaction Publishers.

Heidegger, Martin and Karl Jaspers. (1990), *Briefwechsel 1920–1963*, Walter Biemel und Hans Saner (eds.), Frankfurt: Klostermann.

Jaspers, Karl. (1919), *Psychologie der Weltanschauungen*, Berlin: Springer.

Jaspers, Karl. (1947), *Von der Wahrheit*, Munich: Piper.

Jaspers, Karl. (1949), *Vom Ursprung und Ziel der Geschichte*, Munich: Piper.

Jaspers, Karl. (1951), *Rechenschaft und Ausblick: Reden und Aufsätze*, Munich: Piper.

Jaspers, Karl. (1956), *Philosophie*, Berlin: Springer.

Jaspers, Karl. (1957), *Die großen Philosophen*, Munich: Piper.

Jaspers, Karl. (1963), "Lionardo als Philosoph," in *Philosophie und Welt: Reden und Aufsätze*, 211–72, Munich: Piper.

Jaspers, Karl. (1999), *Die geistige Situation der Zeit*, Berlin: de Gruyter.

Jaspers, Karl, Dominic Kaegi, and Reiner Wiehl, eds. (2016), *Korrespondenzen*, Göttingen: Wallstein.

Jaspers, Karl and Heinrich Zimmer. (1993), "Briefe 1929–1939," *Jahrbuch der Österreichischen Karl-Jaspers-Gesellschaft*, 6: 7–32.

Joas, Hans. (2014), *Was ist die Achsenzeit? Eine Wissenschaftliche Debatte als Diskurs über Transzendenz*, Basel: Schwabe.

Jullien, François. (2004), *Detour and Access: Strategies of Meaning in China and Greece*, Sophie Hawkes (trans.), New York: Zone Books.

Kroll, Jörn. (forthcoming), "Open Sky: Open Society: Zhuangzi and Jaspers on Understanding and Communicating without Closure," *Existenz*.

Levinas, Emmanuel. (1979), *Le temps et l'autre*, Montepellier: Fata Morgana.

Ludz, Ursula, ed. (2002), *Menschen in finsteren Zeiten*, Munich: Piper.

Ma, Lin. (2007), *Heidegger on East-West Dialogue: Anticipating the Event*, New York: Routledge.

May, Reinhard. (1996), *Heidegger's Hidden Sources: East-Asian Influences on His Work*, Graham Parkes (trans.), London: Routledge.

Meyer, Thomas. (2017), "Mit leichter Hand," *Zeit*, 23 February. Available online at: https://www.zeit.de/2017/07/karl-jaspers-korrespondenzen-gesamtausgabe-philosophie

Nakayama, Tsuyoshi. (1998), "Jaspers und die Mystik," in Richard Wisser and Leonard Ehrlich (eds.), *Karl Jaspers's Philosophy: Rooted in the Present, Paradigm for the Future*, 179–84, Würzburg: Könighausen and Neumann.

Nelson, Eric S. (2017), *Chinese and Buddhist Philosophy in Early Twentieth-Century German Thought*, London: Bloomsbury Academic.

Parkes, Graham, ed. (1987), *Heidegger and Asian Thought*, Honolulu: University of Hawaii Press.

Raffoul, François and Eric S. Nelson, eds. (2013), *The Bloomsbury Companion to Heidegger*, New York: Bloomsbury Academic.

Rémusat, Jean-Pierre Abel. (1823), *Mémoire sur la vie et les opinions de Lao-tseu, philosophe chinois du VIe siècle avant notre ère, qui a professé les opinions communément attribuées à Pythagore, à Platon et à leurs disciples*, Paris: Imprimerie Royale.

Roetz, Heiner. (1992), *Die chinesische Ethik der Achsenzeit: Eine Rekonstruktion unter dem Aspekt des Durchbruchs zum postkonventionellen Denken*, Frankfurt: Suhrkamp.

Saner, Hans. (1988), "Jaspers' Idee einer kommenden Weltphilosophie," in Leonard Ehrlich and Richard Wisser (eds.), *Karl Jaspers Today. Philosophy at the Threshold of the Future*, 75–92, Lanham: University Press of America.

Schwartz, Benjamin. (1975), "The Age of Transcendence," *Daedalus*, 104.2: 1–7.

Sheehan, Thomas, ed. (2010), *Heidegger: The Man and the Thinker*, New Brunswick: Transaction Publishers.

Sundermeier, Theo. (1996), *Den Fremden verstehen: Eine praktische Hermeneutik*, Göttingen: Vandenhoeck.

Teoharova, Genoveva. (2005), *Karl Jaspers' Philosophie auf dem Weg zur Weltphilosophie*, Würzburg: Königshausen & Neumann.

Thornhill, Chris. (2002), *Karl Jaspers: Politics and Metaphysics*, New York: Routledge.

Waldenfels, Bernhard. (2016), *Grundmotive einer Phänomenologie des Fremden*, Frankfurt: Suhrkamp.

Wenning, Mario. (2014), "Heidegger and Zhuangzi on the Nonhuman: Towards a Transcultural Critique of (Post)Humanism," in Chloë Taylor and Neil Dalal (eds.), *Rethinking the Non-Human*, 93–111, New York: Routledge.

Wenning, Mario. (2017), "Vom Ursprung und Ziel der Zweiten Achsenzeit," *Jahrbuch der Österreichischen Jaspers Gesellschaft*, 30: 111–29.

Wenning, Mario. (2018), "Jaspers on Exemplary Individuals," *Studi Jaspersiani: Rivista Annuale della Società Italiana Karl Jaspers*, 6: 151–67.

Wisser, Richard and Leonard Ehrlich, eds. (1998), *Karl Jaspers's Philosophy: Rooted in the Present, Paradigm for the Future*, Würzburg: Könighausen and Neumann.

Wohlfahrt, Guenter. (2003), "Heidegger and Laozi: *Wu* (Nothing): On chapter 11 of the *Daodejing*," *Journal of Chinese Philosophy*, 30.1: 39–59.

PART THREE

Mature Encounters: A Forest of Ideas

8

Heidegger and Daoism:

A Dialogue on the Useless Way of Unnecessary Being

Bret W. Davis

1. Introduction

The intent of this chapter is to unfold—to bring to light and further develop—the largely implicit dialogue that Heidegger began with the two foundational texts of Daoism, the *Daodejing* 道德經 and the *Zhuangzi* 莊子. Heidegger's familiarity with these Daoist texts goes back to at least the 1920s. In fact, one of the key expressions of *Being and Time* (1927), "*In-der-Welt-sein*" (being-in-the-world), was coined not by Heidegger but by the German translators of Okakura Kakuzo's *The Book of Tea*,[1] a copy of which Heidegger reportedly received in 1919.[2] In a chapter entitled "Daoism and Zennism," Okakura wrote that "Chinese historians have always spoken of Daoism as the 'art of being in the world,'"[3] a phrase that Marguerite and Ulrich Steindorff rendered into German as "Kunst des In-der-Welt-Seins."[4] Heidegger revealed his familiarity with Martin Buber's 1910 edition of the *Zhuangzi* in 1930 when in conversation he referred to the story of the happy fish in chapter 17 of the *Zhuangzi* in order to explain his understanding of being-with (*Mitsein*) others.[5]

As interesting as such evidence of early contact may be, Heidegger's dialogue with Daoist thought really gets underway in the pages—even if kept mostly between the lines—of *Country Path Conversations* (*Feldweg-Gespräche*), a set of three dialogues Heidegger composed at the end of the war (1944–45).[6] *Country Path Conversations* is a pivotal text in Heidegger's path of thought; in it one finds Heidegger critically rethinking the basics of his earlier hermeneutical phenomenology. In particular, in *Country Path Conversations* more than anywhere else, one witnesses Heidegger's turning away from associating thinking with willing—an association he had himself explicitly embraced in the first half of the 1930s—and his development of the critique of technology central to his later thought.[7]

A year after he composed *Country Path Conversations*, Heidegger endeavored to co-translate the *Daodejing*. Yet the *Daodejing*'s resonance with and influence on his thought can be clearly discerned already within *Country Path Conversations* itself. Daoism's critique of willful artifice and call for a return to natural and non-coercive action (*wuwei* 無為) accord with Heidegger's critique of the "will" (*Wille*) and his alternative comportment of "releasement" (*Gelassenheit*) introduced in *Country Path Conversations*. Moreover, Heidegger's notion of "path" or "way" (*Weg*), which appears not only in the title but also throughout the text of *Country Path Conversations*, clearly reverberates with the central Daoist notion of *dao* 道. The final resonance between the *Daodejing* and Heidegger's later thought to be discussed in the first half of this chapter pertains to the limits as well as delimiting power of language.

The second half of this chapter pursues convergences and, in the end, divergences between Heidegger's later thought and the second foundational text of Daoism, the *Zhuangzi*. This will be done initially by way of examining Heidegger's startling quotation of a passage from this text at the very conclusion of *Country Path Conversations*, a passage on "the use of the useless" (*wuyong zhi weiyong* 無用之為用) or, in Heidegger's rendering, "the necessity of the unnecessary" (*die Notwendigkeit des Unnötigen*). This quotation is especially significant given that Heidegger wrote to his wife at the time that the notion of "the unnecessary" that he found in this ancient Chinese text "is what I mean by 'Being.'"[8]

After returning once again to convergences between Heidegger and Daoism regarding the limits and delimiting power of language, this time with reference to the *Zhuangzi*, the chapter ends by flushing and fleshing out some crucial divergences between the "fundamental attunements" (*Grundstimmungen*) of Heidegger and the *Zhuangzi*. Whereas, starting in the 1930s, Heidegger speaks in somber terms and tones with the poet Hölderlin of the need for a "holy mourning" of the loss of the old gods in order to anticipate a new arrival of the divine, and of the fundamental attunement of "reticence, shock, and diffidence" as being proper to our transitional times at the end of the Occidental history of metaphysics as we prepare for a leap into another way of being, the *Zhuangzi* speaks in irreverent and playful terms and tones of "leaping into the boundlessness" of the ubiquitous Way, and of "free and easy wandering" in its "unbordered vastness." Regardless of which of these attitudes the reader ends up finding more compelling, by explicating Heidegger's largely implicit and still nascent dialogue with Daoism, in this chapter we venture a few steps down the path of what Heidegger once called "the inevitable dialogue with the East Asian world."[9]

2. Venturing into the Inevitable East–West Dialogue

On only a very few occasions did Heidegger attempt to write in the form of dialogues or conversations.[10] The first of these attempts was *Country Path Conversations*, a set of three dialogues written at the end of the war that Heidegger called, in a letter to his wife, his "Plato book."[11] These dialogues marked the end of nearly a decade of intensely solitary and often cryptic manuscripts, beginning with *Contributions to Philosophy: Of the Event*.[12] It is as if, in these imaginary conversations, Heidegger is preparing not only to share the most intimate and far-reaching dimensions of his path of thought but also to develop that path in conversation with others—and, moreover, given the implicit and, in the end, explicit references to Daoism, with other traditions of thought.

During the decade leading up to *Country Path Conversations*, in addition to writing his volumes of private manuscripts and notebooks, in his public lectures Heidegger carried out a somewhat more exoteric dialogue with ancient Greek and modern German philosophers and, importantly, with Hölderlin's poetry. We also know that, during this time, Heidegger intensified his covert conversations with East Asian texts and scholars. These conversations had been underway since the early 1920s, yet they had waned in the mid-1930s when Heidegger—aligning his philosophy for a time with his own unorthodox vision of "the inner truth and greatness" of National Socialism,[13] a vision that rejected biological racism yet was at times reprehensibly anti-Semitic and at bottom resolutely ethnocentric.[14] In 1936 Heidegger was still xenophobically concerned with "the protection of the European peoples from the Asiatic."[15] In the late 1930s, however, his interest in East Asian thought was evidently rekindled, notably through his contact with Nishitani Keiji (1900–90), a Kyoto School philosopher who was studying in Freiburg between 1937 and 1939, whom Heidegger invited to his home on the weekends to teach him about Zen.[16] Heidegger broke the silence on his decades-long dialogues with various Japanese thinkers when, occasioned by a visit from the literary scholar Tezuka Tomio (1903–83), in 1955 Heidegger composed "From a Conversation on Language (1953–4): Between a Japanese and an Inquirer."[17] It is not difficult to surmise the need Heidegger felt to compose this particular text in the form of a dialogue; it is, after all, a dialogue concerned with the very possibility of dialogue between two radically different traditions, two radically different languages or "houses of being," in only one of which did Heidegger feel at all at home.

In the course of his "From a Conversation on Language," Heidegger suggests that the "entirely different" Western and East Asian linguistic "houses of being" may ultimately "well up from a single source,"[18] and the conversation ends by calling for a shared attunement to an originary silence.[19] Radical cross-cultural dialogue would, it is suggested, need to be accompanied by an even more radical diasigetics, a conversing through silence.[20] Perhaps we might say, in light of Heidegger's claims that the Japanese understood his references to "the nothing" (*das Nichts*) better than did his fellow Europeans,[21] that the dialogue in question is between two different linguistic houses of the same "nothing" that makes way for the disclosure of linguistically determined beings by withdrawing its indeterminate abundance. As Heidegger suggests in *Country Path Conversations*, the paths on which we humans walk and talk afford us, at best, simple "vistas"—or "clearings"—that reveal "just a bit of the abundance" of the surrounding "self-veiling expanse" that abides in the "forest."[22]

Having elsewhere examined the resonances (and some dissonances) between Heidegger's conception of the nothing and that of the Zen thinkers of the Kyoto School,[23] here I shall explore the resonances (and some dissonances) between some of Heidegger's key thoughts, such as *Gelassenheit*, *Weg*, and *das Unnötige*, with key Daoist notions such as *wuwei*, *dao*, and *wuyong*. Before discussing these connections, however, some further reflections on hermeneutical questions of influence and translation are called for.

Although presented in a somewhat prosecutorial manner, Reinhard May's *Heidegger's Hidden Sources: East Asian Influences on His Work*, together with Graham Parkes's valuable supplementary essay, "Rising Sun over Black Forest: Heidegger's Japanese Connections," well document the influence that Heidegger's study of Daoism and Zen exerted—mostly tacitly—on his thought. Beyond the scholarly question of whether Heidegger should have better cited his sources, however, is the philosophical question of how we should understand such influences. In this regard we should attend to a statement Heidegger once made about influence:

> It is the prerogative of great poets, thinkers, and artists that they alone are capable of letting themselves be influenced ... Whatever the Greats give they do not have by way of their originality, but rather from another origin [*Ursprung*], one that makes them sensitive to the "influence" of whatever is originary in other Greats.[24]

The context of this remark is Hölderlin's "ability to be influenced by Pindar and Sophocles—and that now means, to listen in an originary and obedient manner to whatever is originary in the foreign from out of his own origin."[25]

In this context Heidegger also speaks of translation. "Tell me what you think of translation," he remarks, "and I will tell you who you are."[26] Heidegger goes on to tell us what he thinks:

"Translating" ["*Übersetzen*"] is not so much a "*trans*-lating" ["Über-*setzen*"] and passing over into a foreign language with the help of one's own. Rather, translation is more an awakening, clarification, and unfolding of one's own language with the help of an encounter with the foreign language. Reckoned technically, translation means substituting one's own language for the foreign language, or vice versa. Thought in terms of historical reflection, translation is an encounter with a foreign language for the sake of appropriating one's own language.[27]

Specifically, Heidegger is speaking here of the need for the Germans to "learn the Greek language so that the concealed essence of our own historical inception can find its way in the clarity of our word."[28] It is Hölderlin who taught Heidegger that "the free use of one's own" becomes possible only by way of an encounter with the foreign. Hölderlin claimed that in order for the Germans to freely use what is proper to them, namely "the clarity of presentation," they must also learn what is natural not to them but to the Greeks, namely "the fire from heaven" or "holy pathos."[29]

Following Hölderlin, Heidegger was concerned first and foremost with the dialogue between the ancient Greeks and the modern Germans. However, Heidegger also states that this "dialogue with the Greek thinkers and their language . . . remains for us the precondition of the inevitable dialogue with the East Asian world."[30] Thus we can speak of an arc spanning the twin dialogical orientations of Heidegger's thinking—an arc that extends back to the Greeks and then over to East Asia.

Gadamer, who has said that "Heidegger studies would do well to pursue seriously comparisons of his work with Asian philosophies," suggests as a reason for the sparsity of explicit references to Asian thought in his texts that a German scholar of Heidegger's stature would be hesitant to refer to a thought he could only read in translation.[31] Heidegger himself, in his letter to the director of the conference held at the University of Hawaii in 1969 on the theme of "Heidegger and Eastern Thought," after stating that "again and again it has seemed urgent to me that a dialogue take place with the thinkers of what is to us the Eastern world," wrote that "the greatest difficulty in this enterprise always lies, as far as I can see, in the fact that with few exceptions there is no command of the Eastern languages either in Europe or in the United States."[32] As the present volume exemplifies, this situation has fortunately improved over the past few decades.

Heidegger reportedly once claimed in conversation that "for the process of the encounter between Occident and Orient I suppose 300 years [is needed]."[33] If he meant for the process itself, this is not an unreasonable estimate. One thinks of the centuries it required for the radically different traditions that stem from Athens and Jerusalem to be interwoven in Europe, and for the Indian tradition of Buddhism to be appropriated by the Chinese. To be sure, advances in transportation and communication technologies have drastically sped up the pace of cross-cultural encounters. But speed and ease are hardly any guarantee of depth; in fact, they may well be inimical to it. As Heidegger would say, technological facility can make cross-cultural encounters facile, and geographical proximity is no guarantee of genuine nearness.

In any case, Heidegger did not only cautiously approach but on a number of occasions boldly ventured into dialogue with East Asian thought. Most explicitly in "From a Conversation on Language," and mostly implicitly in texts such as *Country Path Conversations*, we find Heidegger not just preparing for but actually engaging in what he called "the inevitable dialogue with the East Asian world."

Heidegger's longstanding interest in Daoism led to his collaboration with a Chinese scholar who had translated the *Daodejing* into Italian. After meeting Heidegger in 1942, Paul Shih-Yi Hsiao (Xiao Shiyi 蕭師毅) recalls having "Now and then ... handed him parts of my translation of the [*Daodejing*] into Italian," and during the summer break of 1946, their plans to work on a collaborative translation of the *Daodejing* into German materialized when Hsiao "met [with Heidegger] regularly every Saturday in his cabin on top of Todtnauberg."[34] They began to translate the "chapters concerning the [*dao*]," but only managed to translate eight such chapters, and unfortunately their translations have not been recovered. Years later, Heidegger reportedly said that it was Hsiao who did not want to continue. This may have been because of what Hsiao referred to as "a slight anxiety that Heidegger's notes might perhaps go beyond what is called for in a translation."[35]

Heidegger himself wavered on whether to venture to translate or to respect the untranslatability of terms such as *dao*. At one point in his later writings Heidegger refers to *dao*—alongside *logos* and his own *Ereignis*—as an example of a "guiding word" that cannot be translated.[36] Yet elsewhere Heidegger is not only willing to translated *dao* as *Weg*, he even goes so far as to say that "The *Dao* could thus be the Way that moves everything [*der alles be-wëgende Weg*], that from which we might first be able to think what reason, mind, meaning, *logos* properly—i.e., from their own essence—mean to say."[37] In the word *dao*, Heidegger seems to have heard, on the cusp of an originary silence, an indication of what he calls in his "From a Conversation on Language" the "single source" that makes dialogue and translation among even the most different languages possible.[38]

For our part, triangulating between the sibling languages of German and English on the one hand and Chinese, a language belonging to a very different language family on the other, we need to take care that we remain hermeneutically attuned to both the perilous pitfalls and fecund possibilities of translation and cross-cultural dialogue. Venturing further down the path of a dialogue between Heidegger's thought and Daoism, we must take care to be neither too timid nor too rash.

3. *Weg* and *Dao*: Heidegger's (Largely Implicit) Conversation with the *Daodejing*

Let us begin by examining the resonances with—and unmistakable influences from—the *Daodejing* that are implicit in *Country Path Conversations* and sometimes made explicit elsewhere in Heidegger's corpus.

It is highly significant that Heidegger's interest in the Daoist classics is rekindled precisely during his turn away from understanding the relation between human being and being in violent and voluntaristic terms, namely in terms of a militant bringing to a stand of the overpowering onslaught of being,[39] and his concomitant turn toward understanding this relation in terms of a non-willful releasement (*Gelassenheit*) to a letting-be (*Seinlassen*).[40] While he borrows the term *Gelassenheit* from Meister Eckhart, Heidegger's stress on non-willing (*Nicht-Wollen*) in *Country Path Conversations*, and his understanding of *Gelassenheit* as a kind of "higher activity" that in fact lies beyond the very "distinction between activity and passivity" defined by the "domain of the will,"[41] bear unmistakable affinities with the notion of *wuwei*—non-doing or non-coercive activity—in the *Daodejing*.[42] Another common theme to be explored is that of a movement of returning to rest in a "Way" (*Weg*, *dao*). For both Heidegger and the *Daodejing*, this Way is not a transcendent being that lords its Will over us, but rather a natural self-unfolding or "enregioning" (*Vergegnis*) of a surrounding "open-region" (*Gegnet*) that lets us be as we release ourselves unto its middle-voiced occurrence.[43]

To begin with, let us look at the obvious, though unacknowledged, connection between Heidegger's discussion of the emptiness of a jug and chapter 11 of the *Daodejing*. In the latter we read: "One molds clay to make a vessel. Yet the vessel is useful because of what is not there . . . Thus while we profit from what is there, it is useful because of what is not there."[44] In *Country Path Conversations* we read: "This nothingness of the jug is really what the jug is."[45] This nothingness or emptiness that is the essence of the jug is in turn said to be brought to abide in the expanse of the whole gathering involved in the event of drinking, that is, in the expanse of "the festival," which in turn belongs to the open-region—that free expanse that gathers all gatherings.[46]

A few years later, in the 1949 lecture "The Thing," the emptiness of the jug again plays an important role in Heidegger's thought.[47] In fact, already in *Contributions to Philosophy* (1936–8) Heidegger had spoken of the "hollow middle" of the jug as "what determines, shapes, and bears the walling action of the walls and their surfaces. The walls and surfaces are merely what is radiated out by that original open realm." Setting it on par with Plato's cave allegory, and in place of "the guiding notion of light," Heidegger uses the emptiness of the jug as a way to speak not just of the essence of a thing but of "the openness of the open" as a "clearing for self-concealment."[48] Here the emptiness of the jug is used as an allegory for the recessive yet vital dimension not just of a being (*ein Seiendes*) but of the open-region of being (*Sein*) or, as Heidegger writes using an archaic spelling, of beyng (*Seyn*). In order to emphasize being's difference from beings, Heidegger sometimes refers to it as "the nothing" (*das Nichts*).[49] The nothing is not a nihilistic privation of being but rather, as Heidegger writes in *Contributions to Philosophy*, "the essential trembling of beyng itself and therefore *is* more than any being."[50]

In order to emphasize the temporally dynamic character of being, Heidegger sometimes refers to it as "the way." Daoists also understand the *dao* in terms of an indeterminate nothingness or emptiness that engenders and harbors determinate beings. In the *Daodejing* we are told that "beings are engendered by the nothing [*you sheng yu wu* 有生於無]," and that "the *dao* is an empty vessel [*chong* 沖], yet use can never fill up its abyssal depth."[51]

Among the many other references to the *dao* in the *Daodejing*, let me single out two more passages for their resonances with Heidegger's later thought:

> The Great Way flows everywhere, able to move left and right. The ten thousand things depend on it for their existence and it does not reject them. It accomplishes its work while remaining anonymous. It clothes and nourishes the ten thousand things, without becoming their master [*zhu* 主].[52]

> The Way never coercively does anything [*wuwei*], and yet it leaves nothing undone. If princes and kings can abide by this, the ten thousand things will naturally develop of their own accord.[53]

Let us now look at some resonant passages from Heidegger's *Country Path Conversations* and other texts. The notion of path or way (*Weg*), as we have said, appears not only in the title but also frequently in the text of *Country Path Conversations*. For example, in the second conversation, after emphasizing that "*from everywhere we must continually turn back to where we properly already are*," the Tower Warden asks: "Do you not notice that we are already walking on the ever reliable country path?"[54] In the first conversation, the Guide speaks of "the silent course of a conversation that moves [*bewegt*] us," and the following exchange ensues:

SCHOLAR: Which indeed means that it brings us onto that path which seems to be nothing other than releasement [*Gelassenheit*] itself.

GUIDE: And yet releasement is something like rest.

SCHOLAR: From this it has suddenly become clearer to me how movement on a way [*Be-wegung*] comes from rest and remains engaged in rest.

GUIDE: Then releasement would not just be the way [*Weg*], but rather the movement (on a way) [*Bewegung*].

SCHOLAR: Where does this strange way go, and where does the movement befitting it rest?

GUIDE: Where else than in the open-region, in relation to which releasement is what it is?[55]

The repose of *Gelassenheit* is not a quietism in the sense of a refraining from action. Rather, there is a stillness, a rest, that is not opposed to action but, like the eye of a storm—or, to use images that occur both in the *Daodejing* and in the *Zhuangzi*, the empty "hub of a wheel" (*gu* 轂) or "hinge of the *dao*" (*dao shu* 道樞)[56]—that is the heart and hearth of action done naturally, without artifice or coercion (*wuwei*). Heidegger writes: "Rest here does not mean the cessation of activity . . . Rest is a grounded repose in the steadfastness of one's own essence."[57] Indeed, this "rest is the hearth and reign of all movement."[58]

One may be reminded of Aristotle's *energeia*, the state of being-at-work of something that has attained to its essence.[59] Yet Heidegger is critical of the notion of "work," especially of the modern ethos of "work and achievement" where work has come to be seen as the positive, with leisure or rest as the negative. This is a reversal, he says, of the understanding of the ancients, "for whom all work was only the interruption, and that means the negation, of leisure, *neg-otium*."[60]

What is at issue is thus a movement that rests in an emergence from and return to that dynamic matrix in which all things belong.

GUIDE: Things rest in the return to the abiding-while of the expanse of their self-belonging.

SCHOLAR: Then can there be a rest in the return, which is after all a movement?

GUIDE: Indeed there can, if the rest is the hearth and the reign of all movement.[61]

In this way the open-region "bethings" (*bedingt*) things and "enregions" (*vereignet*) humans.[62] The restful movement of the latter is what is called "releasement" (*Gelassenheit*).

GUIDE: Releasement comes from the open-region, because releasement properly consists in the human remaining released to the open-region, and doing so by means of the open-region. The human is released to it in his essence, insofar as he originally belongs to the open-region. He belongs to it, insofar as he is inceptually a-propriated to the open-region, and indeed by the open-region itself.[63]

Once again we can hear unmistakable resonances with the *Daodejing*:

> Attain to the extremity of emptiness [*xu* 虛] by steadily maintaining stillness. The myriad things creatively arise, and I watch them turn back. Having grown and flourished, each one returns home to its root. Returning to the root is what is called stillness [*gui gen yue jing* 歸根曰靜].[64]

Daoist sages are able to see the movement of returning to stillness that is the way-being of beings because they have attuned themselves to the stillness that is at the heart of this movement.

At the end of the second of the *Country Path Conversations*, the Teacher says: "We have long been moving ourselves [*uns . . . bewegen*] on a between-field [*Zwischenfeld*]," and the conversation continues:

GUEST: You mean between fields on the country path [*Feldweg*]?
TEACHER: That would be splendid.
TOWER WARDEN: But it is not so; to walk on the country path [*auf dem Feldweg gehen*] does not yet necessarily mean to celebrate this path [*diesen Weg begehen*]—
TEACHER: such that it moves us.[65]

What is the "it" which moves us? Evidently it is the field-path of the open-region. Yet if we understand this path or this region as a being, perhaps as the highest being, then we are still thinking in terms of an ontic opposition of beings and thus in terms of the activity or passivity of one being vis-à-vis another. What is at stake is not a matter of obeying the Will of the Way—as if it were a transcendent subject who lords its will over us—but rather a matter of attuning ourselves to and thus participating in its spontaneous movement.

Heidegger accordingly distances his notion of *Gelassenheit* from the use of this term in Christianity, where its sense remains within "the domain of the will." For German Christian mystics, *Gelassenheit* signifies the serene state of mind attained through a *releasement from* one's own egoistic self-will and a corresponding *releasement unto* the Will of God. Even Meister Eckhart, according to Heidegger, thinks of *Gelassenheit* within the domain of the will.[66] The Scholar in the first of Heidegger's *Country Path Conversations* says that "what we are calling releasement evidently does not mean the casting off of sinful selfishness and the letting go of self-will in favor of the divine will."[67] He later asks, "but how is releasement related to what is not a willing?" and the following exchange ensues:

SAGE: After all that we have said of the bringing to abide of the abiding expanse, of the letting rest in the return, and of the regioning of the open-region, the open-region can hardly be spoken of as will.

SCHOLAR: That the open-region's enregioning and bethinging essentially exclude themselves from all effecting and causing already shows how decisively all that pertains to the will is foreign to them.[68]

Heidegger attempts to think that in which the movement of things and humans rest, not as a transcendent being, but rather as a surrounding open-region, an abiding expanse that is not a static space but rather a dynamic way that affords us our meandering field-paths.

In a later text, Heidegger explicitly mentions *dao* in his attempt to express this most central of his thoughts.

[T]he way belongs in what we are here calling the region. Intimatingly said, the region is the regioning of the clearing that frees, wherein all that is cleared and freed, and all that conceals itself, together attain the free expanse. The freeing and sheltering character of this region is the way making movement [*Be-wëgung*] that yields those ways that belong to the region . . . The region is first a region in that it provides ways. The region moves [us] along a way [*Sie be-wëgt*] . . . The word "way" probably is a primordial word [*Urwort*] of language that speaks to the meditative mind of humans. The guiding word in the poetic thinking of Laozi is *Dao* and means "properly" way . . . The *Dao* could thus be the Way that moves everything [*der alles be-wëgende Weg*] . . . the Way that draws everything onto its path. All is Way.[69]

The *Daodejing* tells us that all beings depend on the Way and yet, "being always without desire [*wuyu* 無欲]," it "does not become their master."[70] Insofar as one is "capable of non-coercive action [*wuwei*]," we are told, one is able to "lead without lording over."[71] In doing so we are following the manner of the *dao*, whose movement is compared with the inconspicuous power of water that "benefits the ten thousand things without contending with them."[72] People are to model themselves on the Earth, which in turn models itself on Heaven, which in turn models itself on the Way. The Way, for its part (which is not in fact a part but rather the dynamic whole in which everything else participates), models itself only on its own "natural spontaneity" (*ziran* 自然).[73]

For Heidegger, in order to return to an attentive attunement to the natural movement of this non-willful Way, one has to let go of the will (*Wille*). As a transitional step toward this releasement of and from the will, one must paradoxically "will non-willing." That is to say, one must move through and beyond "willfully renouncing willing" in order to release oneself to a mode of being that "does not at all pertain to the will."[74] Analogously, the *Daodejing* says that "sages desire to be without desire" in order to return to the Way that is "always without desires."[75] In this freedom from desire, the sage returns to a state of "unhewn wood [*pu* 樸]."[76] "Without desire one attains peaceful tranquility, and the world settles itself of its own accord."[77]

Yet this peaceful tranquility does not issue in an inactive quietism. Rather, as we have seen Heidegger say, this "rest is the hearth and reign of all movement."[78] By attuning ourselves to this hearth of stillness in the midst of movement, we can stir up a different kind of motivation. By returning to the root, the empty hub of the wheel of the Way, we can allow our desires to stem from and be guided by that movement of the Way which is itself without desire. The opening chapter of the *Daodejing*, after saying that the nameless *dao* is the beginning of Heaven and Earth—i.e., of the primal distinction that opens up a world of differences—says that the named *dao* is the mother of the myriad things. It then tells us that whenever we are "without desire we observe its mystery," and whenever we are "with desire we observe its delimited manifestations."[79]

The crucial questions for practice as well as thought are: How can we move among the Way's manifestations without masking over its mystery? How can we remain attuned to the heart of stillness that allows for the most efficacious movement? In the words of the *Daodejing* that Heidegger especially asked to be written out in decorative calligraphy: "Who can, settling the muddy, gradually make it clear? Who can, stirring the tranquil, gradually bring it to life?"[80] How can we act without a subjective will and without subjecting ourselves to a transcendent Will? How can we let ourselves into an engagement (*Sicheinlassen*) with a letting-be (*Seinlassen*) that, it turns out, is the very source of our releasement (*Gelassenheit*)? How can we let our desires stem from and remain rooted in that which is without desire? In refining such questions and thereby intimating answers, both the *Daodejing* and Heidegger's path of thought bring us, step by step and again and again, to the limits of what we are able to think and say; in other words, to the limits as well as to the delimiting power of language.

4. The Limits and the Delimiting Power of Language

This brings us to a final resonance between the *Daodejing* and Heidegger's later thought. It is noteworthy that Heidegger's explicit references to the *dao* are found in his collection of essays entitled *On the Way to Language*. Eventually giving his entire Collected Edition the motto "ways—not works," Heidegger must have been intrigued by fact that *dao* can mean both "way" and "to say."

The character *dao* is often used as a verb to mean "to tell" in the sense of "to show the way," to explain how to do something or how to get somewhere.

Historically, the Daoist sage has been described as a member of the *daojia* 道家, that is, one who belongs to the school, family, or house of the *dao*. Only one who houses and is housed by, embodies and inhabits the Way is able to serve as a guide to others. A guide is intimately familiar with a way and thus can lead others down it, as distinct from a "scholar" who studies pathways traveled by others or a "scientist" who follows an established method of knowing and measuring things objectively. Heidegger uses the term *Weiser* in the first of the *Country Path Conversations* in the sense of a "guide" rather than its typical meaning of a "wise man" who possesses wisdom (*Weisheit*). Heidegger's *Weiser* is someone who can show (*weisen*) the way, the manner (*Weise*) of doing something, in this case the manner of proceeding down a path of thought that leads into unknown regions.[81]

In contrast to previous and contemporaneous uses of the term *dao* to mean a method of achieving some end, whether it be a method of farming or of cultivating virtue, the Daoists used the word somewhat ironically to indicate that which cannot be reduced to a set method to achieve a preconceived end. The ultimate Way precedes and exceeds our human intentions to contrive and control. How, then, can the Way be known or shown when it is not a specific method for achieving a definite end? Like Heidegger's *Weiser*, the Daoist sage does not seek to objectively know and definitively name the ultimate Way, but rather to "go-into-nearness" to it and let it guide our thought and action.[82]

The *Daodejing* famously begins by saying that "the *dao* that can be said [literally *dao*-ed] is not the abiding *dao*."[83] This inceptual text of Chinese thought begins, in contrast to the Gospel of John, with the self-effacing claim that in the beginning was *not* the Word, that the Way and the Life cannot be identified with the Logos. And yet, the opening chapter of the *Daodejing* goes on to say, this nameless origin of the primal distinction between Heaven and Earth, when named, is the mother of the ten thousand things. Language allows things to be; but language itself springs from something nameless, something that can only be named with a pseudonym, such as "*dao*."

> There is something nebulous yet whole, born before Heaven and Earth. Tranquil and void, it stands alone, unchanging. Going around everywhere, it is never exhausted or endangered. It may be regarded as the mother of all under Heaven. I do not know its name. Sheltering it with a pseudonym, I call it *dao*.[84]

Is Heidegger's being more closely wedded to language than is the *dao* of the *Daodejing*? To be sure, language plays a crucial role in Heidegger's thought. Heidegger calls on us to remain "on the way to language." And yet, the path of Heidegger's thought leads us not only to appreciate the delimiting power of language but also to peer beyond its limits. For Heidegger, while it is language that discloses the being of beings, it is silence that attunes us to the concealed dimension of being (or beyng, *Seyn*) which enables that linguistic disclosure to eventuate in the first place.

In the "Essence of Language," Heidegger meditates on Stefan George's lines: "So I renounce and sadly see: Where word breaks off no thing may be [*So lernt ich traurig den verzicht: Kein ding sei wo das wort gebricht*]."[85] It is language that allows things to be. Language is the house of being. Poetry is the temple in the center of the "precinct" (*Bezirk, templum*) wherein the determinations of a clearing of unconcealment are first marked off (*bezirkt, temnein, tempus*) by the word.[86] Language, in other words, domesticates being; it allows the world to be meaningful and thus makes our lives livable. But what about the wider field, the open-region, in which the poetic precinct is marked off and the linguistic house of being is built? What about what Maurice Merleau-Ponty calls "the wild region" (*la région sauvage*) that frees one from being a prisoner in one's own culture and enables one to communicate with other cultures?[87] If "language is the house of being,"[88] as Heidegger claims, a house is a home, replies the Zen philosopher Ueda Shizuteru (1926–2019), only in the process of leaving and returning to it; otherwise it is a bird cage or a prison house.[89]

Heidegger, in fact, does not simply equate language with being. Language, he says, is "the language of being like clouds are the clouds of the sky."[90] The clouds in this image are like visible, delimited configurations of the wide open—and in itself invisible—sky. The blueness of the sky is, as it were, a trace, a subtle determination, that hints back into the pure openness of the sky, the sky that withdraws from all perception, like the darkness of a starless and moonless night. The poet can name being only because he or she "reaches sooner into the abyss" of this starless night. "The poet could never go through the experience he undergoes with the word if the experience were not attuned to sadness [*die Trauer*], to the mood of releasement [*Gelassenheit*] into the nearness of what is withdrawn but at the same time held in reserve for an originary advent."[91]

In the final paragraph of the first of his solitary manuscripts, *Contributions to Philosophy*, Heidegger writes: "Language is grounded in silence."[92] Near the beginning of that text he writes: "Words fail us; they do so originally and not merely occasionally." And yet, he goes on to say, "this failing us is the inceptual condition for the self-unfolding possibility of an original (poetic) naming of being." He then asks himself: "When will such a time come?"[93] Some eight years later, in a note included in the supplements to the first of the *Country Path Conversations*, he writes: "Of all goods the most dangerous is language, because it cannot keep safe the unspoken—(not because it veils too much, but rather because it divulges too much)."[94] Language is the house of being; it domesticates a world for us. But in doing so it covers over the originary ground of silence; speaking inevitably betrays the unspoken. And yet, in an adjacent note Heidegger writes: "Where else could the unspoken be purely kept, heeded, other than in true conversation."[95]

In the third of the *Country Path Conversations*, Heidegger suggests that "*logos* originally means gathering," such that the essence of the human as *zōon logon echon* "consists in being in the gathering, namely, the gathering toward the all-unifying One," which is "the divine itself."[96] This all-unifying One, however, is not "the monotonous homogeneity of the indistinct," but rather: "What is selfsame can only be what is different; indeed the purest selfsame rests in the most different. I would almost like to assert the reverse: The different rests in the pure selfsame."[97]

We can thus surmise that it is through conversation between those who are most different that we can re-attune ourselves to the One that gathers all in such a manner that lets us be in our differences. Can we not infer that it is by way of East–West philosophical dialogue that we are best able to attune ourselves to the formless open-region that surrounds all of our culturally and linguistically formed horizons, to the *dao* as "the Way that moves everything . . . the Way that draws everything onto its path"?[98]

5. Zhuangzi's Use of the Useless and Heidegger's Necessity of the Unnecessary

We will return to the topic of language and silence later on. For now, let us turn our attention to the end of *Country Path Conversations*, where Heidegger suddenly and quite unexpectedly quotes a passage from the *Zhuangzi* on "the necessity of the unnecessary." The quotation is particularly surprising insofar as it caps off a discussion of the special historical role to be played by the Germans as "the people of poets and thinkers" who "in the noblest manner wait" upon the coming of the word, the word that would determine anew the essence of humanity. The Germans purportedly must set out again on the patient path of becoming who they truly are, having been led astray into a devastating nationalism that self-assertively "wills," rather than nonwillfully "waits" on, its essence.[99] The German *Volk* is said to be able to

> squander its essence purely on the unnecessary. For what is more unnecessary than the waiting that waits on the coming? What is more necessary than getting down to business with the given facts, remaking what is present at hand, and moving forward what has existed heretofore?[100]

The conversation continues as follows:

OLDER MAN: In other words, that factual sense of reality which they claim lets humans first stand with both feet squarely on the ground.

YOUNGER MAN: That sense which drives peoples to secure a place for themselves on the earth, a place on which they can stand fast and create close to the facts in order to be effective and validated. And yet, nonetheless, this necessary matter [*Nötiges*] of theirs can never be without the unnecessary [*das Unnötige*].

OLDER MAN: Such that the necessity of the unnecessary [*die Notwendigkeit des Unnötigen*] would remain to be thought.[101]

The unnecessary is not what we need in the manner of all the daily necessities that drive us about in the business and busyness of our lives in a world of predetermined meanings and goals. Rather, "the unnecessary requires us and our essence like the sound . . . requires the instrument which gives it off."[102] It would be the calling of the Germans to "learn to know the necessity of the unnecessary and, as learners, teach it to the peoples [*den Völkern*] . . . And for a long time this may perhaps be the sole content of our teaching: the urgent need and the necessity of the unnecessary."[103]

It is thus all the more striking that, in this context of speaking of the special historical endowment and task of the German people, the Older Man concludes the conversation by quoting a conversation he claims to have copied down in his student days from "a historiological account of Chinese philosophy":

The conversation goes like this:
The one said: "You are talking about the unnecessary."
The other said: "A person must first have recognized the unnecessary before one can talk with him about the necessary. The Earth is wide and large, and yet, in order to stand, the human needs only enough space to be able to put his foot down. But if directly next to his foot a crevice were to open up that dropped down into the underworld, then would the space where he stands still be of use to him?"
The one said: "It would be of no more use to him."
The other said: "From this the necessity of the unnecessary is clearly apparent."[104]

The conversation retold here can be found in chapter 26 of the *Zhuangzi*.[105] Brook Ziporyn translates it as follows:

Huizi said to Zhuangzi, "your words are useless!"
Zhuangzi said, "it is only when you know uselessness that you can understand anything about the useful. The Earth is certainly vast and wide, but a man at any time only uses as much of it as his two feet can cover. But if you were to dig away all the earth around his feet, down to the Yellow Springs, would that little patch he stands on be of any use to him?"
Huizi said, "it would be useless."
Zhuangzi said, "then the usefulness of the useless [*wuyong zhi weiyong* 無用之為用] should be quite obvious."[106]

The *Zhuangzi* frequently refers to a huge twisted tree as both an example and an analogy for the usefulness of being useless. "It is precisely because it is so useless that it has lived so long."[107] "The lacquer tree is useful and thus it is cut down. Everyone knows how useful usefulness is, but no one seems to know how useful uselessness is."[108] Only the "spirit man" is said to know how to rely on the same worthlessness as such a worthless tree.[109]

At the end of the first chapter of the *Zhuangzi*, in another dialogue with his logician friend Huizi, Zhuangzi is told: "I have a huge tree which people call the Stink Tree. The trunk is swollen and gnarled, impossible to align with any level or ruler. The branches are twisted and bent, impossible to align with any T-square or carpenter's arc . . . and your words are similarly big but useless." Zhuangzi responds:

> Why not plant it in our homeland of not-even-anything [*wu heyou zhi xiang* 無何有之鄉], the vast wilds of open nowhere [*guang mo zhi ye* 廣莫之野]? Then you could loaf and wander there, doing lots of nothing there at its side, and take yourself a nap, far-flung and unfettered, there beneath it. It will never be cut down by ax or saw. Nothing will harm it. Since it has nothing for which it can be used, what could entrap or afflict it?[110]

We generally attend only to the limited ground directly under our feet at this moment, that is, only to what is deemed useful or necessary in our current horizon of understanding; and we understand and use things according to their position in the network of meanings, according to the role they play in our concerned dealings with things. But "is it not absurd to judge [the tree] by whether it does what is or is not called for by its position, by what role it happens to play?"[111]

According to the early Heidegger of *Being and Time*, we understand beings first and foremost as "equipment" (*Zeuge*) in a world, that is to say, in a "totality of significations" structured by a chain of "in-order-to" links leading to an ultimate "for-the-sake-of-which" (*Umwillen*), the life-project projected by our will (*Wille*).[112] However, in *Country Path Conversations*, having turned away from the voluntaristic undertones of his earlier thought to a fundamental attunement of *Gelassenheit*, in implicit consonance with the Daoist *wuwei* and with explicit reference to a passage from the *Zhuangzi*, Heidegger now stresses that without the surrounding undisclosed and apparently "useless" and "unnecessary" expanse of earth[113]—the "open-region" or "open nowhere"—we could not move, that is to say, we could not look out beyond our current horizons to open up new ways of understanding and experiencing the world. And this includes new ways of seeing trees. Rather than first and foremost seeing the forest as "timber,"[114] the later Heidegger calls on us "for once to let [the tree] stand where it stands . . . Because to this day, thought has never let the tree stand where it stands."[115] Where it stands, Zhuangzi would say, is not in a world centered on us and structured by our pragmatic concerns and technological *teloi*, but rather, like us, it originally stands in its and our "homeland of not-even-anything, the vast wilds of open nowhere."

In "Wege zur Aussprache" (1937), Heidegger writes that philosophy involves a kind of

> knowing the essence of things, which is always concealing itself anew, by leaping ahead and opening up new domains and viewpoints for inquiry. Precisely for this reason this knowing is never directly useful. It only ever has an indirect effect, in that philosophical meditation prepares new perspectives and standards for all our comportments and decisions.[116]

In this sense, all our scientific and everyday dealings with "facts," with things as they are disclosed within our current horizons of understanding, depend on philosophy's wider outlook, which must remain ever attuned to the usefulness of the useless. Lost in the rat race of managing apparent necessities, we cover over the more profound need we have of "the unnecessary." "Running around amidst beings" (*Umtrieben an das Seiende*),[117] we remain oblivious of our primal relation to being (*Sein*).

Around the time he was writing *Country Path Conversations* (the last conversation bears the date May 8, 1945), Heidegger wrote to his wife, in a letter dated March 2, 1945: "On the essence of the unnecessary (which is what I mean by 'Being') I recently found the short conversation between two Chinese thinkers that I'm copying out for you."[118] On June 27 of that year, just before departing Messkirch and Wildenstein to return to what had become occupied Freiburg, Heidegger gave a talk entitled "Poverty" (*Die Armut*) to a small audience, a talk in which he developed further the idea of the necessity of the unnecessary by way of interpreting the following two passages from Hölderlin's essays:

> For us everything is concentrated upon the spiritual, we have become poor in order to become rich.[119]

> Neither from himself alone, nor solely from the objects that surround him, can the human being have the experience that more than a mechanical course, that a spirit, a god, is in the world. But he can indeed experience this in a more lively relationship, exalted above pressing needs, in which "he" stands with that which surrounds him.[120]

The gist of Heidegger's speech is conveyed in the following lines:

> To be truly poor means to be such that one is deprived of nothing except what is unnecessary . . . To be truly deprived means not to be able to be without what is unnecessary and thus immediately and exclusively belonging to what is unnecessary . . . What is unnecessary is what does

not arise out of a necessity or need [*Not*], that is, what does not arise out of compulsion [*Zwang*], but out of what is free and open [*das Freie*] . . . What is freed is what is released into its essence and protected from the compulsion of necessity. What frees in freedom averts or overturns in advance necessity. Freedom is that which [in this sense] turns necessity [*Das Freiende der Freiheit wendet zum voraus die Not ab oder um. Die Freiheit ist das die Not Wenden*] . . . Freedom means averting or overturning necessity [*Not-Wendigkeit*], insofar as what frees is not necessitated by a need and is thus what is unnecessary . . . Now, beyng is what lets each and every being be what it is and how it is, and is thus precisely that which frees, that which lets each being rest in its essence, thus safeguarding it.[121]

This talk on "Poverty" is a rich supplement to the end of *Country Path Conversations*. What is of particular importance to us here is the convergence that occurs between Heidegger's interpretations of Hölderlin and the *Zhuangzi*. This convergence, mediated by Heidegger's own thinking, is surely a remarkable event of intertraditional cross-fertilization. What is especially remarkable is that, at the end of *Country Path Conversations*, the usual pattern of Heidegger's text is reversed, such that it is the Chinese source that appears on the surface while Hölderlin remains in the background. It also appears that, in this case, given that the talk on "Poverty" was presented a month and a half after the third conversation was completed, Heidegger's reading of the *Zhuangzi* may have informed his reading of Hölderlin rather than, or at least as much as, the other way around.

6. Heidegger's Somber vs Zhuangzi's Playful Attunement

Of course, we should not merely celebrate convergences without also taking into account divergences. We cannot simply conclude that the *Zhuangzi* and Hölderlin have been synthesized in Heidegger without also engaging in a *diairesis* that shows how this resonating sameness also implies dissonant difference. Genuine dialogue, after all, entails not only a *Horizontverschmelzung* but also, at the same time, an *Auseinandersetzung* or at least a clarification of the alterity of different ways of thinking and experiencing. Since fully staging a critical dialogue between the *Zhuangzi* and Heidegger's thought is beyond the scope of what can be done here, I will have to restrict myself to sketching, in broad and bold strokes, a few indictors.[122] Indeed, given the limited space I have remaining to venture into this vast topic, I will need to proceed somewhat recklessly. As Zhuangzi says, "I'm going to try speaking some reckless words. How about listening just as recklessly?"[123]

Let us return to the issue of language before turning to the issue of temperament and tone. At the end of chapter 26 of the *Zhuangzi*—the chapter from which Heidegger quotes at the end of *Country Path Conversations*—Zhuangzi asks: "Where can I find a man who has forgotten words so I can have a few words with him?"[124] Here, I would like to suggest, we find intimated both the proximity to and the distance from Heidegger. First the proximity: Both agree that language occurs as a movement between silence and speech. The speaking of language, we might say, takes place in a wider field of silence, just as useful things require a wider field of uselessness. For Heidegger, primordial speech, poetic naming, stems from a silent attunement to "the peal of stillness [*das Geläut der Stille*]."[125] Determinate things come to presence and are preserved in words; yet words devolve into "idle chatter" when their silent origin—the withdrawing or self-concealing indeterminate fullness of being—is forgotten.

Analogously, in the *Zhuangzi* we are told:

> When the Way is seen clearly, that just means that it has not really been encountered, so debate about it is no match for silence. The Way cannot be learned, so hearing about it is no match for plugging up your ears . . . The Way cannot be heard; whatever is heard is not it. The Way cannot be seen; whatever is seen is not it. The Way cannot be spoken; whatever is spoken is not it. Know that what forms has no form. The Way corresponds to no name.[126]

The Way, the *dao*, as we have seen both the *Daodejing* and Heidegger say, is a provisional name for the unspoken "mystery of mysteries" that allows "thoughtful saying." Hence, what is at issue is a circulating movement between silence and speech or, as the Zen philosopher Ueda Shizuteru puts it, an irreducible movement of "exiting language and exiting into language."[127] The *Daodejing* says that "inversion [*fan* 反] is the movement of the *dao*,"[128] and in the *Zhuangzi* we read of "the Great Return [*da gui* 大歸]": "The formless goes into form; the formed goes back into the formlessness."[129] This circulating movement characterizes the relation between silent attentiveness to the nameless and nebulous dynamic whole of the *dao* and linguistic determinations of its provisional parts.

According to the *Zhuangzi*, words ensnare us; in using them we all too easily end up getting used by them, caught in our own trap. "A fish trap is there for the fish. When you have got hold of the fish, you forget the trap . . . Words are there for the intent. When you have got hold of the intent, you forget the words."[130] This is why Zhuangzi wants to have a few words with a man who has forgotten words. His emphasis is on the forgetting of the words in order to return to the fluidity of the *dao*, in order to freely move with and within the movement of the world. Words come and go as a natural part of this spontaneous process, but in holding on to them they end up holding us up.

Now, while the Daoist understanding of the movement between going forth into the linguistic delimitations of form and silently returning to a formless wellspring of possibilities resonates, as we have seen, with the thought of Heidegger and the poetry of Hölderlin, I think there is also a difference in stress, a difference in predominant orientation, and, especially with regard to the *Zhuangzi*, a difference in tone and fundamental attunement. Whereas Heidegger and Hölderlin mourn the loss of originary words and reverently wait upon the arrival of new ones, the *Zhuangzi* both playfully undermines old ossified words and impishly innovates new and unusual ones.

In *The Event*, a private manuscript written in 1941/2, Heidegger suggests that the orientation of the thinker and the poet are opposite and complementary. Whereas "thinking is a becoming at home in being un-homelike," poetizing is a "becoming at home out of being un-homelike."[131] The thinker opens us up to the silent abyss (*Abgrund*); the poet grounds it with a new name. Heidegger's thinker anticipates and defers to the poet; the thoughtful journey into the abyss is for the sake of a poetic return. On the whole, one could say that the tandem movement between Heidegger's thinker and poet accords with the twin comportments toward language found in the *Zhuangzi*.

However, the fundamental attunement Heidegger claims is appropriate to our Occidental onto-historical epoch is strikingly different from that of this ancient Chinese text. The fundamental attunement of the other inception (*der andere Anfang*) of post-metaphysical thinking, Heidegger writes in *Contributions to Philosophy*, entails "restraint [*die Verhaltenheit*], shock [*das Erschrecken*], and diffidence [*die Scheu*],"[132] and elsewhere he says that the fundamental attunement of Hölderlin's poetry is "holy mourning [*heilige Trauer*]," understood as a "resolve to renounce the gods of old" that is at the same time a "resolute readiness for awaiting the divine" to return.[133] For Heidegger, in short, both the thinker and the poet are needed in a time of need, and they respond to the necessity of the unnecessary with "pain" and "suffering" in an "attunement of a holy mourning in readied distress."[134] For Heidegger, the journey along the path of thought and poetry is a sober occasion. "Sobriety," he writes in an essay on Hölderlin, "is the sensibility that is always ready for the holy."[135] And in *Country Path Conversations* we are told that thinking is "the festival of sobriety."[136] The *Zhuangzi*, on the other hand, in order to explain the manner in which the sage "harbors himself in naturalness [*cang yu tian* 藏於天]" such that nothing can harm him, uses the analogy of a drunken man who falls from a cart but remains uninjured.[137] For the *Zhuangzi*, moving in tune with the Way is not a matter of sobriety, pain, suffering, or mourning, but rather, as the title of its first chapter announces, a playful process of "free and easy wandering" (*xiaoyao you* 逍遙遊).

Not unlike the later Heidegger, the *Zhuangzi* calls for a freedom that would come from a letting go of the will and a return to that in which we belong, a return to our place of participation in the natural movement of a Way, the fundamental or rather abyssal character of which cannot be ultimately fathomed or reduced to fixed formulas. But the mood of Zhuangzi's recovery of freedom is very different; it is playful, ironic, and often audacious. Not only would Zhuangzi readily accept Heraclitus's invitation to find the divine in the kitchen, to a reverent inquirer wanting to know where to look for the *dao* he ends up irreverently saying: "It is in the piss and shit."[138]

The authors of the *Zhuangzi* call for a return to a primordial naturalness covered over by what is seen as the artificiality of Confucian culture. The problem is not that we lack words that let things be; the problem is that words have become rigid borders that separate things from each other and from us. The problem is not that we need "grounders of the abyss [*Gründer des Abgrundes*]";[139] the problem is that the creative abyss has been covered over and stifled with too much grounding.

Both Heidegger and Zhuangzi compare thinking and language to cultivating fields, but the different manners in which they speak of this is revealing. Heidegger ends his "Letter on Humanism" with the following lines: "With its saying, thinking lays inconspicuous furrows in language. They are still more inconspicuous than the furrows that the farmer, slow of step, draws through the fields."[140] Zhuangzi's contemporary Mengzi 孟子 (Mencius) spoke of cultivating the innate goodness of the human heart with a similar metaphor: The farmer cannot get sprouts to grow faster by pulling on them; he has to "let" them grow in an attentive manner that is neither simply active nor simply passive.[141] Among Confucians, Mencius is closest to the Daoist preference for naturalness over human artifice. But even he is still too Confucian, too cultivated, too ritualistic, for Zhuangzi.

Zhuangzi speaks of the cultivated field of language in the following manner. "The Way has never had sealed borders, and words have never had consistency. It is due to [the establishment of a definition of] 'this' [as opposed to 'that'] that there are [now] rigid boundaries."[142] The word translated here as "rigid boundaries" is *zhen* 畛, which literally indicates the ridges in rice paddies. What Zhuangzi apparently laments is the *overcultivation* of the field, which covers over and rigidifies the original fluidity of the *dao* and of language.

Like so much of the *Daodejing* and the *Zhuangzi*, this can be understood as a critique of Confucianism, whose Way involves methods of cultivating the moral traits of benevolence (*ren* 仁), righteousness (*yi* 義), and ritual (*li* 禮). The *Daodejing* speaks of the decline from the spontaneously natural Way into artificial Confucian morality as follows: "When *dao* is lost, then there is virtue. When virtue is lost, then there is benevolence; when benevolence is lost, then there is righteousness; when righteousness is lost, then there is ritual."[143] The first half of the traditional version of the *Daodejing* is accordingly focused on the *dao*, and the second half on virtue (*de* 德). "Virtue" can be used as a translation of the Daoist *de* insofar as we understand it in its literal meaning of "power," here the native power effortlessly displayed by a thing or person when it remains in accord with the Way that generates and flows through all things. "The *dao* generates beings and *de* nourishes them ... The *dao* is revered and *de* is valued not because this is commanded but rather always just spontaneously so."[144] The *Daodejing* accordingly calls not for forward progress in the elaboration and cultivation of moral virtues, but rather for a radical return to the virtuosity that naturally issues from dwelling in accord with the Way.

In a similar manner, the *Zhuangzi* proclaims that "the ancients" returned all the way to a point prior to the establishment of artificial boundaries between things.

> The understanding of the ancients really got all the way there. Where had it arrived? To the point where, for some, there never had existed so-called things ... Next, there were those for whom things existed but never any definite boundaries between them. Next were those for whom there were boundaries but never any rights and wrongs. When rights and wrongs waxed bright, the Way began to wane.[145]

It is important to point out that, although there are "primitivist" strands in some later chapters of the *Zhuangzi*, the author(s) of the "Inner Chapters" and the later chapters written in their vein are not simply nostalgic for a bygone age. Even when they strategically employ primitivist tropes, the predominant voices of "Zhuangzi" and his surrogates in the text, it seems to me, do not simply want to return people and fields to the wild and to forbid farming and cultivation. Rather, they suggest that their (and they would surely also say our) society has gone too far in the direction of artificial cultivation such that people need to return, not to a static and silent state of formlessness, but rather to the very movement of going forth into form and returning to formlessness. After all, it is this ceaseless movement of inversion between speech and silence, form and emptiness, that is the *dao*.

The *Zhuangzi* is especially critical of the Confucian doctrine of the "rectification of names" (*zhengming* 正名), according to which names should be fixed, by the ruler, in order to clearly indicate distinctions, relations, and duties. This doctrine was championed by Xunzi 荀子, the Confucian counterpart of Mengzi and sharp critic of the Daoists. Xunzi thought that human nature was naturally bad and in need of artificial rectification. His preferred metaphor was not agricultural but rather technological, namely forcefully "steaming and bending ... wood straight as a plumb line into a wheel."[146]

The *Zhuangzi*, on the other hand, agrees with the *Daodejing* in thinking that humans should emulate the *dao*, which models itself only on its own natural spontaneity.[147] It also agrees that this natural spontaneity of the *dao*, while providing the power of naming, cannot itself ultimately be named.

According to the *Zhuangzi*, it is the rigid distinctions we make between "this" and "that," solidified through unequivocal linguistic codifications, that alienate us from the fluid movement of the *dao* and the ability to freely respond to the situation at hand by way of balancing perspectives. "Thus the sage uses various rights and wrongs to harmonize with others and yet remain at rest in the middle of Heaven the Potter's Wheel [*tian jun* 天鈞]."[148] "Heaven" (*tian*) in the *Zhuangzi* means the natural Way of things, and the sinograph for "Potter's Wheel" (*jun*), Ziporyn points out in a footnote, also means "equality." "The two meanings converge in the consideration of the even distribution of clay made possible by the constant spinning of the wheel."[149] The constant spinning of the wheel refers to the fluid assumption of various perspectives as appropriate to shifting circumstances. In a related metaphor for finding the pivotal empty center of flexible response-ability, the *Zhuangzi* says: "When the hinge is fitted into the socket, it can respond endlessly."[150]

Let us now imaginatively ask: What would Heidegger say to Zhuangzi, and how would Zhuangzi respond to Heidegger? After all, thinking about what they would say to each other can help us think about what they have to say to those of us who read them both. Heidegger would presumably say that Zhuangzi does not understand that we in the modern West and Westernizing world are living in a time of urgent need (*Not*)—a need ironically evinced precisely in our apparent lack of need (*die Not der Notlosigkeit*)[151]—a time of distress in the face of the flight of the gods and the abandonment of beyng, a time when originary language is reticent to speak. For Heidegger, the proper relation to the unnecessary is, after all, one of distressful need; modern humans in particular urgently need to learn to let language speak so as to ground the abyss of the unnecessary.

Zhuangzi, on the other hand, wrote at a time when, he felt, too much had already been said; too many established names had already been used and had covered over the creative wellspring of the nameless and useless. And he would probably think that a *Gesamtausgabe* of more than a hundred volumes is too much to write in any circumstance, especially if what really matters is, as Heidegger himself claimed, "simple saying."[152] Zhuangzi would probably think that Heidegger's concern with grounding the abyss is still captive to the will to fathom and found the ground of things that Heidegger himself criticizes.[153] Heidegger's thought prepares for a leap (*Sprung*) into another inception, an inception that is thought to require a grounding of the abyss. Yet Zhuangzi would playfully prod: Why not just let go into the abyss? In other words: "Leap into the boundless [*wujing* 無竟] and make it your home!"[154]

Zhuangzi would probably think that Heidegger is holding himself back from unreservedly letting go into the natural Way of the great expanse of the "open-region." In *Country Path Conversations* Heidegger writes: "The expanse carries us to what is objectless, and yet also keeps us from dissolving into it."[155] And later on: "In waiting, the human-being [*das Menschenwesen*] becomes gathered in attentiveness to that in which he belongs, yet without letting himself get carried away into and absorbed in it."[156] For Zhuangzi, however, one need not fear dissolving or being absorbed into the Way, insofar as it is the creative source as well as the solvent of provisional distinctions and fluid identities.

"Having emptied my will," Zhuangzi says, "I have no destination and no idea of where I have arrived at . . . I ramble and relax in unbordered vastness [*panghuang hu pinghong* 彷徨乎馮閎]."[157] In this leap into a "playful wandering in the great void [*you hu taixu* 遊乎太虛],"[158] would one lose oneself, one's humanity, one's linguistic and ethnic identity, even one's very— and very Western, especially American, insistence on—individuality? Is this what it would mean to become what the *Zhuangzi* calls "the Consummate Person [who] has no fixed identity, the Spirit Man [who] has no particular merit, [or] the Sage [who] has no fame"?[159] It would seem not since, after all, we meet the most colorful array of strikingly unique characters throughout the *Zhuangzi*. It seems that, in wandering freely through the dense forests and vast beaches of the open-region, we would not simply come to disdain or avoid the horizonal places that give our lives meaning and the borderlines that provide us with personal and political identities— but we would gain the freedom to use all these markers of identity without being used by them, to draw these lines in the sand rather than set them in stone, to casually camp out rather than willfully wall ourselves up in our current cultural clearings.

Perhaps one would then become more genuinely capable of entering into a dialogue between traditions of thought and language, having found one's true home in a never-ending journey of going forth and returning—not to a land determined by blood, soil, language, or tradition, but rather to the unbordered vastness of the open-region, the formless nothing that we all share in common as the nameless wellspring of all our different ways of being and speaking.

Let me end with that suggestion, and with some corresponding questions. The *Zhuangzi* was, to be sure, written in a very different time and place. But does that mean that it is decidedly less, or potentially more significant for us? It apparently means that it is less useful, less necessary. After all, we don't need to read an ancient Chinese text to go about our business in the modern Western and Westernizing world. But might doing so help awaken us to the necessity of the unnecessary, the usefulness of the useless? If we want to attune ourselves to the all-encompassing open-region, should we not look as far as possible beyond our current horizons? If we want to understand the universe—the unbordered vastness—that we all share in common, should we not engage in a conversation with what is most different? Such has been the intent of this chapter, which has attempted to nurture the nascent dialogue between Heidegger and Daoism, and in particular to show how together—across great distances and differences—they have much to teach us regarding the Useless Way of Unnecessary Being.

Notes

1   Kakuzo Okakura, *Das Buch vom Tee* (Leipzig: Insel-Verlag, 1919).

2   Tomonobu Imamichi, *In Search of Wisdom: One Philosopher's Journey*, (Tokyo: LTCB International Library, 2004), 123.

3   Kakuzo Okakura, *Cha no hon / The Book of Tea* (Tokyo: Kodansha, 1998), 92–3. "Taoism" has been changed to "Daoism." The Japanese translator of Okakura's English text renders this phrase as *yo ni sho suru no jutsu* 世に処する の術, a Japanese parsing of the Chinese-Japanese (*kanbun* 漢文) phrase Okakura presumably had in mind, *sho sei jutsu* 処世術.

4   Okakura, *Das Buch vom Tee*, chapter 3; accessed online at: http://gutenberg. spiegel.de/buch/das-buch-vom-tee-9294/4. See Dennis Hirota, "Okakura Tenshin's Conception of 'Being in the World'," *Ryūkoku Daigaku Ronshū* , 478 (2011): 11. Hirota claims that the phrase *chushi* 處世 (Japanese: *shosei*; note that 処 is the modern Japanese simplification of 處) can be found in chapter 9 of the *Zhuangzi*, but I have been unable to find it there or indeed anywhere in the *Zhuangzi*. It seems to have first appeared in later texts such as the *Huainanzi* (second century BCE). See https://ctext.org/pre-qin-and-han?searchu=處世. David Chai informs me that the term subsequently appeared in many of the traditional commentaries on the *Zhuangzi*, starting with Cheng Xuanying 成玄英 (fl. seventh century).

5   Heinrich Wiegand Petzet, *Encounters & Dialogues with Martin Heidegger 1929–1976*, trans. Parvis Emad and Kenneth Maly (Chicago: University of Chicago Press, 1993), 18.

6   Martin Heidegger, *Gesamtausgabe*, vol. 77; Martin Heidegger, *Country Path Conversations*, trans. Bret W. Davis (Bloomington: Indiana University Press, 2010).

7   On this crucial turn in Heidegger's path of thought, see Bret W. Davis, *Heidegger and the Will: On the Way to Gelassenheit* (Evanston: Northwestern University Press, 2007); and Bret W. Davis, "Returning the World to Nature: Heidegger's Turn from a Transcendental-Horizonal Projection of World to an Indwelling Releasement to the Open-Region," *Continental Philosophy Review*, 47.3 (2014): 373–97. For an introduction to this topic, see Bret W. Davis, "Will and Gelassenheit," in *Martin Heidegger: Key Concepts*, ed. Bret W. Davis (New York: Routledge, 2014), 168–82.

8   Martin Heidegger, *Letters to His Wife: 1915–1970*, ed. Gertrud Heidegger, trans. R.D.V. Glasgow (Cambridge: Polity, 2008), 187.

9   Martin Heidegger, *Vorträge und Aufsätze* (Pfullingen: Neske, 1994), 43; Martin Heidegger, *The Question Concerning Technology and Other Essays*, trans. William Lovitt (New York: Harper and Row, 1977), 158. For an attempt to concisely present the relevance of Heidegger's thought to cross-cultural philosophy, and vice versa, see Bret W. Davis, "East-West Dialogue after Heidegger," in *After Heidegger?*, eds. Gregory Fried and Richard Polt (London: Rowman & Littlefield, 2018), 335–45.

10 Other than *Country Path Conversations* and "From a Conversation on Language (1953/54): Between a Japanese and an Inquirer" (Martin Heidegger,

Gesamtausgabe, vol. 12, 79–146; Martin Heidegger, *On the Way to Language*, trans. Peter D. Hertz [New York: Harper and Row, 1971], 1–54, translation of the title modified), the only other text in this form is "Das abendländische Gespräch: 1946/1948" (Martin Heidegger, *Gesamtausgabe*, vol. 75, 57–196), an unfinished dialogue written in the wake of *Country Path Conversations*.

11 Heidegger, *Letters to his Wife*, 187.

12 Martin Heidegger, *Gesamtausgabe*, vol. 65; Martin Heidegger, *Contributions to Philosophy (From the Event)*, trans. Richard Rojcewicz and Daniela Vallega-Neu (Bloomington: Indiana University Press, 2012).

13 Martin Heidegger, *Gesamtausgabe*, vol. 40, 152; Martin Heidegger, *Introduction to Metaphysics*, trans. Gregory Fried and Richard Polt (New Haven: Yale University Press, 2014), 122.

14 On Heidegger's ethnocentrism in the 1930s and beyond, and on his turn (or return) to an interest in East–West dialogue starting in the late 1930s, see Bret W. Davis, "Heidegger on the Way from Onto-Historical Ethnocentrism to East-West Dialogue," *Gatherings: The Heidegger Circle Annual*, 6 (2016): 130–56.

15 Martin Heidegger, "Europa und die deutsche Philosophie," in *Europa und die Philosophie*, ed. Hans-Helmut Gander (Frankfurt: Vittorio Klostermann, 1993), 31.

16 See Bret W. Davis, "Heidegger and Asian Philosophy," in *The Bloomsbury Companion to Heidegger*, eds. François Raffoul and Eric S. Nelson (New York: Bloomsbury Academic, 2013), 460.

17 Martin Heidegger, *Gesamtausgabe*, vol. 12, 79–146; Heidegger, *On the Way to Language*, 1–54.

18 Ibid., 85 and 89; Ibid., 5 and 8.

19 Ibid., 144; Ibid., 52–3.

20 See Bret W. Davis, "Heidegger's Orientations: The Step Back on the Way to Dialogue with the East," in *Heidegger-Jahrbuch 7: Heidegger und das ostasiatische Denken*, eds. Alfred Denker *et al.* (Freiburg/Munich: Alber Verlag, 2013), 177–80.

21 See Harmut Buchner (ed.), *Japan und Heidegger* (Sigmaringen: Thorbecke, 1989), 225; see also Ibid., 166.

22 See Heidegger, *Gesamtausgabe*, vol. 77, 184 and 205; *Country Path Conversations*, 120 and 132.

23 See Davis, "Heidegger and Asian Philosophy", 463–8.

24 Martin Heidegger, *Gesamtausgabe*, vol. 53, 62; Martin Heidegger, *Hölderlin's Hymn "The Ister"*, trans. Will McNeil and Julia Davis (Bloomington: Indiana University Press, 1996), 50.

25 Ibid.; Ibid.

26 Heidegger, *Gesamtausgabe*, vol. 76; Heidegger, *Hölderlin's Hymn "The Ister"*, 63.

27 Heidegger, *Gesamtausgabe*, vol. 80; Ibid., 65–6.

28 Heidegger, *Gesamtausgabe*, vol. 81; Ibid., 66 (translation modified).

29 See Martin Heidegger, *Gesamtausgabe*, vol. 39, 290–4; Martin Heidegger, *Hölderlin's Hymns "Germania" and "The Rhine"*, trans. Will McNeil and

Julia Davis (Bloomington: Indiana University Press, 2014), 263–7; Heidegger, *Gesamtausgabe*, vol. 53, 168–70; Heidegger, *Hölderlin's Hymn "The Ister"*, 134–7; and Martin Heidegger, *Erläuterung zu Hölderlins Dichtung* (Frankfurt am Main: Vittorio Klostermann, 1996), 82–8; Martin Heidegger, *Elucidations of Hölderlin's Poetry*, trans. Keith Hoeller (New York: Humanity Books, 2000), 107–13. For an explication and critique of Hölderlin's and Heidegger's understanding of the proper mode of cross-cultural encounter as a matter of "homecoming through the foreign," see Bret W. Davis, "Heidegger on the Way," 139–44.

30 Heidegger, *Vorträge und Aufsätze*, 43; Heidegger, *The Question Concerning Technology*, 158.

31 From Gadamer's personal correspondence with Graham Parkes, as recorded in the latter's introduction to *Heidegger and Asian Thought* (Honolulu: University of Hawaii Press, 1987), 5, 7.

32 Winfield Nagley, "Introduction to the Symposium and Reading of a Letter from Martin Heidegger," *Philosophy East and West*, 20.3 (1970): 221. See also Martin Heidegger, *Gesamtausgabe*, vol. 9, 424; Martin Heidegger, *Pathmarks*, ed. William McNeill (Cambridge: Cambridge University Press, 1998), 321; and Heidegger's statement quoted in Willfred Hartig, *Die Lehre des Buddha und Heidegger: Beiträge zum Ost-West-Dialog des Denkens im 20 Jahrhundert* (Konstanz: Universität Konstanz, 1997), 15–16.

33 Hellmuth Hecker, "Ein Spaziergang mit Heidegger," in Hartig, *Die Lehre des Buddha und Heidegger*, 269.

34 Shih-Yi Hsiao, "Heidegger and Our Translation of the *Tao Te Ching*," in *Heidegger and Asian Thought*, ed. Graham Parkes (Honolulu: University of Hawaii Press, 1987), 93, 96.

35 Ibid., 98.

36 Martin Heidegger, *Identität und Differenz* (Stuttgart: Neske, 1999), 25; Martin Heidegger, *Identity and Difference*, trans. Joan Stambaugh (New York: Harper and Row, 1969), 36.

37 Heidegger, *Gesamtausgabe*, vol. 12, 187; Heidegger, *On the Way to Language*, 92 (translation modified).

38 Ibid., 89; Ibid., 8. See Davis, "Heidegger's Orientations," 179–80.

39 See Heidegger, *Gesamtausgabe*, vol. 40, 105 and 115; Heidegger, *Introduction to Metaphysics*, 153 and 166–7.

40 See the references in note 7.

41 See Heidegger, *Gesamtausgabe*, vol. 77, 108–9; Heidegger, *Country Path Conversations*, 70.

42 See *Daodejing*, chapters 2, 3, 10, 37, 43, 48, 63. Translations from the *Daodejing* are my own. I have benefited from consulting a variety of translations, including that by P.J. Ivanhoe and Bryan Van Norden (eds.), *Readings in Classical Chinese Philosophy* (Indianapolis: Hackett, 2005), 163–203.

43 See *Daodejing*, chapters 8, 16, 25, 34, 37, 48, 51, 62, 73; and Heidegger, *Gesamtausgabe*, vol. 77, 108–9, 122–3, 142–4; Heidegger, *Country Path Conversations*, 70, 79–80, 92–4.

44 *Daodejing*, chapter 11.

45 Heidegger, *Gesamtausgabe*, vol. 77, 130; Heidegger, *Country Path Conversations*, 85.

46 Ibid., 137; Ibid., 89.

47 Martin Heidegger, *Gesamtausgabe*, vol. 79, 7–11; Martin Heidegger, *Bremen and Freiburg Lectures*, trans. Andrew J. Mitchell (Bloomington: Indiana University Press, 2012), 7–10.

48 Heidegger, *Gesamtausgabe*, vol. 65, 338–9; Heidegger, *Contributions to Philosophy*, 268–9.

49 "Nothingness itself, however, is being [*Das Nichts selbst aber ist Sein*]." Martin Heidegger, *Gesamtausgabe*, vol. 71, 121; Martin Heidegger, *The Event*, trans. Richard Rojcewicz (Bloomington: Indiana University Press, 2013), 103.

50 Heidegger, *Gesamtausgabe*, vol. 65, 256; Heidegger, *Contributions to Philosophy*, 209. On the many other references to the "the nothing" in Heidegger's thought, see Davis, "Heidegger and Asian Philosophy," 463–4. Note that, beginning in the 1930s, Heidegger sometimes uses the archaic spelling of *Seyn* (beyng), instead of *Sein* (being), in order to indicate that he is referring to the originary appropriating event of revealing/concealing rather than to "beingness" (*Seiendheit*) in the sense of a metaphysical essence or ground of beings.

51 *Daodejing*, chapters 40 and 4.

52 Ibid., chapter 34.

53 Ibid., chapter 37.

54 Heidegger, *Gesamtausgabe*, vol. 77, 177–8; Heidegger, *Country Path Conversations*, 115.

55 Ibid., 118; Ibid., 76–7.

56 *Daodejing*, chapter 11; Zhuangzi, *The Complete Works of Zhuangzi*, trans. Burton Watson (New York: Columbia University Press, 2013), 10.

57 Heidegger, *Gesamtausgabe*, vol. 53, 23; Heidegger, *Hölderlin's Hymn "The Ister"*, 20.

58 Heidegger, *Gesamtausgabe*, vol. 77, 115; Heidegger, *Country Path Conversations*, 75.

59 See Aristotle, *Metaphysics*, 1050a.

60 Heidegger, *Gesamtausgabe*, vol. 77, 69; Heidegger, *Country Path Conversations*, 44.

61 Ibid., 115; Ibid., 75.

62 Heidegger, *Gesamtausgabe*, vol. 77, 122–6, 139–43; Heidegger, *Country Path Conversations*, 80–2, 90–3.

63 Ibid., 122; Ibid., 79.

64 *Daodejing*, chapter 16.

65 Heidegger, *Gesamtausgabe*, vol. 77, 202; Heidegger, *Country Path Conversations*, 131.

66 In Davis, *Heidegger and the Will*, chapter 5, I argue that Heidegger's passing critique hardly does justice to Eckhart's notion of *Gelassenheit*, and specifically to the manner in which Eckhart breaks through and beyond a standpoint of deference to the Will of a transcendent God.

67 Heidegger, *Gesamtausgabe*, vol. 77, 109; Heidegger, *Country Path Conversations*, 70.

68 Ibid., 143; Ibid., 93.

69 Heidegger, *Gesamtausgabe*, vol. 12, 186–7; Heidegger, *On the Way to Language*, 91–2 (translation modified).

70 *Daodejing*, chapter 34.

71 Ibid., chapter 10; see also Ibid., chapter 51. The phrase "lead without lording over" is Ivanhoe and Van Norden's felicitous translation of "*zhang er bu zai* 長而不宰."

72 *Daodejing*, chapter 8.

73 Ibid., chapter 25.

74 Heidegger, *Gesamtausgabe*, vol. 77, 107; Heidegger, *Country Path Conversations*, 66.

75 *Daodejing*, chapters 64 and 34.

76 Ibid., chapters 15, 19, 28, 32, 37.

77 Ibid., chapter 37.

78 Heidegger, *Gesamtausgabe*, vol. 77, 115; Heidegger, *Country Path Conversations*, 75.

79 *Daodejing*, chapter 1.

80 Ibid., chapter 15, as quoted in Hsiao, "Heidegger and Our Translation," 100.

81 See Heidegger, *Gesamtausgabe*, vol. 77, 84–5; Heidegger, *Country Path Conversations*, 54.

82 "Go-into-nearness" translates "*In-die-Nähe-gehen*," which is the German translation eventually given for the Greek title of the first of the *Country Path Conversations*. That title is a one-word fragment by Heraclitus: Αγχιβασίη. See Heidegger, *Gesamtausgabe*, vol. 77, 152–5; Heidegger, *Country Path Conversations*, 99–102.

83 *Daodejing*, chapter 1.

84 Ibid., chapter 25.

85 Heidegger, *Gesamtausgabe*, vol. 12, 156; Heidegger, *On the Way to Language*, 60.

86 Heidegger, *Gesamtausgabe*, vol. 5, 310; Martin Heidegger, *Poetry, Language, Thought*, trans. Albert Hofstadter (New York: Harper and Row, 2001), 132.

87 Maurice Merleau-Ponty, *Signs*, trans. Richard McCleary (Evanston: Northwestern University Press, 1964), 120.

88 Heidegger, *Gesamtausgabe*, vol. 9, 313; Heidegger, *Pathmarks*, 239.

89 Shizuteru Ueda, *Zen—kongen-teki ningen* (Tokyo: Iwanami, 2001), 387. See Bret W. Davis, "Expressing Experience: Language in Ueda Shizuteru's Philosophy of Zen," in *Dao Companion to Japanese Buddhist Philosophy*, ed. Gereon Kopf (New York: Springer, 2019), 713–38.

90 Heidegger, *Gesamtausgabe*, vol. 9, 364; Heidegger, *Pathmarks*, 276.

91 Heidegger, *Gesamtausgabe*, vol. 12, 159; Heidegger, *On the Way to Language*, 66.

92 Heidegger, *Gesamtausgabe*, vol. 65, 510; Heidegger, *Contributions to Philosophy*, 401.

93 Ibid., 36; Ibid., 30.

94 Heidegger, *Gesamtausgabe*, vol. 77, 159; Heidegger, *Country Path Conversations*, 104.

95 Ibid.; Ibid.

96 Ibid., 223–4; Ibid., 145.

97 Ibid., 88–9; Ibid., 56.

98 Heidegger, *Gesamtausgabe*, vol. 12, 186–7; Heidegger, *On the Way to Language*, 91–2 (translation modified).

99 Heidegger, *Gesamtausgabe*, vol. 77, 206–7, 233–5; Heidegger, *Country Path Conversations*, 133, 152–3.

100 Ibid., 234; Ibid., 152–3.

101 Ibid., 234; Ibid., 153.

102 Ibid., 237; Ibid., 155. See also Ibid., 227, 232; Ibid., 148, 151.

103 Ibid.; Ibid., 155.

104 Ibid., 239; Ibid., 156.

105 Like the *Daodejing*, traditionally attributed to Laozi and so also called the *Laozi*, the *Zhuangzi* was composed by a number of authors, some of them more and some less closely connected with the person Zhuangzi who may have composed the first seven of the thirty-three chapters—however, some scholars now think that even those first seven "Inner Chapters" were composed by more than one author. In any case, what concerns us here is the consistency of thought rather than the identity of authorship. Following the example of the text itself, I will sometimes use "Zhuangzi" as a name for the collective authorship of the central and consistent lines of thought in the text.

106 Zhuangzi, *Complete Works*, 231; see also *Zhuangzi: The Essential Writings with Selections from Traditional Commentaries*, trans. Brook Ziporyn (Indianapolis: Hackett, 2009), 112.

107 Ibid., 30; Ibid.

108 Ibid. 33; Ibid., 32.

109 Ibid. 31; Ibid.

110 Ibid., 6; Ibid., 8.

111 Ibid., 31; Ibid.

112 See Martin Heidegger, *Sein und Zeit* (Tübingen: Max Niemeyer, 1993), 63–88; Martin Heidegger, *Being and Time*, trans. John Macquarrie and Edward Robinson (New York: Harper and Row, 1962), 91–122; and Davis, *Heidegger and the Will*, 32–40.

113 On the roles that self-concealing "earth" and encompassing "nature" play in Heidegger's turn from a voluntaristic projection of a meaningful "world," see Davis, "Returning the World to Nature."

114 Heidegger, *Sein und Zeit*, 70; Heidegger, *Being and Time*, 100.

115 Martin Heidegger, *Was heißt Denken?* (Tübingen: Max Niemeyer, 1984), 18; Martin Heidegger, *What is Called Thinking?*, trans. J. Glenn Gray (New York: Harper and Row), 44.

116 Martin Heidegger, *Denkerfahrungen 1910–1976* (Frankfurt am Main: Vittorio Klosterman, 1996), 18.

117 Heidegger, *Gesamtausgabe*, vol. 9, 116; Heidegger, *Pathmarks*, 92.

118 Heidegger, *Letters to His Wife*, 187.

119 Martin Heidegger, *Gesamtausgabe*, vol. 73/1, 5; Martin Heidegger, "Poverty," trans. Thomas Kalary and Frank Schalow in *Heidegger, Translation and the Task of Thinking*, ed. Frank Schalow (New York: Springer, 2011), 3.

120 Ibid., 7; Ibid., 5 (translation modified).

121 Ibid., 8–9; Ibid., 6–7 (translation modified).

122 In particular, I will not be able to pay due attention either to the mellowing tone and attunement in Heidegger's thought between the later 1930s and the 1960s or to the significant differences in tone and attunement between the *Daodejing* and the *Zhuangzi*.

123 Zhuangzi, *The Complete Works*, 16; Zhuangzi, *The Essential Writings*, 18.

124 Ibid., 233; Ibid., 114.

125 Heidegger, *Gesamtausgabe*, vol. 12, 27; Heidegger, *Poetry, Language, Thought*, 207.

126 Zhuangzi, *The Complete Works*, 184; Zhuangzi, *The Essential Writings*, 89–90. Here and in other quotations from this text, I have changed Ziporyn's translation of *dao* as "Course" to "Way."

127 See Davis, "Expressing Experience."

128 *Daodejing*, chapter 40.

129 Zhuangzi, *The Complete Works*, 181; Zhuangzi, *The Essential Writings*, 89 (translation modified).

130 Ibid., 233; Ibid., 114.

131 Heidegger, *Gesamtausgabe*, vol. 71, 330; Heidegger, *The Event*, 286 (translation modified).

132 Heidegger, *Gesamtausgabe*, vol. 65, 22 and 395–6; Heidegger, *Contributions to Philosophy*, 19 and 313–14.

133 Heidegger, *Gesamtausgabe*, vol. 39, 94–5; Heidegger, *Hölderlin's "Germania" and "The Rhine,"* 85–6.

134 Ibid., 182; Ibid., 166.

135 Heidegger, *Erläuterung zu Hölderlins Dichtung*, 77; Heidegger, *Elucidations of Hölderlin's Poetry*, 98.

136 Heidegger, *Gesamtausgabe*, vol. 77, 137; Heidegger, *Country Path Conversations*, 89.

137 Zhuangzi, *The Complete Works*, 146; Zhuangzi, *The Essential Writings*, 78 (translation modified). Ziporyn translates *tian* 天 more literally as "the Heavenly." As he tells us in his Glossary of Essential Terms, in the *Zhuangzi*

this term refers to "the spontaneous and agentless creativity that brings forth all beings" and whose "action is effortless and purposeless." Zhuangzi, *The Essential Writings*, 217.

138 Zhuangzi, *The Complete Works*, 182; Zhuangzi, *The Essential Writings*, 89.

139 Heidegger, *Gesamtausgabe*, vol. 65, 7; Heidegger, *Contributions to Philosophy*, 8. It is important to point out that Heidegger is decidedly not calling for a ground in the "metaphysical" sense of "beingness" as a bedrock of constant presence. Noting a passage where Heidegger says of the grounders of the abyss that "their seeking loves the abyss, in which they know the oldest ground" (Heidegger, *Gesamtausgabe*, vol. 65, 13; Heidegger, *Contributions to Philosophy*, 13), John Sallis comments: "For those who question, being grounders of the abyss does not mean installing a ground that would cancel the abyss as archaic ground, as an abysmal ground older than beingness as ground." John Sallis, "Grounders of the Abyss", in *Companion to Heidegger's Contributions to Philosophy*, eds. Charles Scott *et al.* (Bloomington: Indiana University Press, 2001), 189.

140 Heidegger, *Gesamtausgabe*, vol. 9, 364; Heidegger, *Pathmarks*, 276.

141 Ivanhoe and Van Norden, *Readings in Classical Chinese Philosophy*, 127.

142 Zhuangzi, *The Complete Works*, 13 (my translation); Zhuangzi, *The Essential Writings*, 16.

143 *Daodejing*, chapter 38.

144 Ibid., chapter 51.

145 Zhuangzi, *The Complete Works*, 11–12; Zhuangzi, *The Essential Writings*, 14.

146 Ivanhoe and Van Norden, *Readings in Classical Chinese Philosophy*, 248.

147 *Daodejing*, chapter 25.

148 Zhuangzi, *The Complete Works*, 11; Zhuangzi, *The Essential Writings*, 14.

149 Ibid.

150 Zhuangzi, *The Complete Works*, 10; Zhuangzi, *The Essential Writings*, 12.

151 See Heidegger, *Gesamtausgabe*, vol. 65, 107; Heidegger, *Contributions to Philosophy*, 85.

152 Heidegger, *Letters to His Wife*, 182; see also Heidegger, *Gesamtausgabe*, vol. 9, 364; Heidegger, *Pathmarks*, 276.

153 See Heidegger, *Gesamtausgabe*, vol. 77, 164; Heidegger, *Country Path Conversations*, 106.

154 Zhuangzi, *The Complete Works*, 17.

155 Heidegger, *Gesamtausgabe*, vol. 77, 206; Heidegger, *Country Path Conversations*, 132.

156 Ibid., 226; Ibid., 147.

157 Zhuangzi, *The Complete Works*, 182–3; Zhuangzi, *The Essential Writings*, 89. Here I have combined and modified the translations by Watson and Ziporyn.

158 Ibid. 183; Ibid. (translation modified).

159 Ibid., 3; Ibid., 6.

References

Buchner, Harmut, ed. (1989), *Japan und Heidegger*. Sigmaringen: Thorbecke.

Davis, Bret W. (2007), *Heidegger and the Will: On the Way to Gelassenheit*, Evanston: Northwestern University Press.

Davis, Bret W. (2013), "Heidegger and Asian Philosophy," in François Raffoul and Eric S. Nelson (eds.), *The Bloomsbury Companion to Heidegger*, 459–71, New York: Bloomsbury Academic.

Davis, Bret W. (2013), "Heidegger's Orientations: The Step Back on the Way to Dialogue with the East," in Alfred Denker *et al.* (eds.), *Heidegger-Jahrbuch 7: Heidegger und das ostasiatische Denken*, 153–80. Freiburg/Munich: Alber Verlag.

Davis, Bret W. (2014), "Returning the World to Nature: Heidegger's Turn from a Transcendental-Horizonal Projection of World to an Indwelling Releasement to the Open-Region," *Continental Philosophy Review*, 47.3: 373–97.

Davis, Bret W. (2014), "Will and *Gelassenheit*," in Bret W. Davis (ed.), *Martin Heidegger: Key Concepts*, 168–82, New York: Routledge.

Davis, Bret W. (2016), "Heidegger on the Way from Onto-Historical Ethnocentrism to East-West Dialogue," *Gatherings: The Heidegger Circle Annual*, 6: 130–56.

Davis, Bret W. (2018), "East-West Dialogue after Heidegger," in Gregory Fried and Richard Polt (eds.), *After Heidegger?*, 335–45, London: Rowman & Littlefield.

Davis, Bret W. (2019), "Expressing Experience: Language in Ueda Shizuteru's Philosophy of Zen," in Gereon Kopf (ed.), *Dao Companion to Japanese Buddhist Philosophy*, 713–38, New York: Springer.

Hartig, Willfred. (1997), *Die Lehre des Buddha und Heidegger: Beiträge zum Ost-West-Dialog des Denkens im 20 Jahrhundert*, Konstanz: Universität Konstanz.

Heidegger, Martin. (1962), *Being and Time*, John Macquarrie and Edward Robinson (trans.), New York: Harper and Row.

Heidegger, Martin. (1968), *What is Called Thinking?*, J. Glenn Gray (trans.), New York: Harper and Row.

Heidegger, Martin. (1969), *Identity and Difference*, Joan Stambaugh (trans.), New York: Harper and Row.

Heidegger, Martin. (1971), *On the Way to Language*, Peter D. Hertz (trans.), New York: Harper and Row.

Heidegger, Martin. (1975–), *Gesamtausgabe*. Frankfurt am Main: Vittorio Klostermann. Cited by the following volume numbers: (5) "*Holzwege*", (9) "*Wegmarken*", (12) "*Unterwegs zur Sprache*", (39) "*Hölderlins Hymnen 'Germanien' und 'Der Rhein'*", (40) "*Einführung in die Metaphysik*", (53) "*Hölderlins Hymne 'Der Ister'*", (65) "*Beiträge zur Philosophie (Vom Ereignis)*", (71) "*Das Ereignis*", (73/1) "*Zum Ereignis-Denken*" (vol. 1), (75) "*Zu Hölderlin / Griechenlandreisen*", (77) "*Feldweg-Gespräche (1944/45)*".

Heidegger, Martin. (1977), *The Question Concerning Technology and Other Essays*, William Lovitt (trans.), New York: Harper and Row.

Heidegger, Martin. (1984), *Was heißt Denken?*, Tübingen: Max Niemeyer.

Heidegger, Martin. (1993), "Europa und die deutsche Philosophie," in Hans-Helmut Gander (ed.), *Europa und die Philosophie*, 31–41. Frankfurt: Vittorio Klostermann.

Heidegger, Martin. (1993), *Sein und Zeit*, Tübingen: Max Niemeyer.

Heidegger, Martin. (1994), *Vorträge und Aufsätze*, Pfullingen: Neske.

Heidegger, Martin. (1996), *Denkerfahrungen 1910–1976*. Frankfurt am Main: Vittorio Klostermann.

Heidegger, Martin. (1996), *Erläuterung zu Hölderlins Dichtung*, Frankfurt am Main: Vittorio Klostermann.

Heidegger, Martin. (1996), *Hölderlin's Hymn "The Ister"*, Will McNeil and Julia Davis (trans.), Bloomington: Indiana University Press.

Heidegger, Martin. (1998), *Pathmarks*, William McNeill (ed.), Cambridge: Cambridge University Press.

Heidegger, Martin. (1999), *Identität und Differenz*, Stuttgart: Neske.

Heidegger, Martin. (2000), *Elucidations of Hölderlin's Poetry*, Keith Hoeller (trans.), New York: Humanity Books.

Heidegger, Martin. (2001), *Poetry, Language, Thought*, Albert Hofstadter (trans.), New York: Harper and Row.

Heidegger, Martin. (2008), *Letters to His Wife: 1915–1970*, Gertrud Heidegger (ed.), R.D.V. Glasgow (trans.), Cambridge: Polity.

Heidegger, Martin. (2010), *Country Path Conversations*, Bret W. Davis (trans.), Bloomington: Indiana University Press.

Heidegger, Martin. (2011), "Poverty," Thomas Kalary and Frank Schalow (trans.), in Frank Schalow (ed.), *Heidegger, Translation and the Task of Thinking*, 3–10, New York: Springer.

Heidegger, Martin. (2012), *Bremen and Freiburg Lectures*, Andrew Mitchell (trans.), Bloomington: Indiana University Press.

Heidegger, Martin. (2012), *Contributions to Philosophy (From the Event)*, Richard Rojcewicz and Daniela Vallega-Neu (trans.), Bloomington: Indiana University Press.

Heidegger, Martin. (2013), *The Event*, Richard Rojcewicz (trans.), Bloomington: Indiana University Press.

Heidegger, Martin. (2014), *Hölderlin's Hymns "Germania" and "The Rhine"*, Will McNeil and Julia Davis (trans.), Bloomington: Indiana University Press.

Heidegger, Martin. (2014), *Introduction to Metaphysics*, Gregory Fried and Richard Polt (trans.), New Haven: Yale University Press.

Hirota, Dennis. (2011), "Okakura Tenshin's Conception of 'Being in the World'," *Ryūkoku Daigaku Ronshū*, 478: 10–32.

Hsiao, Shih-Yi. (1987), "Heidegger and Our Translation of the *Tao Te Ching*," in Graham Parkes (ed.), *Heidegger and Asian Thought*, 93–103, Honolulu: University of Hawaii Press.

Imamichi, Tomonobu. (2004), *In Search of Wisdom: One Philosopher's Journey*, Tokyo: LTCB International Library.

Ivanhoe, P.J. and Bryan Van Norden, eds. (2005), *Readings in Classical Chinese Philosophy*, Indianapolis: Hackett.

Laozi. *Daodejing*. Available online at: https://ctext.org/dao-de-jing

May, Reinhard. (1996), *Heidegger's Hidden Sources: East Asian Influences on His Work*. Graham Parkes (trans.), New York: Routledge.

Merleau-Ponty, Maurice. (1964), *Signs*, Richard McCleary (trans.), Evanston: Northwestern University Press.

Nagley, Winfield. (1970), "Introduction to the Symposium and Reading of a Letter from Martin Heidegger," *Philosophy East and West*, 20.3: 221.

Okakura, Kakuzo. (1906), *The Book of Tea*, New York: Duffield and Company.

Okakura, Kakuzo. (1919), *Das Buch vom Tee*, Marguerite Steindorf and Ulrich Steindorf (trans.), Leipzig: Insel-Verlag.

Okakura, Kakuzo. (1998), *Cha no hon / The Book of Tea* (a bilingual edition), Asano Akira (trans.), Tokyo: Kodansha.

Parkes, Graham, ed. (1987), *Heidegger and Asian Thought*, Honolulu: University of Hawaii Press.

Petzet, Heinrich Wiegand. (1993), *Encounters & Dialogues with Martin Heidegger 1929–1976*, Parvis Emad and Kenneth Maly (trans.), Chicago: University of Chicago Press.

Sallis, John. (2001), "Grounders of the Abyss," in Charles Scott *et al.* (eds.), *Companion to Heidegger's Contributions to Philosophy*, 181–97. Bloomington: Indiana University Press.

Ueda, Shizuteru 上田閑照. (2001), *Zen—kongen-teki ningen* 禅一根源的人間 [Zen: Originary Human Being], volume 4 of *Ueda Shizuteru shū* 上田閑照集 [Ueda Shizuteru Collection], Tokyo: Iwanami.

Zhuangzi. (2009), *Zhuangzi: The Essential Writings with Selections from Traditional Commentaries*, Brook Ziporyn (trans.), Indianapolis: Hackett.

Zhuangzi. (2013), *The Complete Works of Zhuangzi*, Burton Watson (trans.), New York: Columbia University Press.

9

Heidegger and Zhuangzi:

The Transformative Art of the Phenomenological Reduction

Patricia Huntington

1. Introduction

In the *Zhuangzi* 莊子, we find a text that is both delightful in its literary fancy and demanding as an orientative guide to life.[1] The phenomenological method here adopted aligns itself with other literary, hermeneutic, and metaphorical treatments. Without ignoring the skeptical aspects of the text, such approaches demonstrate that the *Zhuangzi* promotes a rich program of spiritual transformation as an art of living. These delightful stories issue powerful challenges through a series of jolts that deprive the reader of commonsense (natural) attitudes, expose the relativity of customs and local perspectives, brush aside artificial labels, befuddle knowledge that is commonly inherited and relied upon, and even arrest analytical acumen. There have been detailed applications of the Husserlian forms of the phenomenological, eidetic, and transcendental reductions to various Eastern philosophies and meditative practices.[2] My aim will be conservatively limited to treating the phenomenological reduction, in its hermeneutic rendition in Heidegger and as applied to the *Zhuangzi*, as a practice of de-cultivation rather than of psychological and moral cultivation that builds up capacities developmentally under the design and direction of critical reason. The *Zhuangzi* can be read as enacting a practice of reduction in both textual and soteriological terms. My explicit aim will be to show that a program of un-learning generates newfound virtues and powers (*de* 德) that escape the purview of a life directed exclusively by the power of rational discernment.

The path of de-cultivation nourishes receptive openness and solitariness in Heidegger, while the *Zhuangzi* significantly expands this repertoire to include powers such as unknowing, trust in the Dao 道, nondual correlative perception, and the adoption of non-purposive or nontelic aims. Because this art of non-rational transformation yields a sustainable way of life that integrates all our powers, it can be considered superior to that of the deliberate forms of cultivation that amplify the power of reason alone.

2. Natural Attitudes or Cicadas and Doves

From both phenomenological and Zhuangzian standpoints, people operate at a cicada-and-dove level in our natural attitudes and everyday approaches to life. Fish cannot become birds, and birds do not fly ten thousand *li*. The adult mind is secure in its standing as a rational agent and center of moral will; it has abandoned childish dreams. Yet phenomenology shows us that first-order empirical senses of life (facts) are anything but natural (things-in-themselves), while Zhuangzi pokes fun at such attitudes as artificial conventions, learned modes of valuation rooted in the acquired belief in "an autonomous heart-mind over and above its affective states" that puts the child's mind to rest.[3] Throughout this commentary, I will use the lyrical phrase "cicadas and doves" to capture both naïvely-held beliefs and more critically developed worldviews that preserve this separation of the discriminating mind from affect, intuition, and vital force as well as spiritual contact with life as it emerges in its transformative power.[4]

The "natural attitude" is a technical term inherited from Husserlian phenomenology. It denotes the commonsense operative assumption that we experience and know the world as it exists outside and independent of the human mind.[5] Yet the intentional or co-relational nature of consciousness shows that, even as objective phenomena are not reducible to mental constructs, we only know phenomena (objectively) as they appear finitely within and are actively constituted by the field of human awareness (subjectivity).[6] Because the objects of consciousness (*noema*) and acts of conscious awareness (*noesis*) arise concurrently, "facts" and "things" are not simply facts and things. Phenomena are, rather, encrusted in histories of interpretation, cultural attitudes, and socialized forms of evaluation. The perceiving consciousness, that actively inherits such natural understandings, is not truly primordial but instead reflects the suppositions, preferences, beliefs, and theories of an acquired outlook.

My intent is not to detail the complexities of the eidetic and transcendental forms of reduction but instead to emphasize the reduction as a transformative practice that progresses from phenomenological suspension (epoché) to intuitive apprehension. Even though it remains within the scope of reflective activity, Husserl develops the phenomenological reduction as a technique that strips away the prejudices and cultural encrustations of the natural attitude, purifies perception, and restores a presuppositionless apprehension of things-in-themselves. This technique begins with the phenomenological epoché that suspends or brackets all beliefs and theories about the world that we take for granted. Through this detachment from suppositions, phenomena can then be described and analyzed as they arise immediately in "essential intuition."[7] The technique of eidetic variation imaginatively represents manifold variations of how a particular phenomenon arises in human experience in order to perform the eidetic reduction; that is, apprehend and judge it by its eidetic or invariant qualities (*eidos* or essences). Because consciousness plays an active role in the meaningful construction of phenomena, Husserl took an additional step through the transcendental reduction to examine the intentional structures of pure consciousness. Ramakant Sinari clarifies that Husserl "is predominantly interested in comprehending that line of demarcation which separates consciousness in the act of positing essences from consciousness reflecting this or that."[8]

This Husserlian notion of the natural attitude can illuminate Heidegger's view that "Dasein is its world" with several qualifications. First, in the expanded hermeneutical approach of Heidegger, we begin with the situated nature of human existence as a whole and not merely consciousness. As François Raffoul states, "if all there is is life, thought cannot be an external gaze *upon* life, from a position outside life."[9] Second, although it would be nice to say that world and subjectivity, rather than consciousness and its intended object, are co-relational, the language of co-relationality gives the falsifying impression that subject and environment first exist as independent and separate things, only then to be brought into mutual relation. Dasein and world are not co-relational because Dasein is its world.[10] Third, the hermeneutic turn within phenomenology through Heidegger, Sartre, and Merleau-Ponty repudiates the idea that we can return to a presuppositionless apprehension of things. To claim that Dasein is its world means that human existence has an inherently projective structure and is thus interpretive (*Auslegung*) in both prethematic (prepredicative) dealings and thematic (predicative) modes of conceptualization. Interpretation arises actively through "the working-out of possibilities projected in understanding," whether the aims are practical (to care for an animal) or theoretical (to create a science of animals).[11] The epoché or suspension of everyday assumptions cannot thus lead back to world-less, pre-interpreted, or un-projected (transcendental) apprehension of the invariant determinants of things. The reduction must be reconfigured as a step-back that initiates a regular practice of perceiving the limitations of our finite and interpreted views of all things.

In the Heideggerian context, the "natural" (Husserl) becomes the "everyday" (Heidegger), and the reduction is reconfigured as a step-back and not a technique "which makes possible the disclosure of a pure, absolute transcendental consciousness with no relationship to the world in order to be."[12] Everyday assumptions include more than the fallacy of thinking we know facts outside subjective consciousness. These include the basic notions that encompass our sense of being-in-a-world: (1) that we are isolated selves who first exist substantially before socialization; (2) that we stand in a world like an object placed in yet separate from a container; (3) that the preexisting empirical world is a brute and uninterpreted datum; and (4) that we manufacture language as a tool to represent this otherwise brute and mute reality. All four of these operative assumptions reflect dichotomized abstractions or, as Zhuangzi might put it, artificialities that cover over the nature of their production and of our primordial non-dichotomous experience of phenomenal existence.

However useful these everyday assumptions may be to collective survival and individual success, they create in conceptual terms a false division between self and world. And in practical terms, they produce a fractured and alienating sense of separation from others and the lifeworld. These conceptual dichotomies uproot us from the elemental experience of the creative co-constituting and interpretive nature of being-in-a-world (human existence) before it reifies into dualities. At this point Heidegger converges in broad terms with the *Zhuangzi*: critical disputes over the worldviews and ideological commitments that are built upon this uprootedness begin from a faulty starting point and cannot repair alienation from self, others, life, and the world.

Heidegger's version of a phenomenological reduction confronts us with a hermeneutic dilemma. Can there be a science of being if Dasein is its world? *Being and Time* answers in the affirmative. Because the step-back engages us in the phenomenal reality that human experience emerges out of nothingness or the inexhaustibility of horizons of meaning, it seems to leave us with only competing worldviews. Yet Dasein can become transparent to its existence by projecting the horizon of interpretation upon our outermost possibility, death.[13] Death awareness, when lifted to the surface and brought to bear on our lives, thrusts us back upon the nature of human finitude. There are two intertwined levels to the projective nature of human existence, ontic and ontological. Ontic projections pertain to specific goals, aims, and purposes, while the ontological articulates the fact that human existence reaches projectively beyond any one world-horizon into the very font of unconcealment or disclosedness as such. The generative condition for the possibility of all world-horizons of interpretation is that we reach into nothingness at both the point of origination (the upsurge of life) and cessation (death). Actively living out of death awareness, while strenuous, roots us in a fragile, ever-elusive, and enigmatic compliance with the fact that we know things only finitely within our field of awareness.

Although in Husserl, the phenomenological reduction ultimately leads to the transcendental study of the noetic structures of consciousness, the hermeneutic turn in phenomenology treats the subject in holistic terms as an affective, embodied, and driven being and as embedded in the forces of culture and history. This turn thickens our grasp of the depth and force of cultural conditioning and attenuates the desire to arrive at a pure standpoint. By reversing the thrust that collapses death awareness (ontological nothingness) into purposive aims (socialized ontic worldviews), the hermeneutic step-back inaugurates a process of de-cultivation or un-learning. The phenomenological reduction cannot be merely a technique that purifies consciousness because it involves a confrontation with mortality as a necessary moment in delivering us to transparency to a never-ending engagement with the mystery of the disclosure of being (life). Without equating Heidegger and Daoism, we can note a similarity with the enigmatic nature of the Dao as Laozi 老子 describes it in his *Daodejing* 道德經: the Dao that can be named is not the constant Dao (*changdao* 常道).[14] We can touch its originating power and virtue but not conceptualize it without remainder.

3. Practice: Dislodging Cicadas and Doves

Even though *Being and Time*'s primary aim of developing a fundamental ontology remains conceptual, Heidegger's philosophy encourages an exploration of the transformations produced through a lived practice of reduction. Elsewhere I have criticized the Heideggerian model of authenticity (*Eigentlichkeit*) for reinstating a positive paradigm of self-cultivation, rather than adhering to a rigorous path of de-cultivation; I have argued that it leaves intact a residual sense of a preexisting self.[15] Manifold scholars have examined a tension between Heidegger's ontology and the intersubjective model of authentic engagement with finitude. A bone of contention for East Asian thinkers like Tetsurō Watsuji is that fundamental ontology does not begin by articulating a completely nondual sense of interdependence, namely, that selves are empty of intrinsic nature.[16] Like Watsuji, Erin McCarthy, Lawrence Vogel, and others, I find irresolvable tensions in *Being and Time*.[17] Yet focusing on the rich practice of the reduction, rather than tensions between ontology and intersubjectivity, allows me to highlight the practice of de-cultivation in the early Heidegger as a way to engender an elemental form of virtue.

Rather than treat a Heideggerian variant of the reduction as landing us in some form of relativism or skepticism, a phenomenological approach understands the step-back to recover a bearing; that is, a dispositional orientation to discourse and life that allows the anxious drive for security to surface. Because transparency does not deliver us to a final, fixed, and absolute standpoint, a fundamental and *angst*-producing insecurity suffuses human life. Typically, this *angst*—anxiety over no-thingness or the lack of an unchanging basis for judgment—drives people to seek conceptual security by one of two means: either by turning commonplace "cicada-and-dove" worldviews into absolute standpoints or, where a reflective sense of the limits of perspective obtains, by compulsively defending one's viewpoint.[18]

The evasion of finitude, when unacknowledged, infects argumentation and yields stubborn or questionable outcomes: the driven need to be right belies an extraneous excess of self-affirmation, the impulse to embrace a final worldview betrays want of arbitrarily terminating the process of growth, the inability to sustain expansion of the field of phenomenality belies stubbornness. Insofar as existential *angst* is not confronted, the impetus to security will taint conceptual debates, close down the field of phenomenality (what can be perceived or what counts as evidence), and impose an arbitrary limit on dialogue. Moreover, abstracting from primordial openness produces staunch resistance to awakening from everyday attitudes that are culturally inherited and reinforced by worldly aims. As valuable as it is to dispute worldviews reflectively and abstractly, a practice of stepping back examines the underlying attitudes and rigid dispositions betrayed in the laughter of the cicada and the turtle dove, the self-pride of small wisdom, the puffed-up words of Jie Yu, the sounds of the shrill and quarrelsome. While understandable, our anxious dealings with the world bind us ever more thoroughly to narrow and closed worldviews, and reductive modes of interaction.

Given that it does not nullify the need to evaluate and argumentatively assess the importance of moral values, political ideologies, or social aims, we might ask what value lies in this step-back? Is openness simply a more holistic and contextualized way to capture reflective life? I suggest not. The value, I propose, lies in an elemental form of virtue/power (*de*) that cannot be produced through cultivation (socialization) but only through de-cultivation; that is, a practice of reduction or fasting of mind and heart. Eric Nelson exemplifies the nourishing of such virtue in terms of Heidegger's grasp of individuation. One commonplace and shared understanding is that we are all individuated because, as adults, we have formed personalities, autonomous moral capacities, independent ideas, and the ability to determine and achieve practical aims. Yet this hard-won "natural attitude" proves to be a form of cicada-and-dove-like ignorance because it takes for granted that individuation is completed at base, even if we can enlarge critical understanding and build a more rectified character on top of that base. Rather than treat individuation as the outcome of psychological development and socialization, Nelson shows that, for Heidegger, individuation arises only when we break with this commonplace attitude: "The uniqueness of the self and things does not arise from the imposition of a view, prescription, or imperative ... but emerges in letting the world be encountered."[19]

Heidegger's emphasis on individuation (*Vereinzelung*), mineness (*Jemeinigkeit*), and solitude (*Einsamkeit*) demonstrates that radical individuation "is a becoming finite."[20] It inheres in the active process of realizing one's finitude rather than through the formation of capacities. Holding oneself open for finitude transforms fear and anxiety into receptivity to the unpredictable and allows one to grow stable in meeting the unknown, however much it might jolt one uncomfortably into yet new shifts in perspective. It progressively dissolves the psychic protections of artificial constructs and defensive patterns of ideation. "Solitude is a condition not of escaping the world but of encountering it."[21] Lawrence Vogel accentuates the arduous nature of living authentically. To take up one's finitude authentically, rather than hide behind social conventions and the limitations of the adult mind, means to stand "open to the structures of existence" and to take "hold of ... existence in light of the constraints of history, embodiment, and morality."[22] Because social conventions seem to "disburden one of the anxiety-producing responsibility," we resist holding ourselves open in the vulnerabilities of finitude.[23] Nelson's insightful explication enables us to comprehend how commitments to a worldview, even when rationally developed, can be pinned to a near-untouchable set of assumptions and psychic formations that ward off *angst*. These inevitably harden beneath the adult capacity to be self-governing; they uproot and restrict the power of rational life by producing a zone of indifference that proves incorrigibly difficult to dislodge. Everyday modes of being make one "indifferent to that which would throw light on the character and plight of [one's] own existence."[24]

The step-back, understood as a practice of authentic individuation, fosters not simple psychological acceptance of finitude but an active comportment, a "taking up, safeguarding, and preserving of finitude."[25] Critical suspension of beliefs does not suffice to eradicate anxiety and indifference. The reduction can only fulfill itself through a strenuous practice that fosters the elemental power, in solitariness, to remain aware of finitude, to sustain an attitude of willingness to persist in being shown one's finitude (illusions), and to bear it well. This willingness expresses itself in the virtuous receptivity that welcomes what comes without defensive or indifferent acts of rational repudiation. Such stability does not come from socialized character but instead from the genuine dissolution of *angst* and the restoration of child-like wonder in non-discriminate openness.[26] One might hear in these Heideggerian concerns the echo of Zhuangzi's radical mockery of such patterns of "rational" development. Such a bearing might also capture Zen Master Dōgen's view that life is one continuous mistake because it shows that, however rational we may be, we can and often are mistaken in our way of being-in-the-world, and not simply through lapses in a logical process of ideation.[27]

To further develop an understanding of the reduction as a constant return to openness that fosters an elemental *de* requires that we supplement Heidegger in two directions, one social and one spiritual. By turning to the *Zhuangzi*, I directly address the latter but not the former. The Heideggerian step-back takes us to the fact that our individual identities are bound up with "cultural heritage—its possibilities, its patterns of living and doing, its stories and interpretations."[28] Each of our cicada-and-dove belief systems is related to that larger historical horizon of interpretation or, as Charles

Guignon puts it, "shared medium of intelligibility."[29] Yet Heidegger presupposes a homogenous cultural horizon and writes a grand meta-narrative of Western thought, as Latina feminists Dorothy Leland and Mariana Ortega, and as comparative thinkers, including Eric Nelson, have shown. The practice of un-learning that nurtures a mature and liberating individuation needs to be pursued in the cultural domain through a dialogical and communicative practice with others whose stories about history and whose cultural sensibilities differ from one's own. It calls for a conceptual model that reinterprets the step-back as a step into "world-traveling."[30] Holding oneself open would lead into a series of reductions that might illuminate racial, ethnic, cultural, sexual, and other entrenched biases. The willingness to sustain the uncanny discomforts of world-traveling would prove vital to transformation. Zhuangzi's "ease in wandering" (*xiaoyaoyou* 逍遙遊) must, in this light, be understood to move beyond the likes of comfort and the dislikes of discomfort, and thus support the enabling orientation that permits one to value each.

4. Phoenixes, Butterflies, and Dream

Unlike Husserl and Heidegger, the *Zhuangzi* is not burdened by the aim to produce philosophy as rigorous science or develop a fundamental ontology. The literary movement of the text can thus conform to and prepare reception of the paradigmatic way of life it espouses.[31] The *Zhuangzi* can be seen as undertaking the phenomenological reduction in a hermeneutic sense in two corresponding aspects, textual and soteriological. The opening chapters can be understood as *enacting* a preliminary step-back through clearing away discriminations and desires. Analyzed as deliberate enactments that lead the reader to "disengage" the discriminating, planning, and goal-oriented mind, the literary art of the *Zhuangzi* "engage[s] the intuitive or aesthetic functions of the mind."[32] By disarming the analytic mind, this textual reduction prepares the reader for the soteriological paradigm that presents the fasting of the mind and effortless (*wuwei* 無為) or natural action (*ziran* 自然) as a proscribed way of living. The *Zhuangzi* returns us to a way of nourishing *de* that inheres in being or the generative matrix of life rather than by adherence to prescriptive courses (*dao*s) like those of the Confucian or Mohist schools that mold behavior developmentally to attain specific moral or social ideals.[33] By articulating a robust and transformative art of following *tian* 天 (Heaven), the *Zhuangzi* demonstrates that it is possible to live in the world by not-knowing and through relinquishing purposive aims.

Robert Allinson's definition of spiritual transformation helps to clarify a radical view of "free and easy wandering" that is neither irrational nor reducible to aesthetic play, even though one lives without pre-designed aims in life. Spiritual transformation effectuates a change in "perspective" that alters the mind and "takes one beyond all viewpoints" or particular beliefs.[34]

This transformation in perspective, attitude, and orientation is "noetic, but not intellectual" (i.e., not the result of philosophical explanation or logical deduction); irreducible to psychological insight (because it "removes an entire mental block" and not only emotional conflicts); and non-mystical (since it cannot depict a static union where "all distinctions vanish").[35] It is not an adjustment within interpersonal and social relations conventionally understood through a shared world-horizon but a dramatic liberation from the world-horizons that bind one to constrained forms of affective and mental change. We could call such a radical and complete transformation "mystical" in the qualified sense that James Sellmann does; that is, not as static mergence with the cosmos but rather as being restored to life in "continuity with the particulars of nature."[36] Spiritual transformation requires a deliberate release from discrimination ("so" and "not so"), ordinary emotions (joy and sorrow), likes and dislikes (desirous preferences), and entry into a way of unknowing and trust. The mockery of Zhuangzi forms a part of the ease of wandering, yet this ease emerges through a serious program of fasting and the cultivation of willingness to live from the larger perspective of the oneness of things.

4.1. Textual Reduction

The opening chapters can be said to enact a phenomenological reduction through two broad steps: (1) suspending the habit of discrimination and (2) dismantling the desire to realize an ideal self. Among the plethora of transformative metaphors in the *Zhuangzi*, the mythical phoenix Peng and the butterfly dream frame the first two chapters and all that falls within (the cicada and the little dove, the story of the hand balm, the chirping of birds). This framing strikes a blow at conventional ideals, and the dualities they rest upon, by positing the preposterous idea that one could undergo a great transformation, like Peng, that seems impossible to fathom from all customary standpoints. Because the *Zhuangzi* imparts a model of living that stands at odds with normal ways of cultivation, it must initially generate disorientation and then shatter the shared, commonsense orientation to accomplishment that underlies all life projects, beliefs, and viewpoints, whether one valorizes the life of virtue or that of the scoundrel. This orientation treats life's journey as a planned and goal-oriented quest to attain an ideal form of selfhood (the butterfly dream).

That the cicadas and doves scoff at the transformation of a fish into the phoenix Peng in chapter 1 (Carefree Wandering) signals that the trained adult mind can only regard such carefree living as ludicrous, impossible to attain or, even worse, a gaudy display of arrogance. "Where does he think *he's* going?" taunts the little quail.[37] Having been trained to rule over perception, judgment, and decision, the adult mind cannot entertain an order of liberation, greatness, and distinction that exceeds all it assumes to be rationally and humanly attainable. Considered through the lens of phenomenological reduction, the story cannot facilely promote greatness (Peng) over smallness (cicadas, doves, and quails). Rather, it cautions the reader not to confound any worldly notions of grandeur with the promise of carefree wandering, which Peng enters only after he is diminished and moves beyond dichotomous distinctions into the sea.

Peng, when seen as cicadas do, is symbolic of everything great that humans desire to emulate, yet he remains "dependent upon things for survival" and does not point beyond "worldly desires."[38] When transplanted into the world-horizon of the southern sea, Peng appears dwarfed by the sea's vastness. By showing that even Peng's apparent majesty might appear inconsequential by other cultural standards, Zhuangzi nullifies the cultivated and learned heart-mind that measures great and small against one constructed horizon of value or another.[39] These passages draw the reader to place under an existential epoché assumptions of great and small ("so" and "not so") and to quiet the "petty desires and selfish grievances" born out of and which keep us bound to them.[40]

The butterfly dream progresses further to unearth the relation between rational ideals and desire. It plays upon a symbol of an unfathomable and irreversible transformation. Halting discrimination at its logical limit, the image of the caterpillar-turned-butterfly captivates the heart-mind with its profound longing to become so grandiosely transformed as truly to become distinguished. Discriminations, as treated in the *Zhuangzi*, hinge not on the source unknown (Dao) that unites, relativizes, and contextualizes them but rather on a singular ranking. The discriminating mind produces world-horizons by prioritizing aims according to ideal ends or an idea of the best life. This projected ideal, in turn, underwrites desire and gives vent to competitive ambition. Through the dream scenario, Zhuangzi treats all specific aims as harnessing an elemental desire to become outstanding, literally to stand out above others. Whether pursued toward good or bad, prominent or humble, social or anti-social, conventional or unconventional forms of distinction, the desire for distinction orients us to measure ourselves against others through the rankings we adopt. It thus misses the mark of the great transformation heralded in the story of Peng.

Understood as an embodied form of the phenomenological reduction, the *Zhuangzi* stages the dream in a manner that unleashes and toys with the reader's desire to identify with the butterfly. Positioned like bookends, the story of Peng and the butterfly dream draw the reader through a process of (1) stilling the cognitive impetus to make distinctions, (2) discovering the hidden motivational ambitions that prove the rational quest to be less righteous than it pretends, and (3) finally to a shattering of the very quest to know the self. This final blow moves from the suspension of discrimination and the unmasking of desire to a possible reorientation and dramatic transformation. It prepares the disoriented and shattered heart-mind to accept the possibility of a radically alternative path, not simply that of un-learning rather than upbuilding but also of unknowing and forgetting the self.

The heart-mind compulsively questions, who am I really, Zhuang Zhou (i.e., Zhuangzi) or the butterfly? By calling into question the ambition that taints discrimination, the *Zhuangzi* challenges the very quest to know oneself through fulfilling one's ambition. The reduction is brought to a head when the machinations of calculative planning and goal-oriented activity are pared down to this circular and irresolvable anxiety over who I am really. Like manifold linguistic distinctions before it, Zhuangzi does not resolve the dream-question of selfhood but instead foils the cognitive and emotional desire to know who I am in advance of action. This forces the reader to suspend the customary pattern of an agential doer who wields the power to fashion an ideal image of self and, in a pre-designed manner, take steps to become this exemplary self.

These textual reductions teach that entry into a genuinely great transformation (*dahua* 大化) cannot be rationally planned, self-governed, or rooted in the comparative mind. Moreover, this literary art squelches the surreptitious inclination to turn the butterfly into a spiritually ideal measure of true selfhood.[41] By depriving us of what we unconsciously seek—to become superior either in worldly terms or through transcendent escape from the world—this tight little story, translated into six sentences, with neither commentary nor elaboration, uncovers the hidden motivations of the rational life.[42] The *Zhuangzi*'s stance inaugurates a shift away from the view that the discriminating mind is the sole agent of change. A necessary condition for entering into a co-creative life is to proceed without knowing; that is, to relinquish dreams of self-attainment.

4.2. Soteriological Reduction: The Paradigmatic Practice

The examples of Cook Ding 庖丁 and the fasting of the mind (*xinzhai* 心齋) have received manifold treatments as articulating a *paradigmatic life* practice. Zhuangzi, I have suggested, cannot *conceivably* propose Cook Ding as exemplifying a sustainable spiritual practice, rather than an occasional virtuosic performance, without first bringing the heart-mind to a stop. And the story of the fasting of the mind begs the question whether a non-purposive way of living can in fact be sustainable. How can Yan Hui (a disciple of Confucius) teach men of worldly station to be ethical without proposing a standard or assuming right demeanor? In the hands of the *Zhuangzi*, the reduction, by restoring contact with *tianji* 天機 (Heavenly mechanism), unveils the prospect of realizing a profound trust in life and its promptings as a practiced way of being-in-the-world. This transformation in modality of living proves sustainable based on several factors: unknowing, trust, nondual perception, and intrinsic aims.

In the *Zhuangzi*, the step-back does not merely suspend but ultimately deposes discrimination and desire as the faculties that play the *governing roles* in action. Taken as a practice of reduction, the fasting of the mind empties out the senses, the heart, the mind, the desire to correct the misguided. "Don't listen with your ears, listen with your mind. No, don't listen with your mind, but listen with your spirit. Listening stops with the ears, the mind stops with recognition, but spirit is empty and waits on all things. Dao gathers in emptiness alone. Emptiness is the fasting of the mind."[43] The cicadas and doves in our minds balk at the idea that a non-purposively-oriented life could form a sustained way to be in the world. It seems utterly naïve to commandeer life without the protections of knowledge, without developing strategies for survival, and without reliance upon past experience to show us how to handle new situations.

Edward Slingerland's notion that there is a "normative order" (*tianji*) and an irrepressible force of Dao buried beneath all interpreted and linguistic horizons is important in this context. Freedom from goal-oriented and desire-driven lifestyles rests on the experience of the Dao or the Heavenly mechanism as a guiding force and as a font of action.[44] A non-purposive orientation need not land us in aimless pursuits because action can stem from a font other than desire and be guided by powers other than the discriminating intellect. This font and power emerge through an alignment between the self and life. That Heaven proves "normative," in the sense that following it might prove the best way to live, must be discovered along the way and cannot be known in advance by discrimination, abstract judgment, or even divination.

Cook Ding, like other stories of skilled know-how, exemplifies this process of developing an intuitive orientation that is no longer suppressed and controlled by the reflective capacity. Cook Ding's skill emerges through a progressive series of epoché from the ears to the heart-mind to *qi* 氣 (vital breath, energy). Slingerland details this as a movement that first relinquishes ordinary sensory responses (I don't look with my eyes), then releases "discriminating knowledge" (listening with the heart-mind) until Cook Ding can listen "with the *qi*" or spirit. Listening with the heart-mind articulates the standard way we acquire skill through reliance on knowledge of the parts of the ox. The *Zhuangzi*, however, considers this kind of knowledge to be a blunt instrument that easily "butchers" the outcome because a preconceived and set plan cannot adapt to the concrete fact that this particular ox does not fit neatly into a scheme or ideal essence of ox. Listening with spirit, by contrast, allows the cook effortlessly to sense spaces between the joints and thus gracefully avoid clumsy mistakes and butchered results.[45]

One could gloss this path of reduction, following Husserl, as a return to pure subjectivity and a primordial intuition that apprehends things-in-themselves. But what matters in the *Zhuangzi* is that contact with the irrepressible Heavenly mechanism releases, stimulates, and nourishes one's irrepressible "spiritual" powers or *de*. For this reason, an entirely new form of life becomes possible. A.C. Graham argues that "Zhuangzi's ideal is to have no choice at all, because reflecting the situation with perfect clarity you can respond in only one way."[46] James Sellmann emphasizes the organismic power to live and die with the alterations of things.[47] There may be, even for Zhuangzi, multiple fitting responses and certainly multiple variations of the authentic person's (*zhenren* 真人) virtuosic style of cutting an ox, yet Graham and Sellmann converge on the point that an apt response arises out of the interplay between life and the person, and is not rooted in planning, knowledge, and past experience. Slingerland underscores that such a *non-rational or unknowing* manner of being can be likened to that of the artist who sees the creative process more as one of discovery than attainment. One discovers rather than designs "the proper way pigments on a canvas are to be combined to reflect a landscape, or the way a knife is to be wielded if an ox is to be butchered."[48]

This co-creativity does not rest exclusively upon primordial intuition (Husserl) or the mystery of disclosure (Heidegger) but upon the power of this generative matrix and our own natural inherence in it. That the way of *unknowing* is not a prescription for an irrational, impulsive, and blind life, or "a purely egotistic pastime," as Robert Allinson argues, can be explained through the virtues it produces.[49] By relinquishing a projective pattern for decision, the fasting of the mind inaugurates *a more intelligent way of living*. However ironic it may seem, the *Zhuangzi* counsels that one begins to "know the limits of things" or acquire authentic understanding only through this dynamic engagement with life.[50] Proof of the superiority of this non-rational way can be found in the dynamic, soft, and adaptable capacity to respond in a fitting manner, and not force or "butcher" things, overwhelm the field of action, or press people beyond their breaking point. By contrast, the discriminating mind, bent on its preconceived agenda, inevitably overrides the natural flow and presses past what the situation can bear. Such a manner of moving against life inevitably retards growth. The ambitious underpinnings of a self-directed life gather everything into its domain of rational mastery. The "natural" way, though not without artistry or even elements of deliberate intent, reverses and undoes this habitual and self-conscious pattern of lording over life.

The fasting of the mind grows credible when we articulate the growth it engenders. The "forgetting the self"—by fasting away the seemingly essential power to make distinctions and "do" action—nurses the *virtues of trust and delight*.[51] Trust is an elemental form of virtue that grows out of receptivity because one discovers through practice, and retrospectively, that things progress better if one does not overpower but rather meets what the situation calls forth and permits. Trust in *tian* (illumination) engenders trust in the authentic life through strengthening the virtue of being able to follow, sense, apprehend, and delight in the wild, strange, and fortuitous alterations of things. It solidifies *a non-anxious way of moving* through life because it dispels the mistake of the discriminative mind in thinking that we must abstractly determine the ideal way to proceed; it relieves the heart-mind of the hefty weight of laying out courses of action and straining to discipline the uncontrollable outcomes of events. Rational fears dissolve, since emptying the mind and forgetting the self do not yield irresolute and dissolute conduct. Instead, they foster a solid yet supple attentiveness that allows life to nourish growth in oneself, in others, and in situations. This mode of being-in-the-world produces consistency in meeting the field of action with joy and unexpected delight but without utilizing contrived effort to straighten character. It "stabilizes" a non-interfering orientation, in the way that improvisational virtuosity does, by repeated unscripted performances; that is, by eliminating preferences and pre-designed strategies for attainment. And it enhances reception of the strangeness of others and things.

The *Zhuangzi,* I wish to suggest, considers the hallmark of intelligence to be creative adaptability to the unexpected alterations of things. "The understanding of the ancients really got all the way there" refers not simply to the equalizing of viewpoints but to "the point where, for some, there had never existed so-called things."[52] This marks the moment when *eidetic* reduction nullifies itself as a quest for cognitive classification and a path of knowing, for it is the point where the discrimination of things can be seen to reside in the naming and labeling of them, calling them a "this" which implies a "that." This point constitutes the pivot around which the mind can be freed for the ultimate reduction, namely, to move non-dually with the transformation of things. The *Zhuangzi* "would not define rightness in any one particular way but would instead entrust it to the everyday function [of each being]."[53] Instead of a quest for essences, the *Zhuangzi* shows a way of life that can flourish by embracing the *immeasurable proportions of things.*

The non-rational life gives birth to the virtues of "correlative nondual thinking" that harmonize, as James Sellmann argues, with the "nondual, two-sided flip-flop environment in which a life is lived."[54] "The correlative nondual point of view . . . perceives the interdependency of opposites, such as the Peng bird and the turtle dove."[55] It also captures the way the mind generates the opposite out of phenomena: "thinking of the small turns into thinking of the big."[56] I would extend this analysis to include the immeasurable ways that nondual thinking generates adaptable action that, when befitting a circumstance, is big when needed, small when fitting, low-lying if necessary or standing-up as prompted. And it permits a thoroughly embodied manner of appraising things in context. Things, in effect, are not captured by a single measure. Peng is big when placed in the North and small when placed in the South. The discriminating mind that carries over a previous label and judgment that conceives Peng as a static essence impedes and generates interference in how things arise and call for response in the present situation. Peng changes diachronically relative to situation and to its opposite.

Yet because small and large are also not discrete names, nondual perception includes synchronous and immeasurable facets to the two-sided interdependence of opposites. The liberated mind can see the tallness in the small. Even a cicada acquires its form, beauty, power, and greatness from the Dao. It can discern the smallness of all that the world considers grand. It can intuit the hidden in the visible bones of the ox, recognize the virtue of the lame person who ascribes no blame to the Dao, and find the exemplar in the monstrous or odd. From the perspective of *unknowing*, one's virtue, in the ethical sense, emerges through fasting away the preferences of the bloated heart that cannot transcend a dualistic, non-contextual, and non-dynamic manner of evaluating things. The *Zhuangzi* certainly confounds the usual ways of discriminating, since gourds can be tubs and a balm for chapped hands can serve the fiefdom.[57] "Only the man of far-reaching vision . . . has no use of categories, but relegates them all to the constant."[58]

Earlier I noted that integration into the generative matrix of life makes the non-rational life possible. Action can stem from spirit. The Dao can lead beyond set measures and release one for the adaptive intelligence that can apprehend, in light of Heaven, the situated size of things. Yet such a life, if it is to be sustained in a thoroughgoing manner, must be lived ever more fully for *intrinsic aims*. There may be no discernible *telos* or extrinsic cosmic purpose to the generative Dao because it gives us no foundation on which to project the standards of ideal character formation, development of civilization, or moral coda. Yet it does not follow that the generative Dao realizes no intrinsic, non-purposive, natural, or autotelic ends, namely, to nourish, liberate, and transform. The fasting of the mind, understood as a transcendental reduction, performs a dance with the Dao. In this dance, the extensive reach out into life pursuits must constantly shed extrinsic aims in order to discover and be fortified anew by the intrinsic lessons that life bestows.

Finally, this path of de-cultivation must engender an integration of powers that otherwise fall fallow under domination of the discriminating mind or "self," powers such as the intuitive, sensitive, feeling, vital, and spiritual aspects of human being as well as those of nondual perception and thought. The living *movement of return* to the essentially creative font of effortless action could be said to marshal all our powers conjointly or in unique combinations as the circumstance demands. Even though the Cook Ding passage seems to give special significance to *qi* or vitality as the spontaneous force of free action, overemphasis on *qi* would have two undesirable outcomes. It would give undue credence to the prospect that the *Zhuangzi* promotes mindless forms of spontaneity. Edward Slingerland clarifies that effortless action is not unaware or blind but rather unself-conscious and unscripted.[59] Overemphasis on vitality would equally neglect the other faculties involved in correlative nondual perception, trust in the Dao, and the virtues of practical knowing that the non-rational life fosters.

To the degree that one can speak of individuation in the context of the *Zhuangzi*, it must be as a process of self-forgetting that unifies one with the generative matrix of the Dao and unleashes the fuller array of powers that enable one to follow Heaven and respond to the unexpected. In the *Zhuangzi*, integration cannot refer to a psychological view, as this would mimic the kind of Confucian or Mohist patterns of development that he scorns. The term "individuation" normally starts to collapse at the point that partaking in the creative processes of life unfolds through forgetting the self's power to impose a plan and assert its separateness. Heidegger shows that genuine individuation arises only through de-cultivation and the growth of virtues that openness produces. Zhuangzi might add that we acquire and lose "individuation" as we transform along with and adaptively respond to the immeasurable and wild transformation of things.

5. Conclusion

Examining the *Zhuangzi* through the lens of the phenomenological reduction shows a number of reasons to globalize philosophy and re-examine the nature of philosophy as an academic discipline. The *Zhuangzi* encourages the Western academic to break with a narrow conception of rationality, and even to take disciplined reasoning less seriously. If, as the *Zhuangzi* intends to show, the pretentions that underlie rational life impede or limit the growth of humanity, then it proves conceivable that an ideal path of learning might progress not only from moral cultivation to taking reflective distance on cultivation but also from reflective life to a liberation from attachments to the reflective life. Engaging the Daoist tradition debunks the idea that there is one sole path to the attainment of an enlightened orientation. Even though the cultivation of a rational life may benefit most individuals in a given society, it may not be recommended that every individual take a direct path into reflective life, since not all people are intellectually inclined. If the aim of philosophy is not finally enjoyment of critical debate but rather self-transformation, then it can proceed in various ways. A transformational approach can dissolve attachment to any native bent, and thus open a person to an integration of powers that would introduce balance into her overall orientation to life. The intellectual cannot be exempted from the task to safeguard finitude. The *Zhuangzi* detects the need to combat the stubborn barriers to self-examination that, ironically, the pursuit of the reflective life can erect.

The *Zhuangzi* and the Daoist tradition invite a rejuvenated sense that the ultimate value of philosophy lies in its power to orient us to live a better life and to effectuate transformative attitudes and outlooks. Anchoring philosophy in a liberated relation to one's primary bent, rather than prizing one bent over another, engenders an appreciation of other modes of thinking, manifold ways of arriving at insight, and creative methods of edification. In addition to decentering analytical reasoning as the sole path to enlightenment, this lineage leads one to consider the importance of utilizing a host of rhetorical, didactic, literary, paradoxical, textual, analytic, and hermeneutical modes of thinking to advance the vocation of philosophy. It dismantles the presumption that Western philosophy has long held to be the Queen of the sciences. It challenges philosophy as a discipline to adapt to demands of the global era and correct its collusions with Western forms of cultural imperialism.

Among the more illuminated legacies of Western thought we can include political liberties, constitutional democracies, and conceptions of basic human rights. Axiomatic to the Daoist heritage is a robust understanding that life conditions change. Old paradigms must give way to paradigm shifts, even as core intuitions and aspects of the past may need to be preserved in that shift. What once heralded progress and ascension may now impede growth and productive change. There has always been an underside to the European Enlightenment, so evident in the long-standing harms of colonization, uneven development, cultural imperialism, and the denigrating treatment of non-Western philosophies as infantile. The global situation calls for the promotion of dialogical models of decision-making, the implementation of new metrics of poverty and wealth that do not singularly prize material assets and consumerist lifestyles, and the preservation of cultural continuity, spiritual wisdom, and collective relations to land among indigenous and other post-development communal formations around the globe. Precedents and models for these shifts have been conceived by Western and non-Western thinkers, philosophers and scientists, activists and people. Yet these newly conceived models emerged not through hypothetical reasoning by its lights alone but rather through genuine engagement with and listening to the (excluded) voices of others.

If Western philosophy is to play a viable role on the global stage—by correcting imbalances in global development, meeting the environmental emergency, circumventing the crisis that the Oil Peak will generate, and defeating cultural imperialism—it must reconceive itself as a practice of intercultural dialogue. Such a practice would arguably be anchored, as Zhuangzi teaches, in child-like openness and a humble sense of finitude. Much philosophizing speaks about but neglects to engage the other—at home, in the South or in the East. Yet the obvious cannot readily be dismissed. The cultural other plays an irreplaceable role in revealing to Western thinkers both the richness and the drawbacks of their intellectual heritage. The assumption that any culture can make this assessment on its own does not hold up to scrutiny. Actual intercultural dialogue thrusts one back upon unflattering discoveries of faulty suppositions, intense attachments to them, deeply embedded racist or ethnocentric habits, and *angst*. Even a lifetime of sincere self-examination cannot guarantee that deeply internalized patterns of thought have been sufficiently dislodged to maintain reflective awareness in the face of other cultural logics or excluded perspectives. The very jesting of the *Zhuangzi*, the delight it takes in poking fun at the quest for rational life, the quick-witted way it stops abstract reason short in its tracks could easily be dismissed and cast aside as unworthy of attention by the philosopher in pursuit of conceptual debate. This too might evoke bellyaching laughter and glee from Zhuangzi, since it so eloquently expresses the underlying sensibility of much Western philosophy that only those traditions that can match its rationality merit engagement in worthy discourse.

Notes

1   Kwok-Ying Lau develops a rich phenomenological expression of this orientative character of Chinese philosophy in his *Phenomenology and Intercultural Understanding: Toward a New Cultural Flesh* (Dordrecht: Springer, 2016).

2   For an overview, see: Julia Jansen and Wenjing Cai, "Husserlian Phenomenology: Current Chinese Perspectives," *Comparative and Continental Philosophy*, 10.1 (2018): 2–6; and D.P. Chattopadhyaya, Lester Embree, and Jitendranath Mohanty (eds.), *Phenomenology and Indian Philosophy* (Albany: State University of New York Press, 2019).

3   Kim-Chong Chong, *Zhuangzi's Critique of the Confucians: Blinded by the Human* (Albany: State University of New York Press, 2016), 2.

4   Sellmann points out that *bianhua* 變化 refers not only to transformations "of form and shape (*bian* 變) . . . but also entails a complete renewal of the experience of life's meaning (*hua* 化)." See James D. Sellmann, "Transformational Humor in the *Zhuangzi*," in *Wandering at Ease in the Zhuangzi*, ed. Roger Ames (Albany: State University of New York Press, 1998), 170.

5   Edmund Husserl, *Ideas Pertaining to a Pure Phenomenology and to a Phenomenological Philosophy*, First Book, (The Hague: Nijhoff, 1982), 27–8.

6   Ibid., 88–9.

7   Edmund Husserl, *Ideas: General Introduction to Pure Phenomenology* (London: George Allen & Unwin Ltd., 1931), 49, cf. 131. For a general description of the evolution of the reduction in Husserl, see Dermot Moran and Timothy Mooney (eds.), *The Phenomenology Reader* (New York: Routledge, 2002), 12–16.

8   Ramakant Sinari, "The Method of Phenomenological Reduction and Yoga," *Philosophy East and West*, 15.3–4 (1965): 219.

9   François Raffoul, "Factical Life and the Need for Philosophy," in *Rethinking Facticity*, eds. François Raffoul and Eric S. Nelson (Albany: State University of New York Press, 2008), 75.

10 Martin Heidegger, *Sein und Zeit* (Tübingen: Niemeyer Verlag, 1985), 84. For the English translation, see Martin Heidegger, *Being and Time* (New York: Harper and Row, 1962). I follow the standard method of citing marginal page numbers so that the references correlate to the German passages.

11 Ibid., 148. In all life activities, human beings operate interpretively; that is, by projecting a horizon of possibility (a world of cleaning) within which things appear meaningfully "as" something (a dust cloth) and "in order to" (for the

sake of tidying up) (Ibid., 148–9). On this hermeneutic ground, Heidegger claims that "[i]t is not the case that man 'is' and then has, by way of an extra, a relationship-of-Being towards the 'world'—a world with which he provides himself occasionally" (Ibid., 84).

12 Francis Seeburger, "Heidegger and the Phenomenological Reduction," *Philosophy and Phenomenological Research*, 36.2 (1975): 213.

13 Heidegger, *Being and Time / Sein und Zeit*, 231–5.

14 Laozi, *Daodejing*, chapter 1. Available online at: https://ctext.org/dao-de-jing

15 Patricia Huntington, "A Huayan Critique of Heidegger: The Quest for a Non-Obstructed Mitdasein," *Journal of the Pacific Association for the Continental Tradition*, 1 (2018): 8–11 and 15–18.

16 Tetsurō Watsuji, *Watsuji Tetsurō's Rinrigaku: Ethics in Japan* (Albany: State University of New York Press, 1996), 9–15.

17 Erin McCarthy, *Ethics Embodied: Rethinking Selfhood through Continental, Japanese, and Feminist Philosophies* (Lanham: Lexington Books, 2010), 20–6; and Lawrence Vogel, *The Fragile "We": Ethical Implications of Heidegger's "Being and Time"* (Evanston: Northwestern University Press, 1994), 7–9, 19–20, and 24–7.

18 David Wong, "Zhuangzi and the Obsession with Being Right," *History of Philosophy Quarterly* 22.2 (2005): 98–9.

19 Eric S. Nelson, "Heidegger and the Ethics of Facticity," in *Rethinking Facticity*, eds. François Raffoul and Eric S. Nelson (Albany: State University of New York Press, 2008), 131.

20 Ibid.

21 Ibid.

22 Vogel, *The Fragile "We,"* 94.

23 Ibid., 13.

24 Nelson, "Heidegger and the Ethics of Facticity," 133.

25 Ibid., 132.

26 This is nicely expressed in Chai's comments that the *Zhuangzi* "espouses a philosophy of self-forgetting, a de-labelling of knowledge as we know it, so that one may return to the naïve state of innocence we experience as children; the carefree wandering of *xiaoyao*." David Chai, *Early Zhuangzi Commentaries: On the Sounds and Meanings of the Inner Chapters* (Saarbrücken: VDM Verlag Dr. Müller, 2008), 1.

27 Taigen Dan Leighton, *Cultivating the Empty Field: The Silent Illumination of Master Hongzhi* (Boston: Tuttle Publishing, 2000), 4.

28 Dorothy Leland, "Conflictual Culture and Authenticity: Deepening Heidegger's Account of the Social," in Nancy J. Holland and Patricia Huntington (eds.), *Feminist Interpretations of Martin Heidegger* (University Park: The Pennsylvania State University Press, 2001), 110.

29 Quoted in Leland, Ibid., 115.

30 Mariana Ortega, *In-Between: Latina Feminist Phenomenology, Multiplicity, and the Self* (Albany: State University of New York Press, 2016), 51–8 and 87–116.

The concept of "world-traveling" comes from María Lugones, "Playfulness, 'World'—Traveling, and Loving Perception," *Hypatia*, 2.4 (1987): 3–19.

31 A fruitful comparison of literary techniques in the later Heidegger and the *Zhuangzi* falls outside the scope of this chapter.

32 Robert Allinson, *Chuang-Tsu for Spiritual Transformation: An Analysis of the Inner Chapters* (Albany: State University of New York Press, 1989), 23.

33 Zhuangzi, *Zhuangzi: The Essential Writings with Selections from Traditional Commentaries* Brook Ziporyn (trans.) (Indianapolis: Hackett Publishing, 2009), xiii.

34 Allinson, *Chuang-Tzu for Spiritual Transformation*, 8.

35 Ibid., 8–9.

36 Sellmann, "Transformational Humor," 170.

37 Zhuangzi, *The Essential Writings*, 4.

38 Chai, *Early Zhuangzi Commentaries*, 37; cf. Zhuangzi, *The Essential Writings*, x.

39 Chai argues that Zhuangzi "instills in the reader a sense of our own diminutiveness as human beings while encouraging us to move beyond our petty desires and selfish grievances." Chai, *Early Zhuangzi Commentaries*, 37.

40 Ibid.

41 Zhuangzi, *The Essential Writings*, 21.

42 The additional passages on dreaming reinforce the view that it matters not whether we are dreaming. Zhuangzi suggests "still, there may even be a greater awakening after which you know, that this, too, was just a greater dream." P.J. Ivanhoe and Bryan Van Norden, *Readings in Classical Chinese Philosophy*, 223. Their translation, however, captures the point that awakening may be from lesser to more apt perspectives, but the process cannot be said to have a limit. It thus fits with other translations: "I don't know whether you are awake or you are dreaming." Zhuangzi, *Chuang-Tzu: Basic Writings*, Burton Watson (trans.) (New York: Columbia University Press, 1996), 85. See also "When I say you are dreaming, I am dreaming too" in Ibid., 43.

43 Zhuangzi, *Basic Writings*, 54. This story appears in chapter 4 of the text (*renjianshi* 人間世) and has Confucius teaching his disciple Yan Hui the arts of mental fasting.

44 Edward Slingerland, *Effortless Action: Wu-wei as Conceptual Metaphor and Spiritual Ideal in Early China* (Oxford: Oxford University Press, 2003), 195–203.

45 Ibid., 201.

46 A.C. Graham, *Disputers of the Tao: Philosophical Argument in Ancient China* (La Salle: Open Court, 1989), 190.

47 Sellmann, "Transformational Humor," 171.

48 Slingerland, *Effortless Action*, 201.

49 Allinson, *Chuang-Tzu for Spiritual Transformation*, 7.

50 Zhuangzi, *Basic Writings*, 46; Zhuangzi, *The Essential Writings*, 21.

51 On the essence of the human, see Slingerland, *Effortless Action*, 181.

52 Zhuangzi, *The Essential Writings,* 14.

53 Ibid., 13.

54 Sellmann, "Transformational Humor," 164.

55 Ibid.

56 Ibid., 166.

57 Zhuangzi, *Basic Writings*, 28–9.

58 Ibid., 37.

59 Slingerland, *Effortless Action*, 8.

References

Allinson, Robert. (1989), *Chuang-Tzu for Spiritual Transformation: An Analysis of the Inner Chapters*, Albany: State University of New York Press.

Ames, Roger, ed. (1998), *Wandering at Ease in the Zhuangzi*, Albany: State University of New York Press.

Chai, David. (2008), *Early Zhuangzi Commentaries: On the Sounds and Meanings of the Inner Chapters*, Saarbrücken: VDM Verlag Dr. Müller.

Chattopadhyaya, D.P., Lester Embree, and Jitendranath Mohanty, eds. (1992), *Phenomenology and Indian Philosophy*, Albany: State University of New York Press.

Chong, Kim-Chong. (2016), *Zhuangzi's Critique of the Confucians: Blinded by the Human*, Albany: State University of New York Press.

Graham, A.C. (1989), *Disputers of the Tao: Philosophical Argument in Ancient China*. La Salle: Open Court.

Heidegger, Martin. (1962), *Being and Time*. John Macquarrie and Edward Robinson (trans.), New York: Harper and Row.

Heidegger, Martin. (1985), *Sein und Zeit*. Tübingen: Niemeyer Verlag.

Holland, Nancy J. and Patricia Huntington, eds. (2001), *Feminist Interpretations of Martin Heidegger*, University Park: The Pennsylvania State University Press.

Huntington, Patricia. (2018), "A Huayan Critique of Heidegger: The Quest for a Non-Obstructed *Mitdasein*," *Journal of the Pacific Association for the Continental Tradition*, 1: 5–23.

Husserl, Edmund. (1931), *Ideas: General Introduction to Pure Phenomenology*, W.R. Boyce Gibson (trans.), London: George Allen & Unwin Ltd.

Husserl, Edmund. (1982), *Ideas Pertaining to a Pure Phenomenology and to a Phenomenological Philosophy*, First Book, F. Kersten (trans.), The Hague: Nijhoff.

Ivanhoe, P.J. and Bryan van Norden, eds. (2001), *Readings in Classical Chinese Philosophy*, Indianapolis: Hackett Publishing.

Jansen, Julia and Wenjing Cai. (2018), "Husserlian Phenomenology: Current Chinese Perspectives," *Comparative and Continental Philosophy*, 10.1: 2–6.

Laozi. *Daodejing*. Available online at: https://ctext.org/dao-de-jing

Lau, Kwok-Ying. (2016), *Phenomenology and Intercultural Understanding: Toward a New Cultural Flesh*, in *Contributions to Phenomenology* (vol. 87), Dordrecht: Springer.

Leighton, Taigen Dan. (2000), *Cultivating the Empty Field: The Silent Illumination of Master Hongzhi*, Boston: Tuttle Publishing.

Leland, Dorothy. (2001), "Conflictual Culture and Authenticity: Deepening Heidegger's Account of the Social," in Nancy J. Holland and Patricia Huntington (eds.), *Feminist Interpretations of Martin Heidegger*, 107–27, University Park: The Pennsylvania State University Press.

Lugones, Maria. (1987), "Playfulness, 'World'—Traveling and Loving Perception," *Hypatia*, 2.4: 3–19.

McCarthy, Erin. (2010), *Ethics Embodied: Rethinking Selfhood through Continental, Japanese, and Feminist Philosophies*, Lanham: Lexington Books.

Moran, Dermot and Timothy Mooney, eds. (2002). *The Phenomenology Reader*, New York: Routledge.

Nelson, Eric S. (2008), "Heidegger and the Ethics of Facticity," in François Raffoul and Eric S. Nelson (eds.), *Rethinking Facticity*, 129–47, Albany: State University of New York Press.

Ortega, Mariana. (2016), *In-Between: Latina Feminist Phenomenology, Multiplicity, and the Self*, Albany: State University of New York Press.

Raffoul, François. (2008), "Factical Life and the Need for Philosophy," in François Raffoul and Eric S. Nelson (eds.), *Rethinking Facticity*, 69–85, Albany: State University of New York Press.

Seeburger, Francis. (1975), "Heidegger and the Phenomenological Reduction," *Philosophy and Phenomenological Research*, 36.2: 212–21.

Sellmann, James D. (1998), "Transformational Humor in the *Zhuangzi*," in Roger Ames (ed.), *Wandering at Ease in the Zhuangzi*, 163–74, Albany: State University of New York Press.

Sinari, Ramakant. (1965), "The Method of Phenomenological Reduction and Yoga," *Philosophy East and West*, 15.3–4: 217–28.

Slingerland, Edward. (2003), *Effortless Action: Wu-wei as Conceptual Metaphor and Spiritual Ideal in Early China*, Oxford: Oxford University Press.

Vogel, Lawrence. (1994), *The Fragile "We": Ethical Implications of Heidegger's "Being and Time,"* Evanston: Northwestern University Press.

Watsuji, Tetsurō. (1996), *Watsuji Tetsurō's Rinrigaku: Ethics in Japan*, Yamamoto Seisaku and Robert E. Carter (trans.), Albany: State University of New York Press.

Wong, David. (2005), "Zhuangzi and the Obsession with Being Right," *History of Philosophy Quarterly*, 22.2: 91–107.

Zhuangzi. (1996), *Chuang-Tzu: Basic Writings*, Burton Watson (trans.), New York: Columbia University Press.

Zhuangzi. (2009), *Zhuangzi: The Essential Writings with Selections from Traditional Commentaries*, Brook Ziporyn (trans.), Indianapolis: Hackett Publishing.

10

The Reader's Chopper:

Finding Affinities from Gadamer to Zhuangzi on Reading

Sarah A. Mattice

1. Introduction

Reading is a skill and a practice that many take for granted. Words and letters are all around us; the visual world is saturated with things to read. For many fully literate adults, reading is such a fundamental skill that we do not remember clearly not being able to read.[1] Once we have learned to read, something foundational about our existence in and engagement with the world has been fundamentally altered, forever. Cognitive scientists and psychologists describe this as an "irreversible" process, because once it has really taken hold, or become automatic, we read without even trying—even sometimes when we are trying not to, as in the case of the Stroop Effect[2]—and we try to read even in cases where we know what we are seeing is not "readable"—as in Xu Bing's 徐冰 (1955–) art installation piece "Book of the Sky."[3]

In this chapter, I follow in the methodological footsteps of twentieth-century literary giant Qian Zhongshu 錢鍾書 (1910–98), who often wrote of the importance of *datong* 打通, creating connections and breaking down or through barriers between previously un-associated material by identifying unusual correspondences or affinities.[4] In this chapter, my aim is to contribute to the ongoing conversation on the ethics of reading, by putting alongside one another material from such diverse sources as cognitive science, European phenomenology, contemporary humanities, jazz music, and classical Chinese philosophy, to name a few. Although reading is an irreversible, mostly automatic process that many of us take for granted after we are literate, reading well can be a rich ethico-aesthetic practice that we self-consciously attend to as part of a larger, transformative process of living well.

2. Contemporary Research on Reading

"What happens when we read?" is a bad scientific question.[5]

When Daniel Willingham, author of *The Reading Mind*, says that "what happens when we read" is a bad question, he does not mean that we should not be investigating what happens when we read, as he notes that scientists have been trying to do just that, from a variety of perspectives, for more than a century. One reason he says that it is a bad scientific question is that reading is too complex—it is made up of so many different sub-processes, like vision, memory, grammar, language comprehension, vocabulary, emotion, and so on—and so we should ask questions of the individual sub-processes, and really understand those before moving on to the larger activity. Another reason it is a bad question, according to Willingham, is that understanding what happens when we read requires us to know what happens, and we might not always be the best judge of that.

> The history of psychology shows that it's easy to be fooled when you try to describe a task . . . Here's a simple example. When we read it feels as if we move our eyes smoothly—we sweep from the start of a line to the end, and then snap back to the far left of the page for the next line. That impression is easily disconfirmed by watching the eyes of another person as she reads. Her eyes don't move smoothly, but instead jump from one spot to the next, usually a distance of seven to nine letters. That's so easily observed it's probably been known for centuries. But even that observation—jumping movements, not smoothly tracking—is an incomplete description. In fact, your eyes are not always pointing at the same letter when you read. About half the time each eye looks at a different letter. They may even be slightly crossed.[6]

Although it may be a "bad" question, we do know a lot about how we read, not only as Willingham describes above, about the workings of our eyes, but about technical reading things like fonts and sizes and slants and colors (on paper and on screen, and how they differ in terms of readability), about reading pedagogy and the importance of not only letter recognition and word vocabulary but also background knowledge to reading comprehension, and about reading and memory and just how little of what we read most of us actually retain. Researchers are also studying things like whether or not people commonly experience inner speech while they read, or how often they actually visualize passages from the text that they are reading.[7]

And, of course, as we are now fully immersed in the digital age, we are learning more and more about how very different reading is not just on a screen, but online, with hypertext and links and multitasking that does make reading online an overlapping but somewhat different skillset than reading offline. We also know that when we read on screens, we tend to read in a Z or F pattern,[8] not every line, and that we pay significantly more attention to the left side of the screen than the right: about 80 percent of our eye attention goes to the left half of the screen.[9] The fact that researchers have spent significant time and energy tracking down this information is not just good for web designers who want to redesign their pages so that people really see all their good information, but it is also useful for people who study reading habits of students. Imagine a page of text in print and a page of text as a PDF; now imagine you've put a patch over the lower right corner of the text on the PDF. This is basically what the F pattern of reading does on a screen— our eyes read the top lines, and the left sides of things, but we don't spend as much time or attention with the lower right-hand corner of a page. Now imagine this is how you read (without being aware of it) a twenty-page document. It is no wonder that basic reading comprehension, recall, and other reading tests are noticeably better with print than digital reading, and the F pattern is not even the only issue. A number of researchers have also studied the tactile experience of holding a book or paper in hand, being able to flip back pages in a book, or hold a page and move between pages, or put a finger at one spot in a text—all of these physical aspects of reading with print materials do seem to make a difference.[10]

Cognitive neuroscientist Dr. Maryanne Wolf, Director of the Center for Dyslexia, Diverse Learners, and Social Justice in the Graduate School of Education and Information Studies at UCLA, explains that her research

> depicts how the present reading brain enables the development of some of our most important intellectual and affective processes: internalized knowledge, analogical reasoning, and inference; perspective-taking and empathy; critical analysis and the generation of insight. Research surfacing in many parts of the world now cautions that each of these essential "deep reading" processes may be under threat as we move into digital-based modes of reading.[11]

Wolf is careful to note that she is not blaming technology per se, but rather that we need to pay attention to the environment in which our brains are developing and the practices we consistently privilege. She explains,

> If the dominant medium advantages processes that are fast, multi-task oriented and well-suited for large volumes of information, like the current digital medium, so will the reading circuit. As UCLA psychologist

Patricia Greenfield writes, the result is that less attention and time will be allocated to slower, time-demanding deep reading processes, like inference, critical analysis and empathy, all of which are indispensable to learning at any age.

However, as the *Atlantic*'s Jordan Weissmann pointed out:

The Pew Research Center reported . . . that nearly a quarter of American adults had not read a single book in the past year [2013]. As in, they hadn't cracked a paperback, fired up a Kindle, or even hit play on an audiobook while in the car. The number of non-book-readers has nearly tripled since 1978.[12]

In other words, while it may be tempting for some Luddites to raise an anti-digital reading alarm, given what we know about low numbers of readers, and about high adult illiteracy rates in the United States, focusing on how to help make reading a more self-conscious, reflective practice in whatever medium it is found might be the best approach. For my purposes here, I am interested in a contemporary conversation concerning the ethics of reading—not books vs. e-readers or audiobooks vs. comic books or stories vs. poems vs. non-fiction or any of that, but about the role that practices of reading might play in an ethical life, broadly conceived.[13] For that conversation, with contemporary research as an important motivating force, we begin with philosophical reflection on the experience of reading, with an eye toward how that may contribute to this larger project.

3. Reading from a Phenomenological Perspective

While much of the literature on phenomenology of reading is concerned with either literary criticism or reading education, for our purposes here I want to draw attention to a strand of thinking that focuses on phenomenology of reading with a more philosophical bent. Georges Poulet's 1969 essay, "Phenomenology of Reading," opens by exploring some of the differences between a book and a vase, concluding that while the vase obliges you to remain outside of it, "on the other hand, take a book, and you will find it offering, opening itself. It is this openness of the book which I find so moving . . . In short, the extraordinary fact in the case of a book is the falling away of the barriers between you and it. You are inside it; it is inside you; there is no longer either outside or inside."[14] He continues, exploring the way in which the consciousness of another "welcomes me, lets me look deep inside itself, and even allows me, with unheard-of license, to think what it thinks and feel what it feels."[15] While Poulet is somewhat uncritical about whether he means this consciousness is the consciousness of the author(s), the author(s)' intention, the book itself, or a more metaphoric sort of connection through the book to other persons—real, living, dead, imagined, fictional, etc.—his point centers on the feeling, both of intimacy and of a sort of displacement, created by the act of reading certain kinds of text in a certain way.

Poulet describes the way in which he is drawn into a fully interior world of language as he reads (fiction), a world where the difference between himself as subject and the external world of objects is blurred or reduced. In explaining what he calls the "remarkable transformation wrought in me through the act of reading," Poulet puzzles over the idea that in reading, he is "thinking the thoughts of another"; he is the "subject of thoughts other than my own."[16] There is a certain style or habit of reading with total commitment, and Poulet finds that, on careful phenomenological examination, this leads to a sort of dispossession of the self, evident in reading either a popular thriller or a work of "high" literature. Poulet explains that this dispossessed self is "a consciousness astonished by an existence which is not mine, but which I experience as though it were mine."[17]

Building critically on Poulet's work, Wolfgang Iser's 1972 "The Reading Process: A Phenomenological Approach" argues that in reading, "text and reader no longer confront each other as object and subject, but instead the 'division' takes place within the reader himself. In thinking the thoughts of another, his own individuality temporarily recedes into the background."[18] But, whereas Iser argues that Poulet draws from this the conclusion that in reading, which is understood as a kind of identification or internalization, the author's life story and the reader's individual disposition must be absent, Iser suggests that this is the wrong way to understand this phenomenon. In reading, in making this division within ourselves where we "take as a theme for ourselves something we are not," we are reshaping ourselves to increasingly accommodate the unfamiliar.[19] He explains:

> someone else's thoughts can only take a form in our consciousness if, in the process, our unformulated faculty for deciphering those thoughts is brought into play—a faculty which, in the act of deciphering, also formulates itself . . . The need to decipher gives us the chance to formulate our own deciphering capacity . . . [reading literature] entails the possibility that we may formulate ourselves and so discover what had previously seemed to elude our consciousness. These are the ways in which reading literature gives us the chance to formulate the unformulated.[20]

In other words, Iser, following a more hermeneutic line than Poulet, considers reading a creative practice involving the text, the community, the reader's anticipations, recollections, imagination, and her ability to make space for the unfamiliar within herself—to not only comprehend but also decipher and formulate for herself words, thoughts, language, ideas, narratives, stories, and so on that are not her own.

Although Iser does not directly reference Hans-Georg Gadamer's philosophical hermeneutics, it is clearly visible in the architecture of his phenomenological account of reading. While there is a great deal that could be said concerning Gadamer's hermeneutics and the phenomenology of reading, here we can focus on his metaphor of conversation for the activity of understanding, where the paradigm case of understanding is understanding a text. For Gadamer, understanding is

> a reciprocal relationship of the same kind as conversation. It is true that a text does not speak to us in the same way as does a Thou. We who are attempting to understand must ourselves make it speak . . . the chief thing that these apparently so different situations—understanding a text and reaching an understanding in a conversation—have in common is that both are concerned with a subject matter that is placed before them . . . Every conversation presupposes a common language, or better, creates a common language . . . To reach an understanding in a dialogue is not merely a matter of putting oneself forward and successfully asserting one's own point of view, but being transformed into a communion in which we do not remain what we were.[21]

Working out the understanding-as-conversation metaphor has several implications for the phenomenology of reading, on Gadamer's account. In order to be in a position to listen to the other conversation partner—the text—we must ourselves actively do something with it in order to be in a position to listen. For Gadamer, the conversation is not a passive metaphor, but one that implies significant effort and skill on the part of the reader. As he notes, the "rigor" of hermeneutical experience is "uninterrupted listening"— in other words, making the text speak is precisely putting oneself in a position to listen as openly as possible, without imposing oneself or any other interruptions, onto what it has to say.[22] It also implies not only that we listen, but that like in a real conversation, we are genuine participants, readers who must follow the thread of the conversation where it goes: "a genuine conversation is never the one that we wanted to conduct . . . Understanding or its failure is an event that happens to us."[23] So while the conversation metaphor is not passive, it does suggest some of the ways in which once we engage seriously in reading, we are swept up in the experience in ways that are not in our control, and are transformed as a result of the experience.

Not only is listening a crucial part of the conversation of reading, for Gadamer, but because of his interest in the phenomenology of language, he sees the conversation of understanding as one that happens primarily with relation to active speech. Gadamer writes, "Reading with understanding is always a kind of reproduction, performance, and interpretation. Emphasis, rhythmic ordering, and the like are part of wholly silent reading too.

Meaning and the understanding of it are so closely connected with the corporeality of language that understanding always involves an inner speaking as well."[24] We need not take him to be making an empirical claim here, but rather to be suggesting that we attend to the embodied, rhythmic vitality of language as we encounter it in the practice of reading, even when that reading is not literally out loud.

Furthermore, given Gadamer's commitments to the historically effected consciousness and the hermeneutic circle, it is no surprise that he, along with Iser and others, would see a necessary connection between reading and application, or the idea that the meaning one creates, from a conversation or from a text, is always already involved with the reader: "a person reading a text is himself part of the meaning he apprehends. He belongs to the text that he is reading."[25] That is, not only does the reader bring her own background, language, history, and cultural context to the text, but she also brings her anticipations and expectations about the text, the connections she makes between part of the text and a memory or experience, and how she, personally, integrates herself, the text, and the larger context together into a meaningful moment. How could she not be part of the meaning she apprehends? This also accounts for how our experiences of re-reading a favorite text, like having a conversation with a good friend, can be familiar and yet reveal something new or unexpected—while the literal text may not have changed (although our friend likely has), because we have continued to live and grow and have new experiences, we bring a new set of possibilities to the text, and so we bring the potential for new connections and new meaning to our conversation with it.

Contemporary art director, designer, and typesetter Peter Mendelsund takes up the phenomenological thread in his latest book, *What We See When We Read*. While not a work of academic philosophy, the phenomenological elements of this text are fully integrated with the subject matter, through images, backgrounds, and fonts that change from page to page and topic to topic, as one would expect from an iconic textual artist and observer. Mendelsund describes the experience of reading in this way:

> When you first open a book, you enter a liminal space. You are neither in this world, the world wherein you hold a book (say, this book), nor in that world (the metaphysical space the words point toward). To some extent this polydimensionality describes the feeling of reading in general— one is in "many places at once."[26]

While this is similar in many respects to Poulet and Iser, Mendelsund is here making a subtle shift in his description of reading. In invoking the language of polydimensionality and liminality, Mendelsund has pointed us away from the pure interiority of Poulet's description, which seemed to exist not in a single dimension but in a kind of no-space, where the distance between subject and object has been entirely dissolved.

Mendelsund brings us back into our bodies, in holding the book, and yet also reminds us of the ways in which reading can draw our attention away from the physicality of the activity into the world of the book, and the ways in which we can be in different places in different ways at the same time, without necessarily having merged or lost something. He writes:

> When I read, my retirement from the phenomenal world is undertaken too quickly to notice. The world in front of me and the world "inside" me are not merely adjacent, but overlapping: superimposed. A book feels like the intersection of these two domains—or like a conduit; a bridge; a passage between them.[27]

Again, the language here is reminiscent of Poulet and Iser, but with slight differences. Mendelsund's description resists the easy collapse of the phenomenal world into the "interior" world—in describing these worlds as overlapping, and the book as a passage, he is allowing each to maintain its own sensibility while acknowledging the reality of the feeling that the distinction between them has broken down.

Mendelsund's text meanders in, around, and through questions connected to what we see, hear, smell, taste, touch, and feel when we read. In particular, he makes a strong case for a connection between the visual and the auditory: "I would suggest that we *hear* more than we see while we are reading."[28] In the context of the passage in which he writes this, Mendelsund has asked his readers to consider what happens when we read the opening lines of *Moby-Dick*: "Call me Ishmael." He is drawing our attention to our having been addressed, and asking us to think about what that means. While it is possible that he is making a claim about inner speech vs. visualization, I think that like Gadamer, he is trying to get us to attend to the connection between being readers and being listeners, not to literal sound but to listening as a metaphor for reading.

When Mendelsund suggests that we "hear" more than we see, part of what he is relying on is both experience and research into the way our senses attempt to reproduce literary description—in knowing what Anna Karenina looks like from how she is described in the novel, you are familiar with her and yet, if asked to sketch her, may not really be able to provide much detail. Or, if a scent is described, although we usually say we can bring that scent to mind, we are often making a metaphoric or analogous move from something in our own experience, which may or may not match the intended scent. Mendelsund suggests that part of how we can make sense of these synaesthetic moves is that although we use our eyes to read (generally), the connections are made through a kind of neural-auditory mode. Seeing the words does not necessarily entail reading—the understanding that comes with reading requires, for him, a kind of *listening* to the language as it is presented.

In thinking about his description of reading as a movement into a polydimensional, liminal space, a space between, and of reading as a kind of hearing, Mendelsund seems to be inviting us to consider music as a source metaphor for making sense of some of the phenomenal aspects of reading. As American jazz pianist Craig Taborn reflects, "[music] is a way of connecting to things beyond ... it always suggests a liminal space, or the quicksilver spaces between things."[29] Here, Taborn's description of music as always suggesting the spaces between or connecting things gives us a way to understand Mendelsund's claim that entering a book puts us in-between— we are in-between or polydimensional in much the same way, perhaps, that music puts us in-between or in many places at once, aiding us to reach out of ourselves and to be reached in ourselves at once.

Taborn continues, thinking about both the experience of playing music and of listening to music as:

> really an art of memory ... the way sound works, you play a note, and then that note is gone, and you've played the next note, and the concept of memory, the consequence of a melody is based on you remembering what the note that happened before was, it's all memory. You never hear a whole piece at once, you can't.[30]

Taborn's description of listening to a piece of music here is phenomenologically astute—although it comes from his extensive experience, his ability to explain the experience in a way that resonates not only with other musicians or music listeners but also with the experience of reading points to the power of Mendelsund's claim about hearing and reading. A significant portion of the activity of reading, too, is an art of memory. As Willingham notes, "reading depends on memory."[31]

Reading and listening aren't just about memory, though. "It's all imagination. You hear a note, and you're like, I like this melody, and then you can sing it back, but you're singing back your memory of what it sounded like, and it subtly shifts and alters even in that process."[32] Taborn's description here is reminiscent of Iser's account of reading, and also of the Gadamerian roots of Iser's hermeneutic approach to phenomenology in general.

As is the aim with most phenomenological projects, the thread here, from Poulet and Iser to Gadamer and Mendelsund, is not naïvely descriptive. Each of these authors is drawing our attention to what it is like to read, what we are like when we read, as part of their larger concerns about what it means to be human, to be the sort of beings who are drawn to find and make meaning in the world around us and with one another. Reading, by its very nature, is an activity of both meaning and connection. It directs us out of ourselves and brings others to us. Even something as simple as a road sign can be profoundly intimate or profoundly alienating, as anyone who has ever been lost can attest. The phenomenological project is also a call to consider the value of certain habits of reading.

4. Toward an Ethics of Reading

[R]eading is a practice that raises questions of ethical significance.[33]

The natural continuation of this thread of phenomenological reflection on reading is found in Michelle Boulous Walker's *Slow Philosophy: Reading Against the Institution*. In this text, Walker surveys a number of major figures in continental philosophy, from Emmanuel Levinas and Luce Irigaray to Simone de Beauvoir and beyond. Walker's main purpose in the text is to develop an account of an ethics of reading. She argues that

> what slow reading allows is an open relation to the complexity of the world we inhabit. In this it partakes of a love of wisdom and philosophy as a way of life. By granting us unhurried time, we are able to open out to the world. It is this openness that permits us what is ultimately an ethical relation with our world. Openness to otherness, to strangeness, to complexity is what *constitutes* ethics. And slowness, in this sense, is what enables this openness.[34]

Walker sets the stage for her argument by looking at the trend that understands reading primarily under a technological or scientific model of information acquisition, which draws on "mining" or "extraction" metaphors: as you read, mine the text for the key information, extract the parts that will be on the test, etc.[35] On this sort of model, according to researcher Peggy Kamuf, the activity of reading is simply a "technique for capturing information."[36]

Walker uses the current trend toward reducing reading to a technology of information capture to motivate the project of considering connections between reading and complexity. She draws on work by Hans Ulrich Gumbrecht: "Gumbrecht makes a positive link between reading and complexity, arguing that a certain slow and careful reading ... makes it possible for us to confront—I would say 'encounter'—high levels of complexity, thus resisting the temptation to reduce and simplify the issues at hand."[37] Reading, then, becomes one of the key practices that exposes students (and all of us) to complex issues that are not easily or obviously resolvable into simple or straightforward solutions. She writes, "reading is thus re-figured in his work as a kind of bitter-sweet exposure or openness to complexity, one that inevitably takes its time."[38] Given a certain ethical perspective, this is a very desirable habit to inculcate—both the sense of ethical complexity and the sense of the value of not rushing ethical decisions.

Walker is not alone in suggesting that haste is not a virtue. From philosophers like Paul Cillers to contemporary psychologists like Iain McGilchrist, a number of thinkers have argued that the ability to pay a certain quality of attention to what one is doing is crucial to success, and rushing compromises that ability. Walker also notes that this quality of attention, which may be habituated through certain kinds of reading practices, is definitely not habituated by other kinds of reading practices, especially the online skimming and multitasking common in contemporary students. Drawing on work from Mark Bauerlein, she notes that:

> The basic skills of concentrated attention, uninterrupted thinking and receptivity are lacking in an alarmingly large proportion of first-year students. In an effort to counter this trend Baurlein makes the case for developing habits of slow reading aimed to accustom high school students to the attentive mode that complex material demands.[39]

An ethics of reading, then, involves a certain kind of habituation into a slow and concentrated reading practice, one where we are continually and repeatedly engaging with irreducibly complex material, material that encourages us to return to it with new questions, concerns, and ideas, but that resists reduction to simple interpretations.

To appreciate some of the problematic ethical implications of the information capture/mining model of reading, we need look no further than the example given by Peter Brooks, Sterling Professor Emeritus of Comparative Literature at Yale University and Andrew W. Mellon Foundation Scholar at the University Center for Human Values and the Department of Comparative Literature at Princeton University, for the purpose of his seminar "The Ethics of Reading and the Cultures of Professionalism"—the Torture Memos.[40] As Brooks explains:

> I began by evoking the Torture Memos because in that case the disastrous results of not reading—of merely pretending to read while in fact inserting one's own prejudices and preferred outcomes between the reader and the text—are so clear and so horrible . . . Though the consequences of other sloppy, misguided, pernicious interpretations may not be so spectacularly awful, they can skew everything that follows in their wake.[41]

In other words, one of the dangers of reading to "mine" for information is that when one mines, one already knows what one is looking for. Having decided ahead of time what to look for not only precludes the text from revealing itself as it is, but also reinforces whatever one approaches it with. Brooks continues, "the issue of the Torture Memos and my classroom experience in interpreting legal texts led me to claim that the humanities can, and at their best do, represent a commitment to ethical reading."[42]

Here, Brooks gives a real-life, concrete example of the kind of predicament that is directly related to how we read—with what quality of attention, with what purposes, with what appreciation of the complexity of the issues at hand, and with what sense of consideration for and openness to others. Brooks, very much in line with Walker's project, continues, explaining that "reading as a self-conscious practice—'reading in slow motion,' as it has been called—tends to suggest the inadequacies of the simple and the certain."[43] Here, he brings in the same idea of slowness, of the need for viewing reading as a practice, one that is attended to self-consciously, and one that has a direct relationship with complexity.

Brooks is careful to note that in talking about an ethics of reading, he is not talking about the idea that reading "good" books somehow makes one a "good" person, or that in order to be a "good" person one must read. Rather, he notes, "what I want to defend is not a product but a process and a practice. The practice of reading itself, pursued with care and attention to language, its contexts, implications, uncertainties, can itself be an ethical act."[44] That is, in reading in the manner suggested by Brooks—slowly, self-consciously, attentively, without imposing our own meaning on the text—we are habituating profoundly important ethical patterns. In the act of reading we are interpreting what is happening, we are giving a reading of the circumstances, and in doing so "we must constantly submit what we want the text to mean to the constraints of the lexicon, the historical horizon, and the text as a whole. This submission to culture as something beyond one's individuality is itself a discipline."[45] Here, we have not only Walker's sense of openness and complexity as part of the ethics of reading, but also a sense, returning from the earlier phenomenologists, of the way in which this kind of reading practice puts oneself in a relationship with others, where one's own wants are not the sole determiner of things.

Charles Larmore, a participant in one of Brooks's symposia on ethics in reading, continues on this somewhat Levinasian theme: "The most basic fact about our relation as readers to texts is that this relation is asymmetrical. We can read the text, but the text cannot read us."[46] Texts, he argues, are vulnerable to their readers in a number of different ways, especially in terms of rushed or poor readings. Larmore continues, "our ethical character shows itself most clearly in how we treat the vulnerable, since they cannot make it in our interest to treat them well. Though I will not go so far as to say that a bad reader cannot be a good person, I doubt that a habitually careless or deliberately manipulative reader will be one."[47] Larmore has here added a very interesting dimension to an ethics of reading. If, as Walker and Brooks have argued, reading as a practice has an importantly ethical dimension and/or can be an important part of an ethical life, then habitually reading poorly (carelessly or manipulatively) would seem to be a sign of habits that are not confined to practices of reading. In other words, if practices of reading can positively habituate other ethical aspects of one's life (not rushing to judgment on complex issues, for instance), then habitually careless or prejudicial reading would seem to be a potential sign of habitual carelessness or prejudicial activity elsewhere as well.

In thinking about reading having a more direct connection to ethics, Elaine Scarry, also a participant in one of Brooks's symposia, writes on the connection of literature and poetry, specifically, with empathy, deliberative thought, and beauty. In terms of empathy, she is well in line with other thinkers, who have argued similarly for the idea of "the capacity of literature to exercise and reinforce our recognition that there *are* other points of view in the world, and to make this recognition a powerful mental habit."[48] Narrative, in particular, is particularly powerful for eliciting empathy, especially in circumstances where other forms of argumentation have not been successful.[49] She notes that the way literature/poetry develops empathy and how it develops deliberative thought are actually very similar:

> the claims made about dispute greatly resemble what we can say about empathy. What they have in common is not just the recognition that there are multiple points of view, two sides to every coin, but also the chance to practice, and thereby to deepen and strengthen that recognition . . . both dispute and empathetic narrative require one to think counterfactually, to think the notion that one does not oneself hold to be the case.[50]

That is, reading about certain kinds of disputes, in poetry or literature, can help us practice deliberative thought, because it requires us not only to recognize that different points of view exist, but to actually play out different perspectives. As Iser suggested earlier, this enables the expanding of our cognitive capacities—by reading certain kinds of things, we are able to think in new and different kinds of ways. In particular, since good deliberation requires that we be able to recognize multiple perspectives and follow premises out to their conclusions, when we read literature and poetry, we are able to deliberate better, according to Scarry, and that is crucial for public, democratic ethical progress.

Scarry argues that in addition to empathy and deliberative thinking, reading (literature and poetry) is also important for ethics because of its connection with beauty. This is perhaps the least intuitive but most sophisticated of her points. She writes:

> beauty interrupts and gives us sudden relief from our own minds. Iris Murdoch says we undergo "an unselfing" in the presence of a beautiful thing; "self-preoccupation" and worries on one's own behalf abruptly fall away. Simone Weil refers to this phenomenon as a "radical decentering." I call it an "opiated adjacency," an awkward term but one that reminds us that there are many things in life that make us feel acute pleasure (opiated), and many things in life that make us feel sidelined, but there is almost nothing—except beauty—that does the two simultaneously. Feeling acute pleasure at finding oneself on the margins is a first step in working toward fairness.[51]

The earlier phenomenologists all wrote of the "sidelined" sort of feeling in reading, and each perhaps hinted at the great pleasure they found in reading, but Scarry is the first to explicitly connect these together—part of the acute pleasure of reading is precisely in the feeling of being sidelined by the presence of beauty, in being swept along in something that is not yours, in stretching your cognitive capacities beyond where they were yesterday, in being drawn into that liminal space where you, too, are intimate with greatness for a moment and yet it is not about you. As a moment of motivation for ethical practice, beauty is particularly powerful.

5. Zhuangzi Transforms Reading

Not only is beauty an important motivation for ethical practice, but focusing on beauty highlights an important gap in what has been discussed to this point. What is missing from the ethics of reading so far is an explicitly aesthetic dimension. Reading, in the sense we've been discussing, is neither an algorithmic process nor a simple skill. Rather, it is a complex, embodied, holistic set of phenomena, an approach to the intentionality of an other or others, embedded in an artifact, that cannot be reduced to a procedural operation. Furthermore, through the act of reading, reader, text, and culture are mutually transformed and mutually transform one another. This aesthetic dimension and context are crucial for the ethics of reading; as Judith Butler notes in her response to Brooks's symposia, the question now for all those who want to resist the "embattled humanities" discourse and broader cultural dismissal of the humanities is: "what now is the value of our values?"[52] An ethics of reading cannot hope to respond to this question without a robust aesthetic dimension, as "value" and questions of value are not reducible to questions of ethics, but are connected to lived experience through aesthetic processes. An ethics of reading also cannot hope to be successful without having roots in more than one intellectual tradition. As a text that plays with questions of value and use, interpretation and language, and that sees what in common Western philosophical vocabulary are called epistemological, ethical, and aesthetic values as necessarily intertwined, the Classical Chinese Daoist text *Zhuangzi* 莊子 is not only a pleasure to read but also an important text for intervening in this conversation.

While the *Zhuangzi* does not have much to say, directly, about the activity of reading, it has a great deal to say about skillful and aesthetic practices, about language, and about how to live well.[53] In the history of Chinese art and aesthetics, it is one of the single most influential texts, not only in terms of its poetic discussion of aesthetic issues such as creativity, transformation, and spontaneity, but as a work of art in its own right, one which has served as a repository of inspiration for generations of artists—literary, visual, and auditory. The character of Zhuangzi or Zhuang Zhou is the paradigm example of an artist-philosopher at play, and the *Zhuangzi* is a consummate work in and of aesthetics. Contemporary philosopher Li Zehou explains:

> Zhuangzi may still be considered the first in the history of Chinese art to
> have discovered and given attention to the aesthetic principles of artistic

creation and appreciation, in particular as concerns those creative phenomena that seem almost miraculous in skill, impossible to grasp or formalize, and difficult to describe or articulate . . . Zhuangzi's philosophy is, in and of itself, aesthetic in character.[54]

This is a text that presents the ceaseless transformations of the world as a model on which human beings can draw inspiration for playfully transforming themselves and their world in resonance with the constant changes of the cosmos.[55] The text is organized into thirty-three chapters, each of which contains stories, poems, songs, short essays, and other prose comments. The first seven chapters are often referred to as the "inner chapters" and historically were thought to have been authored by Zhuang Zhou himself. While contemporary evidence now suggests that many hands were at play, even in the inner chapters, the text as a whole might be thought of as a collected set of the work of various jazz masters, riffing on similar themes. In what follows, I draw on four stories from different sections of the text, to think about what a Zhuangzian perspective might add to our discussion of the ethics of reading.

5.1. Wheelwright Pian

One of the few points in the text that does directly discuss books and reading is the story of Wheelwright Pian. So the story goes, the Duke of Huan is reading a book, likely on a topic we might classify as "ethics," at the top of the hall when the Wheelwright puts down his tools and goes to ask what the Duke is reading. The Duke replies that he is reading the words of a sage, but when asked if the sage is alive, replies that the sage is dead. The Wheelwright criticizes this as reading "the dregs of the men of old," and when asked by the Duke to explain himself or die for his insolence, he says:

> Speaking for myself, I see it from the perspective of my art. In making a wheel, if I chip too slowly, the chisel slides and does not grip; if too fast, it jams and catches in the wood. Not too slow, not too fast; I feel it in the hand and respond from the heart, the mouth cannot put it into words, there is a skill in it somewhere that I cannot explain to my son and that my son cannot learn from me. This is how in my seventy years I have grown old making wheels. If the men of old and their untransmittable messages are dead, then what my lord is reading is the dregs of the men of old, isn't it?[56]

While this story is often taken as a critique of texts, language, and reading, I think the critical element here is not so much about the fact that the Duke is reading, and not "doing," but that the Duke at once says that the sage is dead, and that his words are worth reading. From the Wheelwright's perspective, what is found in the book is mere "dregs of old" *if* the Duke thinks that he can mechanically read and reproduce the sage's advice for living well (his ethics) without himself creatively adopting and making live the sage's words. Reading without concern for self-and-world transformation, and without an acknowledgment of both the aesthetic (non-algorithmic) and what we might call the hermeneutic application, is the object of the critique. In other words, fixed words are mere dregs, while transforming words are more than mere text. Wheelwright Pian is making a phenomenological point here about the necessary embodiment of skill, and the fact that learning and skill require aesthetic personalization. If the sage is really dead, then what is left to feel in the hand and respond to from the heart? On the other hand, if the book is a real connection, through language, through a meaning-making activity, to the life of another, then treating that other as "live" is precisely what makes possible a transmission, not of a message, but of the potential of a way of life that must be lived to be understood.

5.2. Cook Ding

Cook Ding, the butcher whose story is found in chapter 3 of the *Zhuangzi*, is often taken as a paradigm exemplar of Zhuangzian Daoism:

> Cook Ding was butchering an ox for Lord Wenhui. His hand touched, shoulder leaned in, foot stamped on the ground, putting pressure with his knee, with a hiss! With a thud! The chopper as it sliced never missed the rhythm, now in time with the Mulberry Forest dance, now with an orchestra playing the Qingshou. "Ah, excellent!" said Lord Wenhui. "Your skill has reached such heights!" Cook Ding set down the chopper and replied, "What I care about is *dao*, this goes beyond skill. When I first began to butcher oxen, wherever I looked I saw nothing but oxen. After three years, I no longer saw an entire ox. Now, I use the numinous to encounter it, and do not use the eye to see it. The senses know where to stop, the numinous continues on. I rely on natural patterns, cleave along the main seams, let myself be guided by the main cavities, go by what is inherently so. I skillfully pass through without hitting any tendons or ligaments, not to mention solid bone. A good cook changes his chopper once a year, because he hacks. A common cook changes it once a month, because he smashes. Now I have had this chopper for nineteen years, and have butchered several thousand oxen, but the edge is as new as if it just came from the grindstone. At that joint there is space between, and the blade's edge has no thickness; if you take what has no thickness and put it into the space between, then, there is more than enough room in there for the edge to roam about. This is why after nineteen years the edge of my chopper is as new as if it were fresh from the grindstone."[57]

Cook Ding's description of his career as a butcher can be easily likened to a reader's progression, from learning letters and words and sounding out each unfamiliar word to the ease and familiarity of a reader who hardly even recognizes that she is engaged in *doing* anything when she reads. The ease, the joyful dance of the embodied practice of Cook Ding's care for *dao*, how things are and how they should be, which is skillful and yet not mere skill, lends an aesthetic richness to the language of reading. If we were to read as Cook Ding butchers, how would we read? We would read with a direct care for the embodied nature of the activity, with a dance-like rhythm and grace; we would recognize that reading is part of a larger project of caring for *dao* and nourishing life; we would be guided by the particulars of the situation without imposing ourselves upon it; and we would pay careful attention to the empty spaces and places. We can see these empty spaces in Mendelsund's account of when as readers we are asked "not to see," or to "imagine the unimaginable" or to "understand a character by what they are not."[58] The relationship between the silence that births a tone and the void that words emerge from reminds us that often it is the play or interplay between what is present and what is absent that creates meaning.

The empty spaces and places, for the butcher the joints of the animal, the openings between muscle, bone, ligament, and fiber, for the reader are perhaps what is unsaid, unwritten, and yet what underlies and holds together the story, the description, or the argument; they are also the meaning that is yet-to-be-determined, the space for significance to emerge from the particulars of the given text, rather than through the imposition of a fat chopper that would get very dull indeed shoving its prejudgments through the text. The experienced reader's chopper, guided by what is absent as much as what is present, does not hack or smash but moves through the text with the agile precision of a very slim blade. The novice's chopper, on the other hand, may need frequent sharpening.

In building on this last point, we would especially take care to go slowly when the going was difficult, as Cook Ding relates:

> "However, each time I come to something complicated, I see the difficulty and cautiously prepare myself; my gaze settles, activity slows down, there is a slight movement of the blade—and the tangle unravels, like a clod of earth crumbles to the ground. I stand with chopper in hand, look around leisurely and with satisfaction, then clean the blade and put it away."[59]

Although we have had reference before to complexity, this is the first opportunity we have had to reflect phenomenologically on the experience of reading something difficult, something where slowness is not a general virtue but a particular demand, and where the best response to success might be to put down the book for a while. And, since we are not all of Cook Ding's superior skill and experience, the tangle might not unravel on the first try. It may in fact take a great deal of patience and repeated effort to unravel, so we might need his leisurely satisfaction with even small amounts of progress.

5.3. Potter's Wheel

In chapter 2 of the *Zhuangzi*, the text is particularly critical of points of view that seem to take an arbitrarily fixed or dogmatic stance on how things are or should be, without careful reference to the circumstances and particulars of the surrounding context. One of the most famous stories from this chapter is called "Three in the Morning," and tells of the anger of a group of monkeys at learning that their daily ration of seven nuts will be split into three in the morning, four in the evening, and their delight when the trainer switched it to four in the morning and three in the evening instead. Commenting on this, the text reads: "Thus, the sage uses various rights and wrongs to harmonize with others and yet remains in the center of the sky-like potter's wheel."[60] In switching the number of nuts in the monkey's meals, the trainer did not make any substantive change—the monkeys still got seven nuts total, but because he paid careful attention to their conditions, he was able to make their circumstances that much better. The image of the sky-like potter's wheel, or the potter's wheel of the heavens (*tian* 天), is a powerful metaphor for the way certain kinds of activity can make the best use of their immediate circumstances. As Brook Ziporyn notes:

> The character here used for "Potter's Wheel" also means "equality." The two meanings converge in the consideration of the even distribution of clay made possible by the constant spinning of the wheel: the potter's wheel's very instability, its constant motion, is what makes things equal. Note also that Chinese cosmology considers Heaven, the sky, to be "rotating": the stars and constellations turn in the sky, and the seasons—the sky's varying conditions—are brought in a cyclical sequence. The turning of the seasons is what makes things exist and grow. The turning of the Potter's Wheel sky brings life, as the potter's wheel creates pots.[61]

While it may be common to think of reading as a linear sort of activity, from point A to B, from start to finish, the spinning of the potter's wheel is a very apt image for the practice of reading. The potter's wheel maps well onto an hermeneutic circle, describing the sort of recursive relation Iser mentions between a line of text, the reader's imagination, larger text itself, the broader cultural context, and the reader's return through the text, which is not a passive process happening to the reader but an active, dynamic, and creative process in which reader, text, language, context, and culture—hand, clay, water, motion, and wheel—all act together transforming one another and being transformed by one another into a new experience. In addition, we can take the hermeneutic dimension of the wheel also to have a temporal aspect, keeping in mind that reading, like listening to music, is very much an activity of the present moment—the center of the wheel—that stretches back through memory to previously read parts of the text, and into the future through anticipation or expectation of what's coming next, where the present is shaped by the past, and is in the process of shaping what is to come.

One way to read this image is to bring to mind the importance of dynamic instability—the wheel's constant motion is what makes possible both balance on it and creative activity from it. As readers this suggests that we be conscious of our locations, and the difficulty of maintaining one's balance when occupying a position on the outside of the wheel. The empty space in the center allows us to playfully occupy multiple interpretive spaces without becoming fixed to any one in particular. To take this in a more concrete direction, as Brooks notes: "The ability to read critically the messages that society, politics, and culture bombard us with is, more than ever, needed training in a society in which the manipulation of minds and hearts is increasingly what running the world is all about."[62] Occupying the center of the wheel, on this metaphor, then, may allow us not just to take the best advantage of the given circumstances, but to have the necessary interpretive distance to be critical readers of all incoming messages, not taking a friend-or-foe position on the outside of the wheel, or situating ourselves in an echo-chamber where intent and meaning have been determined in advance.

5.4. Fasting of the Heart-Mind

The character of Confucius (Kongzi 孔子) makes several appearances in the *Zhuangzi*. In one of the encounter dialogues of chapter 4, Confucius's favorite disciple Yan Hui has asked for advice about how to serve the Lord of Wei without getting himself killed—a real risk. Confucius is (predictably) skeptical, but finally tells Yan Hui that he must fast the heart-mind (*xin* 心). When asked what that means, he replies:

> Confucius: "If you merge all your intentions into a singularity, you will come to hear with the heart-mind rather than the ears. Further, you will come to hear with the *qi* rather than with the heart-mind. For the ears are halted at what they hear. The heart-mind is halted at whatever verifies its preconceptions. But the *qi* is an emptiness, a waiting for the presence of beings. The *dao* alone is what gathers in this emptiness. And it is this emptiness that is the fasting of the heart-mind."
>
> Yan Hui said, "Before I find what moves me into activity, it is myself that is full and real. But as soon as I find what moves me, it turns out that 'myself' has never begun to exist. Is that what you mean by being empty?"
>
> Confucius said, "Exactly. Let me tell you about it . . . Good fortune comes to roost in stillness. To lack this stillness is called scurrying around even when sitting down. Allow your ears and eyes to open inward and thereby place yourself beyond your heart-mind's understanding. Even the ghosts and spirits will then seek refuge in you, human beings all the more so!"[63]

In his guise here as a Daoist sage, and not a stodgy moralist, Confucius is trying to help Yan Hui figure out how to help others. In order to do that, he suggests, Yan Hui needs to figure out how to stop feeding his heart-mind, the source and activity of his feeling-and-thinking. To do this, Confucius says that he needs to move from hearing with his ears, to hearing with his heart-mind, to hearing with his *qi* 氣 (vital energy), which will allow him to cultivate an emptiness and a stillness that will draw others to him.

In parsing out what this means, Yan Hui says, "it turns out that 'myself' has never begun to exist. Is that what you mean by being empty?" Here, the image of fasting the heart-mind, reading with your *qi*, in concentrated stillness, beyond the preconceptions of your heart-mind, has an additional layer—rather than throwing into doubt the clarity of the subject–object relation, as reading did for Poulet and Iser, here for Yan Hui fasting the heart-mind has perhaps thrown into doubt the existence of his "self" in a strong sense. In an ethics of reading, or reading as part of an ethical life, reflection on what the "self" is and means is crucial, and this is something that certainly would benefit from perspectives from diverse philosophical traditions.

While Scarry takes a key component of the ethics of reading to be taking on other perspectives, from fasting the heart-mind we see also the idea of placing yourself beyond your limited, individualized understanding, and getting beyond the idea of your "self." This can even be seen in Scarry's sense of opiated adjacency, where instead of the feeling of pleasure at one's being sidelined, one might have a feeling of pleasure at being beyond your heart-mind's understanding, empty of yourself. In entering into a liminal space "we" can be "transformed" in important ways that point to the flexible and permeable nature of us as persons. So rather than Poulet's need to "leave the individual behind," reading gives us the opportunity to realize the fiction of the unchanging self. After all, for the *Zhuangzi* one of the most important themes of the entire text is transformation—the constant transformation of the cosmos, but also the potential we have to playfully transform ourselves to meander along with the changes we find around us. An ethics of reading, then, as an aesthetic practice and approach not only to texts, but to any potential sites of meaning and connection to others, whether in images, works of art, persons, or as a way to move about in the world, can be a way to live a response to Butler's question: What value are our values? If they are not to be just the dregs of old, then you will have to see for yourself.

6. Conclusion

Paying attention to the phenomenology of reading has led many thinkers to converge on the importance of reading as a slow, self-conscious practice, one that benefits from repetition and tactile sensation and that gives us the rare opportunity to practice being still. As Mendelsund reflects, "reading mirrors the procedure by which we acquaint ourselves with the world. It is not that our narratives necessarily tell us something true about the world (though they might), but rather that the practice of reading feels like, and is like, consciousness itself: imperfect; partial; hazy; co-creative."[64]

Attending more carefully to this oft-neglected practice can offer us insights into who and how we are. In the Introduction to this chapter I referenced Xu Bing's "Book of the Sky," an installation piece that took four years (1987–91) to complete. This work of art is perhaps one of the most insightful pieces in recent years on many issues, but especially concerning reading. The work is a mixed-media installation featuring books and scrolls printed from hand-carved blocks created by the artist. Each block was created to resemble, but not really be, a character in the Chinese language. The artist then printed the books and scrolls in such a way as to balance word frequency and type, giving the feeling of reading a real text (e.g., "a" and "the" occur more often in sentences than "perchance" or "terrifying"). Each character is meaningless, and yet it produces the illusion of being almost meaningful, nearly readable, just beyond one's reach (if one reads Chinese). As an installation, the ceiling billows with text, the floor is covered in waves of books, the walls flow from one scroll to the next. Moving through it, you are at once immersed in text, and yet never more aware of incommunicability, of the way in which the text resists your almost existential drive to read it. Many Chinese viewers spent hours examining the early exhibits, sure that there were at least some "real" characters mixed in with the fakes.

While there are many things that can be said about this work, from its connection to Xu's time spent working for state propaganda art to Chinese history and block printing, for our purposes there are a few things that stand out. First, there is the phenomenological experience of reading, the way in which the work initiates a connection and makes one try to read it, even when it is obvious that it cannot be read. Your eyes still pore over it as if it were text, as if the characters will soon shift into focus and be meaningful; if you are a calligrapher your hand might even trace some characters to feel the rhythm of the brushstrokes. The opacity of the text is striking—the Chinese Classics were learned through recitation, and while there is a visible rhythm to the organization of the "characters," there is no sound, no reference through the visual to what the text should sound like. Second, the work highlights the context of reading, not only the location, language, history, printing, and so on, but that the very act of reading is a purposeful (if also automatic) act. We read to know, to seek and to find meaning with and through others, and that is always in a larger context. Third, reading is a political activity. As a work of art, Xu's piece is able to suggest this in ways that are perhaps not as clear in a more direct phenomenological analysis. Reading is political in the sense of the privilege of being able to read, the control of what is available to read, and in the Zhuangzian sense of reading as a transformational practice. The piece also encourages reflection on the nature of such a large collection of books—while in the Song and Ming

Dynasties that his work evokes, such large collections would likely have been in private hands, in contemporary times we are lucky enough to have free public libraries, and such institutions have been an important part of not only individual but also cultural transformation. Xu Bing's work prompts us to reflect on the experience, meaning, and significance of reading in our own lives, and as a work of art, it does so in a way that models an ethics of reading, from a work of art to a lived practice and out into our engagements with others.

Finally, the work is called the "Book of the Sky," and while we often take reading to be indicative of human-to-human connection, as Xu hints at with his title we also read the sky, the natural world, and we should perhaps not get so caught up in our own meaning-making activities that we cease to pay attention to the transformations happening around us. I would like to leave you with selections from a letter, written by botanist Robin Kimmerer, as part of a book to young readers:

> I am sitting, on this summer afternoon, in my favorite reading place under the black cherry tree on the hill, looking out over the fields. In the moment before I open a book, I like to just hold it between my palms and remember what an amazing thing it is, a meeting of tree gifts and human gifts on the same page. A place where the reader and the writer meet in reciprocity to create something which has never existed before. A book is an invitation to see the world through another's eyes: blue eyes, black eyes, fiery green wolf eyes.
>
> It feels like the tree is reading over my shoulder, sharing the stories, as it has every right to do, since they are printed on a sheet made of tree cells. Books let us be like trees, don't you think? Seeing beyond the span of our own lives, reading high into the sunlight and deep into the dark fertile soil of imagination. They let us play in their branches or dream in a hammock. If we're lucky our minds will widen with every volume, like growth rings of wisdom. And books attract more books, more ideas— like bright singing birds flocking to a tree of knowledge . . .[65]

Notes

1   While the focus of this chapter is on literate adults, low literacy among adults and children in the United States is a serious issue that has not received significant philosophical attention. Due to space constraints and my own lack of familiarity with the subject, I also do not delve into the interesting philosophical issues surrounding braille or other concerns in phenomenology of reading for the visually impaired.

2   First noted in English by John Ridley Stroop in 1935, the Stroop Effect in psychology described a kind of interference in the reaction time of certain kinds of tasks. One of the most famous demonstrations of this is how much

longer it takes to name (out loud) the color a color word is printed in, when the color it is printed in and the color it spells out are two different colors (e.g., RED, written in black ink, when the task is to name aloud the color of the ink, not the word) of reading aloud the color a word is written in, if the word spelled is a different color than the ink of the word.

3   For images of the work, see: http://www.xubing.com/en/work/details/ 206?year=1991&type=year#206

4   A good introduction in English to Qian's work is Ronald Egan, trans. *Limited Views: Essays on Ideas and Letters* (Cambridge, MA: Harvard University Press, 1998).

5   Daniel Willingham, *The Reading Mind: A Cognitive Approach to Understanding How the Mind Reads* (San Francisco: Jossey-Bass, 2017), 2.

6   Willingham, *The Reading Mind*, 3.

7   See Alan Moore and Eric Schwitzgebel, "The Experience of Reading," *Consciousness and Cognition*, 62 (2018): 57–68.

8   See Kara Pernice, "F-Shaped Pattern of Reading on the Web: Misunderstood but Still Relevant (Even on Mobile)," *Nielsen Normal Group*. Available online at: https://www.nngroup.com/articles/f-shaped-pattern-reading-web-content/

9   See Therese Fessenden, "Horizontal Attention Leans Left," *Nielsen Normal Group*. Available online at: https://www.nngroup.com/articles/horizontal-attention-leans-left/

10 See Anne Mangen *et al.*, "Reading Linear Texts on Paper versus Computer Screens: Effects on Reading Comprehension," *International Journal of Educational Research,* 58 (2013): 61–8. See also the more popularly aimed works by: Naomi Baron, "Do Students Lose Depth in Digital Reading?," *The Conversation*. Available online at: https://theconversation.com/do-students-lose-depth-in-digital-reading-61897; Rachel Grate, "Science Has Great News for People Who Read Actual Books," *Mic*. Available online at: https://mic.com/articles/99408/science-has-great-news-for-people-who-read-actual-books#. PMd5BMAUI; and Maria Torheim, "Do We Read Differently on Paper than on a Screen?," *Phys.org*. Available online at: https://phys.org/news/2017-09-differently-paper-screen.html

11 Maryanne Wolf, "Skim Reading is the New Normal: The Effect on Society is Profound," The *Guardian*. Available online at: https://www.theguardian.com/commentisfree/2018/aug/25/skim-reading-new-normal-maryanne-wolf?fbclid=IwAR28ZJeg3ZcO9TSwYTUWMTiaeTLJ0rTt6iSJmVyA8fajtzTFziyKtj33gZ4

12 Jordan Weissmann, "The Decline of the American Book Lover: And Why the Downturn might be Over," *The Atlantic*. Available online at: https://www.theatlantic.com/business/archive/2014/01/the-decline-of-the-american-book-lover/283222/

13 While traditional phenomenology was not particularly concerned with ethics per se, later developments in existential phenomenology recognize the inextricable connections between the social, political, and intentional spheres of our experience, and so are deeply concerned with how phenomenological inquiry relates to ethical living, and I take this more existential approach to phenomenological inquiry in this chapter.

14 Georges Poulet, "Phenomenology of Reading," *New Literary History*, 1.1 (1969): 54.

15 Ibid.

16 Ibid., 55–6.

17 Ibid., 60.

18 Wolfgang Iser, "The Reading Process: A Phenomenological Approach," *New Literary History*, 3.2 (1972): 289.

19 Ibid.

20 Ibid., 299.

21 Hans-Georg Gadamer, *Truth and Method* (New York: Continuum, 2004), 370–1.

22 Ibid., 461.

23 Ibid., 385.

24 Ibid., 153.

25 Ibid., 335.

26 Peter Mendelsund, *What We See When We Read: A Phenomenology with Illustrations* (New York: Vintage Books, 2014), 61.

27 Ibid., 58.

28 Ibid., 39. In addition, although Mendelsund doesn't make this point, recent research into the causes of dyslexia suggest that it is not a problem with vision, but rather with our phonological system, which is used for processing speech sounds, and which does support his claim here. For more information, see Ellen Ullman, "Cutting-Edge Research to Support Students with Reading Disabilities," *eSchool News: Daily Tech News and Innovation*. Available online at: https://www.eschoolnews.com/2018/02/05/cutting-edge-research-support-students-reading-disabilities/

29 Craig Taborn, "Pianist Craig Taborn on Reinventing Jazz Improvisation," Interview by Steve Paulson, *To the Best of Our Knowledge,* National Public Radio. Available online at: https://www.ttbook.org/interview/pianist-craig-taborn-reinventing-jazz-improvisation

30 Ibid.

31 Willingham, *The Reading Mind*, 5.

32 Taborn, "Reinventing Jazz Improvisation," online.

33 Charles Larmore, "The Ethics of Reading," in *The Humanities and Public Life*, ed. Peter Brooks (New York: Fordham University Press, 2014), 49.

34 Michelle Walker, *Slow Philosophy: Reading Against the Institution* (New York: Bloomsbury, 2017), 31.

35 Ibid., 18.

36 According to Peggy Kamuf's "The End of Reading." This paper delivered at the University at Albany, October 12, 2000. See Walker, *Slow Philosophy*, 18. This rather neatly also subordinates reading as an activity under a combat metaphor ("capturing information"). For more on philosophy and metaphor, see Sarah Mattice, *Metaphor and Metaphilosophy: Philosophy*

as Combat, Play, and Aesthetic Experience (Lanham: Lexington Books, 2014).

37 Walker, *Slow Philosophy*, 19.

38 Ibid., 20.

39 Ibid., 13.

40 See Peter Brooks, "Introduction," in *The Humanities and Public Life*, ed. Peter Brooks (New York: Fordham University Press, 2014), 1.

41 Ibid., 3.

42 Ibid., 1–2.

43 Ibid., 3.

44 Ibid.

45 Ibid., 3–4.

46 Larmore, "The Ethics of Reading," 50.

47 Ibid., 54.

48 Elaine Scarry, "Poetry, Injury, and the Ethics of Reading," in *The Humanities and Public Life*, ed. Peter Brooks (New York: Fordham University Press, 2014), 42. See also David Kidd and Emanuele Castano, "Reading Literary Fiction Improves Theory of Mind," *Science*. Available online at: http://science.sciencemag.org/content/342/6156/377

49 See the preliminary piece by Schwitzgebel and McVey, "Narrative but not Philosophical Argument Motivates Giving to Charity," *The Splintered Mind*, 21 November 2018. Available online at: http://schwitzsplinters.blogspot.com/2018/11/narrative-but-not-philosophical.html

50 Scarry, "Poetry, Injury, and the Ethics of Reading," 45.

51 Ibid., 46–7.

52 Judith Butler, "Ordinary, Incredulous," in *The Humanities and Public Life*, ed. Peter Brooks (New York: Fordham University Press, 2014), 37.

53 While this text does not reflect explicitly a great deal on reading, there are many Chinese philosophical texts that do give explicit attention to the practice of reading. There are also later medieval Daoist practices dealing with the nature of language, reading, and writing that would be fascinating to consider in a longer exploration of this topic.

54 Li Zehou, *The Chinese Aesthetic Tradition* (Honolulu: University of Hawaii Press, 2009), 105.

55 For more on play and Zhuangzi, see chapter 3 of Mattice, *Metaphor and Metaphilosophy*, 2014.

56 Zhuangzi, *Zhuangzi: The Essential Writings with Selections from Traditional Commentaries*, Brook Ziporyn (trans.) (Indianapolis: Hackett Publishing, 2009), chapter 13 (my translation).

57 Ibid., chapter 3.

58 Mendelsund, *What We See When We Read*, 241–2.

59 Zhuangzi, *The Essential Writings*, chapter 3 (my translation).

60 Zhuangzi, *The Essential Writings*, 14 (Ziporyn's translation, modified).

61 Zhuangzi, *The Essential Writings*, 14n16.

62 Brooks, *The Humanities and Public Life*, 2.

63 Zhuangzi, *The Essential Writings*, 26–7 (Ziporyn translation, modified).

64 Mendelsund, *What We See When We Read*, 403.

65 Robin Kimmerer, "Dear Young Reader," in *A Velocity of Being: Letters to a Young Reader*, eds. Maria Popova and Claudia Bedrick (New York: Enchanted Lion Books, 2008), 78.

References

Baron, Naomi. (2016), "Do Students Lose Depth in Digital Reading?," *The Conversation*, 20 July. Available online at: https://theconversation.com/do-students-lose-depth-in-digital-reading-61897

Brooks, Peter, ed. (2014), *The Humanities and Public Life*, New York: Fordham University Press.

Butler, Judith. (2014), "Ordinary, Incredulous," in *The Humanities and Public Life*, Peter Brooks (ed.), 15–37, New York: Fordham University Press.

Fessenden, Therese. (2017), "Horizontal Attention Leans Left," *Nielsen Normal Group*, 22 October. Available online at: https://www.nngroup.com/articles/horizontal-attention-leans-left/

Gadamer, Hans-Georg. (2004), *Truth and Method*, Joel Weinsheimer and Donald Marchall (trans.), New York: Continuum.

Grate, Rachel. (2014), "Science Has Great News for People Who Read Actual Books," *Mic*, 22 September. Available online at: https://mic.com/articles/99408/science-has-great-news-for-people-who-read-actual-books#.PMd5BMAUI

Iser, Wolfgang. (1972), "The Reading Process: A Phenomenological Approach," *New Literary History*, 3 (2): 279–99.

Kidd, David and Emanuele Castano. (2013), "Reading Literary Fiction Improves Theory of Mind," *Science*, 242 (6156): 377–80. Available online at: http://science.sciencemag.org/content/342/6156/377

Kimmerer, Robin. (2018), "Dear Young Reader," in *A Velocity of Being: Letters to a Young Reader*, Maria Popova and Claudia Bedrick (eds.), 78, New York: Enchanted Lion Books.

Larmore, Charles. (2014), "The Ethics of Reading," in *The Humanities and Public Life*, Peter Brooks (ed.), 49–54, New York: Fordham University Press.

Li, Zehou. (2009), *The Chinese Aesthetic Tradition*, Majia Bell Samei (trans.), Honolulu: University of Hawaii Press.

Mangen, Anne *et al.* (2013), "Reading Linear Texts on Paper versus Computer Screens: Effects on Reading Comprehension," *International Journal of Educational Research*, 58: 61–8.

Mattice, Sarah. (2014), *Metaphor and Metaphilosophy: Philosophy as Combat, Play, and Aesthetic Experience*, Lanham: Lexington Books.

Mendelsund, Peter. (2014), *What We See When We Read: A Phenomenology with Illustrations*, New York: Vintage Books.

Moore, Alan and Eric Schwitzgebel. (2018), "The Experience of Reading," *Consciousness and Cognition*, 62: 57–68.

Pernice, Kara. (2017), "F-Shaped Pattern of Reading on the Web: Misunderstood but Still Relevant (Even on Mobile)," *Nielsen Normal Group*, 12 November. Available online at: https://www.nngroup.com/articles/f-shaped-pattern-reading-web-content/

Poulet, Georges. (1969), "Phenomenology of Reading," *New Literary History*, 1 (1): 53–68.

Qian, Zhongshu. (1998), *Limited Views: Essays on Ideas and Letters*, Ronald Egan (trans.), Cambridge, MA: Harvard University Press.

Scarry, Elaine. (2014), "Poetry, Injury, and the Ethics of Reading," in *The Humanities and Public Life*, Peter Brooks (ed.), 41–8, New York: Fordham University Press.

Schwitzgebel, Eric and Christopher McVey. (2018), "Narrative but not Philosophical Argument Motivates Giving to Charity," *The Splintered Mind*, 21 November. Available online at: http://schwitzsplinters.blogspot.com/2018/11/narrative-but-not-philosophical.html

Taborn, Craig. (2018), "Pianist Craig Taborn on Reinventing Jazz Improvisation," Interview by Steve Paulson, *To the Best of Our Knowledge,* National Public Radio, 3 March, Audio 14:35. Available online at: https://www.ttbook.org/interview/pianist-craig-taborn-reinventing-jazz-improvisation

Torheim, Maria. (2017), "Do We Read Differently on Paper than on a Screen?," *Phys.org*, September. Available online at: https://phys.org/news/2017-09-differently-paper-screen.html

Ullman, Ellen. (2018), "Cutting-Edge Research to Support Students with Reading Disabilities," *eSchool News: Daily Tech News and Innovation*, 5 February. Available online at: https://www.eschoolnews.com/2018/02/05/cutting-edge-research-support-students-reading-disabilities/

Walker, Michelle. (2017), *Slow Philosophy: Reading Against the Institution*, New York: Bloomsbury Academic.

Weissmann, Jordan. (2014), "The Decline of the American Book Lover: And Why the Downturn might be Over," *The Atlantic,* 21 January. Available online at: https://www.theatlantic.com/business/archive/2014/01/the-decline-of-the-american-book-lover/283222/

Willingham, Daniel. (2017), *The Reading Mind: A Cognitive Approach to Understanding How the Mind Reads*, San Francisco: Jossey-Bass.

Wolf, Maryanne. (2018), "Skim Reading is the New Normal: The Effect on Society is Profound," The *Guardian*, 25 August. Available online at: https://www.theguardian.com/commentisfree/2018/aug/25/skim-reading-new-normal-maryanne-wolf?fbclid=IwAR28ZJeg3ZcO9TSwYTUWMTiaeTLJ0rTt6iSJmVyA8fajtzTFziyKtj33gZ4

Zhuangzi. (2009), *Zhuangzi: The Essential Writings with Selections from Traditional Commentaries*, Brook Ziporyn (trans.), Indianapolis: Hackett Publishing.

11

Unknowing Silence in Laozi's *Daodejing* and Merleau-Ponty

Katrin Froese

1. Introduction

In the contemporary world, we are drowning in a cacophony of textual voices, thanks in large part to the precipitous rise of social media and an overabundance of available data. But, this surplus of information and text has also been accompanied by a profound sense of meaninglessness and a burgeoning disenchantment, especially as it seems to proliferate without grounding. Nonetheless, we become habituated to this noise and are increasingly uncomfortable with silence and solitude, even though we are in dire need of their counterbalancing effects. Without silence as a companion to language, words themselves are eventually denuded of their meaning and become little more than continuous babble which we are addicted to, despite its unsettling impact. Our language has literally run away from us.

In an environment marked by the excess of speech, Laozi's *Daodejing* 道德經 and the work of Maurice Merleau-Ponty offer a welcome alternative. The need to step back from our linguistic constructs is acknowledged. A primordial silence is once again to become a part of language, and for this to take place, a non-linguistic awareness must be deliberately fostered. In the *Daodejing* stillness is cultivated, and silence also becomes part of the process of naming through the act of continuously renaming and unsettling all settled words. In Merleau-Ponty, silence is a retreat from speaking in order to open up infinite perceptual pathways that lead us to unexpected worlds. This is meaningful in his view because it opens the door to the lived experience of connection, rather than relying on communicative tools alone. However, words do not necessarily function in opposition to silence, there is also a continuous "enfolding" of words into the perceptual experience. The danger arises not from their intermingling, but when we succumb to the temptation to replace perceptual experience with language. The *Daodejing* goes further than this, because it imagines a primordial and silent oneness out of which all particular embodied things emerge. Thus silence not only reminds us of the boundary imposed by language, but of the boundaries of the physical body.

2. Merleau-Ponty

The prevailing view of language assumes that it functions mainly as a communicative tool, which conceptualizes, represents, and enframes experience. This illusory mindset impels us to view silence as little more than a void, signifying ignorance and non-knowledge. However, it is precisely the non-knowing relationship to the world that silence offers, which Merleau-Ponty insists is absolutely essential in order to live a meaningful existence. Silence and speech are placed into polar opposition only when language has detached itself from its corporal moorings to the point where its conceptual abstractions have asserted their primacy. For Merleau-Ponty this amounts to mistaking the secondary end-product of linguistic development for its origins and it dovetails with the fantasy of the omniscient subject to achieve totality, which also functions as a kind of limiting self-enclosure.

According to Merleau-Ponty such an approach glosses over an awareness of language in the process of emergence, wherein it becomes part of our corporal response to the world. Silence resides in the midst of language, attuning us to a plenitude of existence that can never be grasped, nor fully communicated. It represents the confusion out of which language emerges as well as the openness and potential that impels us to speak in the first place. As such, it also functions as an important counterweight to knowledge, reminding us that knowledge itself is only one kind of response to our existence that when taken too far, suppresses the very wonder that gave birth to it in the first place. Silence can keep such wonder alive, reminding us that we are interwoven into a world that "precedes knowledge ... in relation to which every scientific schematization is an abstract and derivative sign-language."[1] In other words, we must stop continuously thinking ourselves out of the world.

The role of silence in Merleau-Ponty is indelibly linked to the primacy of perception, which remains the central theme of his entire corpus. When the phenomenological clarion call to "return to the things themselves" is heeded, we discover that there are no "things" except perhaps as a result of the objectifying acts of consciousness. Instead of privileging consciousness, Merleau-Ponty focuses on perception, which precedes consciousness. Perception is no longer the abstract grasping or apprehension of "things," but a testament to our entanglement in the world. In addition, the predominant role accorded to perception marks a resistance to a life increasingly weighed down by words, which causes the words themselves to be stripped of their meaning. According to the Cartesian framework, the inner world of subjectivity and the world of objects "out there" are starkly demarcated from each other. Since the certainty of objects always eludes us, we retreat into an allegedly "pure world" of thought, forgetting that the inner world of language only emerges through the "outer world." Language gives us the illusion of an inner self when we seek refuge behind its veils. Perhaps it is only in speaking about our perceptions that we begin to assume that perception itself occurs at a distance. In other words, language obscures the nature of perceptual activity. This is why a repeated return to silent perception is absolutely essential: "In the silence of primary consciousness we see not only what words mean but also what things mean, the core of primary meaning around which the acts of naming and expression take place."[2] The emptier language becomes the greater the temptation to ward off this emptiness with the constant flow of words.

Merleau-Ponty vociferously repudiates the observer status we accord to ourselves: "We are caught up in the world and we do not succeed in extricating ourselves from it in order to achieve consciousness of the world."[3] The sense of distance that ensues robs us of meaning and also arrogates to human beings a superior status. Rather than embarking on a quest for knowledge and certainty, Merleau-Ponty launches an investigation to discover what imbues us with a *sense* of meaning. Here the double meaning of the French word *sens* (sense) is instructive, since it refers to both sensation and meaning, thereby already straddling the divide between the conceptual and the corporeal.[4] Merleau-Ponty's philosophy aims to relinquish the obsession with truth in order to return to the roots of pre-objectified world. The Cartesian achievement which had elevated the subject on an epistemological pedestal for Merleau-Ponty is perhaps one primary contributing factor to a profound sense of meaninglessness which pervades the contemporary world.

The terrain of perception is much richer than our barren conceptual categories would permit. Merleau-Ponty remarks that perception is neither passive observation, nor is it an active grasping which remakes the world in our image: "There can be no question of fitting together passivity before a transcendent with an activity of immanent thought. It is a question of reconsidering the interdependent notions of the active and the passive in such a way that they no longer place us before a philosophical antinomy."[5] Each apparently simple act of perception opens up a horizon, arousing "the expectation of more than it contains," and thereby is already "charged with a meaning."[6] As Lawrence Hass points out, the perceptual field is one of excess which "spills out every which way, beyond and around the specific things one attends to."[7] Thus Merleau-Ponty suggests that what exceeds our expectations generates meaning, emerges out of a responsive movement toward an unknown, mysterious world. Meaning is distinct from knowledge. We contribute to the world our own "intentional arc," even by moving in a certain direction, sometimes drawing upon the structures of language that surrounds us in order to do so. Silence is an important part of this process, since it marks an unassuming openness as well as a profound desire for the allure of the unbounded. Thus our "intentional arc" cannot be solely attributed to our subjective intention. Knowledge continuously aspires to transform the unexpected into the expected, but a world in which we cease to be surprised because we are addicted to the Cartesian illusion of certainty, is one that starves us of meaning. The richness of perceptual experience is then reduced to something amenable to measurement and categorization. For example, the label red which we use to characterize an object impels us to forget that the "red patch which I see on the carpet is red only in virtue of a shadow which lies across it, its quality is apparently only in relation to the play of light upon it, and hence as an element in a spatial configuration."[8] It is this poetic field of awareness that perception opens up: "reflection never holds, arrayed and objectified before its gaze, the whole world and the plurality of monads" and "its view is never other than apartial and of limited power."[9] Even the clear contours of a shape only have meaning in relation to a surrounding shapelessness that bring it into relief. Furthermore, we respond to the world affectively before we do so objectively.

Merleau-Ponty also notes that perception preexists the ego: "If I wanted to render precisely the perceptual experience, I ought to say that *one* perceives in me, and not that I perceive."[10] As M.C. Dillon points out, "the perception is primary, only later does reflection step back, disengage itself and transform the world into a spectacle which is viewed from a distance."[11] This means that I am not the agent of perception but rather participate in a process of perception. Merleau-Ponty uses the example of artistic creation to describe this. In "Indirect Language and the Voices of Silence" Merleau-Ponty interprets painting to be a kind of perceiving and being perceived, in which the painter cannot articulate "what comes from him and what comes from things."[12] When I perceive, I also receive and lose myself. What we refer to as the self can be seen as a wave which surges forth and withdraws: "As I contemplate the blue of the sky I am not *set over against* it as an acosmic subject; I do not possess it in thought . . . I abandon myself to it . . . it 'thinks itself' within me."[13] Furthermore, Merleau-Ponty sets art in opposition to what he calls "activism" whereby "only the painter is entitled to look at everything without being obliged to appraise what he sees. For the painter, we might say, the watchwords of knowledge and action lose their meaning and force."[14] We are, according to Merleau-Ponty, "immersed in the visible," which impels us to open ourselves to the world.

A conventional theory of sensation "builds up all knowledge out of determinate qualities" and "offers us objects purged of all ambiguity, pure and absolute."[15] Sight is prioritized as the sensation that is most closely allied to knowledge, but Merleau-Ponty maintains that even our presumptions about what we do when we see are fundamentally mistaken. We assume that sight occurs at a detached distance, which is not the case with senses such as touch and sound that surround and immerse us. But

Merleau-Ponty refuses to uphold the privileged status accorded to sight. He suggests that to "look at the object is to plunge oneself into it,"[16] and when we reflect upon our seeing, we realize that each object is defined only by virtue of its horizon such that every object becomes the "mirror of all others."[17] I do not "see objects" until I concentrate my gaze on a particular, becoming "anchored in it," but this "coming to rest of the gaze is merely a modality of its movement . . . and in one movement I close up the landscape and open the object."[18] Thus the perception of an object depends on the partiality of the gaze, which deliberately allows the surroundings to recede into the background. Each visual fixation, which offers us the illusion of stasis, is in fact the outcome of a certain kind of bodily movement. At the same time, language, which depends upon the ability to objectify, could not occur without the movement of the body that objectifies physically before we can do so intellectually. As such, language mirrors the movements of the body.

When vision is seen as a bodily phenomenon, it can incite an awareness of the deep multiplicity of the world, while the distillation of these experiences into habituated objects and words demands a kind of detachment from experience so that the idea, "like the object," can purport to "be the same for everybody, valid in all times and all places."[19] As a result, "I am no longer concerned with my body, with time, nor with the world . . . I now refer to my body only as an idea."[20] But the idea of the body that is created as a result also allows us to communicate with each other while at the same time marking "the death of consciousness,"[21] and so it opens up the possibility for the creation of a social body. Merleau-Ponty acknowledges that the gaze of another without language would be too unsettling, because there would be no common ground. In the look of the other, I risk becoming a stranger to myself, because the illusion of a coherent self is threatened. I can never see what another sees. Perception is inherently solipsistic, and it is language that attempts to overcome this solipsism: "What is it like when the other turns upon me, meets my gaze, and fastens his own upon my body and my face? Unless we have recourse to the ruse of speech, putting a common domain of thoughts between us as a third party, the experience is intolerable."[22] One need only reflect on the intense discomfort we experience when somebody stares at us in silence to glean the import of these words.

Language is a double-edged sword. The *rationa* structure of sedimented language associated with Cartesian "spirituality" is a much later stage of development that belies its origins. The first uses of language are emotive and gestural, rather than rational and logical: "We speak and we understand speech long before learning from Descartes that thought is our reality. The true dawns through an emotional and almost carnal experience where the 'ideas'—the other's and our own—are rather traits of his physiognomy and of our own, are less understood than welcomed or spurned in love or hatred."[23] Language makes communication and interweaving with others possible, but it also tempts us to take refuge in the illusion of certainty that this second-order experience offers and we "lose contact with the perceptual experience."[24]

In the Introduction to *Phenomenology of Perception*, Merleau-Ponty makes the claim that "to return to things themselves, is to return to that world which precedes knowledge of which knowledge always speaks."[25] We cannot move from certainty within the self, to certainty about the outside world, since the world is there "before any analysis of mine." Before knowledge speaks, before we can even conceive of a consciousness, the world speaks to us *silently*. Thus silence is also a return to pre-egoistic reflection: "When I begin to reflect, I reflect upon an unreflective experience."[26] Merleau-Ponty vociferously denies the existence of an inner world separated from the outer world: "Truth does not 'inhabit' only the 'inner man' or more accurately there is no inner man, man is in the world, and only in the world does he know himself."[27]

In *The Visible and the Invisible* Merleau-Ponty suggests that we engage in a hyper-reflection which is a kind of reflection that returns to pre-linguistic awareness, perpetually relating it to our linguistic ways of being, which would not "lose sight of the brute thing and the brute awareness and would not finally efface them, and would not cut the organic bonds between the perception and the thing perceived with a hypothesis of inexistence."[28] This means that silence would be part of reflection as part of "our mute contact with things, when they are not yet things said."[29] Rather than becoming merely the vehicle for knowledge, thinking becomes a constant interrogation of the world, through which we expose "what in silence it means to say."[30] No conceptual schema can bestow upon the world a singular unity. Instead the world through perception is revealed as "strange and paradoxical."[31] We are transformed through this perceptual act and cannot extricate ourselves from the world "in order to achieve consciousness" of it.[32]

Perception is neither wholly passive nor wholly active and opens up a new surrounding world (an *Umwelt*) and therefore is in itself fundamentally expressive as well as responsive. Our relationship with this *Umwelt* is paradoxical since we are assaulted by it, creating a fissure within ourselves that constantly places our subjectivity under siege. But this inner rift or opening incites within us an impossible thirst for plenitude that drives us to perceive. Perception is also a kind of yearning for the fullness the world offers, while at the same time underlining the impossible possibility of coming together and tearing apart which Merleau-Ponty will later coin the *incompossible*: "The world ceaselessly assails and beleaguers subjectivity, as waves wash round a wreck on the shore. All knowledge takes place within the horizons opened up by perception ... we can never fill up in the picture of the world, that gap which we ourselves are, since perception is the *flaw* in this 'great diamond.'"[33] The image of the great diamond is taken from a poem by Valéry: "Mes repentirs, mes doutes mes contraintes, sont les défauts de ton grand diamant" (My doubts, compunctions, my constraints and checks, these are the flaws of your great diamond).[34] This metaphor highlights the intertwining of suffering, longing and beauty. There is a craving underlying the act of perception, which derives from the weak position of a wounded self, thirsting for a wholeness that will always elude it. It suggests that uncertainty and suffering drive our perceptual curiosity. The quest for knowledge is merely derivative.

Speaking can be a longing to close the gap with words. It too is the child of desire unleashed in perception. When we retreat behind human words, we can easily succumb to the illusion of certainty, and perform an inversion which considers the certainty of words to be primary. However, words are also an expression of uncertainty. Merleau-Ponty cautions us that "philosophy is not a lexicon . . . it does not seek a verbal substitute for the world we see, it does not transform it into something said. It is the things themselves from the depths of their silence, that it wishes to bring to expression."[35] Thus silence in Merleau-Ponty is necessary to create another kind of language, namely an expressive language which would "adjust itself to those figured enigmas . . . whose massive being and truth teem with *incompossible* details."[36] When silence informs language, we do not just speak of the world, the world speaks through us. Merleau-Ponty hints at the possibility of silent speaking.

Perception in Merleau-Ponty is a dialogical relationship to the world. In this sense, it is already a kind of speaking. Silence is no mere absence of sound, but a responsiveness to the plenitude of existence. The active cultivation of silence ensures that language's limiting function does not take over. We speak because we are also spoken to by the world we inhabit. Furthermore, silence constitutes a recognition that there can be no speaking about the world without listening to it. Silence is not inactivity but, rather, is the activity of attunement to that which is necessarily excluded by language. It thereby also ensures the continual transformation and creation of language.

Silence is also a kind of "unraveling of speech" which guards against the excesses made possible by the sedimentation of language, or what Heidegger refers to as idle talk (*Gerede*). This is talk that is primarily repetitive, conventional, and has forgotten that we do not survey (*survoler*) the world, but rather inhabit it. The sedimentation of language impels us to forget that while language is always already there, it also is in a continuous process of emergence. When language becomes automatic, we can easily succumb to the conceptual illusion that language makes sense of the world. In other words, our conceptual certainty is the product of the ossification of habits, particularly when they are socially reinforced: "An attitude towards the world, when it has received frequent confirmation, acquires a favored status for us."[37] Of course all of us are thrown into a world of language from birth and mimic the words of adults. Observing children in the process of learning language reminds us of its expressive nature, since children will often make sounds that have no social meaning but nonetheless have a kind of gestural significance expressing sheer wonder, delight, or even revulsion. Their babbling may not make conceptual sense, but it manifests a meaningful responsiveness to the world they encounter.

Thus the origins of language are poetic rather than utilitarian: "As soon as man uses language to establish a living relation with himself or with his fellows, language is no longer an instrument, *no longer a means; it is a manifestation, a revelation of intimate being and of the psychic link which unites us to the world and our fellow men.*"[38] Language is ontologically grounded in the sounds and gestures of the body according to Merleau-Ponty: "We need then to seek the first attempts at language in the emotional gesticulation whereby man superimposes the given in the world according to man."[39] The notion that signifiers have meaning only in relation to other signifiers, severing the link between signifier and signified, is a later moment in the development of language; however, "conventions are a late form of relationship between men; they presuppose an earlier means of communication and language must be put back into this current of intercourse."[40] Language is above all a musical response to the world, a way to "sing the world's praises and in the last resort to live it."[41] Furthermore, language, at least initially, is not divorced from the body but rather intimately connected to its movements, even if at a later stage of development, language is used to arrest movement in order to generate timeless structures. Merleau-Ponty reminds us of the physical aspects of language, which include a "contraction of the throat, a sibilant emission of air between the tongue and teeth, a certain way of bringing the body into play."[42]

In order to make sense of this idea, it is helpful to turn to the text of the *Zhuangzi* 莊子 since it also underscores the *meaningful* nature of the nonsensical piping of human beings and animals, thereby highlighting that meaning does not inhere in the explanatory function of words, but rather in the responsiveness of words to the cosmos: "Words are not just wind. Words have something to say. But if what they have to say is not fixed, then do they really say something? Or do they say nothing? People suppose that words are different from the peeps of baby birds, but is there any difference or isn't there?"[43] The fact that there is an element of saying nothing in the words, as in the "meaningless" sounds of baby birds, suggests that the origins of human language include a tacit recognition of the radical openness of the cosmos which cannot be contained in words. Therefore the *Zhuangzi* suggests that the most meaningless words of all carry a profound meaning that is forgotten when we saddle them with heavy meanings as we do when they become cumbersome words (*yuyan* 寓言), or heavy/repeated words (*zhongyan* 重言) rather than the goblet words (*zhiyan* 卮言) that express fluidity.[44]

In *The Visible and the Invisible,* Merleau-Ponty goes even further in emphasizing non-linguistic awareness/attunement. The invisible refers to what we would commonly think of as thought, language, and reflection, but by describing it in relation to a physical sensation (vision), he emphasizes the idea that thought is not part of an ethereal sphere divorced from the body, but is instead a sublimation and extension of corporeal activity. The subject–object dichotomy, as well as the dichotomy between consciousness and corporeal existence, are collapsed. Merleau-Ponty understands the body as a dehiscence (*écart*). We open to the outside as we are touched from the inside. There is a constant crossing or intersection between inside and outside as we both touch and are touched, which Merleau-Ponty refers to as the chiasm. The "coincidence" is "never but partial,"[45] meaning that I never grasp the world. Each touching is also a slipping away and this impels us to reach out into the world over and over again. Silence thus is also the process by which the world retreats from our gaze. It is this refusal of the world to surrender to our perception (similar to the conflict between world and Earth in Heidegger) that fuels our desire. Perception, as corporeal participation in being, is also desire which emerges out of the dialectical relationship between presence and absence. The chiasmic encounter highlights the link between desire and perception.[46]

Corporeal entanglement is necessarily ambiguous. My hand is at once both touched and touching, perceived as well as perceiving: "This can happen only if my hand, while it is felt from within, is also accessible from without, itself tangible, for my other hand, for example, if it takes its place among the things it touches, is in a sense one of them, opens finally upon a tangible being of which it is also a part. Through the crisscrossing within it of the touching and the tangible, its own movements incorporate themselves into the universe they interrogate ... It is no different for the vision— except ... that ... the information it gathers [does] not belong 'to the same sense.'"[47] If I try to compartmentalize this process to locate a starting or endpoint, or to subject it to laws of causality which would enable me to identify an agent that acts and an object which is acted upon, I will inevitably fail. I feel one hand through the other. I am perceiving and perceived. There is no internal coherence to the self, only dehiscence: the opening to the other that necessarily entails a splitting within the self. The fact that there is no coherent self is not a source of intellectual stress for Merleau-Ponty. There is no problem of the other, as in Sartre or even Levinas, because the other is part of my internal awareness of myself. Although the notion of a coherent self is a powerful fantasy, such a self could not engage with the world because there would be no open fissures in it that would make meaningful engagement with its *Umwelt* (surrounding world) possible: "There is here no problem of the *alter ego* because it is not *I* who sees, not *he* who sees, because an anonymous visibility inhabits both of us, a vision in general, in virtue of that primordial property that belongs to the flesh, being here and now, of radiating everywhere and forever, being an individual, of being also a dimension and a universal."[48] Thus we do not just see but are "in vision" that anonymously occurs through us. Seeing is not simply something we do; it is also done to us. The flesh for Merleau-Ponty is not mute, dumb matter, but rather an organism that *opens* out into the world and is a "bursting forth of the mass of the body towards the things," which makes me "follow with my eyes, the movements and contours of things themselves."[49]

The chiasmic encounter takes on an even more radical meaning in the text of the *Zhuangzi* in the famous butterfly dream. Here it is not merely one hand touching another that results in a deliberate confusion of identity. Instead, it is one creature transforming into the other in a dream in which Zhuangzi does not "know if he was Zhuang Zhou who had dreamt he was a butterfly, or a butterfly dreaming he was Zhuang Zhou," concluding only "that there must be some distinction" which is called the "transformation of things."[50] As in Merleau-Ponty, this folding of one being into another is meant to undo identity by suggesting that the difference between things *and* their mutual entanglement is a sign of their connective unity. The unity stems neither from the reduction of one to the other, nor from their difference, but rather comes about because of the paradoxical combination of these seemingly opposed tendencies. It is only language which places difference and oneness into an oppositional relationship. Merleau-Ponty's *écart* and Zhuangzi's muddled dream point out that only the paradoxical confusion of these two dimensions allows for transformation. In both texts, identity loses its central place and the process of transformation that occurs because of the encounter is highlighted instead.

Merleau-Ponty also insists that vision is always entangled in other senses and that I never simply see an object, but rather see in constellations: "this red is what it is only by connecting up from its place with other reds about it, with which it forms a constellation, or with other colors it dominates or that dominate it, that it attracts or that attract it, that it repels or that repel it. . . . The red dress *a fortiori* holds with all its fibers onto the fabric of the visible, and therefore onto a fabric of invisible being."[51] The invisible therefore is *part* of the visible. Vision is dynamic, not static. I fix my eyes upon something only by moving away from something else. States of being grab my attention by coalescing in particular ways. It is "less a color or a thing, therefore, than a difference between things and colors, a momentary crystallization of colored being or of visibility."[52] Colors are experienced as affective intensities, not just as abstract distant visual phenomena. It is impossible to separate the affective response to color from its visual cues: "Claudel has a phrase saying that a certain blue of the sea is so blue that only blood would be more red. The color is yet a variant in another dimension of *variatio*, that of its relations with the surroundings this red is what it is only by connecting up from its place with other reds about it, with which it forms a constellation."[53] The emotional intensity of redness is part of the visible experience of it. The invisible underlies the visible.

By suggesting that the visible does not survey from above, but rather is a "grain or corpuscle borne by a wave of Being,"[54] Merleau-Ponty also throws into question the idea that philosophy should mimic science which has traditionally fixed its sights on acquiring a detached bird's eye view. Instead, there is a participation in a varied and multi-layered intercorporeal tapestry. Language is part of this tapestry but we must guard against allowing it to supplant it. That would be akin to equating musical notation with music-making. Quoting from Proust, Merleau-Ponty asserts that one would then be left with "bare values substituted for the mysterious entity he had perceived, for the convenience of his understanding."[55] Meaning and understanding cannot be equated. Merleau-Ponty takes Saussure's notion of the diacritical structure of language, whereby signifiers refer to each other in an endless chain, and applies it to the senses which are also inextricably intertwined, enveloping, pointing, and referring to each other. Instead of the clear categories required by conceptualization, Merleau-Ponty treasures ambiguity, crisscrossing and a "wild being," a notion which, as I will point out below, is similar to the idea of the murky and the obscure in Daoist texts. In seeing one thing, we are at the same time "seeing the invisible" in its multiple dimensions. The invisible is the blurred background that highlights the foreground. It is not absence or Sartre's *néant* but rather a temporary retreat and as such is part of and informs the visible.

Language adds another fold into Being and is an expression of a desire or a movement toward and into the world: "the folding over within him of the visible and the lived experience upon language, and of language upon the visible and the lived experience, the exchanges between his mute language and those of his speech . . . it is the theme of philosophy."[56] Furthermore, such language is called forth "by the voices of silence."[57] The voices of silence in their variegated multiplicity elicit our speech in a manner that is similar to the way in which emotional states can impel us to sing. Such singing is a type of responsiveness that can never be explicated, nor can it generate understanding. But it does generate meaning, which Merleau-Ponty uncouples from knowledge.

Merleau-Ponty replaces the Cartesian quest for certainty with a quest for ambiguity that is vital to maintain the richness of experience. There is a profound paradox that runs through Merleau-Ponty's works on perception. On the one hand, perception is inherently meaningful, and does not require a transcendent abstract justification as its supplement. Yet, at the same time, the interplay between language and silence, which makes reflection upon our perception possible, imbues the experience with a deeper meaning, not because reflection is inherently richer, but because the contrast between the sublimated nature of language and our tangible corporeal existence enables us to be more poignantly aware of the endless depth of perceptual activity. The alienating dimension of language bestows upon silent perception a renewed intensity. In turn, the disintegration of the self that this intensity makes possible, makes us long for the comfort of the social body that language plays a part in creating. Silence is paradoxical. It draws out our voice, and at the same time muffles it, allowing for a kind of melting into our environs that speech undercuts. The undulating relationship between speech and silence is the harbinger of meaning. Glen Mazis describes this relationship as a kind of "pivoting between the invisible of the visible" rather than a retreat into the pre-reflective.[58]

As I have pointed out above, speech also transmits my experience to another, enabling me to become part of and contribute to the creation of a social body. However, when the social transmission of the experience completely eclipses the experience itself, we are left with nothing but empty gestures, devoid of mooring, as is increasingly the case in a world overtaken by social media. One could see the world of social media as an excess of the social that ends up decimating the very social bonds it intends to create. If the social function of language is to remain meaningful, a solipsistic silence must also be maintained. The idea that Derrida takes from Saussure, namely that signifiers refer only to other signifiers, and that the social world is always only a socially constructed one, is rejected by Merleau-Ponty. Language must be grounded, albeit in a "wild being" which is "behind or beneath the cleaves of our acquired culture."[59] Nonetheless, this ground is always shifting. It is silence that repeatedly draws our attention to this perpetually shifting, multi-perspectival, and multi-textured world that we are both drawn to and also repelled by.

3. The *Daodejing*

Silence and stillness play a pivotal role in Laozi's text, the *Daodejing*. Merleau-Ponty uses silence to remind us of the important connection between meaning and the corporal immersion in existence. The *Daodejing* goes even further with a cosmology that underscores the role of silence as part of the process of return to the primordial root of all things. While Merleau-Ponty's primordiality predates the ego and language, primordiality in the *Daodejing* also precedes the development of physical bodies. In the *Daodejing* silence is also pre-perceptual:

> There was some process that formed spontaneously, emerging before Heaven and Earth. Silent and empty, standing alone as all that is, it does not suffer alteration; all-pervading it does not pause. It can be thought of as the mother of Heaven and Earth. I do not yet know its name. If I were to style it, I would call it Dao. And if I were forced to give it a name, I could call it grand.[60]

In the above passage, the word *ji* 寂 means both silent *and* lonely, since it refers to a condition prior to the emergence of the myriad forms of life. The ten thousand things (*wanwu* 萬物), of which we are but one, always long to return to their primal origins. Hence, silence is emblematic of a state before things were distinct from one another, which also can become the source of our longing. According to the *Daodejing*, it is as fundamental to our being as language, which is something we readily forget, especially in a culture that is marked by a surplus of words and text. In other words, the *Daodejing* suggests that even our desire to speak may represent the allure of silence because the plenitude of silence can never be "filled" by speech. Every word we utter falls short and so we frantically search for more fitting words. In fact, the text notes that if "forced (*qiang* 強) to give it a name, I would call it grand." But as soon as the name grand (*da* 大) is bestowed on it, the speaker adopts a plethora of other names that cast doubt on the initial moniker: "Being grand, it is called passing. Passing, it is called distancing. Distancing, it is called returning."[61] The interaction between naming and un-naming or renaming is significant. Through silence we recognize that no name suffices. Thus silence is part of the *action* of naming by unsettling every name. This kind of "deconstruction" is a meaningful process signifying a movement back to the source of all things, which is beyond any single name but at the same time permeates all of them. The primordial oneness gives birth to multiplicity and a fecund naming is part of this process of constant generation and growth. In other words, it draws attention to naming as process rather than focusing simply on "the named."

There are many instances in the *Daodejing* where the importance of *jing* 靜 is underscored. Although this word means silence, it can also mean stillness, calm, and equilibrium. Stillness is the root of movement, even agitated movement: "The heavy is the root of the light, stillness is the lord of agitation (*jing wei zaojun* 靜為躁君)."[62] This passage can be interpreted in multiple ways. One is that frenetic activity (*zao* 躁) is kept in check by *jing* ensuring that one is always drawn back to the silent root. Cultivating the stillness of the body is an important part of this process. Thomas Michael asserts that the "pristine Dao" is related to its inner cultivation within the physical body and that "both are grounded in a physicality that cannot be brushed aside."[63] A second possible interpretation of the passage is that the desire for stillness precipitates the frantic attempt to return to the primordial. Since every action falls short, we engage in unrelenting activity unaware that our nervous movement is a longing for silence.

The *Daodejing* presupposes that harmony is also the most natural state of being, but it is not a harmony that excludes opposition; rather, it emerges out of a process in which opposites flow into each other. This means that even the movement from one extreme to another signifies a natural pull toward equilibrium, just as the door swings around a hinge from one side to another while the hinge itself does not move. The moving opposites always remain connected through the hinge and thus are one.

While the text on one level labels desire a negative force that hinders the return to the Dao, maintaining that a desireless posture enables one to observe the mysteries of things (*gu heng wuyu, yiguan qi miao* 故恆無欲，以觀其秒), it also asserts that desire enables one to "observe boundaries" (*heng youyu ye, yiguan qi suojiao* 恆有欲也，以觀其所徼).[64] Boundaries draw attention to the particular potential of things or their *de* 德. Thus we must move continuously between desire and "desirelessness." The desire manifested in silence is a yearning for a radical openness that impels us to transition through various states rather than settling in any one position. Curie Virag points out that desire is what "incites, animates and furnishes the content of knowing because it represents the workings of the Dao within humans: it is the productive force by which all things come into the world and move towards fulfillment."[65] In contrast, Hans-Georg Moeller argues that desires are identified as the "main cause of war and social disorder in the *Daodejing*."[66] He points out that a desireless stance is necessary among sages as well as being deliberately cultivated in the general populace so as to avoid conflict. However, I argue that the rejection of objectifying desire predicated on acquisition does not constitute the rejection of *all* desire. The above passage attests to the possibility of a desire for fluid and open movement.

In the *Daodejing,* as in Merleau-Ponty, speaking is an *act* that transforms the ten thousand things, sometimes in creative ways that "fold back" into the Dao (to appropriate Merleau-Ponty's language), but also in destructive ways that usher in disequilibrium and mark abrupt departures from the harmonious way of the Dao (of course, even this disharmony experienced by human beings becomes part of the ultimate harmony of the Dao which treats human beings as "straw dogs destined for sacrifice"). The *Daodejing* begins by highlighting the paradoxical nature of language and cautioning us to always speak carefully and tentatively. It throws into question the action of naming while at the same time affirming its importance and vitality:

> Way-making that can be put into words is not really way-making, and naming that can assign fixed reference to things is not really naming. The nameless is the beginning of Heaven and Earth, the named is the mother of the ten thousand things.[67]

There are several ways of interpreting this passage. On the one hand, words cannot possibly capture the eternal Dao (*changdao* 常道), and are but a pale and also misguided imitation of it. Yet, it can also be read in a very different, albeit unconventional way if *chang* is assumed to mean regular or common rather than eternal: "The Dao that can *dao* is not the common Dao, the name that can name is not the regular name." In other words, the Dao that is capable of Dao-ing is not regular because it is continuously adaptive and flexible.[68] The naming that can name is not a congealed word but a fluid one. Naming is always also a renaming. There is a difference between using language adaptively and using it rigidly. Nonetheless, the name is always inadequate to the Dao, and so the only recourse one has is to use words and subsequently undo them, thereby mimicking the ebb and flow of the Dao in language and ensuring that words do not become too entrenched, or sedimented. In order to approximate the stillness of the source, one must be prepared to continually adjust. Thus movement can become a kind of return to the openness of stillness. Sedimented language which all too often bellows into silence, disrupting it rather than growing out of it, obscures the harmonious movement of the Dao.

The *Daodejing* does not vilify speech. Naming itself is a way of participating in the creative generation of the Dao, which is why the named is the mother of the ten thousand things, contributing to their creative proliferation. This is reminiscent of Merleau-Ponty's idea of the poetic and expressive origins of language. A name is no mere label that re-presents things, but rather is a transformative response to the beings of the world. There is a kind of wild fluidity to words, which Merleau-Ponty insists is inscribed in their poetic origins. Habit contributes to their congealment and their poetic roots are quickly forgotten. Perhaps this is why the objectification of the name (or the constant/repeated name) hinders the *process* of naming. The term *changming* 常名 is interesting because it reminds us of the deleterious impact of repetition. But even the seemingly fixed nature of words demands a repetitive movement so that they can be preserved. Merleau-Ponty reminds us that we cannot do without a reservoir of sedimented language in order to be able to speak poetically. The paradoxical oscillation between sedimentation and generation (creation) is a process that both the text of the *Daodejing* and Merleau-Ponty allude to.

The emphasis on the interplay between speech and silence as a form of creative generation also means that the *Daodejing* privileges the obscure rather than the clarity of knowledge. In Merleau-Ponty the obscure takes the form of the overwhelming openness and diversity of experience that is above all fecund, and impels us to form our own "intentional arcs" in response. In other words, our intentionality constitutes a reaction to the confusion arising out of such multiplicity. In the *Daodejing*, obscurity blurs boundaries between things, thereby moving closer to the undifferentiated Dao. The *Daodejing* maintains that the coalescence of the named and the nameless gives rise to the obscure, in part because the clarity of words helps draw attention to the murkiness of the obscure. We swing continuously between clarity and murkiness:

> These two—the nameless and what is named—emerge from the same source yet are referred to differently. Together they are called obscure, the obscurest of the obscure. They are the swinging gateway of the manifold of mysteries.[69]

The *Daodejing* repeatedly highlights the mystery of the cosmos, thereby downplaying and even denigrating attempts to obtain knowledge of it. Knowledge is primarily instrumental because it is used as a mechanism of control, both politically and in relation to the natural world. Mystery in the *Daodejing* and wonder in Merleau-Ponty are *meaningful*. Just as speech without silence can become a dangerous weapon, knowledge without the countervailing impact of mystery can also have ominous effects. Lin Ma points out that *zhi* 知 as rational knowledge is thoroughly resisted in the text. *Zhi* is etymologically related to speech in Chinese since it is a juxtaposition of the radicals for arrow (*shi* 矢) and mouth (*kou* 口). Ma points out that in many instances, *shou* 守 or safeguarding is the preferred phrasing.[70] She highlights one example with this usage which underscores the importance of safeguarding equilibrium: "Extend your utmost emptiness as far as you can, and do your best to preserve your equilibrium" (*shoujing* 守靜).[71]

Closely connected to knowledge in the *Daodejing* is perceptual grasping that can occur when the clearly demarcated "five colors" and "five flavors" assault the senses:

> The five colors blind the eye, the hard riding of the hunt addles both heart and mind, and property hard to come by subverts proper conduct. The five flavors destroy the palate and the five notes impair the ear. It is for this reason that in the proper governing by the sages: They exert their efforts on behalf of the abdomen rather than the eye, thus eschewing one they take the other.[72]

In Daoist meditative practices, the abdomen is the center for focusing one's energies and the place of equilibrium. Energy must be continuously returned to the abdomen in order to prevent it from leaking out of the body. The abdomen is the physical root of stillness within the human body that grounds the other senses and prevents them from being besieged by external stimuli. Thus stillness is not merely an absence of speech, but rather the cultivation of a particular kind of integrative physical energy. Thomas Michael points out that to relinquish human socialization, one must "open oneself up to the energies of the physical world,"[73] and I would argue that physical cultivation of stillness within the body is part of this process. The physical cultivation of a still energy provides a powerful counterweight to conceptual language.

Stillness in Daoism is thus a broader concept than Merleau-Ponty's silence because it is quieting not just of sound but of *all* the senses. It lightens the load not only of speech but also of perceptual grasping, allowing for a kind of perceptive equilibrium. Words are only one form of grasping and their impact is never solely conceptual, since they play a pivotal role in cultivating an anxious desire that precipitates acquisition. Once the five sounds are categorized by language, they are more amenable to grasping. As in Merleau-Ponty, words have a profound impact on the way in which we perceive. This is also why too much studying makes us susceptible to the allure of constant acquisition:

> In studying there is a daily increase, while in learning of Dao there is a daily decrease. One loses and again loses to the point where one does everything non-coercively (*wuwei* 無為).[74]

The unavailability of the Dao to the senses suggests that there is a kind of awareness made possible by the cognizance of their failure to reach what we long for. Thus perceptual failure is an important part of the awareness of the Dao:

Looking and yet not seeing it, we thus call it elusive. Listening and yet not hearing it, we thus call it inaudible. Groping and yet not getting it, we thus call it intangible. Because in sight, sound and touch it is beyond determination, we construe it as inseparably one.[75]

The indeterminacy of the Dao stands in contrast to the determinacy of language:

Ever so tangled, it defies discrimination and reverts again to indeterminacy.[76]

We cannot undo the impact of thinking and naming and completely divest ourselves of our penchant for clarity. But stillness and silence help human beings to blunt the sharper edges of thoughts and words. The swinging gateway represents an ability to pull back, without losing sight of the central hinge. This is a skill that is lost when we immerse ourselves completely in the social world, at the expense of the natural world. What makes language a socially viable tool of communication, namely repetition and ossification, also helps to set human beings against nature. The social use of words, which gives them stability, at the same time disrupts their flow and eventually robs them of their meaning. This means that from a Daoist perspective the social order is often at odds with nature:

As soon as everyone in the world knows that the beautiful are beautiful, there is already ugliness. As soon as everyone knows the able, there is ineptness.[77]

Duality becomes opposition in a social context, when one thing is valorized over another. Furthermore, the act of knowing itself is a social phenomenon. Only social recognition and repetition of the name imbues one with the "knowledge" of words. But the *Daodejing* never ceases to remind us that the ensuing clarity is a delusion. This means that there must be a periodic retreat from the social order to ensure that it does not tip into excess. One must "know when to stop" being a social being and learn to think with nature, rather than against it.

Connected to the balancing effect of silence is the necessary cultivation of non-knowledge since knowledge can be seen as an excess of speech: "Cut off learning and there will be nothing more to worry about."[78] Hierarchy, strife and competition emerge out of a naming that provides us with knowledge since a fixed position automatically invites its opposite. The irony is that even this conflict is part of the relentless desire to return to the equilibrium of the center. In order to ensure that our words do not destroy, we need silence to remind us of a primordial nature that is free of words. Too much knowledge and study are associated with coercion and an excess of Yang 陽 (male, bright, strong, etc.), as compared to Yin 陰 (female, dark, supple, etc.).

Without knowing when to stop speaking, we generate conflict. Acting non-coercively necessitates a retreat from our own language into stillness. The reification of names is dangerous, not only because it undermines the creative, constantly shifting flow of the cosmos, but because the ultimate outcome of this ossification of names is war. The *Daodejing* puts forward the radical idea that the overuse and veneration of language is one of the root causes of deadly conflict. If political leaders were to acknowledge the nameless nature of the Dao, there would be no occasion for strife (of course the irony of this is that they would then also cease to be *political* leaders):

> Way making is really nameless. Although in this unworked state it is of little consequence, no one in the world would dare to condescend to it. Were the nobles and kings able to respect this, all things would defer of their own accord. Heaven and Earth would come together to send down their sweet honey, and without being so ordered, the common people would see that it is distributed equitably.[79]

Recognizing the importance of namelessness goes hand-in-hand with recognizing that knowledge is a threat to the security of the state:

> Those of ancient times who engaged in way-making (Dao) did not use it to edify the common people, but rather to keep them foolish. What makes it difficult to bring proper order to the people is that they already know too much. Thus to use knowledge in governing the state is to be a bane to that state. To use a lack of knowledge in governing the state is to be its benefactor.[80]

This is not a plea to render people ignorant, although the wording of the passage may suggest that this is indeed the case. In comparison to the masses who are enamored with their own knowledge, the person who realizes the unknowable nature of the Dao seems dumb and is also thrust to the social periphery. The wisdom of stillness always makes one an outsider. The masses think they see because they can scale the heights to survey the surroundings (this is reminiscent of Merleau-Ponty's critique of knowledge as *survoler* or surveying from above):

> Most people are happy, happy as though feasting at the *tailao* banquet or climbing some sightseeing tower in the springtime. I alone am so impassive, revealing nothing at all, like a babe that has yet to smile. So listless, as though nowhere to go . . . The common lot see things so clearly, while I alone seem to be in the dark. The common lot are so discriminating, while I alone am so obtuse. So vague and hazy, like the rolling seas; so indeterminate, as though virtually endless.[81]

The wisdom of the sage who cultivates an appreciation for the murkiness of the Dao and retreats into silence appears stupid in relation to the babbling crowd. It is natural for the sage to "speak only rarely" (*xiyan ziran* 希言自然).[82] When words are used to excess, they resemble the "violent winds" which "do not last a whole morning."[83] Silence represents a refusal to see the world through one's communicative tools alone, but in doing so, one is forced into the position of the outsider. In a world overrun with texts and words, such a person is scorned and mocked for her/his rejection of instrumentalism. A non-instrumental stance is open, adaptive, purposeless, and useless in world that prioritizes success and achievement:

> What is truest seems crooked; what is most skillful seems bungling. What is most prosperous seems wanting; what is most eloquent seems halting. Staying active beats the cold; keeping still beats the heat. Purity and stillness can bring proper order to the world.[84]

While the importance of silence in order to procure political peace is underscored in the *Daodejing,* and the text has a tone that is decidedly anti-militaristic, it also raises the possibility that social order and silence are perpetually incompatible and will always remain in tension. We do not have to look far to recognize that the silent leader is an oxymoron. The silent do not wish to lead. While purity and stillness bring harmony to the world, social order may always exclude harmony. Thus while the text tries to find a means of bringing politics into alignment with the silent Dao, it at the same time recognizes the impossibility of doing so. It is perhaps no coincidence that the optimistic tone of Merleau-Ponty's text is achieved only by avoiding a discussion of politics. The *Daodejing*, in contrast, does not avoid this topic and also suggests that the harmony of the Dao may not be something that can ever be fully experienced by social human beings. In this sense, silence could also constitute a recognition that social harmony can never be completely aligned with the harmony of the Dao. But this misalignment also precipitates the desire for return to the Dao.

4. Conclusion

The cultivation of the relationship between speech and silence according to both the *Daodejing* and Merleau-Ponty is necessary to revive the poetic and creative use of language. It signifies an overture or openness to the world that imbues us with a sense of meaning. Mystery and obscurity generate a kind of desire that assists the closure of knowledge. An overemphasis on knowledge risks changing the world into something that can be ordered and controlled, which is why it must be continuously undone. The child, who greets the world with wonder, is not suffocated by the idea that life has no purpose, because it is intuitively preoccupied with its exploration. Meaning in both texts is purposeless and silent. There is no need to endow it with words.

Undoubtedly, language can play a role in this exploratory and creative openness, but only if it also makes room for silence. According to Merleau-Ponty, silence is not a void, or nothingness, but rather a retreat from speech in order to fully engage one's other senses, unencumbered by the conceptual categories that can limit them. In the *Daodejing* it is necessary to attune oneself to the movement and rhythm of the Dao. When we become too engrossed with our own words, then knowledge is easily mistaken for the way things are. We need silence to remind us of perceptual ambiguity and obscurity. For example, speech can impel us to forget that the "discrete" things that are constructed by our minds do not exist, since the ten thousand things flow into each other, continuously changing their shapes. By cultivating silence, which has no boundaries, we can learn to be comfortable with the murky and flowing nature of existence. The *Daodejing* goes further than Merleau-Ponty in underscoring the importance of silence, because there is a cosmological imperative to return to an undifferentiated oneness that is the hinge upon which all the multifarious things of the world converge. Thus stillness, which is also a physical motion, constitutes a return to this root while at the same time making us attentive to the particularity of each moment. Only in silence, which is fundamentally non-differentiated, can we see the irreducibility of all beings to language. Paradoxes have their home in silence. A complete immersion in the world of speech, or to put it in Merleau-Ponty's terms, an invisible world that attempts to deny its roots in the visible, blinds us to nuance and movement.

Furthermore, silence reminds us of the overly instrumental tendencies of an ossified language. Merleau-Ponty's chiasm points out that subjectivity is an illusion since we not only perceive but are perceived: perception is not a method of surveying the world from above, but rather is a connection between things. Once we recognize this, we can begin to act without intention, as the *Daodejing* points out, because we do not know where these connections might lead us. The undifferentiated Dao at the root of things makes possible a radical openness, which in Merleau-Ponty is referred to as "wild being." Meaning comes out of cultivating this openness in the face of which we are all ignorant, as the *Daodejing* points out. Thus we must openly cultivate our ignorance, not just our knowledge. Clichés irk us because we know them too well and they become meaningless with overuse. An instrumental language turns everything into an object that can be easily grasped but such grasping also forecloses the open potential of being that allows interconnection. According to both Merleau-Ponty and the *Daodejing*, it is this interconnection, unpredictable, sometimes wild, and sometimes murky, that makes our existence meaningful. In a social environment that favors unceasing hyperactive babble, the reminder to keep still is a message that should not be ignored.

Notes

1   Maurice Merleau-Ponty, *Phenomenology of Perception* (London: Routledge & Kegan Paul, 1979), ix.

2   Ibid., xvii.

3   Ibid., 5.

4   Reneau Barbaras maintains that Merleau-Ponty never abandons the dualist vocabulary that marks the split between realism and intellectualism, and maintains that the body becomes a site of mediation between the two conflicting strains: "Realism and intellectualism are not so much overcome as pushed to the side, with the result finally that the double negation tends to turn itself into a double affirmation. Far from giving way to a radical reevaluation of the concepts of objective philosophy, the description is actualized in terminology that is simultaneously realist and intellectualist." Reneau Barbaras, *The Being of the Phenomenon: Merleau-Ponty's Ontology* (Bloomington: Indiana University Press, 1991), 6. However, I would argue that the word *sens* is a word that bridges the gap between intellectualism and realism because it is the physical connection to reality, which is also always incomplete and partial, that precipitates the conscious quest for meaning.

5   Maurice Merleau-Ponty, *The Visible and the Invisible* (Evanston: Northwestern University Press, 1969), 43.

6   Merleau-Ponty, *Phenomenology of Perception*, 4.

7   Lawrence Hass, *Merleau-Ponty's Philosophy* (Bloomington: Indiana University Press, 2008), 33.

8   Merleau-Ponty, *Phenomenology of Perception*, 4.

9   Ibid., 61.

10 Ibid., 215.

11 M.C. Dillon, *Merleau-Ponty's Ontology* (Chicago: Northwestern University Press, 1997), 56.

12 Maurice Merleau-Ponty, *Signs* (Evanston: Northwestern University Press, 1964), 58–9.

13 Merleau-Ponty, *Phenomenology of Perception*, 214.

14 Maurice Merleau-Ponty, *The Primacy of Perception: and Other Essays on Phenomenological Psychology, The Philosophy of Art, History and Politics* (Evanston: Northwestern University Press, 1964), 290.

15 Merleau-Ponty, *Phenomenology of Perception*, 11.

16 Ibid., 67.

17 Ibid.

18 Ibid.

19 Ibid., 71.

20 Ibid.

21 Ibid.

22 Merleau-Ponty, *Signs*, 16.

23 Merleau-Ponty, *The Visible and the Invisible*, 12.

24 Merleau-Ponty, *Phenomenology of Perception*, 71.

25 Ibid., ix.

26 Ibid., xi.

27 Ibid., ix.

28 Merleau-Ponty, *The Visible and the Invisible*, 38.

29 Ibid.

30 Ibid., 39.

31 Merleau-Ponty, *Phenomenology of Perception*, xiii.

32 Ibid., 5.

33 Ibid., 241.

34 Paul Valéry, *Collected Works of Paul Valéry* (Princeton: Princeton Legacy Library, 2016), vol. 1: 272.

35 Merleau-Ponty, *The Visible and the Invisible*, 4.

36 Ibid.

37 Merleau-Ponty, *Phenomenology of Perception*, 442.

38 Ibid., 196.

39 Ibid., 186.

40 Ibid., 187.

41 Ibid.

42 Ibid., 194.

43 Zhuangzi, *The Complete Works of Zhuangzi*, Burton Watson (trans.) (New York: Columbia University Press, 2013), chapter 2.

44 Ibid., chapter 27.

45 Merleau-Ponty, *The Visible and the Invisible*, 124.

46 Mauro Carbone maintains that Merleau-Ponty is engaging in a kind of "a-philosophy" in *The Visible and the Invisible* because he attempts to find a language that goes beyond philosophy since the "philosophical formulation tends radically to betray the polymorphism of being." He contrasts this with Hegelian philosophical language intent upon insisting that the absolute is the "identity of identity and non-identity," an identity which can only occur in thought. Philosophy, in Carbone's view, maintains the superiority of the reflected world. Mauro Carbon, *The Thinking of the Sensible: Merleau-Ponty's A-Philosophy* (Evanston: Northwestern University Press, 2004), 36.

47 Merleau-Ponty, *The Invisible and the Invisible*, 133.

48 Ibid., 142.

49 Ibid., 146.

50 Zhuangzi, *The Complete Works*, chapter 2.

51 Merleau-Ponty, *The Invisible and the Invisible*, 132.

52 Ibid.

53 Ibid.

54 Ibid., 136.

55 Ibid., 150.

56 Ibid., 126.

57 Ibid., 127.

58 Glen Mazis notes that Merleau-Ponty's philosophy of perception undercuts all sorts of dualisms including the dualisms of "ideality and materiality, necessity and contingency and empiricism and idealism" and espouses a "felt solidarity" with the world. He uses the term "imaginal" to describe the world between silence and speech. Glen Mazis, *Merleau-Ponty and the Face of the World: Silence, Ethics, Imagination and Poetic Ontology* (Albany: State University of New York Press, 2016), xiii–xiv.

59 Mazis, *Merleau-Ponty*, 121.

60 Laozi, *Daodejing: A Philosophical Translation*, Roger Ames (trans.) (New York: Ballantine Books, 2004), chapter 25.

61 Ibid.

62 Ibid., chapter 26.

63 Thomas Michael, *The Pristine Dao: Metaphysics in Early Daoist Discourse* (Albany: State University of New York Press, 2005), 4–5.

64 Laozi, *Daodejing*, chapter 1.

65 Curie Virag, *The Emotions in Early Chinese Philosophy* (Oxford: Oxford University Press, 2017), 76.

66 Hans-Georg Moeller, *The Philosophy of the Daodejing* (New York: Columbia University Press, 2006), 87.

67 Laozi, *Daodejing*, chapter 1.

68 Most commentaries interpret *changdao* to mean the eternal Dao. For example, Wang Bi notes that: "The Way that can be spoken about is not the eternal Dao, since the eternal cannot be spoken about and named." See Rudolf Wagner, *A Chinese Reading of the Daodejing: Wang Bi's Commentary on the Laozi with Critical Text and Translation* (Albany: State University of New York Press, 2003), 121.

69 Laozi, *Daodejing*, chapter 1.

70 Lin Ma, "Levinas and the *Daodejing* on the Feminine: Intercultural Reflections," *Journal of Chinese Philosophy*, 39.S1 (2012): 165.

71 Laozi, *Daodejing*, chapter 16.

72 Ibid., chapter 12.

73 Thomas Michael, *In the Shadows of the Dao: Laozi, the Sage and the Daodejing* (Albany: State University of New York Press, 2015), 11.

74 Laozi, *Daodejing*, chapter 48.

75 Ibid., chapter 14.

76 Ibid.

77 Ibid., chapter 2.

78 Ibid., chapter 20.

79 Ibid., chapter 32.
80 Ibid., chapter 65.
81 Ibid., chapter 20.
82 Ibid., chapter 23.
83 Ibid.
84 Ibid., chapter 45.

References

Barbaras, Reneau. (1991), *The Being of the Phenomenon: Merleau-Ponty's Ontology*, Bloomington: Indiana University Press.
Carbone, Mauro. (2004), *The Thinking of the Sensible: Merleau-Ponty's A-Philosophy*, Evanston: Northwestern University Press.
Chai, David. (2018), "Thinking through Words: The Existential Hermeneutics of Zhuangzi and Heidegger," in Paul Fairfield and Saulius Geniusas (eds.), *Relational Hermeneutics: Essays in Comparative Philosophy*, 205–19, London: Bloomsbury Academic.
Dillon, M.C. (1997), *Merleau-Ponty's Ontology*, Chicago: Northwestern University Press.
Froese, Katrin. (2018), *Why Can't Philosophers Laugh*, New York: Palgrave Macmillan.
Hass, Lawrence. (2008), *Merleau-Ponty's Philosophy*, Bloomington: Indiana University Press.
Laozi. (2004), *Daodejing: A Philosophical Translation*, Roger Ames (trans.), New York: Ballantine Books.
Ma, Lin. (2012), "Levinas and the *Daodejing* on the Feminine: Intercultural Reflections," *Journal of Chinese Philosophy*, 39 (S1): 152–70.
Mazis, Glen. (2016), *Merleau-Ponty and the Face of the World: Silence, Ethics, Imagination and Poetic Ontology*, Albany: State University of New York Press.
Merleau-Ponty, Maurice. (1945), *Phénoménologie de la Perception*, Paris: Gallimard.
Merleau-Ponty, Maurice. (1964), *The Primacy of Perception: And Other Essays on Phenomenological Psychology, the Philosophy of Art, History and Politics*, James Edie (trans.), Evanston: Northwestern University Press.
Merleau-Ponty, Maurice. (1964), *Le Visible et l'Invisible*, Paris: Gallimard.
Merleau-Ponty, Maurice. (1964), *Signs*, Richard McCleary (trans.), Evanston: Northwestern University Press.
Merleau-Ponty, Maurice. (1969), *The Visible and the Invisible*, Claude Lefort (trans.), Evanston: Northwestern University Press.
Merleau-Ponty, Maurice. (1979), *Phenomenology of Perception*, Colin Smith (trans.), London: Routledge & Kegan Paul.
Michael, Thomas. (2005), *The Pristine Dao: Metaphysics in Early Daoist Discourse*, Albany: State University of New York Press.
Michael, Thomas. (2015), *In the Shadows of the Dao: Laozi, the Sage and the Daodejing*, Albany: State University of New York Press.

Moeller, Hans-Georg. (2006), *The Philosophy of the Daodejing*, New York: Columbia University Press.

Valéry, Paul. (2016), *Collected Works of Paul Valéry*, vol. 1, Princeton: Princeton Legacy Library.

Virag, Curie. (2017), *The Emotions in Early Chinese Philosophy*, Oxford: Oxford University Press.

Wagner, Rudolf. (2003), *A Chinese Reading of the Daodejing: Wang Bi's Commentary on the Laozi with Critical Text and Translation*, Albany: State University of New York Press.

Zhuangzi. (2013), *The Complete Works of Zhuangzi*, Burton Watson (trans.), New York: Columbia University Press.

Zhuangzi. (1998), *Zhuangzi Reader* 莊子讀本, Taipei: Sanmin Shuju.

PART FOUR

A Most Urgent Encounter: Re-Rooting Our Futural Selves

12

Grounding Phenomenology in Laozi's *Daodejing*:

The Anthropocene, the Fourfold, and the Sage

Martin Schönfeld

Phenomenology faces uncertain prospects, not only in the arts and the humanities, but also in relation to the wider spectrum of research programs. Is there a path from its great past to an even greater future? I believe there is—but with the caveat that taking this path would come with two conditions. First, it would require phenomenology to embrace a foundational outlook based on positivism rather than relativism, on objectivity rather than subjectivity, and on realism rather than anti-realism. Second, it would require an orientation toward Eastern ways of thinking, specifically toward Daoism and the ontological model of Laozi's *Daodejing* 道德經. Embracing a realist epistemology and integrating Daoism would allow phenomenology to consolidate its heuristic position. Such a consolidation would let it gain a seat at the interdisciplinary table for managing the crisis of collective existence.

In this chapter, I argue for such a future-oriented consolidation. The argument proceeds from explaining the two conditions toward examining "the fourfold" (*das Geviert*) and "the sage" (*der Weise*), which are neglected concepts in Martin Heidegger's later thought. I describe the need for the conditions and explain how the fourfold and the sage, in a Daoist reading, may satisfy them.

In the first section, I point to an alternative in continental philosophy. It consists of approaches marginalized in the English-speaking world, which, in contrast to the skepticist leanings of postmodern heirs of phenomenology, fit under the conceptual umbrella of dogmatic philosophy. This alternative is better equipped to respond to the civilizational crisis than is the postmodern mainstream. The emergence of this alternative in twentieth-century thought shows that it is possible to think outside the box and yet do so within the horizon of continental philosophy. The possibility of integrating this alternative with Heidegger's late concepts, furthermore, shows that one can pursue a continental alternative without needing to leave phenomenology behind. It merely requires phenomenology to renounce the leanings that make it ill-equipped for the paradigm shift in our lifeworld.

In the second section, I describe how the paradigm shift is documented in the sciences. The universal structure of human existence has changed, and not for the better. At the verge of the third decade of the new millennium, this change is also becoming increasingly hard to miss. When phenomenology first appeared on the scene, environmental impacts were limited to local and regional degradations of the Earth's surface. Understandably, these events were not in the purview of phenomenological research. Only the problem of technology, suggested by Ernst Jünger to Heidegger, put them indirectly at the periphery of phenomenological attention. Now, however, environmental impacts have spread beyond the Earth's surface to the Earth System, affecting its functioning, impairing its integrity, and imperiling civilization.

The section on the paradigm shift adds an interdisciplinary perspective. This puts the question of the future of phenomenology in empirical context. The information presented there may seem obscure without an introduction. Thus an outline beforehand may be useful. Since my argument for the Daoist grounding of phenomenology is intended as a philosophical essay, notes should be kept to a minimum. But since the second section is a report of findings outside philosophy, notes are appropriate there, to document the facts, show the credibility of the sources, and invite readers to compare my account of the meaning of this paradigm shift with the evidence cited.

On the environmental side, our generation is witnessing the sixth mass extinction in Earth history. This event involves not only a loss of biological diversity but also an annihilation of biota to such an extent that it is now manifest in the defaunation of the biosphere. In the past half century, since 1970, the biosphere has lost 60 percent of vertebrate populations in the Global North and 90 percent (not a misspelling) in the Global South. Invertebrate biotas are in similarly dire straits, and for insects, at the bottom at the food chain, and responsible for key biospherical functions such as pollination, the situation is teetering on the verge of catastrophe.

Climate change is intensifying this extinction event, just as defaunation is making climate more sensitive to human forcings. Global warming has reached the point that both icecaps are thinning; that the so-called third pole, the Hindu Kush Himalaya region, is deglaciating; and that ocean currents are slowing down. The polar vortex above the Arctic Circle is weakening, with outflows of polar air to the lower latitudes now occurring every winter. The increase of weather extremes, driven by the thermal energy absorbed through elevated greenhouse gas concentrations in the climate system, is pummeling continents and islands with storms, droughts, and floods; with heatwaves in summer, and deep freezes in winter. As a result, lands in temperate and tropical latitudes are becoming less productive.

On the civilizational side, the lands most vulnerable to the impacts of climate change—in North Africa, South Asia, the Middle East, and Central America—contain also some of the most densely populated regions on Earth. Growing numbers of people are pushed on uncertain migrations, with the majority being children. As rivers run dry, dust bowls grow, and deserts spread, the carrying capacity of the affected regions shrinks. This makes people lose their livelihoods and homes, and forces them to become refugees, seeking shelter elsewhere. The stream of refugees is dividing the host societies which are their destination. Thus in the Global South, economies are being destabilized and nation-states are failing, while in the Global North, doors are closing, walls are going up, and nation-states are battening down the hatches. The growing disparity between haves and have-nots polarizes collective existence, with cascading consequences. One consequence is that the liberal order of the West is succumbing to autocratic regimes. The havoc wreaked on the environment is now blowing back to global civilization.

Prior to the mass extinction and climate change, civilization had impacted nature on the surface, with land conversion and with air and water pollution. Now, human impacts are affecting the ensemble of environmental services and cycles, the totality of the Earth System. (An example of services is the biological productivity of the planet; an example of cycles is the carbon cycle that assimilates CO_2 emissions.) Civilization is dependent on the integrity of the Earth System, and while this is a truism so trivial it hardly merits discussion, it is worth considering that this collective existential dependence is objective, universal, and absolute.

This is the crisis. The upheavals do not spare philosophy. The paradigm shift in our lifeworld imposes a concordant shift on the academy. Postmodern approaches to truth and reality are now obsolete. Relativistic, subjectivist, and anti-realist ways of deconstructing information belong to an earlier age. In the Anthropocene, such skepticist deconstructions are becoming cognitive liabilities. Insisting on them, despite the crisis, also raises ethical concerns.

The philosophical upheaval is illustrated by the precursors to the cognitive approaches that are standard in postmodernity today. For example, with regard to early phenomenology's rejection of psychologism, Edmund Husserl disavowed positivism and embraced a type of subjectivism instead. Seen in the historical context of philosophy protecting its borders against the sciences encroaching from all directions, Husserl's subjectivism, at that time, and in these circumstances, was arguably reasonable.

A generation later, Heidegger's choice of relativism over universalism and his embrace of historicism against progressive alternatives were perhaps not quite so reasonable. But Heidegger made these epistemic choices decades before the planetary crisis would break, and thus his relativism and historicism are features of a more innocent time. In his day, these were philosophical positions and nothing more, without pernicious ramifications.

But that was then. Today, phenomenologists and their allies in the postmodern community who still take the same subjectivist-relativist line that Husserl and Heidegger once did are risking isolation. This is epistemically pointless and ethically irresponsible. Postmodern heirs of Husserl and Heidegger who still declare, during this crisis of collective existence, that objectivity is a myth, that positive evidence can be deconstructed into narratives, that there is always another side to the facts, and that there is no such thing as truth, make themselves into unwitting stooges of the cultural and political forces that are pushing civilization toward the brink. This is neither helpful nor does it represent what phenomenology should be about.

In the third and final section, I describe what phenomenology ought to be about instead. A future-oriented path for phenomenology in the Anthropocene would reorient it toward scientific information by grounding its approach in Daoism. This grounding is made concrete in a Daoist reading of the fourfold and the sage. The motivation of this groundwork is hope. I have faith that phenomenology can get back on track as a future-oriented approach of continental philosophy and join the interdisciplinary project of tackling the Earth System crisis of the Anthropocene. An effective way of doing so, I propose, is to take one's cue from East Asian wisdom, Daoism especially, and Laozi's *Daodejing* in particular. A Daoist turn that is geared toward Laozi (rather than Zhuangzi 莊子 or Liezi 列子) will allow phenomenology to embrace the needed epistemic realism in the spirit of a well-informed ontology.

If phenomenology can find a way out of its anti-realist maze, by using a Daoist map, then the fourfold will constitute the magnetic north, and the sage will function as a compass needle. The fourfold is where phenomenology will have to go, and the sage is the guide on this journey. Traversing on this route, I contend, would empower phenomenology to roll with the punches thrown by the Anthropocene—punches that are swung at all branches of learning now, but that hit the humanities and philosophy harder than others. Capable of deflecting the blows, and freed from the maze, phenomenology could reconnect to other fields, from the arts to the sciences, in the historic enterprise of cultivating a healthier and more mindful human identity. The two Heideggerian concepts, in a Daoist reading, would allow phenomenology to grow out of the subjectivist, relativist reflections that had been its past and mature into an empathy-based, co-evolutionary doctrine of wisdom, which is just what is needed for transitioning to an Ecological Civilization.

1. The Continental Fork: Skeptical vs. Dogmatic Philosophy

If we consider the arc of development of phenomenology from an Anthropocene perspective, one cannot help noticing the gap between its postmodern legacy and the problems that civilization is facing. Indeed, a closer look reveals that the gap is deeper than the surface. If one peers inside, one finds an epistemic machinery underneath, driven by subterranean ontological assumptions, which implicates the legacy of phenomenology in the problems today.

Philosophy has traditionally understood itself as the rational investigation of human existence in the world. Today, this investigation has acquired an empirical dimension. Next to the phenomenological inquiry into being-in-the-world, there is a suite of research programs whose findings have turned conjecture into knowledge, and which have added an aspect of certitude to the existential problematic. This problematic consists of questions of the origin, place, purpose, and destiny of being-in-the-world. Philosophy and the sciences have generated a parallel series of theories and models regarding this problematic. However, this parallel series is parallel only to an extent. In the second half of the twentieth century, one strand of philosophy, the postmodern legacy of phenomenology, veered off into its own direction.

In veering off from the path of science, the postmodern movement did not part ways with analytic philosophy, but diverged from continental philosophy instead. The postmodern divergence does not constitute a split between continental and analytic philosophy (which already occurred in the first half of the twentieth century), but a branching in continental philosophy itself. This branching is also visible in the transcultural geography of thought. Continental philosophy hails from Europe, of course, but its branches point in different directions overseas. The postmodern branch extends from Europe to the Anglophone hemisphere, and is being taught in countries such as Australia, Canada, and the United States. The other branch of continental philosophy, which does run parallel with science, has spread to the Global South instead, and to Latin America in particular. This science-oriented branch has utopian, earthy, and mystical aspects. It was inspired by, and keeps drawing inspiration from, the likes of Meister Eckhart and St. Francis, Baruch Spinoza and Immanuel Kant, Karl Marx and Friedrich Engels, and from Laozi.

The Daoist inspiration is an influence both branches have in common, but is explicit in only one of them. The branch that led from Hegel to Franz Brentano to Husserl absorbed this influence through Heidegger. Tutored by a visiting foreign scholar, Paul Shih-Yi Hsiao (Xiao Shiyi 蕭師毅), Heidegger studied the *Daodejing* and translated parts of it. Comparative scholarship has revealed this influence and its significance.

But this already marks the difference. In the other branch, which involves normative humanism, existential logotherapy, Deep Ecology, and religious existentialism, the Daoist influence had not been a scholarly revelation. It could not have been, because there was nothing to be revealed. The thinkers who embraced Daoism, such as Erich Fromm, Martin Buber, and Arne Naess, had been completely open about their indebtedness to Laozi. Martin Buber taught a seminar on Laozi at the artists' colony at Monte Verità in Switzerland in the 1920s. Zhuangzi makes recurrent appearances in Buber's work. Erich Fromm used a quote from the *Daodejing* as the motto of his work, *To Have or To Be?* and characterized Laozi's role in history as one of the first truly progressive thinkers in *The Heart of Man*.[1] Arne Naess incorporated Daoist ideas in his essays and was outspoken about the "powerful premises" of Chinese philosophy.[2]

By contrast, Heidegger was so reticent about his Daoist inspiration that his conduct borders on plagiarism. This prompted Graham Parkes, the translator of a German monograph—Reinhard May's *Ex oriente lux: Heideggers Werk unter ostasiatischem Einfluss*—to render the English title of the study, deservedly so, as *Heidegger's Hidden Sources*.[3] Apart from Chinese scholars, such as Paul Hsiao, Japanese correspondents, such as Tezuka Tomio, and German friends, such as Ernst Jünger, hardly anyone knew about this influence, despite Heidegger's growing fondness for Daoism in his later life. Jünger, in particular, was amused by the old Heidegger's enthusiasm for Laozi, such as by the quirk that the aging philosopher kept mailing German copies of the *Daodejing* to friends as a gift. But as May and others have shown, this private enthusiasm is in contrast to his public reticence, which made Heidegger credit Western sources, but not non-Western ones, even though Ellen Chan's interpretive analysis[4] and Lin Ma's archival work[5] show how deep Laozi's influence runs in his later thought.

The Daoist influence on the writings of Buber, Fromm, and Naess is obvious, and they, unlike Heidegger, credit their sources. These thinkers represent some of the alternatives to postmodernity—Buber, with his religious philosophy based on Judaism; Fromm, with his normative humanism; and Naess, with his Deep Ecology. Another representative is Victor Frankl, with his existentialist logotherapy. On the non-secular side of the continental alternative there is the religious philosophy based on Christianity. It has flourished in Latin America in the clerical framework of the Roman Catholic Church. This overseas branch of continental philosophy fused with indigenous traditions and converged with Marxism. The Catholic-indigenous synthesis gave the Marxist critique of the political economy a spiritual direction. This critique is tied to solidarity and societal evolution, and it culminated in liberation theology.

Liberation theology is a collective project of philosopher-priests such as Ernesto Cardenal of Nicaragua, Leonardo Boff of Brazil, Gustavo Gutiérrez of Peru, Juan Luis Segundo of Uruguay, and Jorge Mario Bergoglio of Argentina, who was elected in 2013 as Pope Francis I. A distinguishing feature of liberation theology, vis-à-vis postmodernity, is its simple acceptance of science, both over its findings and its epistemology. This difference is not without irony, since postmodernity is secular, while liberation theology is based on faith. But over science, postmodernity bears closer resemblance to evangelical Protestant Christianity, because both evangelicals and postmoderns harbor misgivings over scientific propositions. Both doubt the validity of the scientific Standard Model, which constitutes the peer-reviewed understanding of the natural universe, of Earth's place in the natural universe, and of the human place on Earth. Especially worrisome to evangelicals and postmoderns are the conceptual implications of evolution. Evangelical Protestant Christians are troubled by the idea of an animal pedigree of humankind, and thus by the notion of biological evolution. Postmodern philosophers tend to be troubled by the idea of a civilizational ranking of societies, since they lean toward cultural relativism, and thus harbor misgivings about the notion of societal evolution.

By contrast, liberation theologians do not see any conflict between the Christian Bible and evolutionary biology, and neither are they troubled by the notion of societal evolution. On the contrary, being progressives, societal evolution is their ethical and political desideratum. Marxist doctrines of Dialectical and Historical Materialism put evolutionary biology in a larger metaphysical narrative. Dialectical Materialism anticipates the self-organization of matter, which is studied in cosmology and physics, the emergence of complexity, which is studied in chemistry, and the progression of life from cells to organisms studied in paleontology and biology. Many of the conjectures of Dialectical Materialism are now building blocks of the Standard Model. Historical Materialism has remained more conjectural to date, and unlike Dialectical Materialism, it is also normative. Historical Materialism extends the evolutionary idea to culture and conceptualizes progress as a political and cultural aspiration of societies. Regardless of what one wants to make of this in detail, significant is the attempt of the faithful to resolve a potential conflict with science by offering a creative solution: science tells us that there is evolution in nature, and philosophers and theologians, seconding this, add a friendly amendment: there is and there ought to be evolution in collective human existence as well.

This philosophical harmony with science is also visible in the other, Jewish, branch of religious philosophy. In Buber's case, it is already illustrated in his biography: when he fled from the Nazis, he settled in Palestine and resumed teaching—in a science department. The religious philosopher henceforth taught as a professor of anthropology.

The harmony characterizes the secular strand of the continental alternative as well. Relevant for Fromm's work in normative humanism were the social sciences, such as anthropology, the medical sciences, such as psychology, and the environmental sciences, which inform his blueprint of a human evolution toward sustainability. Frankl's work in logotherapy relates to clinical psychiatry and is generally a reflection on the medical sciences. Naess's work in Deep Ecology is oriented on the eponymous science. Naess is careful to emphasize that Deep Ecology is not reducible to the findings of ecology, since Deep Ecology performs a creative and constructive step beyond the environmental sciences. At the same time, the performance of this step is yet another illustration of the philosophical aspiration to harmony with the science.

As different as the secular and religious variants of the continental alternative are, they have one formal feature in common. In Kantian terms, one could say they represent the dogmatic type of philosophy. In the final paragraph of his magnum opus, *Critique of Pure Reason*, under the rubric, "the scientific method," Kant writes that there are many ways of doing philosophy, but all of them require the need for "systematicity," by which he means that philosophical theories, like scientific ones, must be internally coherent (be non-contradictory) and externally consistent (be in agreement with the facts). The range of philosophies that conform to the scientific method, so understood, is defined by "dogmatism" at one end and by "skepticism" at another. Dogmatism is the affirmation of information; skepticism is its negation. Kant's example for dogmatism is Christian Wolff, and his example for skepticism is David Hume. Answers to the deep questions that occupy the human mind, Kant concludes, are within reach provided philosophy stays between the limits. The middle path between dogmatism and skepticism that Kant prefers and which, as he contends, is the one still open, is the "critical path." Thus there is a range of inquiry, its limits are dogma and doubt, and in between is critique.

From a Kantian point of view, the continental alternative consists of versions of the critical path that run closer to the dogmatic boundary of reason. They are dogmatic in their affirmation of scientific knowledge. Fromm, Frankl, Naess, Buber, and Francis, by this definition, are dogmatists, because they take the results of scientific peer-review at face value. For them, scientific findings are facts, without qualification. They trust in scientific expertise in a fundamentally respectful way. This is not only illustrated in the aspirational harmony just described, but also in specific reactions to scientific progressions, as in the transformation of the Roman Catholic Church under Pope Francis I with regard to climate change. After the Intergovernmental Panel on Climate Change (IPCC) of the United Nations issued the Fifth Assessment Report on the state of the world's climate in 2013 with the updated volume on the physical science basis, and in 2014, with the updated volumes on vulnerability and mitigation, the pontiff responded in 2015 by issuing the encyclical *Laudate Si*—an admonition to the faithful that time on stabilizing the climate is running out, an exhortation that environmentalism is a sacred duty, and an exegetical assertion that stewardship theology is the correct reading of the role of humans in God's creation. This is dogmatic: scientific findings are regarded as facts. And it is philosophy: these facts ground a reflection that opens new vistas.

In sum, dogmatic thinkers do not regard scientific findings as constituting problems or raising questions, or to serve as foils for critical reflection. For dogmatic thinkers, science has the truth of it. Science is the basis, and the purpose of philosophy is to advance conjectures upon and beyond this foundation. For *Laudate Si*, climatology is the basis, and the ensuing reflection leads to the creation of something new: the appropriation of stewardship ethics in Catholic theology. In hindsight, Kant's dogmatic exemplar, Christian Wolff, was a good choice in more ways than one. Chinese philosophy gave Wolff the idea of societal progress congruent with natural evolution, and the dialectical and historical doctrines that Marx and Engels constructed one and a half centuries later go back to Wolff's evolutionary conjecture.

As soon as one conceptualizes the continental alternatives as dogmatic and defines dogmatism as thinking in harmony with scientific findings, the therapeutic aspect comes into view. Dogmatic thinkers conceptualize the love of wisdom as an insight-driven endeavor, which proceeds from the assumption that wisdom is in human reach, and that grasping it will make an existential difference for the better. The meaning of "better," in the therapeutic variants, is oriented on medicine. It concerns the poles of the human condition, sickness and health. Logotherapy, for example, aims to heal damaged souls and broken spirits. It shares with psychotherapy and clinical psychiatry the therapeutic goal of mental health, but it differs from these medical sciences— and thus remains philosophy—in that its conception of this goal is not reducible to mental health in a narrow medical sense. Instead, its goal is a holistic concept, in a broader spiritual sense, which involves also an existentialist dimension, thus warranting the use of metaphorical language on souls and spirits.

The impetus for logotherapy was the therapeutic practice of suicide prevention. In its later iterations, logotherapy concerned trauma management in the context of boundary situations of human existence, such as the exposure to genocide and the capacity of survivors to return to normalcy. Obviously, such exposure is traumatic also in the emotional sense in that it leaves survivors profoundly sad if not despairing. Clinical psychiatry treats such sadness, under the rubric of depression, as a medical condition internal to the patient, stipulated to have physiological or neurological reasons. As such a condition, it can be treated pharmaceutically, and it ought to be cured. Logotherapy, by contrast, targets the type of sadness or depression that is not a medical condition per se, because their presence is arguably a sign of mental health. A survivor who lost her family to genocide and who has not lost her mind should be sad; her depression is not an effect of an internal disorder but a sane response to an external cataclysm.

The existentialist dimension of logotherapy runs parallel to science without being reducible to it. It taps into the universal experience that existence involves luck; that bad things can happen to good people, and no higher meaning can be found for the randomness of evil. Logotherapy responds to this experience with a quasi-proletarian call to work. Meaning is not something dropped in one's lap by the grace of a higher power. Instead, meaning is a sense that one creates and gives to life. These acts of creating and giving are done freely and energetically; they are not one-time gestures but a continuous, daily toil. They are activity understood as hard labor. This activity of giving sense to life (*dem Leben einen Sinn geben*) requires wisdom and courage, as well as wit and stamina. The sense-giving serves survival, well-being, and flourishing. As such, this creation of meaning is subservient to an existential universal.

The integration of dogmatism with therapy reveals a pattern. Logotherapy appeals to wisdom in harmony with science for helping people put their lives back together. Normative humanism appeals to wisdom in harmony with science for realizing a sane society, as Fromm puts it. Liberation theology appeals to wisdom and faith, while accepting the findings of science as positive data, for curing civilization from the disease of social inequality, for mending the rift between the haves and the have-nots. Deep Ecology, finally, appeals to wisdom, inspired by science, for mending the rift between humans and nature caused by economic expansion and population growth. The goal of logotherapy is spiritual health; the goal of normative humanism is a sane society; the goal of liberation theology is a compassionate if not communist social compact, and the goal of Deep Ecology is a sustainable interface of civilization with the Earth System. In each case, the framework of reality is science; the philosophical means is wisdom, and the therapeutic goal is existential flourishing.

The final aspect of dogmatic-therapeutic philosophies is their progressive character. Progressiveness is implicit in the therapeutic dimension, because therapy involves a teleological trajectory, which starts at a given existential or societal situation and ends in the realization of an optimal potential of that existence or society. The trajectory from actuality to potentiality is progressive. This progression is both a movement going forward, from an earlier to a later point, and a movement upward, from a lower level or a worse situation, to a higher level, a better situation.

While the vector of progress in logotherapy is closely aligned with the meaning of progress in medicine, its vector in the other branches it is more aligned with is the meaning of progress in politics, which, by definition, is a leftist concept. Liberation theology, normative humanism, and Deep Ecology are all committed to the thesis of an upwards development in history. While Buber's Jewish thought may seem to have little to do with this vector, once more his biography is illustrative: Buber was not only a Talmud scholar but also a card-carrying socialist, and therefore a progressive par excellence. In the context of justice and rights, this upward development is the evolution from the slaveholder feudalisms of antiquity to the liberal democracies of modernity. In the context of welfare and security, this upwards development is the evolution from market-liberal societies with high levels of inequality to social democratic or socialist societies with low levels of inequality. In the context of sustainability and humaneness, it is the evolution from growth-based capitalistic economies to steady-state ecological economies. As mentioned, the idea of such progressive-evolutionary trajectories grew out of Wolff's reading of the Confucian classics during the early German Enlightenment. Later it was expanded to the Marxist-Leninist doctrine of Historical Materialism. Its contemporary scientific analog is given by various quantitative metrics, such as the Human Development Index (HDI) used by the United Nations Development Program, which measures the height of societal development of nation-states with gauges such as infant mortality, life expectancy, gender equality, years of schooling, and average standard of living differentiated by wealth distribution to adjust for levels of inequality. Another such metric is the Genuine Progress Indicator (GPI) to measure the level of social evolution by qualifying the capitalistic yardstick of Gross Domestic Product (GDP) with criteria such as unpaid labor, community service, environmental integrity, and carbon footprint. HDI and GPI are indices of upward trajectories of existence that are quantifiable rankings of life quality.

The therapeutic and progressive aspects of the dogmatic alternative make the postmodern legacy of phenomenology appear as a conservative and libertarian indulgence. The postmodern branch of continental philosophy, which has been so much better received in the Anglophone Far West than the dogmatic alternatives just described, comprises the liberal approaches whose shared pedigree is phenomenology, in the guise of Heidegger, and which is represented by his students, such as Hans-Georg Gadamer, and his readers, such as Jacques Derrida and Richard Rorty.

Unlike the parallel series of science and philosophy instantiated by analytic thought and by the dogmatic strand of continental thought, postmodernity struck out in its own direction, with theories that have little to do with science and that are often at cross-purposes with its results. In the liberal democracies, this departure from science makes postmodernity converge with political conservativism. This convergence is not coincidental, because postmodernity shares with political conservativism an emphasis on liberty. Whereas dogmatic philosophers operate within self-imposed constraints of reasoning, postmodern philosophers do not. Dogmatic philosophers constrain their reflection by affirming an interdisciplinary basis of knowledge that is external to them, and by embracing a therapeutic goal that serves as a condition of the value of information. While dogmatic philosophers pursue insight-driven endeavors, postmodern philosophers pursue purely heuristic goals with problem-driven endeavors. Dogmatic philosophers strive for a synthesis of information, by connecting the dots in a rational matrix of knowledge and wisdom. Postmodern philosophers, by contrast, strive for an analysis of information, by separating the dots, in a process of deconstruction, which leaves one with an uncertain web of perspectives and narratives.

The postmodern legacy of phenomenology stands in diametrical opposition to the dogmatic philosophies laid out above. In Kantian terms, one could say that postmodernity exemplifies skeptical philosophy. Postmodernity is skeptical in assuming a fundamentally negative stance toward established knowledge. Postmodern skeptics take the information produced by scientific peer-review not at face value. They do not trust in expertise, and they are suspicious of claims to objectivity and rationality. Like political conservatives, postmodern skeptics suspect that such claims are overblown. Political conservatives dismiss the credibility of science through allegations of fraud and corruption (such that climatologists perpetuate the "myth" of global warming in order to "get rich"), but postmodern skeptics dismiss it for more considered and technical reasons: science involves representing and intervening, as Ian Hacking puts it; science is merely a model, as Bas Van Fraassen puts it; and scientific revolutions involve irrational arbitrariness at the very cusp of a paradigm change, as Thomas S. Kuhn puts it. Or, as Bruno Latour, the postmodern disciple of Van Fraassen, sees it: science is merely the attempt at modeling reality and therefore, at best, a simulacrum of reality, but not reality itself. Add to this the long-standing postmodern concern that the scientific community is disproportionately made up of one gender, one class, and one ethnicity, and this simulacrum of reality becomes a fun house mirror, whose reflection is warped by gender-bias and other types of prejudice. Lacking diversity in its community of workers, the community's findings are therefore lacking in diversity, too. When scientists unanimously agree on one monolithic consensus (as over climate change, sustainability, or planetary boundaries), then such mostly male, middle-class, white agreement must surely harbor hidden complexities. For postmodern skeptics, science is only one side of a more complicated story. Only naïve minds—dogmatic thinkers—would be foolish enough to believe in truth and take science by its peer-reviewed word. From a postmodern viewpoint, science is not a simple foundation but a sophisticated challenge instead.

Another difference between dogmatic and skeptical philosophy obtains over wisdom. For postmodern philosophers, wisdom is not within reach, and even the greatest exponent of skeptical philosophy, Socrates, was only in love with wisdom without possessing it, merely knowing that he knew nothing. In the postmodern variant of continental philosophy, the love of wisdom is problem-driven, not insight-driven, and it proceeds from the assumption of the Greek sophists of antiquity that wisdom dissolves into contingency, irony, and, perhaps, also in the solidarity of shared ironic contingencies, as Rorty would have it.

In line with the skepticism and conservativism of postmodern thought, there is also no conception of a genuine progression in the development of cultures. From a postmodern point of view, all cultures deserve respect, and pluralism in the context of tolerance is the shared desideratum. There is accordingly no such thing as a "primitive" culture; older cultures are simply different from modern ones. Hence, there is no "superior" or "inferior" in the postmodern framework. Over its rejection of progressivism, the postmodern heirs of phenomenology remain faithful to Heidegger's historicism. Heidegger maintained (without a shred of evidence, it must be said) that different cultures, representing distinct metaphysical epochs, are inherently incommensurate with one another. It is impossible to make comparisons among them, and each needs to be regarded and appreciated in its isolated uniqueness.

Thus a progressive development, from a lower state to a higher state, with the presupposition that there are universal tools for gauging existence across cultures, is anathema to historicism. This stands in evident contrast to dogmatic variants of continental philosophy, and it results in a nice comparative symmetry: dogmatic philosophers and their scientific peers proceed from the hypothesis that collective existence, whether as societies or as epochs, is defined by material parameters: for example, by the likelihood of infants surviving birth, by the length of average life expectancy, or by the statistical distribution of wealth and access to education, health care, and legal representation. The hierarchical ranking of cultures is determined by how they measure up over life span, equality, literacy, health, and justice. Dogmatic philosophers and their scientific peers operate in a materialistic framework. Skepticist philosophers, by contrast, dismiss the earthy criteria and operate in an idealistic framework.

The idealistic framework of historicism rules out the possibility of an upward trajectory of civil evolution. This points to the final difference of postmodern skepticism. Unlike dogmatic philosophy, there is no therapeutic goal to postmodern thought. Its goal is entirely critical, deconstructive, and context-dependent. Different answers work for different identities, and "better" and "worse" are reducible to context. Instead of the fixed poles of the human condition, sickness and health, and birth and death, postmodern philosophy is interested in the infinite variety of existential identities between. Whatever is better for one set of identities is not necessarily better for another. For postmodern skeptics, the meaning of "better" is irredeemably contextual and subjective. To the extent it is grounded at all, it would be grounded in art.

2. The Dogmatic Turn of the Academy: Enter the Anthropocene

In the scientific series of answers to the question of human existence in the world, we find a growing concern about the increasingly fraught relationship to the natural environment over the past sixty years. This concern started as a worry about human impacts on the natural environment, and evolved into a worry about the blowback of these impacts on humankind. The latest iteration in this series of answers is that the worry has turned into a prediction, and the prediction is turning into observations. The blowback is now happening, and it is jeopardizing our common future.

For the purposes of a Daoist grounding of future-oriented phenomenology, the parting of the ways in continental philosophy is therefore not an innocent split. Or rather, it would have been, had the postwar trajectory of civilization continued indefinitely. In a cultural framework of ever more liberties, ever larger prosperity, and ever greater diversity, one can celebrate postmodernity's libertarian aspirations. As long as the framework keeps expanding, there is no need to tie philosophical inquiry to anything but freedom. Equality will eventually take care of itself; justice is a natural consequence of free markets; and solidarity is not needed in times of plenty. Science is nothing but the competition; it needs to be bested before it bests the arts. The problems of the postmodern heirs of phenomenology identified in the first section would never have come into being if this libertarian dream of the "end of history" culminating in free markets and free people had come to fruition. But since the hope for never-ending human and economic growth was dashed by planetary boundaries such as that of the carbon cycle, the continued libertarian aspirations of postmodernity have turned out to be liabilities.

The answers produced by science have registered the steady deterioration of the human–nature relationship as the decades went by. A first wave of findings, in the 1960s, showed that some species were endangered, some wilderness areas were at risk of destruction, and some regions experienced degradation. All of this seemed to be problems for experts, which could be addressed with better technologies and policies. A second wave, in the 1970s, challenged the hope that this is an expert problem without larger significance for the public. This wave concerned findings of the overshoot of human demand on planetary bioproductivity and environmental services. A third wave of findings, in the 1980s, drove home the message that the overshoot is gaining in existential significance because it caused climate change through the human-induced overshoot of the assimilative capacity of the global carbon cycle.

There was not really a fourth wave of findings after the turn of the new millennium. Instead, the three waves, of regional issues, of a general overshoot, and of global consequences, are now surging ever higher. In the new millennium, the first wave, of biodiversity loss, escalated into the sixth great mass extinction in Earth history. The hemorrhaging of biological diversity has fused with the decimation of common biota to result in an unfolding defaunation of such magnitude that field workers describe it as "biological annihilation."[6]

The second wave, ecological overshoot, has escalated into a conflict between civilization and the biosphere of such intensity that it has made the prevailing growth-based model of market economies unsustainable. The overshoot began in the 1970s when annual human demand on natural supply crossed the maximum annual productivity of the biosphere and the maximum annual capacity of environmental services. Since then, this overshoot has widened. At present, global civilization operates as if it had nearly two planet Earths at its disposal.

By crossing the sustainable yield threshold of service capacity, humankind has altered the quality of its interaction with the Earth System. Before the overshoot, human demand on planetary supply was analogous to consuming the interest accrued by capital stock. Now, in the overshoot, demand on supply is akin to dipping into the stock itself. This reduces the principal and proportionately diminishes interest earnings. When demand exceeds supply, the relationship of human consumers to natural producers grows unstable similar to that of a person who lives off interest earned by savings in the bank, and whose cash withdrawals, year after year, exceed the interest earned, dipping ever deeper into the savings instead. This shrinks the principal on whose presence the person's existence depends. Since the demands remain constant, and since the principal is shrinking, the demands take away ever larger portions of the supply, first slowly, and then swiftly, until supply is gone.

Annual withdrawals in excess of interest earnings can be rational for a person whose unsustainable demand on supply lasts for her lifetime, and who can expect to die before her savings are used up. But rational behavior for senior citizens is not rational behavior for a civilization whose structure is intergenerational. Young adults, children, and infants will be left with a depleted planet and a destabilized Earth System.

That humans transform their environment is not new; it is as old as civilization. New is that the present-day transformation is unprecedented in its rate and magnitude.[7] New is also a qualitative shift: in the past, the environmental transformation involved changes to the biosphere, but now it involves "changes in the structure or functioning of the Earth System."[8]

It is hard to overestimate the implications. The 2019 *Global Risk Report* of the World Economic Forum (WEF) begins with the question: "Is the world sleepwalking into a crisis? Global risks are intensifying but the collective will to tackle them appears to be lacking. Instead, divisions are hardening."[9] The WEF parses the implications as follows:

> Environmental risks continue to dominate the results of our annual Global Risks Perception Survey . . . This year, they accounted for three of the top five risks by likelihood and four by impact. Extreme weather was the risk of greatest concern, but our survey respondents are increasingly worried about environmental policy failure: having fallen in the rankings after Paris, "failure of climate-change mitigation and adaptation" jumped back to number two in terms of impact this year. The results of climate inaction are becoming increasingly clear. The accelerating pace of biodiversity loss is a particular concern. Species abundance is down by 60 percent since 1970. In the human food chain, biodiversity loss is affecting health and socioeconomic development, with implications for well-being, productivity, and even regional security.[10]

The risks of greatest concern—extreme weather, climate change, and biodiversity loss—are entangled symptoms of the human impact on the Earth System. The unprecedented rate and magnitude of this transformation is visible in the human footprint on the terrestrial surface. By the most recent estimate, based on data up to 2018, and released in 2019, "just 5 percent of Earth's landscape remains untouched."[11] By the most comprehensive previous estimate, in 2016, and based on data up to 2015, 19 percent remained untouched.[12] Pristine wilderness is now disappearing at lightning speed, as its reduction from 19 percent to 5 percent in less than five years illustrates.

The loss of wilderness, in the past, was associated with the extinction of rare species. After the turn to the new millennium, a sign that something else was going on, in addition, was the uncanny worldwide decline of honey bees; the so-called colony collapse disorder of bee populations.[13] When biologists turned from measuring biodiversity loss to measuring ecological health, and from counting species to counting populations (e.g., by weighing flying insect biomass caught in malaise traps), a trend came into view that is now called "defaunation" and, informally, "the Great Thinning."[14] In the second decade of the twenty-first century, the Great Thinning spread to common flying insects, with a loss of biomass of 75–82 percent from 1989 to 2015 in some developed countries.[15] As we are approaching the third decade of the century, the Great Thinning affects nearly all wildlife, vertebrates and invertebrates alike. A 2018 index tracking population sizes of vertebrate species (mammals, birds, reptiles, amphibians, and fishes) shows a 60 percent decline in the northern hemisphere since 1970, with a 90 percent decline in the tropics.[16]

This staggering decline, whose full extent became visible only in 2018, is a problem for civilization through the feedback of biota and climate. Nonhuman life and the climate system are interdependent. Types of life shape types of climate, obviously, but more specifically, biodiversity (the variety of species) and biota (the size of populations) shore up climate stability. The converse is also true: the loss of biodiversity and biota weakens climate stability.[17] But it does not stop there, because the positive feedback of declining life and climate change goes both ways; it is bidirectional. The loss of biodiversity and biota drives climate change by making the climate system more sensitive to external forcings such as human carbon emissions. And, climate change drives the loss of biodiversity and biota by sterilizing organisms and impairing reproduction. Climate change causes heat waves, whose longer duration, stronger intensity, and greater frequency have begun to impair plant and insect fertility.[18] Since plants and insects are close to the bottom of the trophic pyramid, this is bound to trigger losses higher up the food chain, and this cascading loss of life loops back into an unstable climate ever more sensitive to human impacts.

While the loss of wilderness, the vanishing of insects, and the vertiginous drop in vertebrate populations all made news in 2018, climate change has steadily continued. In a special report released in October, *Global Warming of 1.5°C* (SR15), the IPCC summarized that for the decade from 2006 to 2015 the average global temperature was 0.87°C higher than temperatures had been in 1750, before the Industrial Revolution (IPCC 2018).[19] In December, the World Meteorological Organization reported that for the decade from 2009 to 2018, the average global temperature was already 0.93°C above the pre-industrial baseline (WMO 2018).[20] According to the WMO, "the 20 warmest years have all occurred in the past 22 years," and "the past four years—2015, 2016, 2017, and 2018—are the four warmest in the series."[21]

The SR15-report was released some months after publication of a landmark study (Steffen *et al.* 2018). This study concluded that warming at 2°C above the baseline may trigger a slide to an inhospitable climate balance, so-called Hothouse Earth, on which civilization at current levels of development and population cannot be sustained anymore.[22] In the SR15-report, the IPCC accordingly revised the upper boundary of our safe operating space downwards. The 2015 Paris Accord had left the aspirational commitments still open, with the goal of stabilizing warming at a range of 1.5–2°C above the baseline, with 2°C as the upper boundary. Since 2018, this so-called two-degree guardrail is no more. In light of the hothouse trajectory, we are now looking at a 1.5°C guardrail. The SR15-report adds that we have about a decade left to make the necessary political and economic adjustments, before the forces set in motion will run away from us.

Making the adjustments would amount to radical action, since roughly 80 percent of global energy needs are presently being met by fossil fuels. CO_2 emissions must be cut by half before 2030 and cease altogether by 2050, otherwise we will sail through the 1.5°C-degree guardrail, beyond which bad things await.[23] The Earth System, the ensemble of environmental cycles and balances, and speaking to us through the scientific community, has issued a categorical demand to the world's policymakers on our collective prospects. We have been handed an ultimatum.

The fraught interface of collective human existence and the natural environment is captured in a figure in the mentioned flagship paper that prompted the United Nations to issue its ultimatum in 2018 (fig. 1).[24] This figure, the "Stability Landscape," of existential trajectories, shows our current situation, the recent past, compared to the backdrop of historical normalcy, and the fork in the road over our common future.

On the left of the Stability Landscape is a trough or a swale, a topological feature that skateboarders call a halfpipe. This is the glacial-interglacial limit cycle. For hundreds of thousands of years, the Earth slalomed down this halfpipe until about half a century ago. The Earth System had been in a stable pendulum swing from one ridge of the halfpipe to another, from ice ages at the left to warm periods (interglacials) at the right.

Had everything else stayed equal, the most recent warm period, the Holocene, would be ending in the foreseeable future. The Earth would have swerved back in the halfpipe through the trough towards the ice age ridge on the left. But something else happened instead: the human overshoot on environmental services such as the carbon cycle. As the carbon cycle could

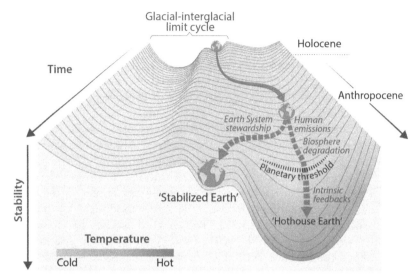

FIGURE 1 *Stability Landscape showing the pathway of the Earth System out of the Holocene and, thus, out of the glacial-interglacial limit cycle to its present position in the hotter Anthropocene.*

not assimilate human carbon emissions anymore, CO_2 concentrations in the atmosphere kept rising, which kept trapping solar radiation, which kept pushing global surface temperatures higher. Thus the human carbon pulse had kicked the Earth outside its halfpipe. Instead of slaloming to the next ice age, it found itself moving from the interglacial ridge into warmer territory. This happened forty years ago. We pushed the Earth System outside its glacial-interglacial limit cycle around 1980.

The far horizon, the backside, of the Stability Landscape shows the recent past of the Earth System: planet Earth, sitting atop the ridge of the halfpipe, but already outside of the halfpipe. Instead of rolling back down into the trough, as programmed into the oscillations of its climate pendulum, the Earth found itself leveraged outside, sitting in unfamiliar terrain, and rolling down an artificially created age of global warming. This is the horizon of the Stability Landscape and the beginning of the story it tells.

In the intervening decades, from policy milestone to policy milestone, from the UN Earth Summit in 1992, to the Kyoto Protocol in 1999, to the Copenhagen talks in 2009, to the Doha Action Plan in 2012, to the Paris Accord in 2015, human carbon emissions have only continued; atmospheric CO_2 concentrations have only gone up, and the Earth kept steadily rolling into ever warmer conditions. Around the turn of the millennium, the human impact on the Earth System had grown so large that the Holocene yielded to the hotter Anthropocene. Meanwhile the Earth careened steadily farther away from its former limit-cycle halfpipe, and as it did, it found itself in a new, warmer gutter, whose trough is defined by deepening instability. The end of the continuous black arrow is where the Earth is now. This is, in one picture, the existential situation we are in.[25]

The Stability Landscape is shown from the vantage point of the future. Looking at the image is as if we were our own posterity and we could look back in time and see, there, in 2018, the Earth having arrived in the new hotter gutter and on track toward a planetary threshold. If it goes over the edge, the Earth will plummet down into the unstable sinkhole of Hothouse Earth. Just as the continuous arrow behind Earth at the fork is the recent past, the dotted arrow in front of the Earth is the near future.

The hatched ridge of the Planetary Threshold is the outer limit of the stable operating mode of the complex system that is our planetary environment. Beyond this limit, nonlinear behavior takes over. This nonlinear behavior is characterized by abrupt changes and by feedback loops kicking in, which will pull the Earth deeper down into the hothouse sinkhole, no matter what we would do then.

In concrete terms, it means this: Earth, outside its former interglacial-glacial halfpipe, is now defined by global mean surface temperatures of *c.* 1°C above the pre-industrial baseline of global temperatures. Global mean surface temperatures are climbing higher, year by year, and the Earth System will be 1.5°C above the baseline not long after mid-century. This would be the point at which Earth, on the straight dotted arrow, crosses the hatched ridge.

If and when Earth adds on this extra 0.5°C level of global warming—the outer boundary of the remaining room for maneuverability of environmental policy—the surface temperatures in the Arctic, which is heating much faster than the rest of the planet, will have become so hot that the permafrost, which, in 2017–18, was thawing only in some spots, will start to melt generally. The permafrost locks in large amounts of semi-decomposed organic material, the giant subarctic compost heap that goes for soil in the tundra. When it melts, the organic material will liquify and its natural chemical breakdown, which is held in suspension by the ice, will continue. This will release methane (CH_4), a greenhouse gas and byproduct of organic decomposition, which, molecule for molecule, is twenty times as potent as carbon dioxide. Greenhouse gas concentrations in the atmosphere will soar, and the planet will heat up so strongly that it will plummet into the Hothouse Earth stage.

Note the steep angle of the walls of the sinkhole. The sinkhole is unstable because of the positive feedback loops that transform human-induced global warming to a runaway process. If and when the permafrost melts and the currently frozen CH_4 is released into the atmosphere, it would be too late for conventional mitigation strategies. Even if, after crossing that boundary, all CO_2 emissions would stop overnight; the global economy would derive all of its energy from sun and wind; all transit would be carbon neutral, with everyone riding bicycles, taking the train, or, perhaps, driving electric vehicles (fueled by batteries charged by sun and wind); and, furthermore, even if the world population would overnight become vegetarian, give up on meat, rewild livestock pastures, plant forests, protect sanctuaries—even if civilization did all this, after crossing the hatched ridge, it would get hotter. The window of opportunity will have slammed shut. The game would be over, and humanity will have lost.

May the patient reader kindly forgive me for this in-depth account, but the point is that this scientific knowledge and this policy response have come into view only in the past year; and that both constitute game changers in the understanding of the human–nature interface. In the past, this interface had been fraught; now, it has become suicidal. In the past, the scientific community had expressed concerns; now, the scientific community has sounded the alarm.

It does not take much imagination to visualize what life on Hothouse Earth would look like. For one thing, the current number of people on Earth is an adaptation to the optimal bioproductivity of Holocene Earth. On Hothouse Earth, however, weather will change to harsher conditions, climate will be hotter, oceans will be more acidic and contain less oxygen, and melting icecaps will release the ice landlocked on the Greenland interior and on the Antarctic continent into the oceans. Cascades of consequences: when the weather turns harsh, agricultural productivity will go down. When the climate turns hotter, most regions on Earth will experience water scarcities, and some regions, such as the Australian outback and the Arab interior, will be so inhospitable that just being outdoors without protection for a duration of time will kill you. When the oceans acidify and deoxygenate, fish stocks will collapse. When the landlocked ice will pour into the seas, beaches and atolls will vanish first, coastal plains will disappear next. The event-cascade will not end here: when agricultural productivity goes down, when water scarcities become chronic, when some areas become uninhabitable, when fisheries collapse, and when the densely populated coastal regions will be flooded, the Great Collapse will begin. Poverty will soar, migration explode, states fail, wars start, and turmoil begin that will last until civilization, or what will be left of it, succeeds at stabilizing at a fraction of its former size. Sure, life will go on, at least for some, and humans have a way of muddling through. But at what cost?

For grasping the extent of the crisis, it will not do to identify the meaning of climate change with mainstream media visualizations such as a bedraggled polar bear on a melting ice flow. This was the past of global warming, when Earth was still slaloming down its halfpipe. But if Earth rolls over the ridge into the sinkhole, the new icon of climate change will be the gun, more likely an AK-47 than an AR-15, since the old Avtomat Kalashnikova is cheap, rugged, and ubiquitous in the Global South. Even children can handle it. On Hothouse Earth, they will.

Lest more fortunate nations in the Global North, such as Canada and Russia, may think they will be spared the worst, they'd better think again.

These will become the destinations for everyone south of them, who will struggle to survive and will migrate as an adaptive response. Russia may cede Siberia to China when the deglaciation of the Himalayas turns the Yellow River and Yangtze into seasonal rivers. Canada will be occupied and annexed by the United States when the Southwest is a desert and the Midwest a dust bowl. Siberia will become a Special Administrative Zone of China, just like Hong Kong, and Canada will become a U.S. territory, just like Puerto Rico. On Hothouse Earth, everyone loses.

This is the crisis. We have ten years to turn things around. Old bourgeois indulgences of anti-realism, relativism, and skepticism, as cultivated by postmodern heirs of phenomenology, are becoming intolerable in the Anthropocene. Faced with the crisis, these indulgences are hooligan attitudes of criminal negligence. They will not do anymore. An alternative is needed, and it must be future-oriented, wise, and aggressive. In short, it must be dogmatic.

3. Grounding Phenomenology in the *Daodejing*

Philosophically provocative about the *Daodejing* is its unabashed naturalism; that is, the epistemic stance according to which natural facts entail ethical values and behavioral norms. To the Far West, historically, naturalism has always seemed improbable; David Hume questioned its logic in the fact–value distinction, and G.E. Moore claimed that inferring values from facts is the "naturalistic fallacy." And yet, this Far Western fallacy is the essence of Daoist wisdom. If one looks at the *Daodejing* for counsel on how phenomenology can get back on track, one finds a suggestion already in the words that link the Way to the sage. These conjuncts are *gu* 故 and *shiyi* 是 以, which mean "therefore" or "this is why." Time and again, the chapters of the *Daodejing* display the same pattern: a stanza about properties of being or Dao 道, followed by a stanza about the conduct of the sage or *shengren* 聖人. Being is of a certain kind, and "therefore" or "this is why" the sage conducts herself accordingly. The sage is wise as she abides in nature.

Perhaps half of the chapters of the *Daodejing* share this inferential pattern. Laozi describes how nature works as a matter of fact, then prescribes what to value and how to act. The sage, in Laozi, is a literary device similar to the gentleman or *junzi* 君子 in Confucianism. Both *shengren* and *junzi* are role models who "show how it is done." If you desire to realize yourself in a human community, look no further than the *junzi*, and if you wish to find yourself in the flow-vector of the universe, then the *shengren* will show you how to go about it. The Confucian gentleman and the Daoist sage represent existence that best corresponds to the environment in which it is placed—the former is the consummate human in a community, and the latter is the enlightened human in the larger ecological, natural, or cosmic environment.

Chapter 5 of the *Daodejing* writes that Nature as such has no humanity (*tiandi buren* 天地不仁). Nature can be cruel or kind, harsh or soft. In this regard, and seen from a cosmic perspective, humans are like straw-dogs or *chugou* 芻狗 in temple ceremonies: they are effigies, which are carried around in pomp and circumstance during the festivities only to be discarded or burnt in celebration at the end. Nature cherishes us, but only for the blink of an eye. The values of nature, to the extent she has any, are ambivalent. And yet, despite this ambivalence, the formal criterion of wisdom is crystal clear: the sage follows nature. Nature is a given way, and *therefore*, the sage abides concordantly. In this ambivalence, the character of this abiding is left open only to an extent. The latitude of choice is constrained by the facts of being and by the norms of conduct.

On the side of being, two properties come into view. One is the claim that Dao is empty yet radiating; it is a void that surges (*dao chong* 道沖), as chapter 4 says. In this regard, it is like chapter 11 speaking of the nave of a wheel from which thirty spokes go to the rim (*sanshi fu, gong yigu* 三十輻, 共一轂). Another is the claim that this spoking of the wheel, this radiation of the Way, creates emergence, structure, and flourishing. The ontogenesis or creation story of Daoism is in chapter 42 of the *Daodejing*. Today, the ancient Daoist schema of self-creation laid out there can be nicely explicated in terms of the scientific Standard Model. Being begins as an energetic void, call it Dao. This singularity, this void, surges in cosmic inflation and generates being or reality as the primordial cosmos (*dao sheng yi* 道生一). The generation of being takes place in a dimensional field, which splits into time and space, cools down to a quantum foam that bubbles into interstices and densities, which condensate into particles, which push and pull one another, until accreting into the building blocks of the present-day universe, its chemical elements, and its celestial bodies. On each step of its way, the primordial being divides and subdivides itself, with one binary unfolding after another (*yi sheng er* 一生二). By successive splits, nature organizes itself, generating higher levels of complexity (*er sheng san* 二生三). Nature creates itself, from chaos to order, and from uniformity to diversity (*san sheng wanwu* 三生萬物). The singularity creates one entity (道生一), then two (一生二), then an interplay (二生三), and finally life and mind, including us (三生萬物).

Is there a lesson for the sage? If this evolutionary arc of emergence (道生一，一生二，二生三，三生萬物) is nature's Way, then ("therefore") the sage better follow suit. Despite its cyclic destructiveness, nature is like a valley spirit (*gushen* 谷神) or a mysterious female (*xuanpin* 玄牝), who gives birth to life in chapter 6 of the text. The void births being, being births diversity, and diversity births life. The Way tends from death to life, from chaos to flourishing, and the wise person mirrors this tendency. The sage favors life over death and flourishing over destruction. Thus the sage favors softness over hardness, gentleness over violence, and peace over war. The sage is not driven by profit or power, but by a reverence for life instead. Throughout the *Daodejing*, Laozi makes clear that the sage is the guardian of life. Today, this Daoist tradition is manifest in the canonization of Laozi as the Guardian Spirit of Ecology by the Chinese Taoist Association.[26]

The task of the wise is to guard life, rather than to toss it to the elements; to let life be, not to stifle it; to cultivate it, not to crush it. Of course, not all Daoist philosophers are as life-affirming and dogmatic about this as Laozi. Zhuangzi and Liezi, who are more popular among postmodern interpreters, exhibit relativistic if not nihilistic values. Some passages in the *Zhuangzi* suggest there is no difference between life and death, and that enlightenment is carelessness. The *Liezi*, furthermore, suggests that selfishness may be wiser than compassion. While such subversive playfulness was entertaining during the libertarian dreams of unlimited capitalistic growth in the Holocene, it is not good counsel as the Earth is rolling toward the ridge of planetary boundaries beyond which the hothouse sinkhole lurks.

For Laozi, the *shengren* is a gardener in the garden of the Dao. Her job is to care for what grows, to nurture the weak, and to protect the small. The *Daodejing* explains how to do this best: by the practice of "non-action" or *wuwei* 無為. For the likes of another great Daoist sage, Liezi, *wuwei* is laissez-faire, but for Laozi, *wuwei* harnesses the flow of being, like a sailor capturing wind in the sails, or a martial artist turning an attacker's fury into the force that neutralizes the assault. Whatever examples one chooses for *wuwei*, Laozi is clear that the style of non-action is one of pliancy (*rou* 柔), and that its form is gentleness. As perhaps the famous dictum from chapter 36 of the *Daodejing* goes: "the soft overcomes the hard, and the weak the strong" (*rouruo sheng gangqiang* 柔弱勝剛強), or as chapter 30 elaborates:

Whenever you advise rulers in the way of Dao, counsel them not to use force to conquer the universe, for this would only cause resistance. Thorn bushes spring up wherever the army has passed, lean years follow in the wake of a great war. Just do what needs to be done, never take advantage of power. Achieve results but never glory in them. Achieve results but never boast. Achieve results but never be proud. Achieve results because this is the natural way. Achieve results but not through violence. Force is followed by loss of strength; this is not the way of the Dao. That which goes against the Dao comes to an early end.[27]

This recap of key points of the *Daodejing* makes it clear where the sage stands vis-à-vis the Stability Landscape of the Earth System in the early Anthropocene. As I have argued in section 2 above, the Earth System is at a fork in the road. One road consists of capitalism, with the practices of extraction, exploitation, and domination, in the spirit of competition and advantage, for the purpose of profit and enrichment. This road has been the Earth System trajectory since the beginning of the Industrial Revolution, and it has pushed nature from its cold–warm cycle up on a warmer ridge, from which it is now rolling toward a hot abyss. The violence our species has been visiting upon nature, by perpetrating climate change and biodiversity decline, goes against the Dao. Capitalistic civilization, with Far Western skeptics and anti-realists in the vanguard, wages war on nature and nonhuman life. This is now pointing us to an early end.

Philosophers faced with the fork in the road must make a choice. Either they continue to embrace the cultural ways that are pushing the planet to the brink, or they embrace an alternative. If they choose the former option, they can try to justify their choice by the epistemic modes of sophistry and reality denial described in the first section. If they choose the latter option, then they will not question reality but embrace it instead; they will cultivate empathy for life on Earth, and they will act and think according to the Dao.

The former and Far Western option makes philosophers into stooges of the libertarian forces that are pushing civilization toward collapse. The latter and Far Eastern option makes philosophers choose solidarity over individuality, compassion over competition, and sustainability over the market. The latter option, furthermore, turns philosophers into future-oriented thinkers grounded in scientific reality. Such philosophers emulate the *shengren*. In doing so—and only in doing so—they guide our world toward a Stabilized Earth destiny.

Analogous to Laozi's *shengren*, Heidegger conceives of *der Weise*. The meaning of the Chinese and German words is the same; both *sheng ren* and *der Weise* mean "sage" or "wise person." Heidegger introduces *der Weise* in *Country Path Conversations* (*Feldweggespräche*, 1944/5). The text is partly a riff on an obscure Greek-Egyptian concept, *áñkhibasié* (ἀγχιβαίη), which fuses the Egyptian *áñkhi*, meaning "near," with the Greek *basié*, meaning "come," into a word that means something like "coming near," "getting closer," or "progressing." This fused concept is not Heidegger's invention; it is the shortest fragment, a single word, by Heraclitus.[28]

The structure of *Conversations* is a dialogue, or rather, a trialogue, of a scholar (*der Gelehrte*), a scientist (*der Wissenschaftler*), and a sage (*der Weise*). English translators have shied away from translating *der Weise* as "the sage"—even though the German *weise* is evidently a homophone cognate to the English "wise." There are reasons for this caution. Heidegger had second thoughts. There is a passage in *Conversations* where he seems to deny that what he means by *der Weise* is what we mean by "sage," and Bret W. Davis, in his translation, accordingly suggests "the guide" instead.[29] In a published excerpt of *Conversations* (1959), Heidegger replaces *der Weise* with *der Lehrer*, which John M. Anderson and E. Hans Freund rightly translate as "teacher."[30] There may well be no ideal translation, considering Heidegger's misgivings. Yet, "sage" is what the German thinker writes. A sage is certainly also a teacher, and it surely fits the role of the sage, as indicated at the beginning of this essay, to serve as a guide in the fourfold. The future-oriented alternatives in section 1, furthermore, underscore this point: the dogmatic thinker is a teacher and guide: informed by insights, inspired by ideas, and contributing to answers. At the same time, all this underdetermines the sage. The sage is more.

What are these other qualities? The sage is not an expert, unlike his interlocutors in *Conversations*—one being a scholarly historian, and another being a natural scientist—and unlike guides or teachers. A guide is an expert in having mastery over a route or a terrain and the information or lore that comes with it. A museum guide knows the exhibits and can tell a story about them. A scout knows the lay of the land and can pick his way through it. A teacher is an expert in a branch of knowledge and in the craft of pedagogy. Different levels of education require different skill sets. For a university teacher, knowledge is most important; for a kindergarten teacher, pedagogy is central. But all teachers as well as all guides are experts, which the sage is not.

Popular culture sheds light on the non-expertise of the sage. In literature, one encounters the sage in the figure of Gandalf in J.R.R. Tolkien's *Lord of the Rings*. Tolkien's figure is carefully drawn; the character has complex traits, which cohere in a well-rounded persona. In Tolkien's tale, each member of the fellowship of the ring is an expert of sorts, and there is accordingly a division of labor in the cast of characters surrounding the ring bearer. One is the ring bearer (Frodo), another is his servant (Sam), a third is a woodsman (Strider/Aragorn), a fourth is a swordsman (Boromir), a fifth can talk to spirits (Legolas the Elf), and a sixth knows the underground (Gimli the Dwarf). Two other Halflings in the fellowship (Merry and Pippin) seem incompetent at first glance, but even they are experts—their interplay adds the indomitable lightheartedness that carrying such a burden needs. It also injects a dose of chaos into the fellowship and the plan, which creates openings for higher powers to intervene and to bring the fellowship the fortune such a venture cannot do without.

Gandalf, however, stands aside. He is not an expert like any of the other members of the fellowship; instead, he is not even part of the fellowship's division of labor. He puffs his pipe and drops the occasional remark, unless being diverted by some business or mission. Then he is off again, but regularly he returns, to check on the fellowship, to aid in the plan, and to come to the rescue when all else seems lost. As Tolkien's sage stands aside, he stands like a leader—even though fellowship has no leader. It is a collective, in which the sage is on equal footing with everyone else. Tolkien's non-hierarchical structure parallels the egalitarian interactions of sage, scholar, and scientist in *Country Path Conversations*.

Neither group is ruled by a leader, but *der Weise* in *Conversations*, like Gandalf in *Lord of the Rings*, is a leader of sorts—a Daoist leader, who acts by non-action and who leads from behind. The sage, as a leader-who-follows, leads and follows the group by his counsel. The experts know certain areas, but the sage sees a bigger picture, which invests him with authority to advise the experts. He does not issue orders but instead suggests answers; he does not possess authority but instead is an authority, and as such he gets along with his companions, whether conversing with experts on a country path or journeying alongside a fellowship through Middle-Earth.

This reveals the positive features of wisdom. First, the sage is a generalist, but this lack of expertise does not make him into an amateur. Instead of being a specialist, he is a master of holistic knowledge. The others are experts; the sage is a holist. Second, the sage is an authority without exerting authority. Laozi's *shengren*, Heidegger's *der Weise*, and Tolkien's wizard are authoritative figures who resist the temptation of authority. They are not corrupted by power or drawn to domination, and neither are they attracted to violence and destructiveness. Third, the sage is soft yet tough. At times, sages may administer a judicious slap, and they see no need to run away from a fight. They have courage and fortitude, and, in the case of Gandalf, they have mettle and valor, yet they are pacifists. Sages are not easily cowed, and this is their strength.

They are also rather old. Age appears to be a fifth feature of the sage, and it seems related to their fortitude. Picturing a "young sage" inevitably fails; one envisions a sagacious youngster and merely sees a wiseass, not a wise person. Age is a symbol, and not a literal condition. For the purpose of utilizing the figure of *der Weise* for a path of phenomenology, it would not do to have an interdisciplinary round table of young to middle-aged climatologists, biologists, agricultural engineers, ecological economists—and then add a senior-citizen thinker.

Age as a symbol stands for knowledge experienced and internalized. The knowledge of symbolic age is not the expertise resulting from study or training, but the reflective outcome of trials and tribulations. This is experience, internalized as suffering processed. The symbolic aging of the sage is that of battle-hardened veterans who had been at the mercy of the elements. The sage is an outdoors character—and one who has been through a lot. His skin is creased; his hide is tough. Yet age as a symbol of suffering processed points to more. A veteran scarred by life is not a sage. Scars must be absorbed, and pain must be digested, and only then wisdom may come into view. This is the sixth feature, and it is visible in Tolkien's tale. Gandalf is not only old, he is also kind. There are laugh lines at the outer corners of his eyes. The hallmark of pain, digested, is serenity and with it, joy. Inner joyfulness opens the mind, widens the heart, and informs one's ethos with wit and warmth. The likes of Gandalf fight against evil, but this fight does not fill them with bile and rancor. The wise age not in bitterness, but in sweetness, and this is the magic of the sage.

But how does one digest pain and age in sweetness in a symbolic fashion? What is the age-related trick for phenomenologists guided by the *shengren* to join peers of the same biological age group at the interdisciplinary round table? Symbolic age can advance beyond biological age through an exercise in cognitive maturity. Part of this exercise is the overcoming of a narrow mind, and thus the liberation from individual expertise. In this regard,

Heidegger's *der Weise* is not another type of scholar or another kind of scientist; he is genuinely different. His distinction is the ability to perceive a total-field image instead of a narrow area of focus. But he is also more than a mere interdisciplinary jack-of-all-trades or whiz-kid generalist, because his cognitive maturity is the ability to sense, within the total-field image, items encountered as what they are in themselves. The sage cognizes items encountered not only in a conventional phenomenological way of attending to the nature of the encounter, but also in the unusual and quasi-magical way of attending to the nature of the encountered. That is, the sage has the ability to switch identities with what he encounters.

In magic or sorcery, trading identities is the first step to conjuring: a wizard calls forth a spirit by a spell, and this calling-forth is possible because the spell links the identity of the one who summons with the one who is summoned. Granted, magic is make-believe, and sorcery only happens in fantasy tales such as *Lord of the Rings*. But the first step to conjuring is also the first step of attending to the nature of the encountered in phenomenological precision. The key is to forge a link, or to connect the dots, and for the cognition of the sage, it is both elementary and advanced.

The elementary aspect of cognition by connection concerns the first, epistemic feature of the sage mentioned—that the sage is a generalist, specifically a holist. Being able to see the big picture is not merely a panoramic vision due to an open mind, but more the result of processing information differently from how experts do it. Experts process information by analyzing it; that is, by isolating a piece of information from its context and dissecting the piece. This is how fine-grained features in the information come into view. Holists, however, process information by synthesizing it; that is, by connecting a piece of information to all other pieces in its context, such that the difference of information and context yields to a network of the given piece of information with all the others connected to it. Processing a piece of information holistically does not bring the piece into focus but instead discloses the web it is linked to. By connecting the dots, patterns in the information come into view. Instead of simply being a panoramic vision resulting from open mind, the big picture thus arrived is the product of a type of rationality that sets wisdom apart from scholarly or scientific expertise. Just as such expertise turns on analytic reasoning, wisdom hinges on synthetic reasoning.

The advanced aspect concerns the last, age-related feature of the sage mentioned above—that the sage is old but kind; that his (symbolic) age is sweet rather than bitter. Being able to assimilate experiences so as to digest the pain requires a panoramic vision that puts the pain encountered into perspective. This vision comes about by trading places of identity. The sage is able to deal with his existential pain in a more mature fashion than an average senior citizen would be able to, since the sage is not just old; the sage is mature, and maturity, *qua* cognitive advancement, amounts to the cultivation of empathy. Empathy is nothing but the ability to switch places between self and other, and to see the world from the vantage point of alterity. Empathy, so cultivated, is the cognitive condition of compassion and benevolence. In this sense, the sage not only "sees" things; the sage "gets" things, too.

Empathy is how the sage can be life-affirming. Theoretically, there is a big picture such as the evolutionary arc of *Daodejing* chapter 42, and the sage abides by it. Practically, the sage abides by the picture since his maturity lends him an empathy so keen that he sees himself in any living being. In literature, on the level of magic, this is how Gandalf can talk to moths and eagles. In philosophy, on the level of epistemology and ethics, this is how the integration of the perspective of the other leads to the appreciation of the other's existential interests, and how it leads from such appreciation to the moral choice of according respect to such interests in well-being and existence, regardless of whether "the other" is an individual life, such as a plant or an animal, or a network, such as an ecosystem. The other merely wants to live. Empathizing with this want, the sage affirms it and chooses to guard it.

Heidegger, in *Country Path Conversations*, coins a term to point to the sensitivity of *der Weise* to the web of being, which is the environmental alterity in which the sage dwells. He calls this cognitive stance *die Gegnet*, a blend of *Gegend*, "region" or "environment"; *gegen*, "against" or "counter"; and *begegnen*, "to encounter." This stance of wisdom involves several facets. One facet is that *der Weise* is someone who picks up on the numinous hints (*Winke*) given to collective existence, and on the basis of this reception, is then capable of pointing to where such hints come from. When the sage points toward the source, he is also able to decipher their meaning and guide (or be wise) in the way that follows best the ideal vector of the numinous hints.[31]

Another facet of this consummate cognitive interface with the environment, the *Gegnet*, is an openness that consists, variously, of waiting (*Warten*), gratitude (*Danken*), attentiveness (*Achtsamkeit*), and letting-go (*Gelassenheit*), in the sense of Meister Eckhart. This is how the magic (*der Zauber*) of wisdom can emerge in the *Gegnet*.[32]

This brings us to the end of reading the Daoist concept of the sage as Heidegger uses it. Our interpretive attempt seeks to suggest to philosophers a future-oriented employment in the collective project of saving civilization from the crisis against the forces that are pushing us ever closer to the edge. In times of crisis, it would be irresponsible for the philosopher to be a skeptic, and it would be pointless to be a better scholar than the scholars, and to be a better scientist than the scientists. The philosopher, schooled in phenomenology, but embracing the dogmatic alternative in the spirit of stewardship, who encounters East Asian wisdom, should be a more mature thinker than the inchoate exemplars of the past century. Such maturity requires the empathy of a consummate environmental interface, whose subjective side Heidegger calls *die Gegnet*, and whose objective side, elsewhere, he calls *das Geviert* or the fourfold.[33]

In conclusion, I hope that two remarks may lead the reader further. They are intended to show that neither the interface (*Gegnet*) nor the fourfold (*Geviert*) is obscure. Both terms, I think, have a secular, interdisciplinary meaning.

Heidegger parses *Gegnet* as "the lingering openness, which gathers everything up and thereby opens itself, such that the openness is sustained and suspended, and in such suspension summoned to let emerge everything in the way it is."[34] He parses *Geviert* as the intersection of the skies (*Himmel*), Earth (*Erde*), the gods (*Götter*), and the mortals (*Sterbliche*). I suggest linking these terms as an epistemic stance vis-à-vis an ontological situation, the stance I hope to have clarified above. Clarifying the situation serves as the appropriate conclusion of this essay.

The ontological situation is that of our Earth System at the verge of the third decade of the twenty-first century, having been pushed out of its halfpipe on a lethal incline by evil forces. This situation, trivially, involves the skies, in terms of rising atmospheric concentrations of greenhouse gases, and thus, it involves the skies in terms of climate change.

It involves, existentially, the Earth, in terms of the double whammy of climate change and biological annihilation, whose positive feedback loops are now jointly affecting cryosphere, hydrosphere, and biosphere alike (ice, seas, and land), to our collective existential detriment.

It involves the mortals, who are just us, and everyone among alterity with whom we can empathetically identify—all living beings, from moths to eagles, from mosquitoes to song birds; in short, all forms of life, from the morbidly obese to the starving, from the superrich to the migrant poor, and from the human to the nonhumans. For mortal all of us are.

Last but not least, it involves the gods, whose identity would remain puzzling if Heidegger were read in disconnect from his hidden Asian sources. In Far Eastern thought, the gods and the numinous hints they rain on hapless mortals, only to be picked up by keen sages, are summed up as *tianming* 天命 or "Mandate of Heaven." Yet, both scholarly renditions are philosophically misleading, which only underscores Heidegger's point.

Western scholars would look at the gods as cultural artifacts and objects of worship in human religions. Eastern scholars would look at *tianming* as the political authority invested in Confucian rulers. But for a future-oriented outlook, seen from a synthetic-rational perspective that seeks to integrate interdisciplinary findings, the gods (Heidegger's *Götter*) are the future vectors at the present fork for mortals on Earth under the sky. One vector, that of the evil gods, consists of unfettered capitalistic, libertarian practices, aided and abetted by postmodern sophistry and skepticism. The vector of evil gods leads down the sinkhole of collective demise.

Another vector, that of good gods, consists of sustainable practices of stewardship, exemplified politically by the People's Republic of China, the Nordic Countries, and the European Union (*sans* Britain, which exits itself to the Far West). This vector, the only arrow that is genuinely future-oriented, is pointed to the wide-open plain of collective stabilization.

Thus, from a secular point of view, the concept of the gods is intrinsically dubious. This leaves philosophers of the future with a choice and a question. The choice is between good and evil, light and dark, demise and survival. The question, addressed to aspiring sages among the phenomenologists of the future, is simply this: which of the two kinds of gods do you pray to?

Notes

1   See Eric Fromm, *To Have or To Be?* (New York: Harper and Row, 1976), and *The Heart of Man: Its Genius for Good and Evil* (New York: Harper and Row, 1964).

2   Arne Naess, "The Place of Joy in a World of Fact," in *The Selected Works of Arne Naess*, ed. A. Drengson (Berlin: Springer, 2005), 2371–82.

3   Reinhard May, *Heidegger's Hidden Sources: East-Asian Influences on His Work*, trans. Graham Parkes (New York: Routledge, 1996).

4   Ellen Chan, "How Daoist is Heidegger?," *International Philosophical Quarterly*, 45.1 (2005): 5–19.

5   See Lin Ma, "Deciphering Heidegger's Connection with the *Daodejing*," *Asian Philosophy*, 16 (2006): 149–71; and "On the Paradigm Shift of Comparative Studies of Heidegger and Chinese Philosophy," *Confluence*, 4 (2016): 81–98.

6   Gerardo Ceballos *et al.*, "Biological Annihilation via the Ongoing Sixth Mass Extinction Signaled by Vertebrate Population Losses and Declines," *Proceedings of the National Academy of Sciences*, 114 (2017): E6089–E6096; doi.org/10.1073/pnas.1704949114

7   Will Steffen *et al.*, "The Trajectory of the Anthropocene: The Great Acceleration," *The Anthropocene Review*, 2.1 (2015a): 81–98, esp. 91.

8   Will Steffen *et al.*, "Trajectory of the Anthropocene," 93.

9   World Economic Forum, *The Global Risks Report 2019*, "Executive Summary," 6.

10 Ibid.

11 Christina Kennedy *et al.*, "Managing the Middle: A Shift in Conservation Priorities Based on the Global Human Modification Gradient," *Global Change Biology* 2019: 1–16 (early pre-publication view), doi.org/10.111/gcb.14549. For a map, cf. Ibid., 5, sec. "Results," figure 1. For a summary, cf. Andrew Freeman, "Just 5 percent of Earth's Landscape is Untouched," *Axios* (2019), 10 January.

12 O. Venter *et al.*, "Sixteen Years of Change in the Global Terrestrial Human Footprint and Implications for Biodiversity Conservation," *Nature Communications* 7 (2016): 12558, doi.org/10.1039/ncomms12558; J.E. Watson *et al.*, "Catastrophic Declines in Wilderness Areas Undermine Global Environment Targets," *Current Biology*, 26 (2016): 2929–34; cf. Kennedy, loc. cit., "4. Discussion," 9.

13 Dennis van Engelsdorp *et al.*, "An Estimate of Managed Colony Losses in the Winter of 2006–2007: A Report Commissioned by the Apiary Inspectors of

America," *American Bee Journal*, 14 (2007): 599–603; Dennis van Engelsdorp *et al.*, "A Survey of Honey Bee Colony Losses in the U.S., Fall 2007 to Spring 2008," *Public Library of Science One*, 3 (2008): e4071, doi.org/10.1371/journal.pone.0004071

14 Rodolfo Dirzo *et al.*, "Defaunation in the Anthropocene," *Science*, 345.6195 (2014): 401–6, doi.org/10.1126/science.1251817. The expression "the great thinning" was coined by Michael McCarthy in *The Moth Snowstorm: Nature and Joy* (New York: New York Review Books, 2016).

15 Brooke Jarvis, "The Insect Apocalypse is Here: What does it Mean for the Rest of Life on Earth?," *New York Times*, 27 November (2018): 2. Cf. also Gretchen Vogel, "Where have All the Insects Gone? Surveys in German Nature Reserves Point to a Dramatic Decline in Insect Biomass. Key Members of the Ecosystem may be Slipping Away," *Science*, 356 (2017): 576–9, doi. org/10/1126/science.aal1160. The entomological paper that set the alarms ringing, the so-called Krefeld Study, is Caspar A. Hallmann *et al.*, "More than 75 percent Decline over 27 Years in Total Flying Insect Biomass in Protected Areas," *Public Library of Science One* (2017), doi.org/10.1371/journal.pone.0185809

16 M. Grooten and R. Almond, eds., Institute of Zoology (London), and World Wildlife Fund, *Living Planet Report 2018: Aiming Higher* (Gland: World Wildlife Fund, 2018), 7–10; cf. also chapter 3, 88–107.

17 Will Steffen *et al.*, "Planetary Boundaries: Guiding Human Development on a Changing Planet," *Science*, 347.6223 (2015b): 1259855, doi.org/10.1126/science.1259855

18 Research on climate change and impaired plant fertility has focused on crop species; e.g., cf. Anida Mesihovic *et al.*, "Heat Stress Regimes for the Investigation of Pollen Thermo-Tolerance in Crop Plants," *Plant Reproduction*, 29 (2016): 93–105, which shows that mild to severe heat stress impairs pollen development. For a summary vis-à-vis global food security, cf. Jerry L. Hatfield and John H. Prueger, "Temperature Extremes: Effect on Plant Growth and Development," *Weather and Climate Extremes*, 10 (2015): 4–10. In late 2018, worrisome experimental evidence of impaired insect fertility induced by climate change was released; cf. Kris Sales *et al.*, "Experimental Heatwaves Compromise Sperm Function and Cause Transgenerational Damage in a Model Insect," *Nature Communications*, 9 (2018): 4771 doi.org/10.1038/s41467-018-072723-z. If the modelled insect–climate link is confirmed by field work, civilization will be in jeopardy.

19 Myles Allen *et al.*, "Technical Summary," 4; "TS1: Framing and Context," in IPCC, *Global Warming of 1.5°C: An IPCC Special Report on the Impacts of Global Warming Above Pre-Industrial Levels and Related Global Greenhouse Gas Emission Pathways, in the Context of Strengthening the Global Response to the Threat of Climate Change, Sustainable Development, and Efforts to Eradicate Poverty* (Geneva: World Meteorological Organization, 2018). Future references are indicated as IPCC *SR15* (2018).

20 World Meteorological Organization (WMO), *State of the Global Climate in 2018: WMO Provisional Statement* (Geneva: World Meteorological Organization, 2018), 1.

21 Ibid.

22 Will Steffen *et al.*, "Trajectories of the Earth System in the Anthropocene," *Proceedings of the National Academy of Sciences* (PNAS) 115 (2018): 8252–9, doi.org/10.1073/pnas.1810141115.

23 For the mitigation window, cf. IPCC *SR15* (2018), loc. cit.: "In model pathways with no or limited overshoot of 1.5°C, global net anthropogenic CO_2 emissions decline by about 45 percent from 2010 levels by 2030 . . . reaching net zero around 2050." Cf. Ibid., *Summary for Policymakers* (approved and accepted 6 October 2018; subject to copy edit); section C "Emission Pathways and System Transitions consistent with 1.5°C Global Warming"; paragraph C1, 15.

24 Will Steffen *et al.*, "Trajectories of the Earth System."

25 See Ibid, 8254.

26 The Chinese Taoist Association (CTA) 中國道教協會 is the formal denomination of Daoism in the People's Republic of China. It is overseen by the State Administration of Religious Affairs. With the embrace of sustainability as an explicitly *religious* goal, it serves as a political platform for environmentalism in China. Laozi's canonization by the CTA in 2006 to the Guardian Deity of Life (*shengtai baohu shen* 生態保護神) follows the CTA's *Qinling Declaration* 秦岭宣言, which states, "Harmony between Heaven, Earth, and Humanity is the crucial guarantee for the sustainability of human activities on earth. It is the highest aim of Daoists. With the environmental crisis getting worse day by day, we have a duty to rethink the role of Daoism in China." Cf. *Alliance of Religion and Conservation*; arcworld.org/downloads

27 Laozi, *Daodejing*, trans. Gia-Fu Feng, Jane English, and Toinette Lippe (New York: Vintage, 2011), 32. The original Chinese reads: 以道佐人主者，不以兵強天下。其事好還。師之所處，荊棘生焉。大軍之後，必有凶年。善有果而已，不敢以取強。果而勿矜，果而勿伐，果而勿驕。果而不得已，果而勿強。物壯則老，是謂不道，不道早已。

28 Martin Heidegger, "Ein Gespraech selbstdritt auf einem Feldweg," in *Feldweg-Gespräche (1944/45)*, (Frankfurt: Klostermann, 2007), 1.

29 Martin Heidegger, *Country Path Conversations* Bret W. Davis (trans.) (Bloomington: Indiana University Press, 2010).

30 Martin Heidegger, "Conversation on a Country Path about Thinking," in *Discourse on Thinking*, trans. John M. Anderson and E. Hans Freund (New York: Harper and Row, 1966), 58–90.

31 Heidegger, "Ein Gespraech selbstdritt auf einem Feldweg," 84–5: ". . . dies schliesst allerdings nicht aus, das seiner ein Weiser ist, mit welchem Wort ich jetzt nicht den Wissenden meine, sondern einen solchen, der dahin zu weisen vermag, von woher den Menschen die Winke kommen; einen solcen, der zugleich die Weise, die Art, weisen kann, wie den Winken zu folgen sei."

32 See Ibid., 99, 100, 108–12, and 113–14 respectively for these terms.

33 See, for example, "Bauen Wohnen Denken" (1951) and "Das Ding" (1950), both in Martin Heidegger, *Vortraege und Aufsaetze* (Stuttgart: Neske, 1997), 139–56 and 157–80; these correspond to Heidegger's *Gesamtausgabe* vol. 7.

34 Heidegger, "Ein Gespraech selbstdritt auf einem Feldweg," 114: "Die Gegnet ist die verweilende Weite, die, alles versammelnd, sich oeffnet, so dass in ihr das Offene gehalten und angehalten ist, Jegliches aufgehen zu lassen in seinem Beruhen."

References

Allen, Myles *et al.* (2018), "Technical Summary" in *IPCC, Global Warming of 1.5°C: An IPCC Special Report on the Impacts of Global Warming Above Pre-Industrial Levels and Related Global Greenhouse Gas Emission Pathways, in the Context of Strengthening the Global Response to the Threat of Climate Change, Sustainable Development, and Efforts to Eradicate Poverty*, Geneva: World Meteorological Organization.

Ceballos, Gerardo *et al.* (2017), "Biological Annihilation via the Ongoing Sixth Mass Extinction Signaled by Vertebrate Population Losses and Declines," *Proceedings of the National Academy of Sciences*, 114: E6089–E6096; doi. org/10.1073/pnas.1704949114

Chan, Ellen. (2005), "How Daoist is Heidegger?," *International Philosophical Quarterly*, 45.1: 5–19.

Dirzo, Rodolfo *et al.* (2014), "Defaunation in the Anthropocene," *Science*, 345.6195: 401–6, doi.org/10.1126/science.1251817

Freeman, Andrew. (2019), "Just 5 percent of Earth's Landscape is Untouched," *Axios*, 10 January.

Fromm, Eric. (1964), *The Heart of Man: Its Genius for Good and Evil*. New York: Harper and Row.

Fromm, Eric. (1976), *To Have or To Be?*, New York: Harper and Row.

Grooten, M. and R. Almond, eds. (2018), *Institute of Zoology (London), and World Wildlife Fund, Living Planet Report 2018: Aiming Higher*, Gland: World Wildlife Fund.

Hatfield, Jerry L. and John H. Prueger. (2015), "Temperature Extremes: Effect on Plant Growth and Development," *Weather and Climate Extremes*, 10: 4–10.

Heidegger, Martin. (1966), *Discourse on Thinking*, John M. Anderson and E. Hans Freund (trans.), New York: Harper and Row.

Heidegger, Martin. (2007), *Feldweg-Gespräche*, in *Gesamtausgabe* (vol. 77), Frankfurt: Klostermann.

Heidegger, Martin. (2010), *Country Path Conversations*, Bret W. Davis (trans.), Bloomington: Indiana University Press.

Jarvis, Brooke. (2018), "The Insect Apocalypse is Here: What does it Mean for the Rest of Life on Earth?," *The New York Times*, 27 November.

Kennedy, Christina *et al.* (2019), "Managing the Middle: A Shift in Conservation Priorities Based on the Global Human Modification Gradient," *Global Change Biology*, 1–16.

Laozi. (2011), *Daodejing*, Gia-Fu Feng, Jane English, and Toinette Lippe (trans.), New York: Vintage.

Ma, Lin. (2006), "Deciphering Heidegger's Connection with the *Daodejing*," *Asian Philosophy*, 16: 149–71.

Ma, Lin. (2016), "On the Paradigm Shift of Comparative Studies of Heidegger and Chinese Philosophy," *Confluence*, 4: 81–98.

McCarthy, Michael. (2016), *The Moth Snowstorm: Nature and Joy*, New York: New York Review Books.

May, Reinhard. (1996), *Heidegger's Hidden Sources: East-Asian Influences on His Work*, Graham Parkes (trans.), New York: Routledge.

Mesihovic, Anida *et al.* (2016), "Heat Stress Regimes for the Investigation of Pollen Thermo-Tolerance in Crop Plants," *Plant Reproduction*, 29: 93–105

Naess, Arne. (2005), "The Place of Joy in a World of Fact," in A. Drengson (ed.), *The Selected Works of Arne Naess*, 2371–82, Dordrecht: Springer.

Sales, Kris *et al.* (2018), "Experimental Heatwaves Compromise Sperm Function and Cause Transgenerational Damage in a Model Insect," *Nature Communications*, 9: 4771 doi.org/ 10.1038/s41467-018-072723-z

Steffen, Will *et al.* (2015a), "The Trajectory of the Anthropocene: The Great Acceleration," *The Anthropocene Review* 2.1: 81–98.

Steffen, Will *et al.* (2015b), "Planetary Boundaries: Guiding Human Development on a Changing Planet," *Science*, 347.6223: 1259855, doi.org/10.1126/science.1259855

Steffen, Will *et al.* (2018), "Trajectories of the Earth System in the Anthropocene," in *Proceedings of the National Academy of Sciences*, 115: 8252–9, doi.org/10.1073/pnas.1810141115

Van Engelsdorp, Dennis *et al.* (2007), "An Estimate of Managed Colony Losses in the Winter of 2006–2007: A Report Commissioned by the Apiary Inspectors of America," *American Bee Journal*, 14: 599–603.

Van Engelsdorp, Dennis *et al.* (2008), "A Survey of Honey Bee Colony Losses in the U.S., Fall 2007 to Spring 2008," *Public Library of Science One*, 3: e4071, doi.org/10.1371/journal.pone.0004071

Venter, O. *et al.* (2016), "Sixteen Years of Change in the Global Terrestrial Human Footprint and Implications for Biodiversity Conservation," *Nature Communications*, 7: 12558, doi.org/10.1039/ncomms12558

Vogel, Gretchen. (2017), "Where have all the Insects Gone? Surveys in German Nature Reserves Point to a Dramatic Decline in Insect Biomass. Key Members of the Ecosystem may be Slipping Away," *Science*, 356: 576–9, doi.org/10/1126/science.aal1160

Watson, J.E. *et al.* (2016), "Catastrophic Declines in Wilderness Areas Undermine Global Environment Targets," *Current Biology*, 26: 2929–34.

World Economic Forum. (2019) *The Global Risks Report 2019: 14th Edition*.

World Meteorological Organization (WMO). (2018), *State of the Global Climate in 2018: WMO Provisional Statement*, Geneva: World Meteorological Organization. *et al.*

INDEX